C000225267

AN EXAMINATION OF
PREHISTORIC STONE BRACERS FROM BRITAIN

Ann Woodward and John Hunter

with

David Bukach, Fiona Roe, Peter Webb,
Rob Ixer, John Watson and Philip Potts

OXBOW BOOKS
Oxford and Oakville

Published by
Oxbow Books, Oxford, UK

ISBN 978-1-84217-438-8

This book is available direct from:

Oxbow Books, Oxford, UK
(Phone: 01865-241249; Fax: 01865-794449)

and

The David Brown Book Company
PO Box 511, Oakville, CT 06779, USA
(Phone: 860-945-9329; Fax: 860-945-9468)

or from our website

www.oxbowbooks.com

A CIP record of this book is available from the British Library

Library of Congress Cataloging-in-Publication Data

Woodward, Ann.
An examination of prehistoric stone bracers from Britain / Ann Woodward and John Hunter with David Bukach...[et. al.].
p. cm.
Includes bibliographical references.
ISBN 978-1-84217-438-8 (hardback)
1. Tools, Prehistoric--Great Britain. 2. Stone implements--Great Britain. 3. Antiquities, Prehistoric--Great Britain. I. Hunter, John. II. Bukach, David, 1971- III. Title.
GN805.W67 2011
936.1--dc23

2011024311

Printed and bound in Great Britain by
Short Run Press, Exeter

Contents

Acknowledgements

The work for this volume was undertaken as part of a wider programme of work at the University of Birmingham with funding from the Leverhulme Trust and with a core team of three: Professor John Hunter (Principal Investigator), Dr Ann Woodward and Dr David Bukach. The team was supported in the field by colleagues from the Open University, Dr Philip Potts, Dr Peter Webb and John Watson (PXRF, Chapter 3), by Dr Rob Ixer (petrography, Chapter 3) and by Fiona Roe (petrography, Chapter 3; Chapter 9; line illustrations, catalogue). The authors are indebted to them for their support, enthusiasm and expertise.

The loans in Scotland were arranged and facilitated by Dr Alison Sheridan, whose help with many other aspects of the Scottish bracer study is gratefully acknowledged, as is the support of Lore Troalen who undertook SEM/EDAX analysis on some of the material at the National Museums Scotland. Tangential to the main bracer project, a sample of Irish bracers was studied, but not chemically analysed, by two team members, Ann Woodward and Fiona Roe in 2006. The authors also drew on unpublished data from *Projet JADE* kindly made available by Dr Alison Sheridan. Comparative studies of Neolithic axe heads were undertaken at the British Museum by Dr Rob Ixer and Dr Vin Davis with the kind support of Dr Gillian Varndell.

Every bracer studied during the main museum tour in England was drawn *de novo* in pencil, without reference to any previous published line illustrations, by Fiona Roe. These pencil drawings were then finalised digitally by Henry Buglass in the University of Birmingham. Most of the available Scottish bracers were drawn in ink by Marion O'Neil, illustrator at National Museums Scotland, and transferred to a digital format. The three bracers housed in the Marischal Museum, Aberdeen were drawn by Jan Dunbar and re-formatted by Henry Buglass. All were converted to a common stylistic format for publication. These appear in the catalogue below together with photographs taken by David Bukach ably supported by Graham Norrie. Much of the illustrative material for the volume was created by Henry Buglass to whom the authors are especially grateful.

The bulk of the material was examined at nine key museums and involved considerable work on behalf of their respective curators in locating and making available appropriate material, and in arranging space for examination often for several days at a time. Without this level of co-operation and support none of this research would have been possible and the authors are especially grateful to the following for their efforts: Gail Boyle (Bristol City Museum and Art Gallery); Paula Gentil (Hull and East Riding Museum); Dawn Heywood (The Collection, Lincoln); Dr Ben Roberts (British Museum, London); Dr Paul Robinson, Dr David Dawson and Lisa Webb (Wiltshire Heritage Museum, Devizes); Paul Robinson (Northampton Museum and Art Gallery); Alison Roberts and Suzanne Anderson (Ashmolean Museum, Oxford); Peter Saunders and Jane Ellis-Schön (Salisbury and South Wiltshire Museum) and Dr Alison Sheridan (National Museums Scotland).

Many objects were loaned from other museums, or recorded individually in museums in order that examination could take place. The authors are grateful to the following for their generosity in making these available, or in taking time to transport them to museums containing larger collections: Rachel Atherton (Derby Museum and Art Gallery); Eva Bredsdorff (Powysland Museum, Welshpool); Dr Chris Chippendale and Anne Taylor (Cambridge University Museum of Archaeology and Anthropology); Dr David Connell (Burton Constable Hall Museum); Neil Curtis (Marischal Museum, Aberdeen); Mary Davis, Jody Deacon and Adam Gwilt (National Museum of Wales, Cardiff); Heather Dowler (Lancaster Museum); Deborah Fox (Worcester City Museum); Jillian Greenaway (Reading Museum and Art Gallery); Giles Guthrie (Maidstone Museum); Robin Jackson (Worcestershire County Council); Claire Jones (English Heritage, Portsmouth); Jane Marley (Royal Cornwall Museum, Truro); Rose Nicholson and Kevin Leahy (North Lincolnshire Museum, Scunthorpe); Emma O'Connor (Lewes Castle and Museum); Fiona Pitts and Rachel Smith (Plymouth City Museum and Art Gallery); Peter Woodward (Dorset County Museum); Leigh Allen and Kelly Powell (Oxford Archaeology); Alan West (Norwich Castle Museum) and Carolyn Wingfield (Saffron Walden Museum). Additionally, Dr Alison Sheridan kindly arranged loans of material from the Hunterian Museum and Art Gallery, Glasgow, the Kelvingrove Art Gallery and Museum, Glasgow, and from Queen's University, Belfast. David Clarke kindly arranged loan of material from Inverness Museum and Art Gallery.

A number of individuals also generously supplied photographs or unpublished information enabling the project to be as complete as possible. These included Dr Steve Burrow (Cardiff); the late Humphrey Case; Peter Cox (AC Achaeology); Emma Durham; Andrew Fitzpatrick (Wessex Archaeology); Dr Sabine Gerloff; Adrian Gollop (Canterbury Archaeological Trust); Dr Volker Heyd; Dr Adam Jackson (RCAHMS); Jan Lanting; Terry Manby; Ges Moody (Trust for Thanet Archaeology); Dr Stuart Needham; Alan Saville; the late Ian Shepherd and John Smythe.

For the use of unpublished results relating to analysis of 14 bracers within *Projet JADE* we acknowledge the help of Michel Errera, Dr Alison Sheridan and all the curators who couriered items to the British Museum for analysis. Dr Vin Davis kindly loaned two samples of Alpine jade for analysis. We are particularly grateful to Professor Mike Parker Pearson for allowing us to use radiocarbon dates from the Beaker People Project prior to publication. In Leiden, we were kindly assisted by Harry Fokkens, Luc Amkreutz, Sasja van der Vaart and Annelou van Gijn. Valuable discussion and advice was also received from Professor Dr Harry Fokkens, Sasja van der Vaart, Alf Webb, Dr Dirk Brandherm and Dr Catriona Gibson. The final text has benefitted greatly from comments kindly provided by Professor Richard Bradley and Fiona Roe, and we are grateful to them for their useful suggestions.

Subsequent to the writing of the main text a further seven bracers were brought to light. We are grateful to Peter Harp, Dr Stuart Needham, Mary Peteranna, Anna Tyacke, Dr Alison Sheridan and Richenda Goffin for bringing these to our attention. It was possible to include brief descriptions of these in an addendum to the main catalogue (ID 155–161).

List of Figures and Tables

List of Figures

List of Tables

1: INTRODUCTION

Ann Woodward and John Hunter

1.1. BACKGROUND

Bracers are thin pieces of fine stone, usually rectangular in shape and pierced with holes at the narrow ends. The number of perforations present is usually two (one at each end) or four, although in some cases the number reaches 12 or 18. The full range of recorded bracer shapes, types and colours is illustrated in the catalogue at the end of this volume. It has been thought, since serious study commenced, that such pieces may have functioned as archer's bracers or wristguards. Most bracers which have been found in archaeological contexts in mainland Britain had been placed in inhumation graves of Beaker date. Such graves date from the Late Neolithic and earliest Early Bronze Age periods, mainly during the second half of the third millennium cal BC.

In use as a wristguard, the stone plate would have been attached to the inner face of the lower left arm, in order to protect the wrist from the rebounding string when a bow was in use. On the other hand Sir Richard Colt Hoare considered such objects to be ornaments (e.g. 1812, 103), and Thurnam observed that several of the antiquarian finds were too wide to have been worn on the wrist (Thurnam 1871, 428–30). Canon Ingram (1867) had noted the positioning of the Roundway find between the bones of the lower left arm, and favoured the wristguard interpretation. Another early discussion of form and possible function was provided by Evans (1897, Ch. 19) who noted early interpretations of bracers as amulets, charms, personal decorations, or aids to cord or rope making, before concurring with Ingram's wristguard hypothesis. However, the British examples were not studied in detail until the 1950s and 1960s when Atkinson prepared a preliminary list. This list can no longer be located but a summary of it, along with the typological scheme that Atkinson had devised, was published by Clarke (1970, 570). It would also seem that Atkinson's list formed the basis for the preliminary list of British examples published by Harbison (1976, 28–31). Since then a few individual bracers have been described in detail (e.g. Robertson Mackay 1980; Whittle *et al.* 1992) but the only overall detailed consideration of the class has been Harbison's (1976) study of the material from Ireland.

There has been no concerted effort made to investigate the morphology and petrography of the British bracers, or the possible sources of the rocks utilised, although a useful listing of the bracers, updating that provided by Harbison, has been compiled by Smith and published electronically (Smith 2006). The debate concerning the possible true function of bracers has continued, and the non-functional hypothesis has been neatly expressed by Case, as follows:

> "*Often highly polished, and in developed forms sometimes embellished with copper and gold, I take stone wristguards to be symbolical renderings of more comfortable workaday leather ones – to have been badges placed or worn sometimes in a non-functional position outside the wrist*" (Case 2004a, 207).

The placing of bracers on the outer lower arm is a major theme of a recent paper by Fokkens *et al.* (2008). Instances of this arm position from Europe and Britain are defined and illustrated, and, employing added information from ethnographic evidence, the authors argued that bracers may have been pieces of exotic decorative equipment – bracelets as opposed to bracers. Other possible functions are also explored, including an association of some of these objects with falconry (Appendix 10.1).

Beaker bracers are not confined in distribution to the British Isles. They occur commonly in many parts of Europe, and it is thought that the type was developed first in Iberia. The general distribution of bracers of varying type in Europe is summarised by Harrison (1980, figs. 36 and 37), and much of the continental material has been listed and considered in detail by Sangmeister (1964; 1974). Aspects of comparison between the British bracers and those on the continent are discussed below (Chapter 9).

1.2 AIMS AND METHODS

This detailed study of bracers forms part of a more wide-ranging research project which has been designed to identify more accurately the significance of burial assemblages from Beaker and Early Bronze Age contexts in England and Wales. The key objective is to produce a detailed analysis of the nature and function of these grave goods and to test the hypothesis that many of the artefacts were originally designed for use as components of ritual costume, or as equipment for use in religious acts and ceremonies. As applied to the bracers, which formed one category within the classes of stone objects studied, the key aims were to produce:

- an illustrated database of the bracers
- a classification of bracers by size, shape and other morphological characteristics
- the characterisation (and possible sourcing) of the raw materials employed
- the determination of their possible function or functions
- an assessment of the incidence and significance of 'antique' items functioning as relics or heirlooms
- an analysis of any patterns of change in use through time and geographical space

A pilot study for the research programme, undertaken in 2004, included a special topic which related to Beaker-age bracers. It was thought that detailed study of a selected sample of 26 bracers, concentrating upon aspects of raw material used, fragmentation and use wear, alongside more traditional study of morphology, might reveal interesting patterns. The results were of great interest and were published promptly (Woodward *et al.* 2006; and for one newly excavated bracer of special interest: Roe and Woodward 2007). In brief, it proved possible to assess the degree of wear, re-fashioning and heirloom status of individual items through a combination of detailed microscopic, petrographic and geochemical analysis; this demonstrated that many of the bracers had been made from rock of two particular types only.

The main three-year programme of research commenced in 2006, and it was decided again to treat the bracers as a special topic. The aim was to compile a database and catalogue for all known bracers, not only those from grave contexts, and to prepare new line illustrations for as many pieces as possible. These drawings would accompany the database of colour photographs which was to be the standard basis for the object record throughout the larger project. The bracer study also departed from the general project design in that it was decided to include the bracers from Wales and Scotland, as well as those from England, so that, alongside the corpus or Irish bracers published previously by Harbison (1976), a total coverage of bracers within the British Isles could be attempted. The distribution of all known bracers in England, Scotland and Wales is shown in Figure 1.1. There is a wide spread from Cornwall and west Wales to north of Inverness in Scotland. Particular concentrations may be discerned in north-east Scotland (around Aberdeen), in the Fens of East Anglia, in the upper Thames valley (around Oxford), in north Kent and in Wessex (especially Wiltshire). Overall, bracers occur more often in eastern England and eastern Scotland, with far fewer examples from Wales, the west Midlands and the south-west. The find spots lie in a variety of highland and river valley locations.

Within the total list of 90 bracers known from England, Wales and Scotland, 16 of these have been lost since discovery, or cannot be located, leaving a total of 74 for study. Of these, 70 have been accessed and physically examined, with the other 4 being interpreted from photographs. Details of the methods by which the various project aims were addressed can be found in Chapter 2. Subsequent to the main analysis of recorded material a further three probable bracers were brought to the attention of the authors: from Armadale, Skye; Dorking Surrey and Flixton, Suffolk, but it has not been possible to include details of these either in the text or the catalogue. It was, however possible to include three other discoveries: from Butterbumps, Lincolnshire; Paul, Cornwall and Walsingham, Norfolk in the catalogue (IDs 155, 156 and 157 respectively), but not in the overall analysis.

Although the bracers from Ireland do not form a key part of this project, coverage of some of the Irish material has been achieved. Primarily, a small number of Irish bracers housed in the British Museum and Scottish museums were studied in detail during the main project itineraries (see Chapter 3. Appendix 3.1). The corpus of Irish bracers published by Harbison in 1976 included line illustrations of all available bracers, totalling 100 items. However few details of colour were recorded, and geological indentifications were only obtained for some of them. It was already known that the Irish bracers tend to differ from other British ones in terms of both shape and colour, with many of them made from red jasper. It was decided that it would be worthwhile to undertake a rapid study of a sample of the Irish bracers in order to consider the specific aspects of morphology, possible petrological identification, use wear and re-modelling. This study encompassed a sample of 33 bracers housed at the National Museum of Ireland, Dublin, studied in 2006. The results have been published separately (Roe and Woodward 2009), but are referred to below.

The results of the main spheres of study form the essential content of this volume. The Catalogue, illustrated with original line drawings and photographs will be found at the end of the volume, and the associated databases are included on the accompanying CD. Details of the petrographic and geochemical methods used in the identification of the rock types are contained in Chapter 2, and the important results obtained form the topic of Chapter 3. Following this there are three chapters which synthesize and analyse the results of studying each available bracer under the microscope. Chapter 4 considers morphology and Chapter 5 the evidence for processes of manufacture. Then Chapter 6 analyses the traces of use wear, the degrees of fragmentation encountered, and the incidence of re-use and re-working of individual bracers.

1.3 PREVIOUS WORK

To set the scene, it may be instructive to consider how some of these themes have been approached previously, both in Ireland and on the continent. Firstly, in relation to the

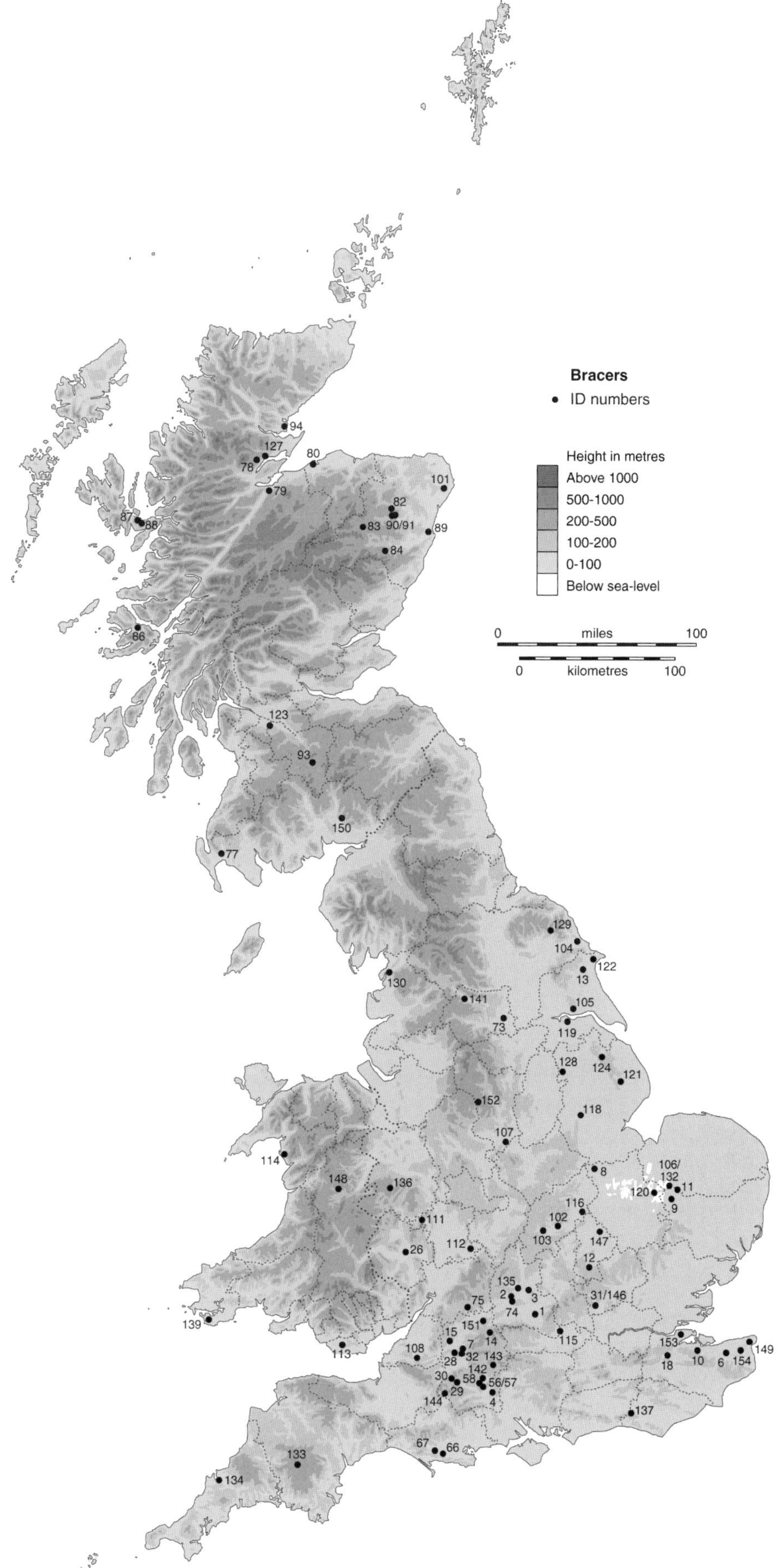

Figure 1.1. Distribution of bracers in England, Scotland and Wales.

identification of raw materials, it can be noted that of the 100 bracers from Ireland listed and studied by Harbison, brief petrological descriptions were obtained for 36 items (Harbison 1976, 31–3, Appendix C). It was notable that most of the bracers analysed were red or grey in colour. Most conspicuous were those manufactured from jasper, several sources of which occur in Ireland, and Harbison noted that several of the others had been made from other pink or red rocks (such as micaceous or silicified siltstones), apparently in an attempt to replicate the red hue of the jasper examples. It is also of interest to note that several of the items at Dublin are made from porcellanite, some of them employing the black variety derived from Tievebulliagh or Rathlin Island. This was the material used to make a group of Neolithic axe heads known as Group IX as defined by the Implement Petrology Group (IPG). Only three of the Irish items analysed are described as being green; one of these was made from steatite while another, from a porphyritic igneous rock, was not thought in 2006 to be a bracer.

Although it has been observed that most continental bracers are made from rocks which are red or grey in colour (Harrison 1980, 92), very few geological identifications for European bracers have been published. The incidence of red and grey bracers amongst the surviving examples for parts of Europe was recorded by Sangmeister (1974). Some recent geological work has been undertaken in Eastern Europe; petrographic identification of 14 bracers from Moravia (Turek 1998) showed that they had mainly been made from Tertiary silicified clay and metamorphic Silurian rocks. These would have derived ultimately from the Palaeozoic Ore Mountains (Krusne Hory), although the raw materials were probably collected as pebbles in stream beds. Turek has also observed that the Moravian bracers are usually made from soft rocks, in strong contrast to those from Britain (Turek pers. comm.).

Very little previous research has been undertaken concerning the possible processes of manufacture for stone artefacts of Neolithic and Bronze Age date (but see Chapter 5.1). However, it is interesting to note that most research covering the topic of drilling holes has been undertaken in relation to artefact types made from amber or jet (e.g. Shepherd 1981 and 1985; Sheridan *et al.* 2003). In relation to bracers themselves some preliminary experimental work, using replica bracers made from slate, has been carried out by Smith (2006), and more extensive experiments have been undertaken by van der Vaart (2009a and b).

The studies of fragmentation and use wear have been inspired by recent research on other classes of Early Bronze Age artefacts. It has been suggested that objects, such as amber beads, that occur in grave assemblages in a fragmentary state may have been pieces from valuable items that functioned as heirlooms or relics (Woodward 2002). In order to study this phenomenon it is necessary to consider the degree of breakage, and also to investigate whether the breaks are ancient or may have occurred either in the soil, at the time of excavation, or during their subsequent curation in stores and museum collections. The fact that fragmentation of bracers had already been noted in the literature suggested that this element of the project proposal might yield some very useful results.

For Europe Sangmeister has listed which bracers in his corpus occurred as fragments (Sangmeister 1974, Tables 4a–g), and this can be expressed as an overall percentage of 12%, from a total of the 262 items listed. Many of the European bracers occur, as in Britain, in Beaker graves, and some of the broken fragments do occur in funerary contexts (e.g. in the Netherlands: Lanting and van der Waals 1976, fig. 23; in Germany: Heyd 1998, abb. 2; in Poland: Makarowicz 2003, fig.10, 1–4 and fig. 15; in Moravia: Kopacz *et al.* 2003, fig. 13.3). These may have been heirlooms. However they also occur on Beaker settlements (e.g. in Hungary: Endrodi 1998, fig. 12,10; in Poland: Czebreszuk 1998, fig. 8). Whether these examples also occurred as heirlooms, in deliberate deposits of a ritual nature, or whether they represent the use and re-use of precious raw materials, is not yet clear. Some of the British bracers also occur in settlement contexts (below).

Harbison had noticed that many of the Irish bracers, about one third in fact, were broken (Harbison 1976, 5–6). Some had been re-bored as smaller bracers, and some of the broken pieces had also been reworked and probably used as pendants. In the Dublin sample studied in 2006 an even higher incidence of breakage (61%) was recorded although a lower number of items had been re-bored as smaller bracers.

1.4 TYPOLOGY

Existing typologies of bracers are complex. The typology originally devised by Atkinson divided the British bracers into three basic groups, long bracers with two perforations (Type A), rectangular examples with two, four or more perforations (Type B), and more complex items (Type C) which were waisted in plan, had four perforations and displayed a strongly concavo-convex profile. Atkinson's subdivisions of Type A, A1 and A2, were subsequently combined by Harbison (1976, 3–4), and Type C2, with V-bored end perforations occurs only in Ireland. Type B is sub-divided into Types B1, with two perforations, Type B2 with four perforations and Type B3 with six or more perforations. All Type B bracers have flat or slightly biconvex sections, although Harbison pointed out that some pieces with slightly concavo-convex profiles do belong to Type B2. Some of these types can be matched amongst the continental material. Thus the complex C1 British bracers conform to Sangmeister B (Sangmeister 1974, 116, abb. 8), Type B1 and some of Type A1 match Sangmeister G and Type B2 are like Sangmeister D. Sangmeister Type A, often with incised decoration, is not represented in Britain; nor are his types E and F, which have some resemblance to British types B2 and B1 respectively, but are more waisted in plan (for further discussion see Chapter 9).

The Atkinson terminology was adopted by David Clarke (1970) and has been used by most authorities since. Recently a more complex coding system has been devised by Smith (2006). This involves the formulation of

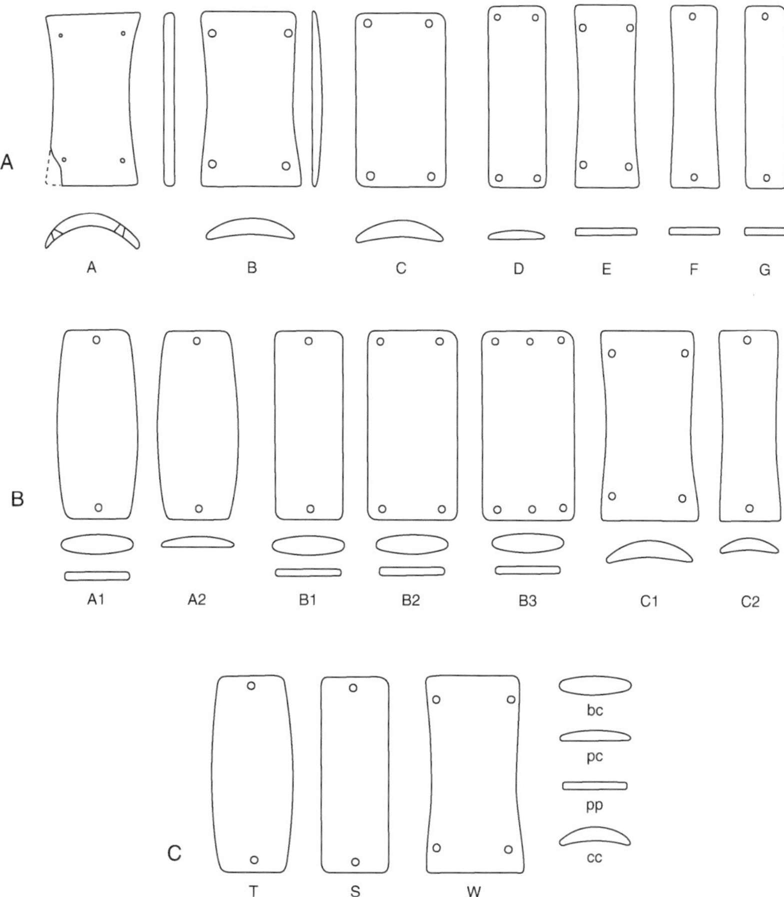

Figure 1.2. Summary of bracer classification systems (after Fokkens et al. 2008): top (A), Sangmeister 1974; middle (B), Atkinson (Clarke 1970); bottom (C), Smith 2006. In Smith's classification a 2-perforation, tapered (T) plano-convex (pc) bracer would be classified as '2Tpc'.

a code for each bracer which summarises three different parameters: the number of perforations; the outline shape and the cross-section. A useful diagram which summarises the three main systems of classification by Sangmeister, Atkinson and Smith, has been provided by Fokkens *et al.* (2008, fig. 1) and is reproduced above (Figure 1.2).

Although the Atkinson system remains useful for descriptive purposes (see Tables 1.1 and 1.2), for the purposes of the present study it was decided to employ none of the existing systems. The programme of research attempts to start from first principles for each section of study; thus the analysis of morphology presented in Chapter 4 does not include existing typological schemes, although it does take into account identified rock type, which is a specific new data source collected during the programme.

1.5 CHRONOLOGY AND CONTEXT

As bracers were current for a period of up to a millennium in Britain, it is important to consider chronological aspects. Until recently, such considerations were based on the recurring associations of bracers in graves with other artefact types which could be dated on typological or other grounds. Such artefacts include Beakers, metal daggers and fancy flint arrowheads. A clear pattern of associations was first appreciated by Clarke, who was able to show that the curved and waisted bracers of Atkinson Type C1 occurred with later Beaker types, whilst the flat Type B bracers were mostly associated with earlier Beaker types. Discussion of these associations was included in his main text (Clarke 1970, 98, 113, 149, 170, 186 and 194–5) and a summary diagram was also supplied (*ibid*, 448, Appendix 3.2). More recently, the overall chronological span of main bracer use in Britain was indicated by Needham, in diagrams depicting the overlapping currency of various artefact classes during the Beaker period (Needham 2005, figs. 11 and 12). Over the last few decades the subject has been further informed by the obtaining of a series of radiocarbon dates, and it is now possible to work some absolute chronology into the argument. In Chapter 7, consideration of the available radiocarbon dates, together with a detailed assessment of the associations of bracers with other dateable artefact types, allows potential correlations with the different rock types to be investigated.

In Ireland a rather different picture emerges with most bracers occurring as stray finds. Many are of the long and narrow two-holed Type A, and Harbison argued that they may have been associated with Food Vessel Bowls rather than Beakers (Harbison 1976, 7–10). Harbison therefore

Table 1.1. Bracers by rock type and Atkinson class.

ID	Site name	County	Atkinson type	Museum
GROUP VI				
1	Dorchester XII	Oxfordshire	C1	Ashmolean, Oxford
7	Hemp Knoll	Wiltshire	C1	British Museum
8	Barnack	Cambridgeshire	C1	British Museum
13	Kelleythorpe	East Yorkshire	C1	British Museum
15	Calne	Wiltshire	C1	British Museum
31	Tring	Hertfordshire	C1	Devizes
73	Ferry Fryston	N Yorkshire	C1	Wakefield
78	Fyrish	Ross & Cromarty	C1	National Museums Scotland
79	Culduthel Mains	Inverness-shire	C1	National Museums Scotland
86	Glen Forsa	Mull	A1	National Museums Scotland
87	Corry Liveras	Skye	C1	National Museums Scotland
89	Borrowstone	Aberdeenshire	C1	Marischal, Aberdeen
91	Newlands, Oyne	Aberdeenshire	B1	Marischal, Aberdeen
101	Ardiffery (replica)	Aberdeenshire	C1	National Museums Scotland
105	Melton Quarry	East Yorkshire	B1	Hull
112	Aldington	Worcestershire	C1	Worcester
116	Raunds	Northamptonshire	C1	English Heritage, Portsmouth
118	Rauceby	Lincolnshire	A1	The Collection, Lincoln
119	Winteringham	Lincolnshire	B3	The Collection, Lincoln
141	Broughton-in-Craven	North Yorkshire	B1	Burton Constable Museum
AMPHIBOLITE				
2	Stanton Harcourt	Oxfordshire	B3	Ashmolean, Oxford
3	Woodeaton	Oxfordshire	probably B2	Ashmolean, Oxford
4	Winterslow Hut	Wiltshire	B3	Ashmolean, Oxford
6	Sturry	Kent	B1	British Museum
10	Sittingbourne	Kent	B1	British Museum
11	Brandon	Suffolk	B3	British Museum
12	Sewell	Bedfordshire	B2	British Museum
14	Aldbourne	Wiltshire	B2	British Museum
18	Offham	Kent	B3	Maidstone
26	Wellington Quarry	Herefordshire	probably B1	Worcs County Council
28	Roundway	Wiltshire	B2	Devizes
30	Sutton Veny	Wiltshire	B3	Devizes
32	Bishops Cannings	Wiltshire	B3	Devizes
66	West Stafford	Dorset	B2	Dorset County Museum
67	Thomas Hardye School	Dorset	B2	Dorset County Museum
74	Gravelly Guy	Oxfordshire	B2	Ashmolean, Oxford
75	Shorncote	Gloucestershire	B	Cirencester
102	Duston	Northamptonshire	B1	Northampton
103	Upper Heyford	Northamptonshire	B1	Northampton
106	Hockwold	Norfolk	B1/A1	Norwich
107	Aston	Derbyshire	B2	Derby
113	Llantrithyd	South Glamorgan	B1	National Museum of Wales
115	Sonning	Berkshire	B3	Reading
121	Calceby	Lincolnshire	B2	The Collection, Lincoln
134	Fox Hole	Cornwall	B2	Truro
137	Pyecombe	East Sussex	B2	Lewes Castle
154	Monkton	Kent	B3	Canterbury Arch. Trust
RED/BLACK				
56	Amesbury Archer (red)	Wiltshire	A/B	Salisbury
57	Amesbury Archer (black)	Wiltshire	A/B	Salisbury
58	Stonehenge (black)	Wiltshire	A1	Salisbury

92	?Scotland (red)		A	Hunterian, Glasgow
94	Dornoch Nursery (red)	Sutherland	A/B	Inverness
108	Ben Bridge (black)	Somerset	A1	Bristol
148	Carneddau (red)	Montgomery	A1	Powysland, Welshpool
153	Cliffe (black)	Kent	A1	British Museum
MISCELLANEOUS				
9	Mildenhall	Suffolk	B2	British Museum
29	Tytherington/Corton	Wiltshire	B3	Devizes
77	Glenluce	Wigtownshire	B1	National Museums Scotland
80	Culbin Sands	Moray	A2	National Museums Scotland
82	Old Rayne	Aberdeenshire	B3	National Museums Scotland
84	Ballogie	Aberdeenshire	A1	National Museums Scotland
88	Broadford Bay	Skye	A1	National Museums Scotland
90	Newlands, Oyne	Aberdeenshire	C1	Marischal, Aberdeen
93	Crawford	Lanarkshire	A	Hunterian, Glasgow
104	nr Scarborough	North Yorkshire	B1	Saffron Walden
111	Lindridge	Worcestershire	B2	Worcester
114	Dyffryn Ardudwy	Merioneth	A	National Museum of Wales
120	Littleport	Cambridgeshire	A1	Cambridge
123	Ferniegair	Lanarkshire	C1	Kelvingrove, Glasgow
133	Archerton Newtake	Devon	B2	Plymouth
135	Cassington	Oxfordshire	B1	Queens University, Belfast
149	Thanet	Kent	B1	Trust for Thanet Archaeology
150	Lockerbie	Dumfries	A	National Museums Scotland
IRELAND				
RED/BLACK				
16	Ireland A (red)		C2	British Museum
17	Ireland B (red)	probably Ireland	A	British Museum
98	Ireland (red)	Antrim	A	Hunterian, Glasgow
99	Ireland (black)	Antrim	A	Hunterian, Glasgow
MISCELLANEOUS				
95	Ireland		A	National Museums Scotland
96	Northern Ireland		A	National Museums Scotland
97	Ireland	Antrim	A	National Museums Scotland
100	Ireland	Westmeath	A	Hunterian, Glasgow

concluded that the Irish bracers dated to the full Early Bronze Age. However subsequent absolute dating for the Food Vessel Bowl series has indicated that these ceramics were current between *c.*2160 and 1930/20 cal BC (Brindley 2007, 250), and thus were contemporary with the main *floruit* of later Beakers (Needham 2005, fig.13).

In order to assemble all the evidence relating to the potential function or functions of the bracers it is also necessary to consider the contexts within which they were found. Firstly there are those examples which were found as stray finds, or on Beaker occupation sites. For those found in graves, the context information includes the types of site or burial from which the bracer was derived, along with any data relating to the age and sex of the body that had been buried. Also important is a detailed consideration of where the bracer had been worn or placed in relation to the lower arm and the body. Finally an investigation of which other artefacts were included in a bracer burial, and where these other artefacts were placed in relation to the body is also of significance. All these sets of evidence are gathered together and analysed in Chapter 8.

Much of the extensive literature on European Beaker graves and sets of grave goods is not available in English. However, some important aspects of Beaker burial customs in eastern Europe have recently been summarised, presented and analysed by Heyd (2007). This paper includes relevant data concerning the division of grave good types by age and gender, and of overall cemetery size and social organisation. A detailed consideration of many of the bracers from western continental Europe, using disparate data gathered from the foreign literature, has been compiled for this project, and is presented as Chapter 9. This addresses

Table 1.2. Bracers of unknown rock type by Atkinson class.

ID	Site name	County	Atkinson type	Museum
122	Bridlington	East Yorkshire	B2	Hull
124	Thoresway	Lincolnshire	A1	Lincoln
126		Lanarkshire	A1	lost
127	Dalmore	Ross & Cromarty	C1	lost
128	Gainsborough	Lincolnshire	B2	Lincoln
129	High Dalby	North Yorkshire	B1	York
130	Bowerham Barracks	Lancashire	A2	Lancaster
132	Hockwold	Norfolk	B3	private possession
136	Black Knoll	Shropshire	B2	unknown
139	Mola	Pembrokeshire	B2	Carmarthen
140		East Yorkshire	B2	Hull
142	Bulford	Wiltshire	unknown	lost
144	Mere	Wiltshire	B1	lost
146	Tring	Hertfordshire	C1	lost
147	Sandy	Bedfordshire	B1	lost
151	Swindon	Wiltshire	unknown	unknown
152	Hartington	Derbyshire	B3	private possession
156	Butterbumps	Lincolnshire	B2	English Heritage
157	Paul	Cornwall	B2	Truro
158	Walsingham	Norfolk	B3	private possession

questions such as where the best parallels for British bracer types may be found, how bracers may have come to the British Isles in the first place, and why the bracers in Ireland are so different from those found in England, Scotland and Wales. This data is woven together with the results from all the project research themes in order to present an overall synthesis for the British bracers. This will be found in Chapter 10.

2: METHODOLOGY

John Hunter, David Bukach, Rob Ixer and Peter Webb

2.1 THE RESOURCE AND INVESTIGATIVE PROGRAMME

The preliminary research for this project necessitated an audit of the existence of bracers and of their locations in various museums. This was conducted through study of excavation reports, previous publications on bracers and Early Bronze Age material, museum catalogues and collections (e.g. Annable and Simpson 1964 for Devizes Museum) and antiquarian volumes (e.g. Evans 1897, Ch. XIX). Material housed in English, Scottish and Welsh museums was visited and lists drawn up of identified bracers together with their locations, reference numbers and other associated data. The museum collections containing groups of bracers were visited first. These were the British Museum, the Ashmolean Museum (Oxford), the Wiltshire Heritage Museum (Devizes) and National Museums Scotland (in Edinburgh). Bracers from many other sites are housed individually in other provincial museums, the National Museums and Galleries of Wales, and, as items from recent unpublished excavations, in various archaeological units. Through a complex process of short loans, as many of these bracers as possible were gathered together for study in four selected museum locations: the Salisbury and South Wiltshire Museum, Northampton Museum and Art Gallery, Bristol City Museum and Art Gallery and The Collection (Lincoln). Altogether bracers from a total of 32 museums and four archaeological units were studied, all within a concentrated study period of four months during 2007 (Table 2.1). A few further bracers were recorded and photographed separately at later dates, as and when they became available for study. For these, selected parameters were recorded, but petrographic and XRF analysis (see below) could not be undertaken. Of the 90 bracers known 16 could not be located; these were either lost, unavailable, or in private collections, although some had published details.

This study does not include the bracers from Ireland, which have been published previously by Harbison (1976). During the study period here, a small number of Irish bracers, housed in the British Museum, National Museums Scotland and the Hunterian Museum and Art Gallery, Glasgow were encountered and listed. These were cross-referred to Harbison's catalogue and were studied in detail. A summary of these eight bracers is included as Appendix 3.1 in Chapter 3. Most bracers from Ireland are housed in Irish museums. Tangential to the main bracer project, a sample of Irish bracers was studied, but not chemically analysed, in 2006. This study was undertaken in order to provide comparative data on the Irish bracers, which are rather different from those from mainland Britain, and also to trial the analysis forms that were being devised for the main research project. The Irish study involved a total of 33 bracers housed in the National Museum of Ireland, Dublin, and the results of this research are published separately (Roe and Woodward 2009).

Few of the bracers discussed here were on museum display; many were in storage, some requiring complex accession procedures. Examinations were conducted on a museum-to-museum basis with the full body of material kindly made available from display and store by the relevant curators in order that the researchers could view the material *in toto*, sometimes over a period of several days. Some loan items were couriered by the relevant museum curators or conservators, while movements of other loans were facilitated by team members.

The research team consisted of seven individuals with different roles to play – microscopy, petrography, non-destructive x-ray fluorescence analysis, magnetic susceptibility, illustration and photography. This reflected the three fundamental parts of the examination and recording process of each bracer: measurement and microscopic investigation (including petrographic examination); x-ray fluorescence analysis and magnetic susceptibility, drawing and photography. The methodologies for the x-ray fluorescence analysis, petrographic analysis, and magnetic susceptibility measurement are detailed below (sections 2.3, 2.4 and 2.5 respectively). The use of portable analytical equipment throughout enabled analysis to be carried out in the museums themselves and thus enabled

Table 2.1. List of all museums or organisations visited, or from where items were loaned (in italics), and numbers of bracers viewed. There is, in addition, a replica bracer from Ardiffery (ID 101) studied at the NMS.

Holding museum or organisation	**No. of bracers**
National Museums Scotland	9
British Museum, London	11
Wiltshire Heritage Museum, Devizes	5
Ashmolean Museum, Oxford	4
Salisbury and South Wiltshire Museum	3
Marischal Museum, Aberdeen	*3*
Dorset County Museum	*2*
Oxford Archaeology	*3*
Northampton Museum and Art Gallery	2
National Museum of Wales, Cardiff	*2*
Worcester City Museum	*2*
The Collection, Lincoln	2
Hunterian Museum and Art Gallery, Glasgow	*2*
Bristol City Museum and Art Gallery	1
Lewes Castle and Museum	1
Inverness Museum and Art Gallery	*1*
Saffron Walden Museum	*1*
Hull and East Riding Museum	*1*
Burton Constable Hall Museum	*1*
Maidstone Museum	*1*
Norwich Castle Museum	*1*
Derby Museum and Art Gallery	*1*
Worcestershire County Council	*1*
Reading Museum and Art Gallery	*1*
English Heritage, Portsmouth	*1*
North Lincolnshire Museum, Scunthorpe	*1*
Royal Cornwall Museum, Truro	*1*
Plymouth City Museum and Art Gallery	*1*
Powysland Museum, Welshpool	*1*
Queen's University, Belfast, (via A Sheridan)	*1*
Cambridge University Museum of Archaeology & Anthropology (plus XRF of 8 Neolithic jadeite axe heads)	*1*
Canterbury Archaeological Trust	*1*
Trust for Thanet Archaeology	*1*
Total bracers studied physically	**70**
Photographs only	
Kelvingrove Art Gallery and Museum	*1*
Lancaster Museum	*1*
Carmarthen Museum	*1*
Lockerbie (via NMS)	*1*
Total number of bracers studied	**74**

the whole examination programme to be undertaken as a single team exercise.

A process of this nature offered significant logistical challenges in addition to those of having the material collected for study and study space made available. Partly for this reason it was agreed that each item should be examined as comprehensively as possible on the one occasion only: this pre-empted the need for a further examination and a repeat of the logistical difficulties and, moreover, meant that the items were only unwrapped and handled on the single occasion. A strict set of Handling Guidelines was formulated, and this was followed by all team members in each museum.

The fact that over 30 museums and units were involved in this process also entailed over 30 different numerical accession systems. As part of the pre-visit programme each individual item was given a project (stone) identification (ID) number for the purpose of the research; this could be cross-referenced with the respective museum accession number concerned and with any other existing classification system that had already been applied (e.g. Atkinson in Clark 1970; Harbison 1976; Smith 2006). The same ID number is used to identify that item throughout this volume. A key feature of the project was that the overview should not only be comprehensive, but also free from pre-existing classification systems. These ID numbers are sequential, but do not represent a complete numerical sequence as the research programme was also concerned with other stone items (e.g. whetstones, sponge finger stones etc.) examined during the same visits. These were also allocated

ID numbers and are published separately under a wider review of the material (Woodward *et al.* in prep.).

2.2 EXAMINATION PROCESS

Each bracer available for study was examined in detail and recorded on a *pro forma* designed specifically for the investigation of bracers; the information was subsequently transferred directly into a relational database (Access). A copy of the *pro forma* is shown in Appendix 2.1 below. Direct transfer from examination to database was rejected as the researchers found that not only did interim transfer of data to paper form allow for easier review and checking, but also that it facilitated annotations of drawings and sketches; in several instances it was found that it was more efficient to sort and analyse paper records than to employ a computer.

A second database was devoted to the contextual data. This covered details of the context of discovery for each bracer, where known, the published reference to any grave plan or other archaeological feature, a copy of the grave plan where available, the details of any associated burial and a listing of any other associated grave goods. The recorded position of each grave good in relation to the body was also listed. This 'assemblage database' is linked to the main database for each bracer by the project ID numbers. Both databases are available on CD media attached to this volume.

Part of the examination was to create a *basic record*; this consisted of the twelve defined contextual, material and typological fields listed in the published catalogue, plus additional fields which would allow any future researcher to obtain more refined details of each object, together with its condition and, where available, its life history. The purpose was to create a record which was both consistent and comprehensive in coverage, which would present data in the most objective manner possible, and which would also allow the researchers to include 'free text' on observations, interpretations and hypotheses which seemed appropriate at the time. An earlier pilot study on a selected body of the material had provided a useful yardstick as to how this might be undertaken, and the detailed *pro forma* was trialled during the study of Irish bracers in Dublin (see above).

Some of the bracers had already been studied or described individually, in varying degrees of detail, in previous publications. Data from these were recorded on the *pro formas* but were reviewed rather than accepted. Any differences that occurred were noted; many of these differences had implications for post-depositional damage or wear. Each record form contained a line drawing of the individual bracer, either from a previous publication or one sketched during the examination. This was roughly to scale and showed both surfaces as well as the profile for working purposes. It allowed the researchers to annotate and number perforations, and to record significant wear, fractures, and any other features deemed to be important during the examination. Every bracer studied during the main museum tour in England was drawn *de novo* in pencil, without reference to any previous published line illustrations. These pencil drawings were then finalised digitally at the University of Birmingham. Most of the available Scottish bracers were drawn in ink at National Museums Scotland, and subsequently transferred to a digital format. The three bracers housed in the Marischal Museum, Aberdeen were also drawn independently. All were subsequently converted to a common stylistic format for publication. These appear in the catalogue below together with appropriate photographs. The latter were taken digitally of each bracer and consisted of basic views (e.g. front and back) with details of any specific feature identified during examination at higher magnification, often with aid of macro extension tubes. Typically this might include characteristic striation patterns, the presence of copper traces identified in a perforation, or a particular marking, flaw or aspect of profile. Photography was undertaken using a Nikon D50 DSLR camera and macro lens and an illuminating copy stand. Lighting was normally placed at oblique angles for specific close-up work in order to best illustrate manufacturing striations and aspects of use wear. Images were captured in RAW image format and imported into image editing software where basic retouching was completed. Colour correction was minimized using daylight light sources, and when necessary was applied on-site using the object for reference.

Part of the comprehensive analysis involved the weight of each item. This was more to create a record than provide a typological criterion, but it would enable future researchers to identify any minor loss not evident visually, or to provide an additional future check on object veracity. Weighing was normally carried out to one decimal place. Colour was also recorded for recognition purposes and was carried out in general terms only for the *pro forma*. It was not felt that recording the detailed shading of items was either useful or feasible at that level of enquiry. Moreover, digital photography allowed colour correction to be carried out while the objects were still available for study. However, geological differences were identified through petrographic examination (below) and required a greater detail of colour measurement for which the Geological Society of America's 'rock-color' charts were employed (below).

Many of the bracers exhibited geological flaws either through rock structure, discolouration or splitting; these were recorded according to character and location for each item and offered interpretation with respect to exploitation and selection of materials. Profile was also recorded from both transverse and longitudinal aspects; this was seen as morphologically significant given that a range of profile types were evident within all geological types (e.g. plano-convex, lentoid etc.) and might have functional or decorative implications.

Dimensional measurements were undertaken using plastic callipers to a theoretical accuracy of 0.1 mm, although in terms of the three largest measurements (length, breadth and thickness) unevenness of reference points would suggest that replicable accuracy was likely to be to the nearest 0.5 mm only. With regard to measurement of smaller features (e.g. facets and ends), a greater degree of accuracy could be argued providing that reference points were clearly visible. In all cases measurements were taken at *maximum* points, although some examples (ie 'waisted' bracers) necessitated measuring minimum points in addition. Perforation measurements were undertaken at three points: the widest diameter of drilling at both front and back respectively, and at the narrowest point of perforation. Not all perforation drillings appeared to be completely circular, in which case diameter measurements were rejected in favour of maximum and minimum records (e.g. $x \times y$ mm) in order to maintain accuracy for this feature.

All observations other than basic measurements were undertaken using a binocular miscroscope (to ×40) with a cold light source which could be adjusted to provide oblique lighting. This enabled manufacturing striations, wear marks, possible re-use and fractures to be interpreted and recorded not only more clearly, but also with a higher degree of confidence. Each item was initially examined visually, its main dimensions recorded and any obvious significant features discussed before being examined microscopically.

Striations were best viewed under the microscope with the light source angled to pick out even the faintest of markings. These were recorded as being either longitudinal, diagonal, lateral, or multi-directional (or in combination) on all surfaces. Their location on each surface (e.g. centre, ends, all over etc.) was also noted. It was also possible to distinguish between striations which were 'regular' in their formation, as opposed to those which were 'irregular' (ie not apparently conforming to any specific pattern or system of application). Moreover, a number of striations could be defined as 'marked' in that they were relatively deeply etched into the bracer surface, as opposed to being 'faint' and hence unfinished and likely to have been unseen. A previous pilot study on a number of the bracers had demonstrated that these were viable definitions and, in most instances, could be made quite objectively. Moreover, the surface finish of the bracers also showed variation; this could be recorded as either 'polished' or 'rough', possibly offering indications of quality of finish or of non-visible surfaces respectively. Rilling, the concentric lines seen within the perforations caused by drilling, was also observed; the bracers were mostly fine-grained and rilling was difficult to see without a microscope. However, in several instances the rilling could be recorded as having been polished or smoothed out as part of a manufacturing or reworking process.

By contrast use wear factors were more difficult to identify, especially on a hard stone material which is likely to have been fastened securely to a perishable material on the forearm rather than moving like a pendant or string of beads. That said, however, many of the bracers exhibited surface scuffing or scratching which was clearly superimposed over the manufacturing striations. These features were also recorded, as was any rounding of the edges or the sides of the perforations which may have reflected use since manufacture. When the full record of each bracer was complete, a general estimate of its degree of wear was attempted. The categories employed ranged from 'fresh' to 'very worn'.

Many of the bracers showed fragmentation either through fracture, chipping or flaking; each element of fragmentation was identified, numbered, recorded and located on the drawing or sketch. In most instances it was also possible to determine whether the damaged elements occurred during manufacture (e.g. during drilling), during use, or post-depositionally. Microscopic analysis usually enabled any weathering to be noted on a damaged section indicating that fracture occurred prior to burial. Reference to previous illustrations of individual bracers, especially in early publications, also provided a useful indicator of any subsequent damage. A general estimate of percentage presence was also made for each item. In the catalogue at the end of the volume this percentage presence was translated into *percentage present at burial* in order to present a more useful criterion for interpretation.

Apart from basic measurement of diameters, perforation data was also recorded with regard to the angle of drilling. Remarkably few holes were drilled vertically (ie at 90° from the bracer surface); most were drilled from an angle, and in several instances the angle of drilling was quite pronounced. This angle was recorded in terms of broad compass orientation using the front/back or top/bottom of the illustrated (drawn) bracer as a reference. For example, perforations could be described as being drilled from the north-east, south-west, or south-south-east etc. according to position. As the top/bottom designation for each bracer drawing was arbitrary, this information could not be used to compare data directly between the different bracers. However, for each individual bracer, the degree of variation of drilling direction could be considered. The direction of drilling has implications both for manufacturing process and/or methods of fastening the bracer to the forearm.

2.3 PORTABLE X-RAY FLUORESCENCE

Compositions of bracers were determined by x-ray fluorescence analysis using a Spectrace TN9000 portable X-ray fluorescence (PXRF) spectrometer. This instrument used radioactive sources to excite the sample and a mercuric iodide detector to measure the fluorescent x-rays. The methodology largely followed procedures described elsewhere (e.g. Potts *et al.* 1997a and 1997b, and Williams-Thorpe *et al.* 1999). Measurements were made with the PXRF analyser in 'lab stand' configuration whereby samples were placed in contact with the instrument over the circular analyser window (active area *c.*16 mm diameter) and are excited sequentially using the radioactive sources Cd-109, Fe-55 and Am-241 for count times of 200, 100 and 40 seconds respectively. X-ray spectra were quantified using the instrument manufacturer's algorithms, the integration of counts from element peak areas obtained by spectrum fitting and a fundamental parameter procedure for matrix correction.

Solid samples, which present a smooth, flat, homogeneous and uncontaminated surface that can be placed in contact with the flat surface (the analytical plane) of the instrument (and cover at least the central 2/3rds of the detector window) are required to provide fully quantitative data. Often, in the analysis of artefacts this ideal is not met, and measured elemental abundances tend to be variably underestimated. The extent to which the data are affected is usually by no more than about 5–10% for fairly flat objects to as much as 15–25%, possibly more, for highly curved objects. As a precaution, elemental ratios, which largely cancel out such effects, are used in preference to measured elemental abundances when comparing artefact compositions. In positioning samples, every effort was made to minimise such deficiencies in quantification by centring the flattest part of a curved surface on the window, and where curvature was cylindrical the flattest dimension was usually placed longitudinally, parallel to the plane of symmetry through the source and the detector.

In some cases, where curvature of the sample resulted in an excessive gap between the sample and the analytical plane, the sample was placed transversely across the analyser to minimise the gap. Consequently, concavo-convex bracers could rarely be presented for analysis in an entirely satisfactory manner. To minimise errors due

Table 2.2. Calibration bias adjustment factors as applied to raw data.

	Multiplier	**± Offset**
K_2O	1.046	-0.35
CaO	1.111	-0.1
TiO_2	1.304	
MnO	0.5	
Fe_2O_3	1.111	
Zn	1	-55
Rb	0.9	8
Sr	1	
Y	1	
Zr	0.909	
Nb	0.906	
Ba	1.2	

Table 2.3. Summary of control sample measurements for AC-E and WS-E.

Ashmolean - Brighton Control data		**AC-E Raw data Average**	**AC-E Raw data St Dev**	**AC-E Expected**	**AC-E Adjusted Average**	**AC-E Adjusted St Dev**
K_2O	%	4.61	0.12	4.49	4.48	0.12
CaO	%	0.42	0.03	0.34	0.36	0.03
TiO_2	%	0.04	0.02	0.11	0.06	0.02
MnO	%	0.12	0.05	0.058	0.06	0.02
Fe_2O_3	%	2.34	0.14	2.53	2.59	0.15
Rb	mg/kg	165	15	152	156	13
Sr	mg/kg	6	7	3	6	7
Y	mg/kg	188	12		188	12
Zr	mg/kg	893	23	780	812	21
Nb	mg/kg	126	7		115	6
Ba	mg/kg	55	13	55	66	16

Ashmolean - Brighton Control data		**WS-E Raw data average**	**WS-E Raw data St Dev**	**WS-E Expected**	**WS-E Adjusted average**	**WS-E Adjusted St Dev**
K_2O	%	1.40	0.08	1	1.11	0.09
CaO	%	8.16	0.20	8.95	8.96	0.22
TiO_2	%	1.75	0.10	2.4	2.29	0.13
MnO	%	0.35	0.07	0.17	0.17	0.04
Fe_2O_3	%	11.74	0.46	13.15	13.04	0.51
Rb	mg/kg	21	10	25	26	9
Sr	mg/kg	392	24	410	392	24
Y	mg/kg	31	9		31	9
Zr	mg/kg	207	16	195	188	14
Nb	mg/kg	25	6		23	5
Ba	mg/kg	335	29	338	402	35

to x-ray counting precision, sample heterogeneity, and instrument positioning, three determinations were normally made; but sometimes only two measurements were taken on small samples or when two measurements were in good agreement. As most of the samples were fine grained, a minimum of two measurements was considered sufficient to account for mineral heterogeneity effects (Potts *et al.* 1997b). Measurements were normally made on the most representative and geometrically suitable surfaces: an average was taken as representative of the sample.

Corrections were made to the average measured concentrations for calibration bias, based on the average deviation from parity between the expected and analysed values of a suite of 20 reference materials analysed as compressed powder pellets. These adjustment parameters are listed in Table 2.2. Major and minor element data (K_2O, CaO, TiO_2, MnO, Fe_2O_3) are reported as percent oxides by mass (m/m%) and trace elements (Rb, Sr, Y, Zr, Nb, Ba) in parts per million by mass (mg kg^{-1}). Although compositions of other elements, such as Cu, Zn and Pb are monitored, concentrations are not normally high enough to be quantitative. Occasionally very high values were noted, suggesting possible mineralization or contamination of the sample.

The comparability of analytical data derived by PXRF during the main period of investigation (Feb–June 07) was monitored by analysing two control samples (powder pellets of a microgranite, AC-E, and a dolerite, WS-E) at the start and end of each operating session. A summary of these data before and after application of the calibration bias correction are listed in Table 2.3. Control charts for the period of analysis, Feb–June 2007, are shown in Figure 2.1. Long term consistency of the data was considered to be satisfactory. The precision limitation of individual measurements is also provided by the standard deviation data which are shown in Figure 2.2.

The effect of measuring uncertainty for ratios plotted in Chapter 3 is shown for the monitor samples in Figure 2.2. It should be borne in mind that the multiple counting of samples reduces the uncertainty that would be associated with an individual measurement, and the resultant error on mean values, by a factor of $1/\sqrt{n}$, where n is the number of measurements. This represents measurement uncertainty for analysis of ideal surfaces – on non-ideal surfaces the uncertainty will generally be larger. The size of uncertainty propagation for ratios depends on relative errors associated with instrumental precision and therefore the magnitude of measured concentrations. For example AC-E has low Sr, close to its detection limits, where the relative error is extremely high, consequently the resulting uncertainty for the Sr/Ca ratio is very large compared to that for WS-E. Thus AC-E provides a pessimistic example, WS-E a slightly optimistic example of uncertainties associated with the Sr/Ca ratio.

2.4 PETROGRAPHY

A total of 62 pieces were studied in detail petrographically by Rob Ixer using a standard ×10 hand lens/low power binocular microscope, but without knowledge of the individual geochemistry of each item. Particular attention was paid to breaks/fractures in the artefact as these provided 'fresh', unpolished surfaces and the true colour of the rock. All lithological features, including mean grain size, presence of clasts, megacrysts, fossils, veining, bedding, laminae and foliation planes were noted and measured. The colour of the polished and any broken, natural surface was recorded and standardised using the Geological Society of America's 'rock-color' chart. Clast grain size within sediments was standardised using the standard grain size scale. A lithological identification for each bracer was made based upon these macroscopic characteristics. In addition the same characteristics were used to group the bracers into lithologically coherent groups. Post-depositional carbonate, silica and limonite coatings on the bracers were noted. Detailed petrographic descriptions were subsequently compiled and these form the petrographic catalogue of bracers presented in Chapter 3 (Appendix 3.5), together with a further nine descriptions made by other members of the team.

2.5 MAGNETIC SUSCEPTIBILITY MEASUREMENTS

Magnetic susceptibility readings were taken using an Exploranium G.S. KT-5 instrument. A minimum sample diameter of 10 cm and thickness of 5 (7) cm, with a smooth flat surface is required to give fully quantitative, accurate measurements. Unfortunately, none of the samples in this study matched this size constraint.

However, corrections can be applied (see Williams-Thorpe and Thorpe 1993) to overcome surface, size and shape deficiencies in many circumstances. However, where shapes are not regular, satisfactory correction can be extremely difficult. For the concavo-convex shaped bracers in particular it would be very difficult to derive other than a very approximate factor for correction. A very rough estimate suggests that corrections for these samples could be as great as a factor of 3 or 4, potentially propagating very large uncertainties.

In some locations, establishing a background 'zero' level can also be very difficult, and, at very low readings, less than about 0.10×10^{-3} SI units, any zeroing discrepancies, possibly of up to 0.03×10^{-3} SI units will degrade results significantly. Results for samples (ID) 118 – 121 may have been underestimated as a result of difficulties in establishing a true background zero at the measuring site.

Raw values, nevertheless as listed in Chapter 3 (Table 3.5, Table Appendix 3.2 and Appendix 3.5) distinguish very successfully, for bracers 5–7.5 mm thick and wider than 25 mm, the presence of Langdale type material, which has a higher raw magnetic susceptibility than for almost all other materials used for UK bracers (see Chapter 3). Samples with lower values than this are either very short, narrow or thin.

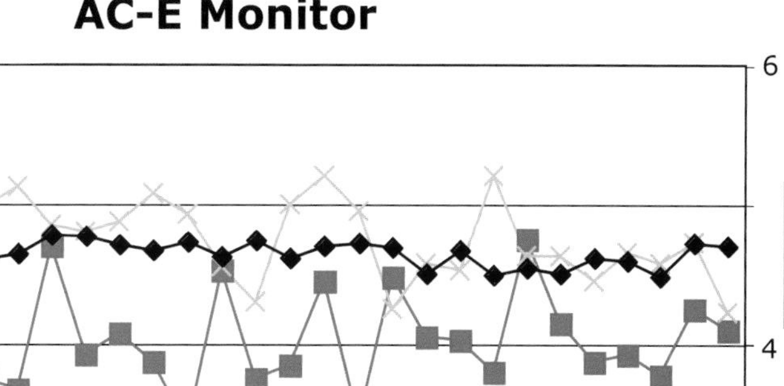
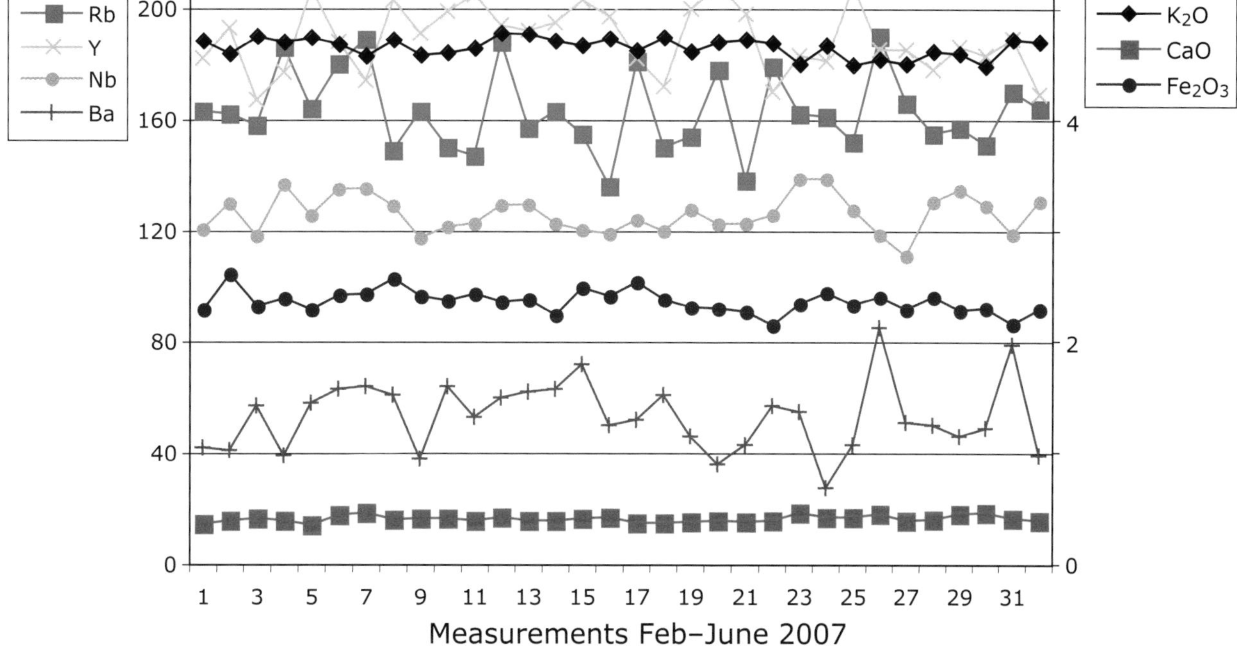

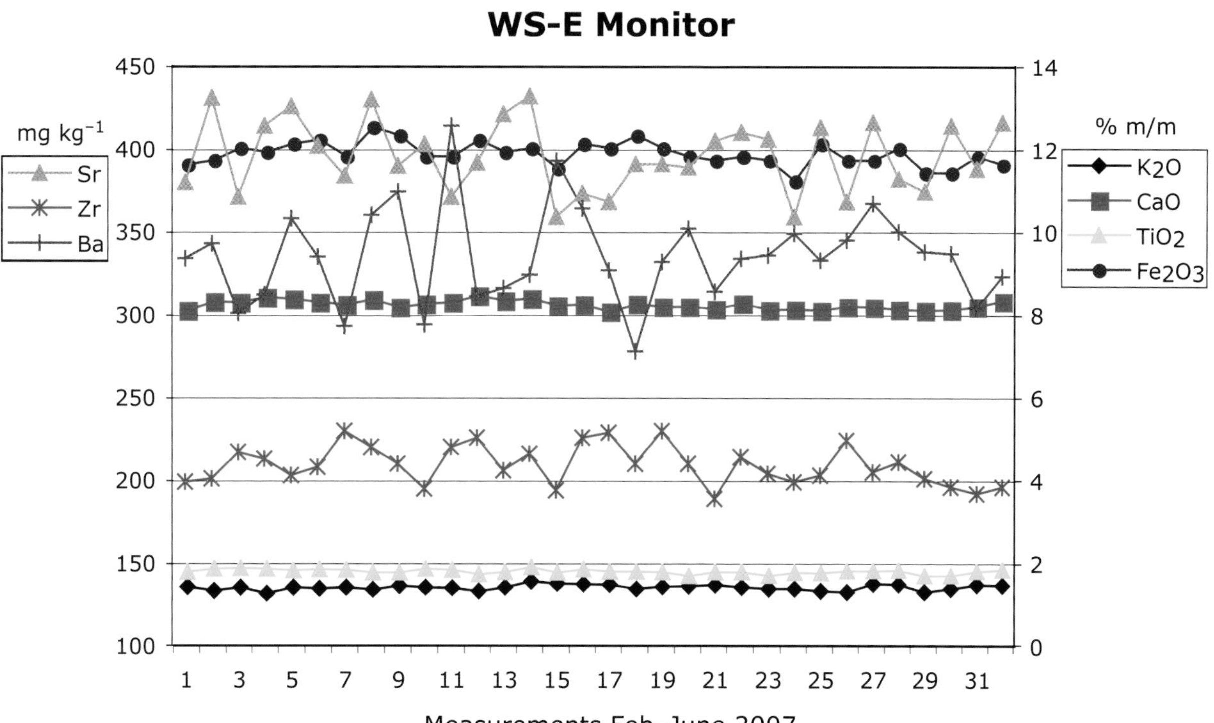

Figure 2.1. Control charts for PXRF operation based on measurements of AC-E and WS-E.

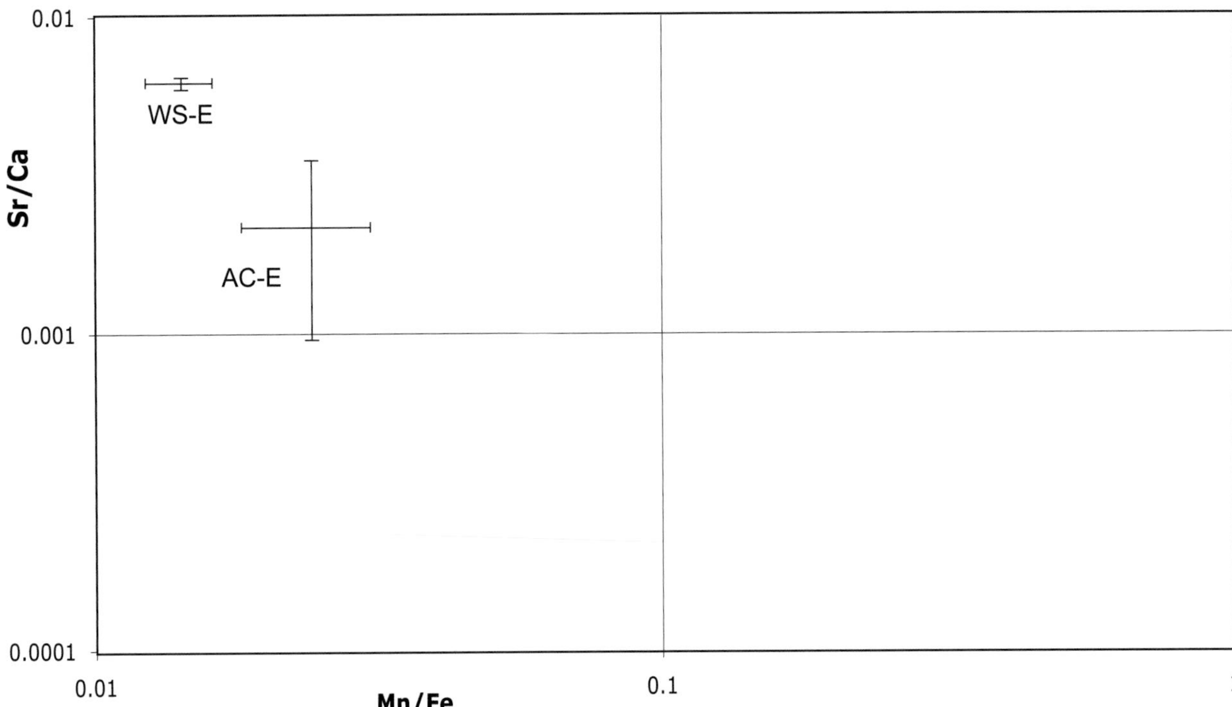

Figure 2.2. PXRF measurement uncertainty for WS-E and AC-E, represented as the standard error of measurement for three determinations (for equivalence with routine analysis).

APPENDIX 2.1. RECORDING PRO FORMA

Appendix Figure 2.1. Front (below) and rear (next page) of bracer recording sheet.

<table>
<tr><td colspan="5">University of Birmingham Institute of Archaeology and Antiquity</td></tr>
<tr><td colspan="5">Leverhulme research project: EBA grave goods</td></tr>
<tr><td>ID number</td><td>County</td><td>Parish</td><td>Barrow number</td><td>Site name</td></tr>
<tr><td>Material
STONE</td><td>Artefact type
BRACER</td><td colspan="3">Number of perforations:</td></tr>
<tr><td>Piggott interment no.</td><td>Corpus type number</td><td colspan="3">Rivets:
Metal stains:</td></tr>
<tr><td colspan="5">References
1</td></tr>
<tr><td colspan="5">2</td></tr>
<tr><td colspan="2">Museum</td><td colspan="3">Museum accession number</td></tr>
<tr><td colspan="2">Weight (g)</td><td colspan="3" rowspan="13">Illustration
Scale
Source</td></tr>
<tr><td colspan="2">Colour</td></tr>
<tr><td colspan="2">Length (mm)</td></tr>
<tr><td colspan="2">Width at mid-point (mm)</td></tr>
<tr><td colspan="2">Width at end 1 (mm)</td></tr>
<tr><td colspan="2">Width at end 2 (mm)</td></tr>
<tr><td colspan="2">Max thickness (mm)</td></tr>
<tr><td colspan="2">Thickness at ends (mm)</td></tr>
<tr><td colspan="2">PERFORATION (most clearly visible example) (mm)
Diam at front
Diam at narrowest
Diam at rear
Form: straight/ hourglass
Placing: symmetric/asymmetric</td></tr>
<tr><td colspan="2">Surface texture</td></tr>
<tr><td colspan="2">Petrology (existing ID)</td></tr>
<tr><td colspan="2">Petrology (macroscopic ID)</td></tr>
<tr><td colspan="2">Petrology (XRF results)</td></tr>
<tr><td>Photo by</td><td>Camera</td><td colspan="2">Photo number</td><td>XRF number</td></tr>
</table>

ID number	**Parish and barrow number**

Form: SHAPE: rectangular/ovoid waisted/slightly waisted/straight side
TRANSVERSE PROFILE: flat/ plano-convex/ concavo-convex (arched)/other
LONGITUDINAL PROFILE: flat/plano-convex/concavo-convex
FACETS: present/ absent flat/ curved location:
ENDS:rounded/faceted
END FACETS: flat/rounded Ht: FACET ANGLES: sharp/rounded
SIDES:rounded/faceted
SIDE FACETS: flat/rounded Ht: FACET ANGLES: sharp/rounded
FLANGES/RIDGES: present/absent form: location:

Fragmentation: % present *Adhesions:*

Fragmentation and damage (including any scratches): (number the breaks if more than one)
front surface:
rear surface:
ends:
corner(s):

Fragmentation: nature of breaks
Break 1: ancient at manufacture/ancient in use/ancient in burial/excavatn. damage/other modern
Break 2: ancient at manufacture/ancient in use/ancient in burial/excavatn. damage/other modern
Break 3: ancient at manufacture/ancient in use/ancient in burial/excavatn. damage/other modern
EXTRA DESCRIPTION

General condition	Very worn/slightly worn/worn/fresh

Traces of manufacture:
SURFACES:
front: rough/ polished/ high polish
rear: rough/ polished/ high polish
STRIATIONS:
front: longitudinal/ lateral/ diagonal/ multi-directional/ other:
faint/ marked
ends/ sides/ all over/ other
regular/ irregular
rear: longitudinal/ lateral/ diagonal/ multi-directional/ other:
faint/ marked
ends/ sides/ all over/ other
regular/ irregular
PERFORATIONS:
first drilling from: front/ rear
any starter holes? Front/ rear/ no
inside perforation (front): smooth/circumferential rilling/other
(rear): smooth/circumferential rilling/other

Wear traces: front:
rear:
ends:
in/around perforations:

Other notes/final comments

Completed by	Date	Entered by	Date

3: ROCKS AND ROCK SOURCES

Rob Ixer, Peter Webb, John Watson and Philip Potts

3.1 GEOCHEMISTRY

3.1.1 Summary

Elemental analysis of lithic artefacts has the potential to provide evidence for recognising artefacts of similar composition for which derivation from the same source material would be a high probability, and, if suitable comparative source material were available, to establish their provenance. In conjunction with petrographic characteristics (Section 3.2), the chemical composition of lithic artefacts may enable rock types to be identified and thus indicate where to look for potential source material.

Sixty-one bracers from England, Scotland and Wales were analysed by portable x-ray fluorescence (PXRF) using procedures outlined in Chapter 2. The results are listed in Table 3.1. Several candidate materials were analysed to test for comparability (Table 3.2), including spotted slates (metamudstones) from Preseli, south-west Wales, Langdale tuff from the Lake District and mudstones from Caerfai Bay, Pembrokeshire. Investigation of bracer compositions and the graphical analysis of data have enabled two large, coherent groups of bracers to be recognised.

One group consists of the 24 samples listed in Table 3.3. They share many chemical and petrographic properties and are thought to be amphibole-bearing metasediments (see 3.1.2). These bracers are generally fine grained, similarly coloured, with hues ranging from pale silvery grey to dark greenish grey; they are sometimes spotted, often mottled and usually have a planar fabric with some degree of fissility. Chemically they are characterized by very low K_2O, Rb and Ba contents; moderate levels of CaO and Fe_2O_3; low to moderate Sr and TiO_2; and moderate Y, Zr and Nb (see bracers of Table 3.3 listed in Table 3.1). Their unusually low values of Sr/Ca (0.0008–0.0025) combined with high levels of Mn/Fe (0.04–0.1) results in a distribution (Figure 3.1) that discriminates them well from other rock types. This plot is particularly effective as Sr substitutes for Ca, and Mn for Fe in rock forming minerals, so that variations in these ratios signify different mineral hosts and different geological origins for the rocks. Candidate materials that were analysed to test for comparability included spotted slates (metamudstones) from Preseli, south-west Wales (Table 3.2) and jadeite (axe head) samples, but neither plot in the same area (Figure 3.2); both types have significant chemical differences, as did altered slates sampled from Perran Beach, Perranporth, north Cornwall. The suite of jadeite Neolithic axe heads chosen was a group of eight examples housed in the Cambridge University Museum of Archaeology and Anthropology. The relevance of jade in this context arises from the work of *Projet JADE*, a European research project investigating the sourcing, production and distribution of Neolithic axe heads of jadeite.

The second group consists of the 18 samples listed in Table 3.4. They too share many chemical and petrographic properties and the rock from which they were derived is a meta-volcaniclastic comparable to the Implement Petrology Committee (IPC) Group VI axe heads which have been provenanced to certain horizons of the Langdale tuffs in the English Lake District (Keiller *et al.* 1941). These bracers are fine grained, texturally more uniform than the previous group, and lack any sign of internal fabric. Their colour ranges from pale bluish grey to dark greenish grey; they often feature fine dark markings and lamination that indicates depositional stratification and sometimes shows effects of dislocation and slippage that occurred before lithification. A common feature is the presence of 0.5–1 mm-sized cavities often with cubic outlines and rusty/limonitic inclusions reflecting former pyrite/pyrrhotite grains. Chemically, the group is typified by fairly high levels of TiO_2 and Fe_2O_3, moderate Rb and Zr, and high Sr and Ba (see bracers of Table 3.4 listed in Table 3.1). In Figure 3.1 they plot as a tight cluster within the range Sr/Ca (0.005–0.009) and Mn/Fe (0.015–0.025). Comparative measurements made on three rock samples of Langdale tuff and reported in Table 3.2, are also plotted on Figure 3.2; although in close agreement with the bracer grouping, they may not represent precisely the same source horizon.

The remaining 19 bracer sample compositions cannot be grouped in any coherent way. Their distribution on Figure 3.1 has no clear patterns. However, in some cases their

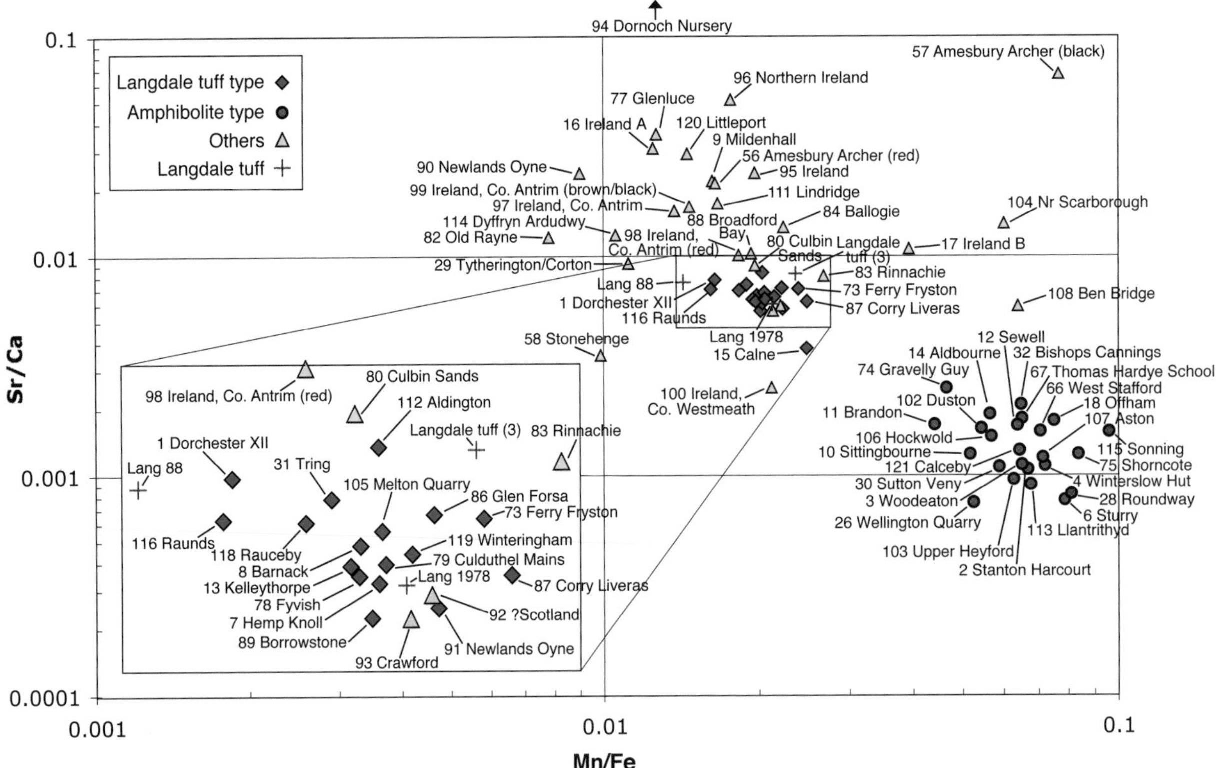

Figure 3.1 Mn/Fe vs Sr/Ca plot of all bracers distinguished individually. In this and the following figures amphibolite type represents the amphibole-bearing metasediments referred to in the text.

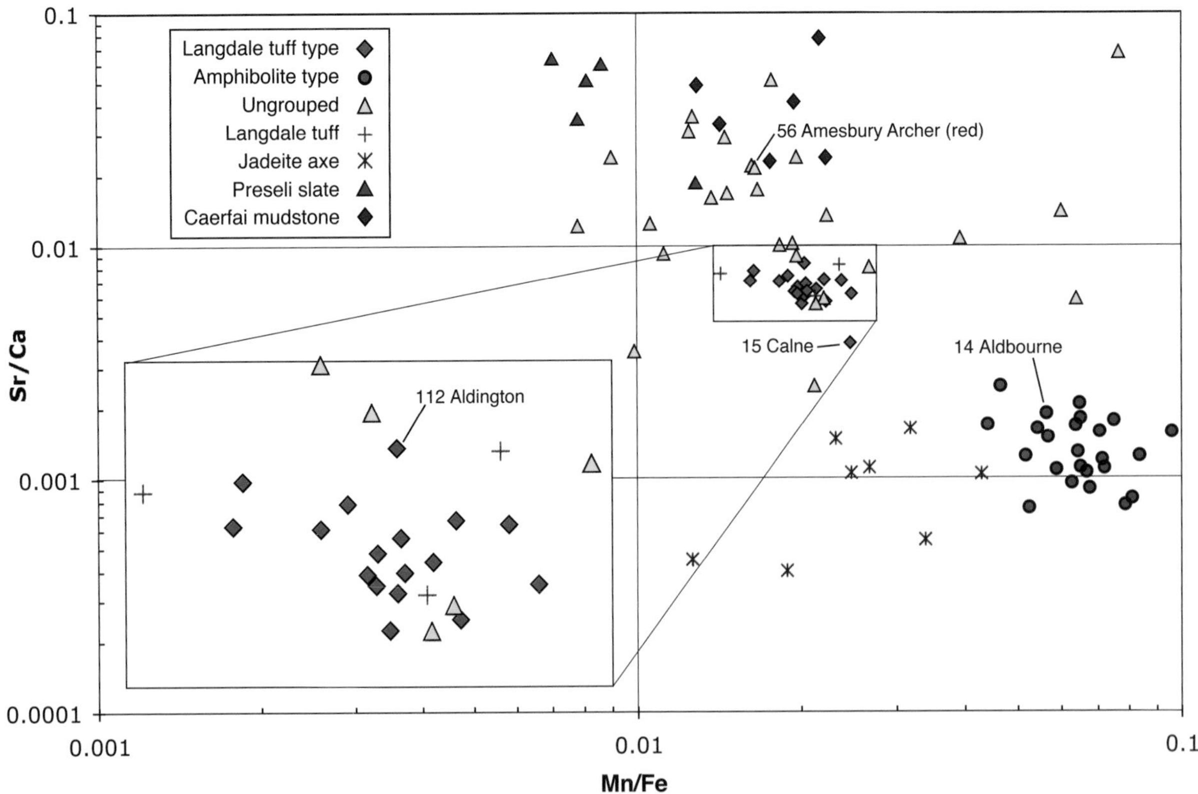

Figure 3.2 Bracers plotted along with comparative samples.

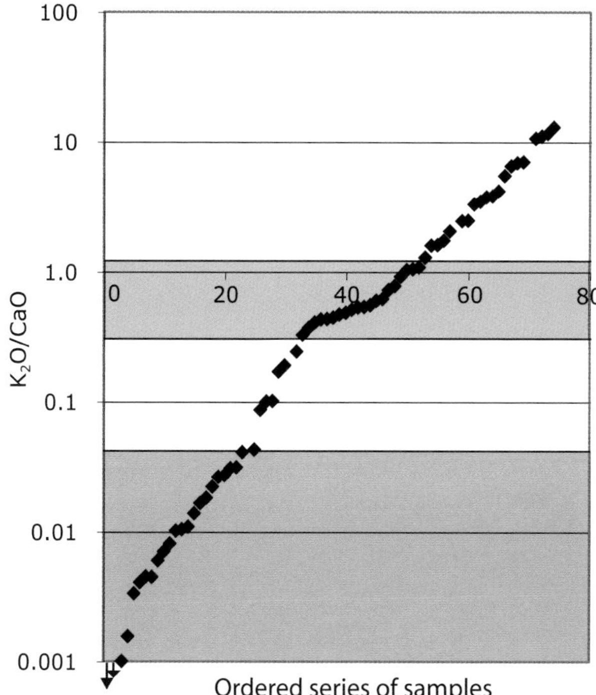

Figure 3.3 Ranked K_2O/CaO ratio values for bracers. The blue band contains the amphibole-bearing metasedimentary bracers and extends to include some samples with low K_2O/CaO values well below the graph. The green band contains the Langdale tuff bracers.

chemistry helps in the broad identification of their source rock type, as discussed further below.

3.1.2 Discussion

Recognition of the groups identified above was aided by the preliminary exercise of ranking samples according to their K_2O/CaO ratios and looking for compositional clusters and natural divisions (Figure 3.3). The groups were then refined by examining other chemical and petrological properties, especially for those samples at the margins of the preliminary groups, to ensure their apparent comparability was justified. The larger group of samples had very low K_2O/CaO values of less than 0.05, whereas the Langdale bracers had K_2O/CaO ratios from 0.4 to 1.0. Within the remaining samples there were no significant natural groups or divisions, their K_2O/CaO ratios ranging from 0.087 to 0.19 and 1.29 to 13.0. The coloured bands on Figure 3.3 contain the groups eventually recognised.

Establishing genuine compositional comparability requires matching of several chemical criteria, as well as other properties, such as petrological characteristics, and therefore for further investigation samples were plotted using several different compositional parameters (see Figures 3.1 to 3.6). Ratios have been used in all plots in an attempt to make valid comparisons of bracer compositional characteristics because the absolute concentrations of

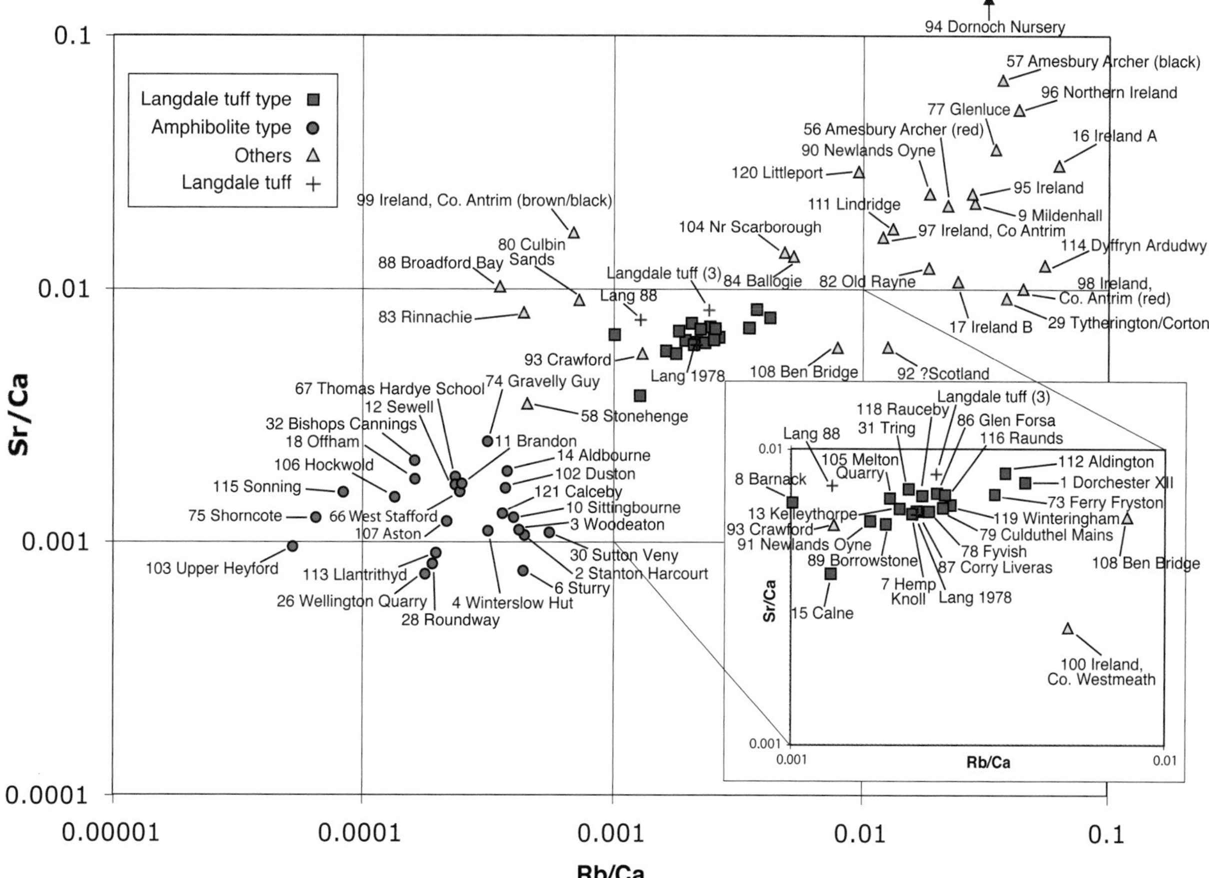

Figure 3.4 Rb/Ca vs Sr/Ca plot of all bracers distinguished individually.

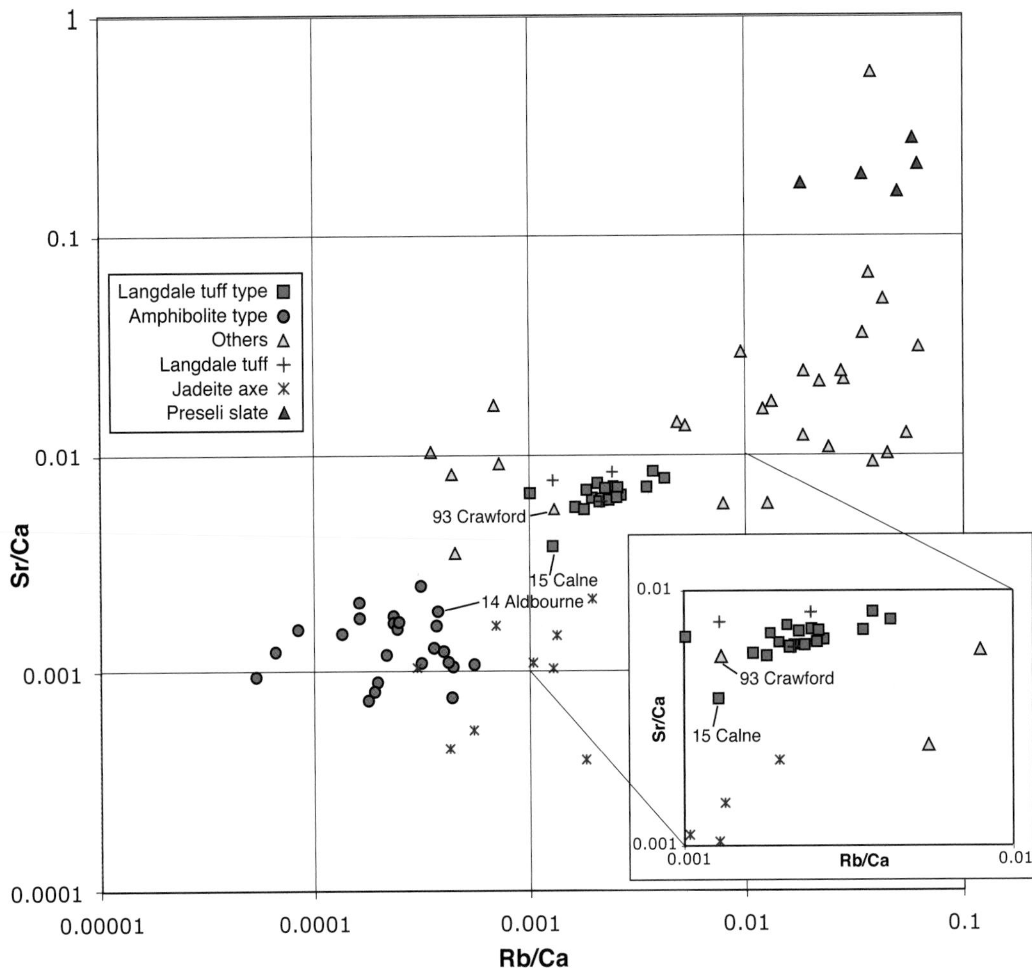

Figure 3.5 Bracers plotted along with comparative samples.

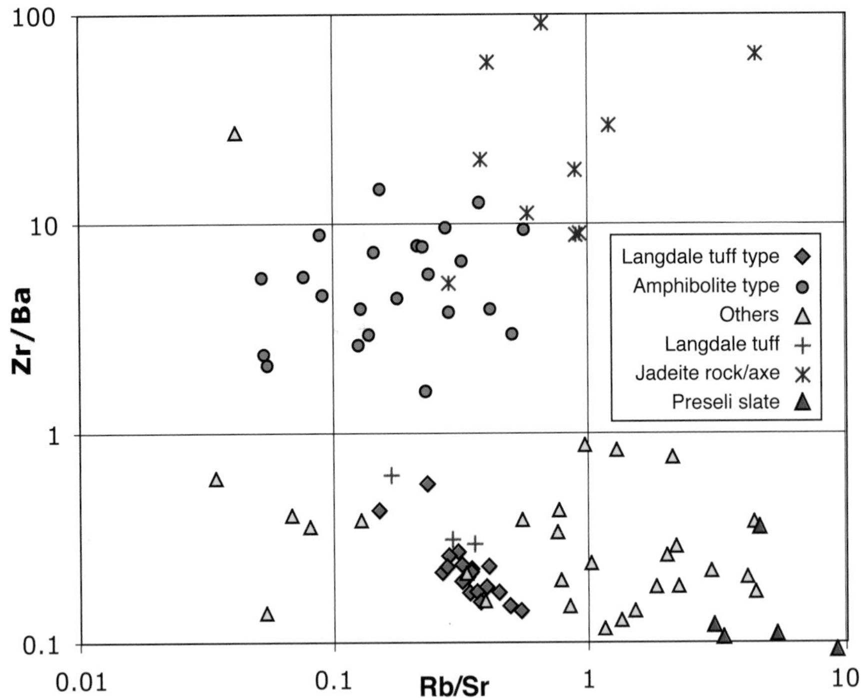

Figure 3.6 Rb/Sr vs Zr/Ba demonstrates that discrimination of the main groupings is possible using other chemical parameters.

constituents cannot always be taken at face value when samples are of different size and shape, as indicated in Chapter 2.4 (PXRF Methodology). Measured concentrations can be expected to be truly representative of the sample only when measurement conditions (affected by sample size, shape, instrument placement, surface irregularities and contamination) are ideal. Obtaining accurate quantitative data is particularly difficult for small and highly shaped items such as the concavo-convex bracers which are common amongst the Langdale tuff group. This should be taken into account when considering the compositional data reported in Table 3.1.

Clearly the groupings of the amphibole-bearing metasedimentary bracers and the Langdale bracers evident on both chemical and petrographic grounds are highly distinctive. Certain individual items may not be compatible in every compositional parameter however, and there may be questions as to their affiliation. For example, ID14 (Aldbourne), was not part of the major group of amphibole-bearing metasedimentary bracers initially selected on K_2O/CaO ratio, but most of its chemical and petrological features are compatible with the group, as is clear in Figures 3.1, 3.2 , 3.4 and 3.5. Its K_2O is unusually high and Y slightly high for the group, whereas other compositional parameters are in the normal compositional range (though CaO and Fe_2O_3 are slightly low). In these latter respects it closely matches the Woodeaton (ID 3) example. On examining several compositional diagrams it was clear that few other bracers plot close to this group of bracers and never consistently did so.

Magnetic susceptibility measurements are all low for this group of bracers, with raw values less than 0.07×10^{-3} SI units (see Table 3.5). However, there is considerable overlap with raw values for the ungrouped bracers.

The recognition of amphibole in this major group of metasedimentary bracers was a result of reflectance spectroscopy analysis of 14 selected samples (Michel Errera pers. comm.). The presence of amphibole, most likely actinolitic, was confirmed by thin section petrography of four of the bracers. The presence of moderate levels of CaO, Fe_2O_3, and minimal K_2O, Rb and Ba is compatible with actinolite-tremolite series amphibole-bearing rocks. These would most likely be Mg-Fe-Ca-bearing metasediments, originally impure carbonate-bearing siltstones – their Sr contents being too low for them to be metabasic rocks. Most of these rocks tend to have a planar fabric as would be expected with the formation of amphibolitic mineralogy under low to medium grade, greenschist facies conditions of regional metamorphism. Subsequent measurement of the Llantrithyd bracer (ID113) in February 2009, using a new form of PXRF instrumentation, a Niton XL3t-900 with He flush to measure 'light' elements has extended our knowledge of its composition and, by association, that of other amphibole-bearing bracers. The data are not fully quantitative on account of surface shape effects being more severe for 'light' element components such as MgO, Al_2O_3 and SiO_2. However, the MgO/Fe_2O_3 ratio of about 2.5, relatively low Al_2O_3 contents (less than 4%), but high SiO_2 (more than 70%) are all compatible with a significant amount (~30–40%) of a tremolite-rich actinolitic amphibole, but even more quartz (50–60%). Such a rock can be regarded as a calc-silicate that had originated as a very silty Ca-Mg limestone and had been subjected to low to medium grade metamorphism.

The Langdale bracers form a particularly tight grouping, particularly in terms of Sr/Ca and Mn/Fe ratios (Figure 3.1 and 3.2). However, the Calne bracer (ID 15) tends to plot away from the rest owing to its high CaO, most likely to be due to surface contamination by visible calcium carbonate encrustation; while the Aldington bracer (ID 112) with a noticeably bleached surface has very low MnO and Fe_2O_3, most likely to be due to leaching of these constituents by weathering. The piece from Kelleythorpe (ID 13) is notably low in several of its chemical constituents (Table 3.1), probably a consequence of the raised placement of the object on the detector, due to the gold studs, but it always plots well within the group in the ratio plots, demonstrating the value of using ratios for characterisation.

Magnetic susceptibility measurements also discriminate the Langdale tuff bracers, their raw values ranging from 0.14 to 0.36×10^{-3} SI units (see Table 3.5) for samples with a thickness of 5–7.5 mm and a width not less than 25 mm, whereas all other bracers (except for three, which are quite different chemically and petrographically) have lower values.

One sample, from Crawford (ID 93), has chemical properties (especially K_2O/CaO ratio) similar to the 'Langdale' group and plots fairly consistently within or close to the main group. However, many compositional abundances are only marginally within range, in particular K_2O, MnO and Ba are quite low despite the measurement being made on a flattish surface from which concentrations are unlikely to be significantly underestimated. There is clear doubt therefore as to whether this sample should be included in the group – indeed, its petrological nature suggests sedimentary affinities differing markedly from that typical of the Langdale tuffs. Its chemical similarity is therefore thought merely to be coincidental.

The samples from Culbin Sands (ID 80) and Ballogie (ID 84) have some chemical features in common with the 'Langdale' group, indeed they tend to plot in the general vicinity in Figures 3.1 and 3.4. However, ID 80 has lower K_2O, TiO_2, and Rb but higher Sr and Zr, and ID 84 has higher K_2O, Rb, Ba, and lower CaO than most of the Langdale group, and is quite different in TiO_2, which is less than 1/10th of the norm for the Langdale group. Petrographically, ID 84 has pale green reduction spots, a feature reminiscent of indurated sediment. Its geochemistry is more compatible with having the composition of shale or metamudstone. The bracer from Broadford Bay (ID 88) is similar to ID 80 in some respects but has even lower levels of K_2O and Ba; it also has lower Fe_2O_3, MnO and Zr. Although these items could have a broadly similar meta-volcaniclastic or metasedimentary origin, they clearly would not have the same source as the Langdale tuffs. The raw magnetic susceptibility for these samples

Table 3.1 PXRF analyses and raw magnetic susceptibility (MS) measurements of British mainland bracers ordered by ascending K_2O/CaO ratio.

Sample ID Sorted K/Ca		**26** **Wellington Quarry** Average (2)	**30** **Sutton Veny** Average (3)	**18** **Offham** Average (4)	**67** **Thomas Hardye Sch** Average (3)	**4** **Winterslow Hut** Average (3)	**2** **Stanton Harcourt** Average (3)	**32** **Bishops Cannings** Average (2)	**121** **Calceby** Average (4)	**74** **Gravelly Guy** Average (3)	**113** **Llantrithyd** Average (3)	**12** **Sewell** Average (3)
K_2O	%	0.0	0.0	0.0	0.0	0.0	0.0	0.0	0.0	0.0	0.0	0.1
CaO	%	7.2	4.3	8.2	5.8	4.8	5.6	7.0	4.8	6.1	4.8	7.1
TiO_2	%	0.4	0.2	0.3	0.4	0.3	0.3	0.3	0.0	0.6	0.2	0.3
MnO	%	0.3	0.2	0.3	0.2	0.2	0.2	0.2	0.2	0.2	0.2	0.2
Fe_2O_3	%	5.4	3.4	3.9	3.6	3.0	3.7	3.5	3.3	4.9	2.7	3.9
Rb	mg/kg	9	17	9	10	11	18	8	12	14	7	12
Sr	mg/kg	39	34	104	76	38	43	105	44	110	31	86
Y	mg/kg	29	22	27	41	28	30	33	28	32	27	27
Zr	mg/kg	101	99	122	135	94	106	115	97	128	75	91
Nb	mg/kg	21	21	24	23	24	18	15	24	24	15	23
Ba	mg/kg	18	33	27	34	25	27	21	10	48	10	31
Raw MS ($\times 10^{-3}$ SI units)		–	–	0.07	0.04	–	–	0.00	0.01	0.07	0.03	0.06
Sample ID **Sorted** **K/Ca**		**115** **Sonning** Average (3)	**10** **Sitting-bourne** Average (3)	**3** **Woodeaton** Average (2)	**66** **West Stafford** Average (3)	**106** **Hockwold** Average (3)	**6** **Sturry** Average (4)	**75** **Shorncote** Average (2)	**103** **Upper Heyford** Average (3)	**107** **Aston** Average (3)	**28** **Roundway** Average (3)	**102** **Duston** Average (3)
K_2O	%	0.1	0.1	0.0	0.1	0.1	0.1	0.2	0.1	0.1	0.2	0.1
CaO	%	6.3	5.0	3.5	4.7	5.2	6.3	9.9	5.1	4.9	7.4	4.0
TiO_2	%	0.3	0.2	0.3	0.1	0.4	0.2	0.2	0.2	0.2	0.2	0.3
MnO	%	0.3	0.1	0.1	0.2	0.2	0.2	0.4	0.2	0.2	0.3	0.2
Fe_2O_3	%	3.0	2.9	2.3	3.4	4.0	3.0	4.7	3.1	2.7	3.9	3.2
Rb	mg/kg	4	14	11	8	5	20	5	2	8	10	11
Sr	mg/kg	72	45	28	53	56	35	89	35	43	43	47
Y	mg/kg	33	26	14	23	24	24	38	26	13	22	26
Zr	mg/kg	113	100	65	107	78	94	116	82	71	86	105
Nb	mg/kg	20	19	13	25	16	20	23	21	13	21	20
Ba	mg/kg	48	15	5	7	9	10	21	39	16	54	13
Raw MS ($\times 10^{-3}$ SI units)		0.00	0.04	–	0.05	0.03	0.06	0.01	0.01	0.03	0.04	0.00

Sample ID Sorted K/Ca		11 Brandon Average (3)	88 Broadford Bay Average (3)	58 Stonehenge Average (3)	83 Rinnachie, Strathdon Average (2)	80 Culbin Sands Average (2)	104 Scarborough Average (3)	8 Barnack Average (3)	15 Calne Average (3)	93 Crawford Average (3)	13 Kelleythorpe Average (3)	91 Newlands Oyne Average (2)
K_2O	%	0.3	0.2	0.4	2.3	0.8	0.1	1.6	3.3	1.9	1.3	2.5
CaO	%	6.7	5.6	5.1	23.1	6.4	0.3	6.4	10.1	5.0	3.3	5.7
TiO_2	%	0.5	0.4	0.2	0.3	0.9	0.1	1.6	1.8	1.3	1.0	1.8
MnO	%	0.2	0.1	0.1	0.0	0.2	0.0	0.2	0.1	0.1	0.1	0.1
Fe_2O_3	%	5.7	2.9	16.6	1.6	9.6	0.5	9.9	5.7	5.0	7.3	7.2
Rb	mg/kg	12	14	16	72	17	11	46	92	46	45	66
Sr	mg/kg	81	408	128	1325	414	30	300	274	197	147	232
Y	mg/kg	34	33	105	305	24	9	41	30	39	17	37
Zr	mg/kg	124	101	33	94	190	68	155	132	166	107	148
Nb	mg/kg	25	23	9	18	29	12	21	20	20	17	20
Ba	mg/kg	17	168	88	682	339	-1	367	644	292	399	541
Raw MS ($\times 10^{-3}$ SI units)		0.07	0.03	0.26	0.10	2.97	0.00	0.36	0.21	0.10	0.19	0.06

Sample ID Sorted K/Ca		89 Borrowstone Average (3)	87 Corry Liveras Average (2)	105 Melton Quarry Average (3)	7 Hemp Knoll Average (3)	119 Winter-ingham Average (4)	86 Glen Forsa Average (2)	31 Tring Average (2)	118 Rauceby Average (4)	116 Raunds Average (3)	78 Fyvish Average (3)	79 Culduthel Mains Average (3)
K_2O	%	2.1	2.8	3.1	2.3	2.8	3.1	2.7	2.8	3.0	2.9	2.8
CaO	%	4.8	6.3	6.6	4.7	5.5	5.8	4.9	5.1	5.0	4.7	3.9
TiO_2	%	1.4	1.6	1.8	1.4	1.5	1.4	1.6	1.7	1.5	1.4	1.4
MnO	%	0.1	0.1	0.2	0.2	0.2	0.2	0.2	0.2	0.2	0.1	0.1
Fe_2O_3	%	6.9	6.2	10.5	8.2	11.0	9.6	9.9	12.6	10.8	7.3	6.3
Rb	mg/kg	62	97	86	71	104	101	72	81	91	79	70
Sr	mg/kg	193	276	322	205	255	294	259	253	250	208	175
Y	mg/kg	18	34	37	35	34	28	38	30	31	22	21
Zr	mg/kg	102	147	152	125	163	156	138	168	141	112	114
Nb	mg/kg	16	20	21	16	25	15	19	24	18	12	14
Ba	mg/kg	528	660	711	580	713	911	608	722	814	719	623
Raw MS ($\times 10^{-3}$ SI units)		0.20	0.17	0.09	0.23	0.02	0.18	0.16	0.05	0.10	0.17	0.14

Continued over the page.

Sample ID Sorted K/Ca		73 Ferry Fryston Average (4)	1 Dorchester XII Average (3)	112 Aldington Average (3)	14 Aldbourne Average (3)	108 Ben Bridge Average (3)	84 Ballogie Average (2)	120 Littleport Average (3)	92 ?Scotland Average (3)	9 Mildenhall Average (3)	111 Lindridge Average (3)	90 Newlands Oyne Average (3)
K_2O	%	2.6	4.1	4.1	4.3	1.3	4.5	1.7	1.1	1.1	2.2	2.8
CaO	%	3.3	4.5	4.0	3.9	1.0	2.8	1.0	0.6	0.4	0.9	0.8
TiO_2	%	1.3	1.7	1.5	0.2	0.2	0.1	0.5	0.2	0.6	0.7	0.7
MnO	%	0.2	0.2	0.1	0.1	0.2	0.1	0.0	0.1	0.1	0.1	0.1
Fe_2O_3	%	7.4	10.4	3.9	2.4	3.6	6.7	2.9	4.7	4.4	5.5	9.0
Rb	mg/kg	82	135	106	11	56	107	68	51	87	84	112
Sr	mg/kg	165	246	237	54	41	271	205	24	66	108	142
Y	mg/kg	23	39	45	41	73	36	20	24	30	34	30
Zr	mg/kg	103	151	130	96	57	195	198	126	325	251	106
Nb	mg/kg	13	20	18	17	13	26	17	13	24	22	22
Ba	mg/kg	690	1074	754	–	450	1246	939	166	395	594	540
Raw MS (× 10^{-3} SI units)		0.20	–	0.22	0.03	0.01	0.08	0.02	0.02	0.12	0.09	0.13

Sample ID Sorted K/Ca		57 Amesbury Archer (black) Average (3)	56 Amesbury Archer (red) Average (3)	82 Candle Hill, Average (2)	94 Dornoch Nursery Average (3)	29 Tytherington/ Corton Average (3)	114 Dyffryn Ardudwy Average (3)	77 Glenluce Average (2)
K_2O	%	1.1	3.4	3.9	1.1	6.3	4.5	3.9
CaO	%	0.3	0.9	0.9	0.2	0.9	0.4	0.3
TiO_2	%	0.2	0.8	1.3	0.5	1.0	0.4	4.0
MnO	%	0.0	0.1	0.0	0.1	0.1	0.0	0.1
Fe_2O_3	%	0.4	7.0	6.0	6.1	8.4	1.7	10.4
Rb	mg/kg	82	139	122	57	249	165	83
Sr	mg/kg	149	134	80	823	59	37	85
Y	mg/kg	23	24	37	20	25	28	21
Zr	mg/kg	89	178	128	119	144	164	365
Nb	mg/kg	19	20	20	17	21	24	76
Ba	mg/kg	234	751	913	297	703	440	421
Raw MS (× 10^{-3} SI units)		0.01	0.04	0.04	0.02	0.10	0.00	0.05

Note: ID 83 was subsequently deemed not to be a bracer, and was excluded from measurements or discussion in other chapters.

Table 3.2. PXRF analyses of comparative geological samples.

Sample ID		Langdale tuff Average (3)	Lang 88 Average (2)	Lang 1978 Average (2)	Preseli slates Average (5)	Caerfai mudstones Average (6)	Jadeite axes Average (6)
K_2O	%	1.7	0.9	2.1	4.5	3.0	0.1
CaO	%	3.4	4.7	4.9	0.1	0.4	3.3
TiO_2	%	1.4	1.7	1.5	1.1	0.8	0.4
MnO	%	0.2	0.2	0.2	0.1	0.1	0.1
Fe_2O_3	%	9.6	12.9	11.2	6.5	6.9	2.7
Rb	ppm	59	43	76	176	115	22
Sr	ppm	201	253	211	40	89	27
Y	ppm	33	35	40	57	25	60
Zr	ppm	165	150	185	241	162	516
Nb	ppm	23	16	29	32	20	22
Ba	ppm	534	239	628	1806	644	27

Table 3.3. List of amphibole-bearing metasedimentary bracers.

ID No	Location	ID No	Location
2	Stanton Harcourt	32	Bishops Cannings
3	Woodeaton	66	West Stafford
4	Winterslow Hut	67	Thomas Hardye School
6	Sturry	74	Gravelly Guy
10	Sittingbourne	75	Shorncote
11	Brandon	102	Duston
12	Sewell	103	Upper Heyford
14	Aldbourne	106	Hockwold
18	Offham	107	Aston
26	Wellington Quarry	113	Llantrithyd
28	Roundway	115	Sonning
30	Sutton Veny	121	Calceby

Table 3.4. List of Langdale tuff bracers.

ID No	Location	ID No	Location
1	Dorchester XII	86	Glen Forsa
7	Hemp Knoll	87	Corry Liveras
8	Barnack	89	Borrowstone
13	Kelleythorpe	91	Newlands, Oyne
15	Calne	105	Melton Quarry
31	Tring	112	Aldington
73	Ferry Fryston	116	Raunds
78	Fyrish	118	Rauceby
79	Culduthel Mains	119	Winteringham

is quite variable and no values match the Langdale range (see Table 3.5).

Ungrouped bracers ('others' in Figures 3.1. 3.4, 3.5 and 3.6) that have distinctive compositional features include the item from Rinnachie (ID 83), not now thought to be a bracer, with very high CaO, Sr and Y, indicating a highly calcic composition – probably a metamorphic calc-silicate rock, taking its lithological features into consideration. However, this piece has been reworked, and there is some ambiguity regarding its use as a bracer. The piece from Stonehenge (ID 58) has high Fe_2O_3 and unusually high Y, but fairly low K_2O, Ba and Rb, and low TiO_2, with particularly low Zr and Nb. It has some features expected of basalt, but its higher raw magnetic susceptibility (0.26 × 10^{-3} SI units) is probably not high enough, and only moderate CaO with low TiO_2 and MnO are not entirely compatible with basalt and an indurated ferruginous marl or concretion remains a strong possibility.

Several of the ungrouped bracers have fairly low abundances of K_2O and CaO along with other major and trace elements. They include pieces from Scarborough (ID 104), Ben Bridge (ID 108) with low TiO_2 and Sr; Littleport (ID 120), ?Scotland (ID 92) with low Sr, Mildenhall (ID 9), Lindridge (ID 111), Amesbury archer (black) (ID 57) and Dornoch Nursery (ID 94), with its unusually high level of Sr. Of these, IDs 9, 94, 104, 108, 111 and 120 are well-lithified? fine sandstones or siltstones. ID104 has particularly low contents of all major and trace elements except for Zr, compatible with being a fine, nearly pure, quartz-rich sandstone. High Zr is a feature of the bracers from Mildenhall (ID 9), Lindridge (ID 111) and Glenluce (ID 77), and may well suggest the presence of detrital zircons. However, whereas ID 9 and ID 111 have several compositional and petrographic similarities, ID 77 differs markedly in several respects, most notably higher K_2O and Fe_2O_3, and extremely high TiO_2, along with significantly high Nb, possibly due to the presence of detrital ilmenite or rutile.

The black Amesbury Archer piece (ID 57) is unusual in its low content of CaO, MnO and especially Fe_2O_3, rather similar to the Scarborough example (ID 104), but unlike ID104 has rather more moderate levels of trace elements, plus K_2O and TiO_2. It has some likeness chemically to the Irish jasper bracers (see Appendix 3.1, Table Appendix

Table 3.5 Raw magnetic susceptibility (MS) measurements for British mainland bracers. Dark grey shading = Amphibole-bearing metasedimentary group; light grey shading = Langdale tuff group. See also Tables 3.3 and 3.4. Note: raw measurements are uncorrected for size and shape of object.

ID	Location	Raw MS (× 10^{-3} SI units)	ID	Location	Raw MS (× 10^{-3} SI units)
32	Bishops Cannings	0.00	6	Sturry	0.06
115	Sonning	0.00	90	Newlands, Oyne	0.06
102	Duston	0.00	18	Offham	0.07
104	Scarborough	0.00	74	Gravelly Guy	0.07
114	Dyffryn Ardudwy	0.00	11	Brandon	0.07
121	Calceby	0.01	84	Ballogie	0.08
75	Shorncote	0.01	105	Melton Quarry	0.09
103	Upper Heyford	0.01	111	Lindridge	0.09
108	Ben Bridge	0.01	83	Rinnachie, Strathdon	0.10
57	Amesbury Archer (black)	0.01	93	Crawford	0.10
119	Winteringham	0.02	116	Raunds	0.10
120	Littleport	0.02	29	Tytherington/Corton	0.10
92	?Scotland	0.02	9	Mildenhall	0.12
94	Dornoch Nursery	0.02	91	Newlands, Oyne	0.13
113	Llantrithyd	0.03	79	Culduthel Mains	0.14
106	Hockwold	0.03	31	Tring	0.16
107	Aston	0.03	87	Corry Liveras	0.17
88	Broadford Bay	0.03	78	Fyvish	0.17
14	Aldbourne	0.03	86	Glen Forsa	0.18
67	Thomas Hardye School	0.04	13	Kelleythorpe	0.19
10	Sittingbourne	0.04	89	Borrowstone	0.20
28	Roundway	0.04	73	Ferry Fryston	0.20
56	Amesbury Archer (red)	0.04	15	Calne	0.21
82	Old Rayne	0.04	112	Aldington	0.22
66	West Stafford	0.05	7	Hemp Knoll	0.23
118	Rauceby	0.05	58	Stonehenge	0.26
77	Glenluce	0.05	8	Barnack	0.36
12	Sewell	0.06	80	Culbin Sands	2.97

3.1), but is very poor in Fe_2O_3 and could well be a silicified siltstone or a chert as it is grey-black rather than red in colour. The ?Scotland piece (ID 92) has similarly low abundances of many major and trace elements but has much higher Fe_2O_3, is dark red and finely crystalline, similar to the Irish jaspers (see Appendix 3.1).

Many of the ungrouped bracers with relatively high K_2O/CaO (>1) are likely to have a sedimentary origin as mudstones and derivatives with moderate to relatively high K_2O along with proportionate Ba and Rb likely to be associated with illite clay or micas. Most of these samples have significant levels of Fe_2O_3, but low Mn/Fe ratios. They include bracers from Newlands, Oyne (ID 90); Amesbury Archer (red) (ID 56); Old Rayne (ID 82); Tytherington/Corton (ID 29) with very high K_2O and Rb; Dyffryn Ardudwy (ID 114) with low MnO, Fe_2O_3 and Sr; Ben Bridge (ID 108) with low Sr but moderately high Y. Most of these are most likely to be indurated, possibly silicified, fine-grained sediments or low to medium grade metamorphic derivatives. The Newlands, Oyne bracer (ID 90) is clearly of metamorphic origin, as it is a porphyroblastic muscovite schist, most likely from the Scottish Grampian Highlands. The Amesbury Archer (red) bracer (ID 56) has chemical similarities to indurated red mudstones from Caerfai Bay, Pembrokeshire (Figure 3.2 and Tables 3.1 and 3.2), which are thought to have been reddened by diagenetic alteration of volcaniclastics. The Dyffryn Ardudwy bracer (ID114) has since been measured for 'light' element components using the new Niton XL3t-900 PXRF instrument. With low MgO, moderate Al_2O_3, high SiO_2 and relatively high K_2O contents, the composition could be closer to that of a K-rich felsic igneous rock rather than a micaceous (meta)sedimentary rock unless it were one that had been extensively altered and silicified. Such felsic igneous rocks are known from parts of Wales.

3.2 PETROGRAPHY

Petrographic examination of 70 bracers (including ID 101 replica which is included in the descriptions below) was able to identify three clear groups of material: bracers of the 'Group VI' type with a probable source in the Lake District, England; those which were amphibole-rich with a likely source (or sources) yet to be precisely defined, and those which conformed to neither, nor which constituted any recognisable petrographical grouping. The majority of the descriptions below resulted from the examination of hand specimens, but a small number (four) could only be viewed from photographs and these are denoted accordingly. Colour definitions used in the following discussion are those of the Geological Society of America's 'rock-color' chart.

3.2.1 Group VI bracers

Macroscopic examination demonstrated that a petrographically coherent group of 18 bracers was dominated by curved examples (i.e. those of concavo-convex section; see also Table 3.4) and comprised those from Dorchester XII (ID 1), Hemp Knoll (ID 7), Barnack (ID 8), Kelleythorpe (ID 13), Tring (ID 31), Ferry Fryston (ID 73), Fyrish (ID 78), Culduthel Mains (ID 79), Glen Forsa (ID 86), Corry Liveras (ID 87), Borrowstone (ID 89), Newlands, Oyne (ID 91), Melton Quarry (ID 105), Aldington (ID 112), Raunds (ID 116) Rauceby (ID 118) and Winteringham (ID 119). The bracer from Calne (ID 15) may also belong to this group, as may a nineteenth bracer from Ardiffery (ID 101) which was only studied in replica.

Within the main group most bracers are greenish-grey (5G 4/1 –5G 6/1), but a few are olive grey (5GY 4/2); all are fine-grained, meta-volcaniclastics characterised by a sub-conchoidal to sub-hackly fracture, thin laminae, sedimentary features including bedding, slumping and small rock clasts, but especially by having limonite pseudomorphs after iron sulphide (pyrite, itself, probably pseudomorphing pyrrhotite) porphyroblasts.

The three bracers from Dorchester XII (ID 1), Aldington (ID 112) and Raunds (ID 116) are petrographically slightly different from the main group in that oxidised iron sulphides are rare or absent. Those from Glen Forsa (ID 86), Rauceby (ID 118) and Winteringham (ID 119) show greater petrographical differences although they are clearly made from volcaniclastic rocks. The Rauceby bracer (ID 118) is brownish grey (5YR 3/2), the example from Winteringham (ID 119) is an olive grey (10Y 3/2) and the Glen Forsa bracer (ID 86) has a partial flaser-like fabric; all differ from the main group in having no obvious limonite pseudomorphs after iron sulphides. The bracer from Calne (ID 15) also lacks any limonite after sulphides but shares enough macroscopic features with the main group possibly to be an outlying member, or to have been made from a very similar lithology.

Lithological identification and provenance

Although none of the bracers of Langdale type has been thin sectioned, macroscopical petrographical comparisons with polished stone axe heads from the English Lake District, defined as Group VI by the Implement Petrology Group (Keiller *et al.* 1941), and with two specimens of rocks collected from a working floor at Langdale suggest that both they and the main group of curved bracers share a common lithology. Their geochemistry is also very similar. 'Total petrography' descriptions of the rocks collected from the Langdale working floor show them to be epidote-bearing, altered volcaniclastics. Other specimens of these volcaniclastics from Langdale were collected in 1978 from scree material at Great Langdale (NY 270072); a petrographical description is detailed in Appendix 3.2. These were two of the three samples used in the geochemical plots (Figures 3.1–3.6).

Dr Vin Davis (pers. comm.) suggests that the bracer raw material is possibly from the Harrison Stickle Tuffs, a horizon within the Seathwaite Fell Tuff volcanic unit of the English Lake District and may have come from the area around Harrison Stickle, or from the south face of the Pike O' Stickle.

Only one bracer of concavo-convex section was not manufactured from Group VI material. This bracer, from Newlands, Oyne (ID 91) is possibly unique in being manufactured from a ?garnet-bearing mica schist. It is the only example to have been made from a medium grained metamorphic rock.

3.2.2 Amphibole-rich bracers

The majority of the flat bracers can also be seen to form a loosely defined group based on the following macroscopical petrographical features: colour; grain size; presence of a planar fabric; presence of spots/mottling, and internal fabric/feel. Most are within the restricted colour range of greenish-grey to olive to bluish grey; this group is also likely to include the bracer from Pyecombe (ID 137) which was confirmed as being amphibole-bearing during *Projet JADE*. A large group of twelve bracers are greenish grey in colour, the majority (9) being between 5GY 7/1 and 5GY 4/1, from Woodeaton (ID 3), Winterslow Hut (ID 4), Sittingbourne (ID 10), Brandon (ID 11), Roundway (ID 28), Bishops Cannings (ID 32), Shorncote (ID 75), Upper Heyford (ID 103) and Llantrithyd (ID 113); the other three lie between 5G 7/1 and 5G 4/1, from Sutton Veny (ID 30), Duston (ID 102) and Aston (ID 107). A small group of four bracers are olive to olive grey, from Sturry (ID 6; 5Y 6/1), Sonning (ID 115; 5Y 4/1), Calceby (ID 121;10Y 7/2) and a greenish yellow example is from West Stafford (ID 66; 10Y 8/2).

A small group of six, light bluish grey bracers have a very restricted colour range. These are from Sewell (ID 12), Wellington Quarry (ID 26) and Gravelly Guy (ID 74), all at 5B 7/1, and from Stanton Harcourt (ID 2) and Aldbourne (ID 14), both at 5B 6/1. The bracer from Thomas Hardye School (ID 67) is the deepest blue (5B 6/2).

All the bracers are fine grained and the majority have a pronounced, thin, planar fabric (foliation) although this is less well-developed in the examples from Woodeaton

(ID 3), Wellington Quarry (ID 26), and Aston (ID 107) and very poorly-developed in the West Stafford (ID 66) example. The main surfaces of the bracer lie along this main foliation. All have darker green spots/mottling except for the pieces from Woodeaton (ID 3), where they are absent and Aldbourne (ID 14) (pale spots), and from Gravelly Guy (ID 74) and Duston (ID 102) where they are poorly-developed. Some have a glassy texture, those from Aston (ID 107) and Sonning (ID 115), or a saccharoidal texture, from Winterslow Hut (ID 4), Sturry (ID 6), Roundway (ID 28), Bishops Cannings (ID 32), Upper Heyford (ID 103) Aston (ID 107) and Llantrithyd (ID 113), and many feel smooth or even talcose. The bracer from Hockwold (ID 106) shares some characteristics with the main group of flat bracers but is yellowish grey (5Y 8/1), has pale spots and is coarser grained than the main group.

The bracer from Aldbourne (ID 14) has pale spots that are closer to white mica porphyroblasts seen in true metasediments (e.g. spotted slates from Carn Menyn) and this, together with its high K content, may suggest that it is different from the majority of the amphibole-rich bracers. Previously thin sections of three bracers have been petrographically described in transmitted light and identified as tremolite fels (Duston ID 102), rhyolite (Upper Heyford ID 103) and nephrite (Sonning ID 115) (Clough and Cummins 1988, 186, 185 and 143). Within this project four bracers (Wellington Quarry ID 26; Shorncote ID 75; Duston ID 102 and Upper Heyford ID 103) were examined and re-examined in transmitted light and two in transmitted and reflected light (ID 26 and ID 75). Petrographically all four are very similar being a very fine-grained amphibole-rich metasediment comprising fibrous amphibole/tremolite-actinolite, quartz and minor sphene. The fine-grained nature presumably allows the bracer to take a good polish, and the fabric allows the bracer to present flattish parallel surfaces.

Fourteen bracers, from Sturry (ID 6), Sittingbourne (ID 10), Brandon (ID 11), Aldbourne (ID 14), Wellington Quarry (ID 26), Sutton Veny (ID 30), Bishops Cannings (ID 32), West Stafford (ID 66), Thomas Hardye School (ID 67), Gravelly Guy (ID 74), Shorncote (ID 75), Hockwold (ID 106), Sonning (ID 115) and Pyecombe (ID 137) were investigated using their reflectance spectra. This investigation was undertaken by *Projet JADE*. This suggested that they were made from amphibole-rich metamorphics and that the main amphiboles were probably tremolite-actinolite. They were found not to match any of the European Neolithic axe heads, raw material samples and working debris of an Alpine origin or reference nephrite material from non-European or Polish sources (Michel Errera pers. comm.).

A low raw magnetic susceptibility ranging up to 0.07 is characteristic of this group.

Lithological identification and provenance

Lithological identification of this group poses some difficulties and merits discussion under three broad headings:

Metasedimentary spotted slates

Although many of the macroscopical features of this group are typical of amphibole-bearing metamorphic rocks including metabasites they are equally characteristic of thermally altered sediments and so, initially, these bracers were identified as being thermally metamorphosed, argillaceous sediments and more especially spotted slates/hornfels (Woodward *et al.* 2006). This was partly based on the macroscopical identification of the green spots as chlorite, rather than amphibole. If the spots are green amphiboles (see below) then hornfels/spotted slate is unlikely. Re-examination of the preliminary geochemical results showed that the 'slates' are potassium-poor and so unlikely to be metamorphosed argillites. In order to investigate further the lithology of this class of flat bracer a series of thermally metamorphosed, spotted, chlorite slates from Carn Menyn in Wales were geochemically analysed alongside the bracers. These spotted slates were chosen as they share many macroscopical features with the bracers, especially the blue-grey ones. The same slates were petrographically described in detail (Darvill *et al.* 2007) and were shown essentially to comprise muscovite, chlorites and quartz, a mineralogy that was confirmed by whole rock X-ray diffraction (XRD, Kinnaird pers. comm.). Geochemical plots show that the Carn Menyn spotted slates and these flat bracers are very different. These results strongly suggest that the flat bracers are very unlikely to be meta-argillites/slates.

Amphibole-bearing metamorphic rocks

Tremolite and actinolite are calcium-magnesium- to calcium-iron-rich members of the amphibole group of minerals and are characteristic of low- to medium-grade metamorphism of basic and ultrabasic rocks or of impure dolomitic limestones. Minor amounts of these amphiboles are widespread in the British Isles as part of the alteration/metamorphism of basic igneous rocks found in Cornubia, Wales, the English Lake District and Scotland. However, other than possibly in Scotland (the Grampians), they do not form fine-grained, compact lithologies as seen in these bracers. The geochemistry data suggest that the flat bracers are made from a metasediment (siliceous meta-limestone/dolostone) rather than a metabasic rock. Tremolite-actinolite-bearing metacarbonates have a yet more restricted distribution in Britain than do their meta-igneous equivalents.

Nephrite jade

Woolley (1983, 256–260) has pointed out that nephrite is not a mineral species, but is the name given to fine-grained, tough, dense, masses of the tremolite-actinolite series of amphibolites. Most nephrite is green, but white also occurs and polished surfaces are somewhat greasy in appearance. Although nephrite is by definition fine-grained and compact there is often a distinct foliation or slatiness allowing for cutting along this foliation and the same foliation causes small scale-like flakes to whiten. This is a feature of some nephrite axe heads and also seen in the bracers from Aldbourne (ID 14) and Thomas Hardye School (ID 67). Many of the bracers, but especially those from Woodeaton (ID 3), Sturry (ID 6), Sittingbourne (ID 10), Brandon (ID 11), Aldbourne (ID 14), Duston (ID 102) and Sonning (ID 115) conform to this definition. Petrographical examination of three bracers, Wellington Quarry (ID 26), Shorncote (ID 75) and Duston (ID 102), shows all are very similar being a very fine-grained amphibolite comprising fibrous amphibole (tremolite-actinolite), quartz and minor sphene. Hence in thin section all three, plus perhaps Sonning (ID 115) could be classed as nephrites with a high degree of confidence. Mineralogically and petrographically Upper Heyford (ID 103) is very similar but is too siliceous to be classed as a nephrite.

Fine-grained but compact tremolite-actinolite amphibole-bearing rocks are rare in Britain but are present in the metamorphic terrains of Highland Scotland. Most nephrites are associated with young mountain belts including those of the Alpine Orogeny. Since no *in situ* British nephrite has been recorded, then a possible origin lies within one of the Alpine Belt mountain chains of Europe-North Africa, although (Michel Errera pers. comm.) probably not in the Alps themselves.

3.2.3 Miscellaneous

Other than the Group VI and the amphibole-bearing metasedimentary group, the remaining bracers form no recognisable petrographical groupings. Hence they have been loosely grouped in terms of their colour and gross lithological characteristics.

It is noteworthy that, other than the two Amesbury Archer bracers (ID 56 and ID 57) and the Stonehenge bracer (ID 58), only one of this group is from Wessex, namely from Tytherington/Corton (ID 29). It is also of note that many of this group have Scottish find spots. Four bracers, from Tytherington/Corton (ID 29), Culbin Sands (ID 80), Broadford Bay (ID 88) and Dyffryn Ardudwy (ID 114) are laminated, greenish grey to olive to yellowish grey, fine-grained metasediments/meta-volcaniclastics. The two non-Scottish ones may be metamudstones. A possible origin for the Tytherington/Corton (ID 29) bracer could be the regionally metamorphosed Lower Carboniferous rocks of Cornubia, and there may be a local Welsh origin for Dyffryn Ardudwy (ID 114) especially as its geochemistry suggests that it may be an acid volcanic, namely a 'rhyolite'. The two Scottish bracers, from Culbin Sands (ID 80) and Broadford Bay (ID 88) are laminated metasediments/volcaniclastics. No provenance is suggested.

Five bracers comprise a sub-group of those that are black or dark grey. The black bracer from Cliffe, Kent (ID 153) is unusual, since it is made from shale which may come from Kimmeridge in Dorset. Four dark grey (N3) bracers are manufactured from siltstone/very fine-grained sandstone; these are from Mildenhall (ID 9), Glenluce (ID 77), Scarborough (ID 104) and Littleport (ID 120). They are olive grey to grey in colour. Fine-grained arenaceous sediments are very common and geological provenancing is impossible, but the ready availability of the sediments might suggest a local/regional origin. Although the pure siltstone used for the Scarborough (ID 104) bracer and the clastic used for the Glenluce (ID 77) bracer could well be local or regional in origin, the indurated siltstones used for the Mildenhall (ID 9) and Littleport (ID 120) pieces are exotic to their find spots. The bracer from Crawford (ID 93), probably a fine-grained sandstone, may also belong to this overall group and, if it is a sandstone, could be local in origin.

Four dark grey (N3) bracers, from Amesbury Archer (ID 57) and Ben Bridge (ID 108), olive black from Lindridge (ID 111) or black (N1) from Stonehenge (ID 58), show lithologies of fine-grained rocks but their grain-size difference suggests they are all from different rocks. Three, from Amesbury Archer (ID 57), from Stonehenge (ID 58) and Lindridge (ID 111) are identified as metamudstones/slates although the Stonehenge (ID 58) example has a raw magnetic susceptibility that is slightly different. Dark metamudstones/slates are common in Britain and hence provenancing is difficult. However, the nearest suitable rocks to the find spots include regionally metamorphosed Lower Carboniferous rocks of Devon and a number of Palaeozoic rocks from South Wales. Other areas would include much of central Wales and the English Lake District. Despite an initial visual resemblance and quite high iron content and relatively high magnetic susceptibility the Stonehenge bracer (ID 58) is not a porcellanite from Northern Ireland, well known as the important Implement Petrology Group IX and a likely source for some of the black Irish bracers (Harbison 1976, 31–33, Appendix C) and certainly the origin of the bracer from Ireland (ID 99). The bracer from Ben Bridge (ID 108) is a slightly coarser grained metasediment with possibly a similar origin to the other three bracers. All the dark grey or black bracers are exotic with regard to their find spots.

The two bracers from Amesbury Archer (ID 56) and Dornoch Nursery (ID 94) are red. A further example, from Carneddau (ID 148) might also be included here, although it is pink rather than red. The fourth red example from ?Scotland (ID 92) is jasper-like and similar to the Irish jaspers; the Amesbury Archer (ID 56) example is an indurated mudstone and the sole, red-coloured English bracer. The latter may be manufactured from Cornubian rocks or those in South Wales. Although red mudstones are abundant and widespread the nearest outcrops to the find spot are in the Devonian and Permo-Triassic sequences of Cornubia and Lower Palaeozoic rocks of South Wales. The Dornoch Nursery example (ID 94) is made from a red fine-grained siltstone and may have been made from local Devonian sediments. The Carneddau (ID 148) example appears to be a bedded fine- to medium-grained micaceous sandstone and as such may have been manufactured from locally to regionally available Lower Palaeozoic sediments.

Two Scottish bracers, from Old Rayne (ID 82) and

Ballogie (ID 84) are greenish grey (5GY 5/1) volcaniclastics with a visual resemblance to the Group VI bracers but ID 84 also has spotting. No geological provenance is suggested for them but they are probably not local. Two further Scottish bracers, from Lockerbie (ID 150) and Ferniegair (ID 123) may be very altered basic lavas as suggested by their fabric as seen in SEM and by partial chemical analyses of some of their mineralogy. These analyses were undertaken at the National Museums Scotland. The mineralogy and petrography of ID 123 especially is consistent with it being a fine-grained altered basic rock (basalt/dolerite).

Two bracers are highly unusual. The bracer from Thanet (ID 149) is made from a grey fine-grained sandstone which is unlikely to be local (the photograph is misleading, since the white flecks are surface adhesions of chalk). The bracer from Newlands, Oyne (ID 90) is unique amongst all the bracers in being manufactured from a fine-grained ?garnetiferous mica schist and may be local. Two further bracers, from Archerton Newtake (ID 133) and Cassington (ID 135), are very fine-grained and possibly could be fine-grained igneous rocks and without closer lithological and geochemical examination remain ungrouped. By contrast, the bracer from Fox Hole (ID 134) is visually clearly of amphibole-bearing type.

APPENDIX 3.1 BRACERS FROM IRELAND

This volume does not include detailed consideration of the bracers from Ireland as these were previously published by Harbison (1976). However, during our study tours of museums in England and Scotland it proved possible to record data for eight bracers from Irish find spots. These are detailed below and illustrated at the end of the main catalogue. The Irish bracers are very different from those of the mainland United Kingdom. They are often red in colour, have only two perforations, are long and narrow in shape and sometimes have end borings (ID 16; Harbison type C2). They also tend to be well finished to a highly regular outline and their cross-sections are often neatly formed to a plano-convex profile. From Ireland there are only two bracers with curved cross-section, approximating to the C1 variety better known from northern Britain (Harbison 1976, nos. 4 and 5). There is a large distinctive group of red two-holed bracers, which are usually made from jasper,

Table Appendix 3.1. Bracers from Ireland housed in The British Museum (ID 16–17), National Museums Scotland (ID 95–97) and The Hunterian Museum, Glasgow (ID 98–100).

ID	Find spot	Harbison number	Type	%	Colour	Rock type	Wear category
16	Ireland	7	C2	100	red	jasper	slight
17	Prob. Ireland	61	A	99	red	jasper	slight
95	Ireland	69	A	99	grey-green	meta-sediment	worn
96	N Ireland	33	A	95	green-grey	meta-sediment	slight
97	Co. Antrim	35	A	100	dark grey/black	mafic/ultramafic	worn
98	Co. Antrim	43	A	100	dark red	jasper	slight
99	Co. Antrim	25	A	99	black/dark grey	porcellanite	worn
100	Westmeath	36	A	99	pink-brown	sandstone	worn

Table Appendix 3.2 PXRF analyses and raw magnetic susceptibility (MS) measurements of Irish bracers, ordered by ascending K_2O/CaO ratio.

Sample ID		99	100	97	17	98	95	16	96
Sorted K/Ca		Ireland, Co. Antrim / Black	Ireland, Co. Westmeath	Ireland, Co. Antrim	Ireland B	Ireland, Co. Antrim	Ireland	Ireland A	Northern Ireland
		Average (2)	Average (2)	Average (3)	Average (3)	Average (3)	Average (3)	Average (3)	Average (3)
K_2O	%	0.0	1.9	1.0	1.5	2.1	7.0	2.2	5.1
CaO	%	0.3	1.8	0.6	0.4	0.3	1.0	0.2	0.4
TiO_2	%	3.0	0.1	0.9	0.3	0.9	0.2	0.4	0.2
MnO	%	0.3	0.1	0.1	0.2	0.1	0.0	0.1	0.1
Fe_2O_3	%	24.4	3.8	10.2	6.2	5.6	2.2	6.8	5.4
Rb	mg/kg	1	72	55	71	105	197	90	120
Sr	mg/kg	31	32	72	31	23	168	44	141
Y	mg/kg	18	22	30	23	17	50	22	27
Zr	mg/kg	202	67	116	60	82	244	88	220
Nb	mg/kg	5	17	16	11	10	25	15	26
Ba	mg/kg	8	235	350	328	474	2110	341	1492
Raw MS ($\times 10^{-3}$ SI units)		9.48	0.05	0.10	–	0.01	0.04	0.03	0.05

and a second set of items which are predominately grey, brown or black in colour.

Dating of the Irish bracers remains problematical, since the few available contexts are not very informative. Harbison noted that many of the stray finds are concentrated in Co. Antrim, corresponding with the distribution of Irish Bowl Food Vessels in that area, and he suggested therefore that the bracers may have been associated more with Food Vessels (Harbison 1976, 8–10). There is now a series of radiocarbon dates for Irish Food Vessels, which places the Bowl Tradition between *c.*2200 and *c.*1800 cal BC at one sigma (Brindley 2007, 74), and this implies a possible chronological overlap with Beakers and so also with the Irish bracers.

The Harbison illustrations are all black and white, and only a small proportion of the bracers had been examined geologically. It was therefore decided to study a sample of Irish bracers afresh in order to compare them with the English, Scottish and Welsh corpus. The sample comprised 35 bracers housed at the National Museum of Ireland in Dublin, and the results of the study are published separately (Roe and Woodward 2009). This appendix will summarise the results of the study of the eight Irish bracers housed in English and Scottish museums and will place those results in the context of the findings of the two more extensive studies. Some basic parameters for these eight bracers are summarised in Table Appendix 3.1.

Most of these bracers conform to the long and narrow shape typical of such items from Ireland, and many also have distinct side or end facets. Only one (ID 99) is wider and more rectangular in outline. The main colours found amongst Irish bracers, both red, and brown to black, are evident and the main rock types known for Irish bracers are also represented. These include the highly distinctive sealing wax red jasper examples, one of porcellanite (the rock used for Group IX Neolithic axe heads) and several grey to brown items made from miscellaneous rocks. All eight bracers are complete or almost complete, with damage resulting from small chips, usually at the ends, suffered in antiquity.

All show well polished upper surfaces, with four categorised as highly polished. Faint polishing striations are usually still visible on the front surface and these vary from longitudinal to diagonal or lateral in direction. Striations on the rear surfaces tend to be much more marked; most often they are longitudinal but diagonal and lateral striations also occur. Rilling is usually visible within the perforations. Within the larger sample of bracers studied at Dublin more jasper items are represented and it is possible to detect differences between the occurrence of striations on the two main groups of bracers: those of jasper and the grey to brown examples. The jasper items are characterised by roughly equal proportions of longitudinal and diagonal striations on the front surface but a marked preponderance of diagonal striations on the rear. Amongst the grey and brown bracers, the dominant directions of striations are rather more diverse. This appears to indicate standardised methods of manufacture for the jasper bracers, and this may have taken place at specific places or workshops (Roe and Woodward 2009, table 1).

Signs of wear usually comprise ancient scratches overlying the polishing striations, but there are two cases of probable thread or thong nicks or notches, and in one case (ID 96) one of the perforations had broken out, following some use of the hole concerned. Overall half of the examples show traces of slight wear and the other four can be classed as worn. It is unusual that all eight bracers are complete or near complete. In the previous studies it was found that a large proportion of the Irish bracers are in fact broken, and indeed many of them have been reworked and refashioned as new artefacts. Sometimes they were reworked at the broken end and supplied with a new perforation in order to produce a refurbished but shorter bracer, but other broken bracers, often half bracers, had not been rebored but the broken ends had been smoothed and repolished in order that such pieces could function as pendants (Roe and Woodward 2009, table 2).

3.1.1 Analysis

Eight Irish bracers were analysed by PXRF; the results are listed in Table Appendix 3.2. They are also plotted in Chapter 3 (Figures 3.1 and 3.4) for comparison with bracers from the United Kingdom mainland. None are from the two main groups of bracers identified in mainland United Kingdom.

There are three red bracers (Ireland, ID 98; Ireland A, ID 16; Ireland B, ID 17) all with fairly low contents of CaO, TiO_2, Sr and Nb. Generally they have moderate levels of K_2O and Fe_2O_3. Visual observation suggests they are jaspers, but their composition suggests that they contain more than just silica and iron oxide.

Two of the other bracers, ID 95 and ID 96 (Northern Ireland) have very high and proportionate levels of K_2O and Ba, tending to suggest they might be indurated or low grade metasediments. The balance of their other constituents is quite similar, suggesting a similar source although they differ somewhat in their appearance. However, they are quite different chemically from Ireland (ID 97), which is lower in K_2O and most trace elements, higher in TiO_2 and Fe_2O_3. Although it has the appearance of a metabasic rock, contents of CaO and Sr are too low for it to be a derivative of most basalts.

Of the remaining Irish bracers, Ireland, Co. Antrim (ID 99), is extremely distinctive petrographically and chemically, with very high Fe_2O_3 and TiO_2; very low K_2O, Rb, Ba and Nb; also fairly low Ca and Sr. With very high raw magnetic susceptibility (9.48×10^{-3} SI units), it is likely to be porcellanite, a thermally altered laterite consisting mainly of iron oxides, silica and mullite.

Finally, the bracer from Ireland, Co. Westmeath (ID 100) has no particularly distinctive features chemically and plots away from other bracers. This may be because of the smooth surface coating that masks the granular rock beneath, which appears visually to be a fine-grained sandstone.

3.1.2 Discussion and catalogue

There are eight bracers which are likely to have been produced from Irish sources; these can be broadly divided according to colour. There is a petrographically tight group of at least three bracers, Ireland A (ID 16), Ireland B (ID 17) and Ireland (ID 98) which are red-coloured (5R 3/4 to 10R 2/2), fine-grained jaspers. A possible further example, from ?Scotland (ID 92), might also be included (see also Appendix 3.5). Visually, the bracers Ireland B (ID 17), and Ireland, Co. Antrim (ID 98) are banded and very similar but ID 16 is finer grained and unbanded. The bracer from Ireland, Co. Westmeath (ID 100) is made from a fine-grained sandstone that was originally pinkish-red but is now weathered to shades of light brown. There is a broad geochemical correspondence between them and they all show a very low magnetic susceptibility characteristic of very silica-rich rocks. No jasper axe heads are recorded from Ireland (Cooney and Mandal 1998). Red jaspers are recorded *in situ* from coastal exposures near Cushendell in Co. Antrim (Holland 1981, 123), within 5 to 10km of Tievebulliagh (Neolithic axe head Group IX origin), or as boulders within drift deposits at Irvinestown, Co. Fermanagh. Hence a local/regional (Ulster) source is possible. Other jasper occurrences occur in the west of Ireland notably in Co. Mayo and Co. Galway (Holland 1981, 85).

Petrographically, there is also a group of green bracers, from Ireland (ID 95), Northern Ireland (ID 96) and Ireland, Co. Antrim (ID 97) based on colour and their fine-grained nature. Macroscopically they appear to resemble the volcaniclastic tuffs of Group VI. However neither their geochemistry nor magnetic susceptibilities are close to those of Group VI. Bracers ID 95 and ID 96 are closer in similarity to each other than they are to ID 97. Group VI axe heads are rare in Ireland, but approximately 20 are known. Green volcaniclastic axe heads possibly from Co. Limerick and the Avoca area of south-east Ireland have been recognised but are relatively uncommon (115 have been recognised; Cooney and Mandal 1998, 69). They are mostly concentrated in Co. Antrim and Co. Limerick.

The final piece, a black bracer from Co. Antrim (ID 99) is of porcellanite. This is the most common Irish Neolithic stone axe head material, but it also has a restricted provenance coming from either Rathlin Island or Tievebulliagh.

CATALOGUE OF IRISH BRACERS EXAMINED

ID 16 IRELAND A

Lithic identification. Jasper.

Description. A homogeneous red (dusky red 5R 3/4) faintly banded jasper with many small pits on thin section surfaces. The magnetic susceptibility is 0.03.

Provenance. Red jaspers are recorded *in situ* from near Cushendell in Co. Antrim and from drift deposits at Irvinestown, Co. Fermanagh. Hence a local/regional source is possible. Other jasper occurrences occur in the west of Ireland particularly in Mayo/Galway. This bracer may have a different provenance to the other three red bracers.

ID 17 IRELAND B

Lithic identification. Jasper.

Description. A very fine-grained homogeneous, red (dusky red 5R 3/4) jasper with 0.8 mm wide sub-parallel, dark bands that may represent dirt in more poorly polished jasper bands.

Provenance. Red jaspers are recorded *in situ* from near Cushendell in Co. Antrim and from drift deposits at Irvinestown, Co. Fermanagh. Hence a local/regional source is possible. Other jasper occurrences occur in the west of Ireland in Mayo/Galway.

ID 95 IRELAND

Lithic identification. A ?volcaniclastic tuff.

Description. A mottled volcaniclastic varying in colour from a yellowish grey (5Y 7/1) to a greenish grey (5GY 6/1). Very small, limonite-rich spots up to 0.1 mm in diameter are rare and the rock is cut by 0.2 mm wide veinlets. It shares macroscopical similarities with Group VI. The magnetic susceptibility is 0.04.

Provenance. An Irish source is possible.

ID 96 NORTHERN IRELAND

Lithic identification. A ?volcaniclastic tuff.

Description. A greyish olive green (5GY 3/2) layered, fine-grained volcaniclastic. The broken and smooth surfaces are the same colour but there is a little limonite coating on the main surfaces. No sedimentary features are seen. It has macroscopical similarities with Group VI. The magnetic susceptibility is 0.05.

Provenance. An Ulster source is unlikely, but could be Irish. However, it is exotic with respect to its find spot.

ID 97 IRELAND (Co. ANTRIM)

Lithic identification. A ?meta-volcaniclastic.

Description. A greenish black (5GY 3/1), very fine-grained rock that is smooth to the touch. It has a faint fabric with streaked/lensoidal darker areas. It has slightly proud darker patches on the surface. The magnetic susceptibility 0.10.

Provenance. An Irish source is possible.

ID 98. IRELAND (Co. ANTRIM, RED)

Lithic identification. Jasper.

Description. A greyish red (5R 4/2) fine-grained, homogeneous jasper. The rock is cut by 0.1–0.2 mm thick dark veinlets. The magnetic susceptibility is 0.01.

Provenence. Red jaspers are recorded *in situ* from near Cushendell in Co. Antrim and from drift deposits at Irvinestown, Co. Fermanagh. Hence a local/regional source is possible. Other jasper occurrences occur in the west of Ireland in Mayo/Galway.

ID 99 IRELAND (Co. ANTRIM, BLACK)

Lithic identification. Porcellanite.

Description. A greyish black (N2), homogeneous porcellanite. The surface, although smooth to the touch, is pitted and has many euhedral, pale 'spots' up to 0.2 mm in diameter. Broken surfaces are shiny due to the high concentration of opaque minerals. The magnetic susceptibility is 9.48.

Provenance. Local/regional porcellanite (Group IX) is found at Tievebulliagh or Brockley, Rathlin Island, both in Ulster.

ID 100. IRELAND (Co. WESTMEATH)

Lithic identification, Fine-grained sandstone.

Description. The surface of the artefact is mottled from a light

brown (5YR 6/4) to a pale yellowish brown (10YR 6/2). However where the surface has spalled off the rock is a pink (pale red 5R 5/2) ?clastic sediment. A sandstone/arkose? The magnetic susceptibility is 0.05.
Provenance. Regional?

APPENDIX 3.2. PETROGRAPHICAL DESCRIPTION OF POSSIBLE LANGDALE SOURCE ROCKS

This description refers to three rock samples from Langdale which were also analysed by XRF (Table 3.2, Langdale tuff, Lang 1978 and Lang 88).

The rock has weathered to a light greenish grey (5G 7/1) and has pronounced 1 mm diameter limonite-rich spots after sulphides. The cut surface is light bluish grey (5B 7/1). In thin section the rock (Lang 88) is a greenish grey (5GY 6/1) with distinct planar bedding/laminations that are cross-cut by irregular, coarser grained, pale-coloured 'bands'. Small, up to 1 mm diameter, sulphide-rich clots are unevenly distributed within the very fine-grained, homogeneous matrix.

A very fine-grained indeterminate matrix carries minor amounts of angular, rock clasts including very fine-grained, feldspathic lavas plus single angular grains of quartz or untwinned feldspar but mainly plagioclase microliths, 20 × 2 to 80 × 4μm in size. Coarser grained irregular areas within the rock lie at high angles to the lamination and may be due to bioturbation and locally are darker green and amphibole-rich.

Epidote is present as abundant, single crystals, up to 0.1 mm in diameter, some with clear cores and cloudy margins and as part of mixed sulphide-silicate metamorphic 'knots'. Here epidote forms rims about the main sulphides mass and is intergrown with green amphibole and with pyrrhotite, chalcopyrite and sphalerite. Pyrrhotite is the most abundant sulphide and occurs as small, up to 40μm diameter tabular or hexagonal crystals or within larger aggregates 200–600μm in size that comprise a few large 100–200μm diameter crystals or mosaics of 10–20μm in size. The aggregates enclose 10 –30 × 2 but up to 80 × 60μm size silicate laths and rare, 5–20μm diameter, pink, euhedral, pentagonal dodecahedral cobaltite and 2–10μm diameter pyrite.

Most pyrrhotite is unaltered but at the edge of the sample pyrrhotite is progressively altered/weathered to thin, 1–5μm wide pyrite or 5–40μm wide marcasite rims, some of the marcasite showing its characteristic tabular habit when replacing pyrrhotite (NPM) or to 20–60μm diameter mixtures of mackinawite and smythite and finally to limonite. Some limonite pseudomorphs are up to 200μm in diameter.

Chalcopyrite is less common than pyrrhotite: trace amounts occur as single crystals in epidote or discrete, 20–40μm diameter grains in the main matrix. Most chalcopyrite however occurs within, or forms 5–30μm wide partial rims to, the large pyrrhotite knots or is associated with pyrrhotite as mixed chalcopyrite-pyrrhotite aggregates up to 80μm diameter, or within 30–150μm diameter pyrrhotite-chalcopyrite±sphalerite or pyrrhotite-chalcopyrite±pyrite mixtures. Pale orange to brown sphalerite is the least common sulphide and only occurs together with pyrrhotite and chalcopyrite. Rare, pale yellow sphalerite occurs as 2–5μm size inclusions in pyrrhotite but most forms 2–40μm wide partial rims to coarse-grained pyrrhotite in association with chalcopyrite.

APPENDIX 3.3. NOTES ON THE SOURCE AREAS OF THE GROUP VI ROCK USED TO MANUFACTURE BRACERS

Two private collections of Group VI Langdale material that had been donated to the Implement Petrology Committee were available for study at the University of York in November 2006. The Geoffrey Taylor collection is a group of about 40 Neolithic axe head roughouts from the Langdale quarry sites, but not accurately located to find spot. In contrast the Stuart Feather collection is a very large collection of debitage and some roughouts and mauls (the latter non-Group VI) from named locations around the various outcrops: Pike O Stickle, Scafell Pike, Glaramara etc. The full distribution of outcrops in the Langdale area is shown by Claris and Quartermaine (1989, fig. 2).

Systematic study of the material showed that Group VI rock with rust coloured spots (limonite pseudomorphs after iron sulphides), as recognised in many of the Group VI bracers, was present in the Pike O Stickle material and that Glaramara (which is further to the north-east), and several of the Taylor roughouts also displayed rust coloured spots. It was observed that the red spotted pieces were all *extremely fine-grained* pieces of tuff, and maybe this is the factor the bracer-makers were interested in, as the finer-grained the tuff, the easier it is to work (in three dimensions) to a fine shape and polish. The occurrence of limonite pseudomorphs is just one component within the vertical variation amongst the tuffs. They can occur in narrow horizontal bands or elsewhere more randomly and therefore probably occur within many outcrops. In other words it is not possible to suggest that the source material for the bracers was obtained from a single working floor at Langdale on the basis of the occurrence of the distinctive limonite pseudomorphs. Possible roughouts for bracers are in fact known amongst the debitage and roughout material recorded from various working areas. These finds are unpublished, but Professor Mark Edmonds has kindly provided the following notes:

> 'Following on from fieldwork conducted over two decades ago (Bradley and Edmonds 1993; Claris and Quartermaine 1989), mapping has continued across the extent of the Seathwaite Fell Tuff formation. The more recent mapping was directed towards the broken and/or discarded roughouts that are a common feature in many exposures. It was geared towards answering specific questions relating to the range of forms represented among the roughouts, further insights into the character of *chaines operatoires* and, finally, the question of distribution and the possible detection of

specific concentrations.

Stretched over several years, it has documented several thousand pieces. It confirms the impression from museum collections and from earlier work, that roughout blades were the primary product of the area and that those blades could take a variety of forms. It also makes clear that many of the so-called 'variant' axes, smaller blades found in Cumbria and across the country, are not simply the result of using and maintaining larger forms. They were, themselves, intended.

While roughout axe blades of various forms dominated the inventories on many exposures, a small number of rather unusual pieces were identified on the crags overlooking the Langdale Valley; specifically, in the area between the Pike O Stickle and Loft Crag. These were also bifacially flaked, but tended to have a very distinctive form, being thin, almost plano-convex in section, with parallel sides, a broad cutting edge and an equally broad butt. They may be roughouts for bracers.

Few of these items were complete, so full dimensions are difficult to establish. However, the majority of the dozen or so examples identified were between 50 and 70mm wide and (where measurable) 140 to 200mm in length. Looked at closely, these pieces reflect skilful working. Edges are generally very carefully trimmed, and flaking is extensive on both principal faces. Also noteworthy is that the difference in height between flake ridges and bulbar scars across the surface of many pieces was very low indeed. In other words, they reflect very careful working, a high degree of control and an attempt to realise the final, ground and polished form during the process of flaking itself.

The possibility that these represent rejected blanks for bracers should certainly be considered. If accepted, it raises a very interesting dimension to arguments about the outcrop and its significance over time. The same areas in which these distinctive forms were recognised are also characterised by the presence of a large number of roughouts, which were being produced from the first half of the fourth millennium BC onwards. If roughout bracers were being made on the same crags some considerable time later, they might reflect a conscious choice; to return to sites of historical, perhaps even ancestral importance, to draw new *tokens of identity* from the stone.'

APPENDIX 3.4. SOURCE ROCK OF CURVED BRACERS AND NEOLITHIC STONE AXE HEADS: A COMPARATIVE STUDY

3.4.1 Introduction and aims

The project has demonstrated that a group of finely made curved bracers of Beaker age (Late Neolithic/Early Bronze Age) were made from grey-green rock derived from the Langdale source in the Lake District of Cumbria. This rock was also used extensively for the manufacture of polished stone axe heads during the Neolithic period, and these were dispersed particularly in Yorkshire and also far into southern Britain and into Scotland (Bradley and Edmonds 1993). Detailed analysis has shown that particular horizons in the Borrowdale Volcanic Group, with distinctive rust coloured spots (oxidised pyrite porphyroblasts) had been selected for making the bracers. The spots are readily detected without the aid of a microscope.

The aim of the study was to determine whether this spotted variant of tuff from Great Langdale was also used to make Neolithic axe heads, and if so, to what extent? In other words, were the makers of the bracers continuing an earlier Neolithic tradition, or seeking out a new source? In order to answer this question it was decided to view a large collection of easily accessible Neolithic stone axe heads. The British Museum collection was chosen as it is one of the largest in the country, and because the axe heads are stored in plastazote pockets in drawers, so can easily be viewed without accessing and opening storage boxes. The study was undertaken by Rob Ixer and Vin Davis, in association with Ann Woodward. A total number of 1440 axe heads, housed in 48 drawers were viewed.

3.4.2 Results

The results are summarised in Table Appendix 3.3 below. Within the large number of axe heads studied only 37 were identified as being made from Group VI rock. No Group VI items were found amongst the collections from Wales, Scotland, Ireland and Jersey.

3.4.3 Conclusions

Firstly, the study confirmed that the spotted variant of Group VI rock has indeed been used for making some Neolithic axe heads. However, this variant was not the typical material for axe manufacture (only 28% of the axe heads viewed in this case study). This is in strong contrast with the bracer materials which are almost always spotted. It can also be concluded that the geographical distribution of Group VI Neolithic axe heads in England is similar to that of the Group VI bracers. In both cases, there are more from the northern counties, followed by the midland counties.

Table Appendix 3.3. Geographical distribution of axe heads of Langdale rock according to type.

County	Group VI not spotted	Group VI spotted
Yorkshire	11	5
Northumberland	5	1
Lincolnshire	2	0
Derbyshire	5	0
Cambridgeshire	3	0
Bedfordshire	1	0
Suffolk	0	1
Oxfordshire	0	1
Greater London	2	0
Totals	**29**	**8**

APPENDIX 3.5. CATALOGUE OF BRACER PETROGRAPHIES

Descriptions are by R Ixer unless otherwise stated as being by A Woodward (AW) or F Roe (FR). Colours are defined according to the Geological Society of America 'rock-color' chart.

ID 1 DORCHESTER XII

Lithic identification. Meta-volcaniclastic.

Description. A fine-grained, greenish-grey (5G 5/1) essentially homogeneous, volcaniclastic rock with a little soft sediment disruption and ?erosion surfaces. Small, 0.3 mm diameter, brown spots are probably oxidised pyrite/pyrrhotite but large pyrite/pyrrhotite porphyroblasts/megacrysts are absent. Smooth to the touch.

Provenance. The rock is a meta-volcaniclastic and is similar in appearance to the Group VI axe head lithologies but lacking the large oxidised pyrite/pyrrhotite porphyroblasts of many other Group VI bracers. The rock may be from the Langdale area of the English Lake District and is exotic with regard to the find spot.

ID 2 STANTON HARCOURT

Lithic identification. A spotted, ?amphibole-rich metamorphic rock.

Description. A light bluish grey (5B 6/1) metamorphic rock with a sub-parallel, planar fabric. The colour is slightly inhomogeneous with rounded, paler, light greenish grey (5GY 8/1) spots, where the surface is damaged/pitted and with diffuse, lensoidal, darker spots, both are 0.5–1 mm in diameter. The under surface has brown stained calcite.

Provenance. The bracer is exotic with regard to its find spot. Macroscopically it has a number of jade-like features. If the bracer was nephrite jade then the nearest recognised sources are continental. Although amphibole-rich metasedimentary rocks are present in the NW Highlands of Scotland, fine-grained, dense, amphibole-rich rocks are rare in the rest of Britain.

ID 3 WOODEATON

Lithic identification. An unspotted, ?amphibole-rich metamorphic rock.

Description. A very, very homogeneous, greenish grey (5GY 5/1) very fine-grained, vitreous rock with a subconchoidal fracture and a very poorly developed, sub-parallel, planar fabric. There is no mottling on the surface and it is very smooth to the touch.

Provenance. The bracer is exotic with regard to its find spot. Macroscopically it has a number of jade-like features. If the bracer was nephrite jade then the nearest recognised sources are continental. Although amphibole-rich metasedimentary rocks are present in the NW Highlands of Scotland, fine-grained, dense, amphibole-rich rocks are rare in the rest of Britain.

ID 4 WINTERSLOW HUT

Lithic identification. A spotted, ?amphibole-rich metamorphic rock.

Description. A faintly mottled metamorphic rock with an overall greenish grey (5G 5/1) colour but with darker, up to 0.5 mm diameter, patches. Thin, dark, 0.4 mm wide and thicker, 1 mm wide, pale veinlets cross-cut the rock; the thicker veinlet is enclosed within 0.1 mm thick, dark margins. The lithology has a planar fabric and where broken has a saccharoidal texture. The artefact is smooth to the touch. The under surface has carbonate concretions adhering to it.

Provenance. The bracer lithology is exotic with regard to its find spot. Macroscopically it has a number of jade-like features. If the bracer was nephrite jade then the nearest recognised sources are continental. Although amphibole-rich metasedimentary rocks are present in the NW Highlands of Scotland, fine-grained, dense, amphibole-rich rocks are rare in the rest of Britain.

ID 6 STURRY

Lithic identification. A spotted, amphibole-rich metamorphic rock.

Description. An inhomogeneous, mainly light olive grey (5Y 6/1) slightly mottled, spotted rock. The rock is saccharoidal in texture and has diffuse, darker green spots 0.4–0.5 mm in diameter. In one third the spots are elongated giving a sub-planar fabric but for most of the bracer the mottling is random. Reflectance spectra suggest the presence of actinolitic amphibole; chlorite minerals are not recognised. The magnetic susceptibility is 0.06.

Provenance. The bracer is exotic with regard to its find spot. If the bracer was nephrite jade then the nearest recognised sources are continental. Although amphibole-rich metasedimentary rocks are present in the NW Highlands of Scotland, fine-grained, dense, amphibole-rich rocks are rare in the rest of Britain.

ID 7 HEMP KNOLL

Lithic identification. Meta-volcaniclastic.

Description. A fine-grained, medium bluish grey (5B 6/1) rock with faint mottling and a non-conchoidal fracture. Small 1 mm diameter pyrite/pyrrhotite altering to limonite is present on the surface of the artefact. The magnetic susceptibility is 0.23.

Provenance. The rock is meta-volcaniclastic and is similar in appearance to the Group VI axe head lithologies. The rock may be from the Langdale area of the English Lake District and is exotic with regard to the find spot.

ID 8 BARNACK

Lithic identification. Meta-volcaniclastic.

Description. A very fine-grained, homogeneous grey olive green (5GY 4/2) non-layered, volcaniclastic rock. The rock has a conchoidal fracture plus very thin, 0.1 mm wide, limonite-rich veinlets cross cutting the matrix. Limonite pseudomorphs after pyrite/pyrrhotite are up to 0.5 mm in diameter; these limonite pits are associated with small circular spalling of the bracer surface. The magnetic susceptibility is 0.36 which is high for this class of bracer.

Provenance. The rock is a meta-volcaniclastic and is similar in appearance to the Group VI axe head lithologies. The rock may be from the Langdale area of the English Lake District and is exotic with regard to the find spot.

ID 9 MILDENHALL

Lithic identification. A dark-coloured siltstone.

Description. A uniform, olive grey (5Y 4/1), thinly bedded, indurated, fine-grained sandstone/siltstone (grain size of less than 187μm) carrying minor amounts of white mica. The magnetic susceptibility is 0.12.

Provenance. Fine-grained sandstones/siltstones are widespread throughout the British Isles. However the bracer is not local to the find spot (unless from the drift) and may be exotic.

ID 10 SITTINGBOURNE

Lithic identification. A spotted, amphibole-rich metamorphic rock.

Description. A faintly mottled, spotted metamorphic rock. Overall it has a dark greenish grey (5GY 4/1) colour with a few random, darker green, solid spots up to 2 mm in diameter. The

rock is cut by thin, darker green silicate and 6–7 mm long by 0.2 mm thick, limonite veinlets. The under surface has calcite staining. Reflectance spectra suggest the presence of actinolitic amphibole; chlorite minerals are not recognised. The magnetic susceptibility is 0.06.
Provenance. The bracer is exotic with regard to its findspot. Macroscopically it has a number of jade-like features. If the bracer was nephrite jade then the nearest recognised sources are continental. Although amphibole-rich metasedimentary rocks are present in the NW Highlands of Scotland, fine-grained, dense, amphibole-rich rocks are rare in the rest of Britain.

ID 11 BRANDON

Lithic identification. A spotted, amphibole-rich metamorphic rock.
Description. A strongly foliated, spotted metamorphic rock with an overall greenish grey (5GY 6/1) colour. Half of the bracer is highly spotted with uniformly distributed spots up to 0.4 mm in size whereas the other half is quite uniform with rare, lensoidal, 3 mm diameter, darker spots. Thin, 0.2–0.3 mm wide, green veinlets cross cut the artefact. The rock has a strong, but thin, 0.1 mm thick, foliation and is clearly metamorphic. Reflectance spectra suggest the presence of actinolitic amphibole; chlorite minerals are not recognised. The magnetic susceptibility is 0.07.
Provenance. The bracer is exotic with regard to its find spot. If the bracer was nephrite jade then the nearest recognised sources are continental. Although amphibole-rich metasedimentary rocks are present in the NW Highlands of Scotland, fine-grained, dense, amphibole-rich rocks are rare in the rest of Britain.

ID 12 SEWELL

Lithic identification. A spotted, ?amphibole-rich metamorphic rock.
Description. A light greenish grey or bluish grey (5G 7/1 or 5B 7/1) faintly mottled metamorphic rock. It is thinly foliated with laminae up to 0.1 mm thick. Some spots/lenses are solid but others have a dark core within a lighter margin but with a dark rim. Thin, *en echelon,* dark green veinlets are present. The underside has thick carbonate concretions. The magnetic susceptibility is 0.06.
Provenance. The bracer is exotic with regard to its find spot. Macroscopically it has a number of jade-like features. If the bracer was nephrite jade then the nearest recognised sources are continental. Although amphibole-rich metasedimentary rocks are present in the NW Highlands of Scotland, fine-grained, dense, amphibole-rich rocks are rare in the rest of Britain.

ID 13 KELLEYTHORPE

Lithic identification. Meta-volcaniclastic.
Description. A homogeneous, dark greenish grey (5GY 4/1) volcaniclastic rock. Thin fractures are infilled with pale carbonate. Limonite pseudomorphs after pyrite/pyrrhotite porphyroblasts are up to 0.5 mm in diameter. The convex surface has concretionary carbonate on it. The magnetic susceptibility is 0.19.
Provenance. The rock is a meta-volcaniclastic and is similar in appearance to the Group VI axe head lithologies. The rock may be from the Langdale area of the English Lake District and is exotic with regard to the find spot.

ID 14 ALDBOURNE

Lithic identification. An amphibole-rich metamorphic rock.
Description. When weathered the surface of the artefact is light bluish grey (5B 6/1) and shows a thin, planar foliation. Where freshly broken the rock is a medium light grey, medium grey or pale blue (N6/N5 or 5B 6/2) and has a saccharoidal texture. The surface of the artefact has abundant dune-like, spalling fractures up to 4 mm in diameter. Reflectance spectra suggest the presence of actinolitic amphibole. The magnetic susceptibility is 0.03.
Provenance. The bracer is exotic with regard to its find spot. It shares macroscopical similarities with the main group of amphibole-rich bracers and is a metasediment. Although amphibole-rich metasedimentary rocks are present in the NW Highlands of Scotland, fine-grained, dense, amphibole-rich rocks are rare in the rest of Britain.No provenance is possible.

ID 15 CALNE

Lithic identification. Meta-volcaniclastic.
Description. A very fine-grained, dark greenish grey (5G 5/1) rock with no internal fabric but a conchoidal fracture. Surface alteration/weathering has caused mottling giving rise to irregular up to 1cm sized, pale olive grey (5Y 6/1) areas. The magnetic susceptibility is 0.21.
Provenance. Macroscopically the lithology is a meta-volcaniclastic but is not a typical Group VI rock. It is more mottled and so superficially resembles amphibolite-rich rocks used for the flat bracers. The rock may originate within the volcanic rocks of the English Lake District. The bracer is exotic with regard to the find spot.

ID 18 OFFHAM

Lithic identification. A mottled ?amphibole-rich metamorphic rock.
Description. Very fine grained with smooth but uneven, mottled pale greenish grey surface (layer ~0.5 mm thick) with much darker, uniformly grey green interior revealed by breakage, and fracturing along irregular surfaces. The edges of broken surfaces have a suggestion of fissility. There is widespread patchy and flecked brown staining (?clay) on parts of surface. The object is similar to the amphibole-rich group. Mottling more apparent than in many others, and may be associated with surface damage or wear. The magnetic susceptibility is 0.07.
Provenance. The bracer is exotic with regard to its find spot. Macroscopically it has some jade-like features. If the bracer was nephrite jade then the nearest recognised sources are continental. Although amphibole-rich metasedimentary rocks are present in the NW Highlands of Scotland, fine-grained, dense, amphibole-rich rocks are rare in the rest of Britain.

ID 26 WELLINGTON QUARRY

Lithic identification. A spotted, amphibole-rich metamorphic rock. Nephrite jade.
Description. A homogeneous, light bluish grey (5B 7/1) spotted metamorphic rock with a sub-conchoidal fracture and a poorly developed planar fabric/foliation. The spots are 0.2–0.4 mm in diameter. The cut surface shows the rock to be a light bluish grey (5B 7/1) and fine-grained with a little limonite staining along some foliation planes. It has a thin, 0.2 mm thick, pale-coloured, weathered rim. In thin section the rock is homogeneous and is a light greenish grey (5G 8/1); locally it shows a poorly developed, lensoidal fabric alongside the pervasive planar foliation.
Microscopical identification. The rock is essentially monominerallic comprising dense, felted, amphibole fibres accompanied by trace amounts of up to 20μm diameter pale-coloured sphene and 1–2μm long TiO_2 minerals. The amphibole is pale brown/colourless, very slightly pleochroic and has interference colours up to the second order suggesting that it is tremolite. Spots are formed from slightly coarser grained amphibole within approximately 100μm long disc-shaped aggregates. Very rare muscovite may

be present. Reflectance spectra confirm the presence of actinolitic amphibole.
Provenance. The bracer is exotic with regard to its find spot. Although amphibole-rich metasedimentary rocks are present in the NW Highlands of Scotland, fine-grained, dense, amphibole-rich rocks are rare in the rest of Britain. Its petrographic and macroscopical properties suggest that this may be a nephrite jade. If the bracer was nephrite jade then the nearest recognised sources are continental.

ID 28 ROUNDWAY
Lithic identification. A spotted, ?amphibole-rich metamorphic rock.
Description. A faintly mottled/spotted, thinly laminated, homogeneous metamorphic rock with a saccharoidal texture. It has a greenish grey (5GY 6/1) surface and 0.5 mm diameter green spots. A little concretionary carbonate is present on the underside of the bracer. The magnetic susceptibility is 0.04.
Provenance. The bracer lithology is exotic with regard to its find spot. Macroscopically it has a number of jade-like features. If the bracer was nephrite jade then the nearest recognised sources are continental. Although amphibole-rich metasedimentary rocks are present in the NW Highlands of Scotland, fine-grained, dense, amphibole-rich rocks are rare in the rest of Britain.

ID 29 TYTHERINGTON/CORTON
Lithic identification. A fine-grained metasediment. 'Slate'.
Description. A uniform, poorly spotted fine-grained metasediment varying in colour from light olive (5Y 6/1) to greenish grey (5GY 6/1). The rock is cross-laminated with pale and dark laminae and has a sub-conchoidal fracture and small up to 2 mm diameter void spaces and rare limonitic spots on its surface. It has a slightly talcose feel. The magnetic susceptibility is 0.10.
Provenance. This is a metasediment, possibly from the Devonian killas of Cornubia. It is exotic with regard to its find spot

ID 30 SUTTON VENY
Lithic identification. A spotted amphibole-rich metamorphic rock.
Description. A greyish yellow green (5GY 6/2), uniform rock with 1 mm diameter, darker brown-green, limonite-rich spots after ?pyrite. The rock is foliated, has a hackly fracture where broken against the foliation, has very faint green spots and is cut by thin, 0.5 mm wide, green veinlets. Reflectance spectra suggest the presence of actinolitic amphibole.
Provenance. The bracer is exotic with regard to its find spot. If the bracer was nephrite jade then the nearest recognised sources are continental. Although amphibole-rich metasedimentary rocks are present in the NW Highlands of Scotland, fine-grained, dense, amphibole-rich rocks are rare in the rest of Britain.

ID 31 TRING
Lithic identification. Meta-volcaniclastic.
Description. A fine-grained, dark greenish grey (5G 4/1) homogeneous rock with faint sedimentary features including the presence of 4 mm long, slightly lensoidal, rock clasts and convoluted bedding/disrupted bedding structures. Up to 3 mm diameter limonitic spots after oxidised pyrite/pyrrhotite are present. The magnetic susceptibility is 0.16.
Provenance. The rock is a meta-volcaniclastic and is similar in appearance to the Group VI axe head lithologies. The rock may be from the Langdale area of the English Lake District and is exotic with regard to the find spot.

ID 32 BISHOPS CANNINGS
Lithic identification. A spotted, amphibole-rich metamorphic rock.
Description. A foliated, mottled metamorphic rock varying in colour from greenish grey (5GY 5/1) to greenish grey (5G 6/1). The rock has small, 1 mm diameter green spots (?megacrysts), a saccharoidal texture and 0.1–0.2 mm thick planar laminae. It has a talcose feel. Reflectance spectra suggest the presence of actinolitic amphibole The magnetic susceptibility is 0.00.
Provenance. The bracer is exotic with regard to its find spot. Macroscopically it has a number of jade-like features. If the bracer was nephrite jade then the nearest recognised sources are continental. Although amphibole-rich metasedimentary rocks are present in the NW Highlands of Scotland, fine-grained, dense, amphibole-rich rocks are rare in the rest of Britain.

ID 56 AMESBURY ARCHER (RED)
Lithic identification. A fine-grained red laminated mudstone.
Description. A red (dusky red 5R 3/4), uniform, bedded, very fine-grained mudstone. The bedding comprises alternating broad red beds enclosing thin, 4 mm wide, darker (blackish red 5R 2/2) slightly coarser grained laminae. Very minor amounts of white mica are visible. The long axis of the bracer is at a steep angle to the bedding. The magnetic susceptibility is 0.02.
Provenance. It is exotic to the find spot. In Britain similar red mudstones are found in the Devonian and Permo-Triassic of Devon and the Cambrian Caerfai Beds in South Wales.

ID 57 AMESBURY ARCHER (BLACK)
Lithic identification.A fine-grained ?sandstone.
Description. A uniform dark grey (N3) indurated, fine-grained (grain size 187μm) ?sandstone The rock is recrystallised and carries very rare white mica. It has spalled along flat, parallel planes. The magnetic susceptibility is 0.01.
Provenance. No provenance suggested but is exotic. The extreme geochemistry suggests it might be very exotic.

ID 58 STONEHENGE
Lithic identification. A fine-grained ?sediment/basalt.
Description. A black (N1), uniform, very fine-grained rock. It has 2 mm long, pale yellow brown, thin lenses on its upper surface suggesting a sediment/metasediment namely a mudstone but a basic lava may be possible. The magnetic susceptibility is 0.26.
Provenance. The lithology is exotic. If it is a mudstone then a Cornubian killas is possible.

ID 66 WEST STAFFORD
Lithic identification. A spotted, amphibole-rich metamorphic rock.
Description. A pale greenish yellow (10Y 8/2) fairly uniform, fine-grained metamorphic rock with very faint, very diffuse, irregularly shaped green spots up to 1 mm in size. The main rock is mottled on a 0.1 mm diameter scale in dark and light green and is cut by a very thin, amphibole-rich, black veinlet. Reflectance spectra suggest the presence of amphibole. The magnetic susceptibility is 0.05.
Provenance. The bracer is exotic with regard to its find spot. Macroscopically it has some jade-like features. If the bracer was nephrite jade then the nearest recognised sources are continental. Although amphibole-rich metasedimentary rocks are present in the NW Highlands of Scotland, fine-grained, dense, amphibole-rich rocks are rare in the rest of Britain.

ID 67 THOMAS HARDYE SCHOOL
Lithic identification. A ?spotted, amphibole-rich metamorphic rock.
Description. A mottled pale blue (5B 6/2), very fine-grained, dense, metamorphic rock with some faint broad banding but no other fabric. Where it is broken the colour is deeper (medium bluish grey 5B 6/1). It has a very thin foliation, and 0.1–0.2 mm (but up to 0.4 mm) diameter spots on its surface that may be 'spalling'. It looks and feels silky. A little post-depositional silica enclosing quartz grains adheres to one surface. Reflectance spectra suggest the presence of amphibole. The magnetic susceptibility is 0.04.
Provenance. The bracer is exotic with regard to its findspot. Macroscopically it has a number of jade-like features. If the bracer was nephrite jade then the nearest recognised sources are continental. Although amphibole-rich metasedimentary rocks are present in the NW Highlands of Scotland, fine-grained, dense, amphibole-rich rocks are rare in the rest of Britain.

ID 73 FERRY FRYSTON
Lithic identification. Meta-volcaniclastic.
Description. A dark greenish grey (5G 5/1) fairly uniform, fine-grained, volcaniclastic rock; it breaks with a hackly fracture and the breaks are the same colour as the surface. The rock shows 4 mm thick bedding and locally autobrecciation? with clasts lying within the fine-grained matrix. Pyrite cubes, up to 1 mm in diameter, are extensively oxidised to limonite. The magnetic susceptibility is 0.20.
Provenance. The rock is a meta-volcaniclastic and is similar in appearance to the Group VI axe head lithologies. The rock may be from the Langdale area of the English Lake District and is exotic with regard to the find spot.

ID 74 GRAVELLY GUY
Lithic identification. A spotted, amphibole-rich metamorphic rock.
Description. The rock is fine-grained, homogeneous and a light bluish-grey (5B 8/1) with slightly mottling and banding. Darker, 2 mm diameter, grey-green patches that may be porphyroblasts are concentrated in layers. The broken edge is medium bluish grey (5B 5/1) and shows that the rock is foliated with thin, planar, laminae. One corner of the bracer has brown-stained ?quartz associated with a thin limonitic rim. Reflectance spectra suggest the presence of actinolitic amphibole. The magnetic susceptibility is 0.07.
Provenance. The bracer is exotic with regard to its find spot. Macroscopically it has a number of jade-like features. If the bracer was nephrite jade then the nearest recognised sources are continental. Although amphibole-rich metasedimentary rocks are present in the NW Highlands of Scotland, fine-grained, dense, amphibole-rich rocks are rare in the rest of Britain.

ID 75 SHORNCOTE
Lithic identification. A spotted, amphibole-rich metamorphic rock. Nephrite jade.
Description. A planar laminated, greenish grey (5GY 6/1) metamorphic rock. Dark green (dusky green 5G 4/2) spots up to 2 mm in diameter have diffuse, irregular edges. The cut surface is a moderate bluish grey (5B 6/1) with a thin, 0.3 mm wide, pale-coloured weathered rim. The rock is very fine-grained and uniform with 0.1 mm wide, greener discs. In thin section the rock is white (N9) and has a very thin foliation and faint paler and darker bands. The magnetic susceptibility is 0.01.
Microscopical identification. It is monomineralic, comprising densely felted amphibole fibres up to 40 x 2μm in size with very rare 1–2μm diameter, white sphene/TiO_2 minerals. The amphibole is colourless and has low interference colours suggesting that it is tremolite. Lath-shaped fibrous amphibole is coarser grained in the paler bands and radiating, coarse grained amphibole with second order interference colours forms 'spots'. Trace amounts of calcite are present on one surface. It is more nephrite-like than Duston although both are very similar. Reflectance spectra confirm the presence of actinolitic amphibole.
Provenance A typical member of the spotted amphibole-rich bracers. The bracer is exotic with regard to its find spot. Macroscopically and microscopically it has nephrite jade-like features. If the bracer was nephrite jade then the nearest recognised sources are continental. Although amphibole-rich metasedimentary rocks are present in the NW Highlands of Scotland, fine-grained, dense, amphibole-rich rocks are rare in the rest of Britain.

ID 77 GLENLUCE
Lithic identification. An unusual siltstone/fine-grained sandstone.
Description. A light olive grey (5Y 6/1), fine-grained, homogeneous, clastic sediment with many small, dark clasts but no fabric. The artefact is rough/gritty to the touch. It resembles a fine-grained cement and is unlike most sediments/metasediments used for bracers. The magnetic susceptibility is 0.05.
Provenance. Without a definitive lithological identification a provenance is unknowable. However, Permian breccias, sandstones and mudstone are local and Lower Palaeozoic sediments are very local to the find spot. If the rock was from the Lower Permian clastic sequence then the bracer could be local.

ID 78 FYRISH
Lithic identification. Meta-volcaniclastic.
Description. A dark greenish grey (5G 5/1) fine-grained volcaniclastic rock with very, very faint inhomogeneities in its internal fabric. It carries 0.5 mm diameter, limonite pseudomorphs after pyrite/pyrrhotite and 0.1 mm wide, dark veinlets. The magnetic susceptibility is 0.17.
Provenance. The local geology comprises Devonian sediments. The rock is a meta-volcaniclastic and is similar in appearance to the Group VI axe head lithologies. The rock may be from the Langdale area of the English Lake District and is exotic with regard to the find spot. Macroscopically it is very like bracer ID 89 Borrowstone; both have characteristic lithologies for this class of bracer.

ID 79 CULDUTHEL MAINS
Lithic identification. Meta-volcaniclastic.
Description. A volcaniclastic rock with a complex mottled surface with slightly darker fine-grained?, angular patches and light greenish grey areas within an overall greenish grey (5G 6/1) colour. Small, 0.5 mm diameter, limonite-stained pits may represent oxidised iron sulphides. The magnetic susceptibility is 0.14.
Provenance. The local geology comprises Devonian sediments. The rock is a meta-volcaniclastic and very typical of the group. It is similar in appearance to the Group VI axe head lithologies. The rock may be from the Langdale area of the English Lake District and is exotic with regard to the find spot.

ID 80 CULBIN SANDS
Lithic identification. A laminated fine-grained ?metasediment/meta-volcaniclastic rock.

Description. A dark greenish grey (5GY 4/1), fine-grained, uniform, indurated, very fine-grained (grain size much less then 187µm), laminated sediment. Thin, dark-coloured laminae/beds up to 1.5 mm in thickness show soft sediment disruptions. The surface colour grades into pale yellowish brown (10YR 6/2) at one end. The magnetic susceptibility is 2.97.
Provenance. Without a definitive lithological identification a provenance is unknowable. The local bedrock comprises Devonian sediments and regionally the rocks are high grade metamorphics, so the bracer is probably exotic with respect to its find spot.

ID 82 OLD RAYNE
Lithic identification. A fine-grained metasediment/meta-volcaniclastic.
Description. A very fine-grained, homogeneous metasediment, the smooth and broken surfaces are dark greenish grey (5GY 5/1). Weathered bands 2 mm wide are an olive grey (5Y 7/1). The break shows that the rock has a planar fabric orientated at about 45° to the flat surfaces. Very thin laminae on the surfaces take a slightly different polish. Visually it shares similarities with some of the Group VI bracer volcaniclastics but is probably a metasediment. The magnetic susceptibility is 0.04.
Provenance. Uncertainty about the lithological identification precludes any meaningful provenance. The local geology is the same as for the nearby Newlands, Oyne (ID 90), namely Dalradian metasediments, schists and gabbros.

*ID 83 RINNACHIE**
Lithic identification. A fine-grained metasediment.
Description. A greenish grey (5GY 6/1), fine-grained, (grain size far less than 187µm), indurated, homogeneous, ?siliceous sediment/metasediment with a moderately well-developed planar fabric. Clastic grains are not visible. The magnetic susceptibility is 0.01.
Provenance. Without a definitive lithological identification a provenance is unknowable. Dalradian metasediments are local to the find spot. Could be local.
** This object was originally viewed as a reworked bracer fragment and analysed accordingly (see Tables 3.1 and 3.5). However, it has since been reinterpreted and no longer considered to be of bracer origin. This description is retained here in order to retain consistency between tables and text. The object was excluded from measurement or discussion in other chapters.*

ID 84 BALLOGIE
Lithic identification. A fine-grained ?spotted meta-volcaniclastic/ ?spotted metasediment.
Description. A greenish grey (5GY 5/1), fine-grained, quite homogeneous, spotted rock. The matrix carries rounded, pale spots up to 0.5 mm in diameter and larger, lensoidal spots up to 3 mm in length, the latter spots are concentrated into bands and some have a darker green core. A little limonite is present but earlier sulphides were not recognised. The magnetic susceptibility is 0.08. Although the bracer has many lithological aspects that are similar to classical Group VI bracers, it differs from them in being spotted so resembling the spotted amphibolite bracers.
Provenance. The local geology comprises Dalradian limestones, mica schists, quartzites and granite. Uncertainty about the lithological identification precludes any meaningful provenance as it might be a metasediment or a fine-grained volcaniclastic of Group VI type.

ID 86 GLEN FORSA
Lithic identification. Meta-volcaniclastic.
Description. A very fine-grained, homogeneous, patchy, greenish grey (5G 7/1) volcaniclastic rock with some sedimentary features and locally a flaser-like fabric. Limonite pseudomorphs after iron sulphides are absent. The magnetic susceptibility is 0.18.
Provenance. The rock is a meta-volcaniclastic but is atypical of the group. The local Mull geology comprises Tertiary basalts and spilites, granites and Liassic sediments. The bracer does not correspond with any Mull rock, however Devonian volcanics/ ?meta-volcanics crop out regionally. The bracer shares similarities in its appearance to the Group VI axe head lithologies. The rock may be from the Langdale area of the English Lake District and is exotic with regard to the find spot.

ID 87 CORRY LIVERAS
Lithic identification. Meta-volcaniclastic.
Description. A homogeneous, fine-grained volcaniclastic rock. The surfaces are mottled with paler patches but are mainly a greenish grey (5G 6/1). The artefact is broken with a hackly fracture and is a greenish grey (5G 7/1). The matrix carries rare, black, lensoidal clasts up to 1.5 mm in length and small, 0.2–0.4 mm diameter, limonite pseudomorphs after ?pyrite/pyrrhotite. A little pale carbonate covers some of the surface of the artefact. The magnetic susceptibility is 0.17.
Provenance. The local geology comprises Jurassic sediments, acid intrusives and Torridonian sandstone with no volcaniclastics. The bracer lithology is exotic with regard to the find spot. The rock is a meta-volcaniclastic and is similar in appearance to the Group VI axe head lithologies. The rock may be from the Langdale area of the English Lake District.

ID 88 BROADFORD BAY
Lithic identification. A fine-grained metamudstone/siltstone/ ?meta-volcaniclastic.
Description. A banded, indurated, fine-grained (grain size is less than 187µm) metasediment with planar bedding and very fine, 0.1 mm thick laminae within beds 1–2 mm wide. Some beds carry crescent-shaped 'mud clasts'. A 4 mm thick, pinkish grey (5YR 8/1) band contrasts with the main dark greenish grey (5G 6/1) of the artefact. Very rare pits after altered pyrite are present. The magnetic susceptibility is 0.03. The rock is probably a metamudstone but may be a volcaniclastic.
Provenance. Without a definitive lithological identification a provenance is unknowable. The local geology is Jurassic and Torridonian sediments and small acid intrusions hence the bracer is unlikely to have been be locally sourced.

ID 89 BORROWSTONE
Lithic identification. Meta-volcaniclastic.
Description. A very fine-grained, homogeneous, mottled volcaniclastic rock that varies in colour from a pale greenish yellow (10Y 8/2) to a greyish olive (10Y 4/2). Sedimentary features are absent but 2 mm diameter, limonitic areas have replaced pyrite/pyrrhotite. The magnetic susceptibility is 0.20.
Provenance. The local bedrock geology comprises Devonian sedimentary sequences intruded by granite. The bracer lithology is exotic with regard to the find spot. The rock is a meta-volcaniclastic and very typical of the group. It is similar in appearance to the Group VI axe head lithologies. The rock may be from the Langdale area of the English Lake District.

ID 90 NEWLANDS, OYNE
Lithic identification. A fine-grained, ?garnetiferous schist.

Description. A dark grey (N3), very dense, fine-grained schist with large muscovites up to 0.5 mm in size and abundant small, euhedral to subhedral, red ?garnets up to 0.2 mm in diameter both within a dark matrix. The magnetic susceptibility is 0.13.
Provenance. The local geology comprises granites, gabbros and widespread Dalradian quartz-mica schists and metasediments. This bracer may be local in origin, certainly regional.

ID 91 NEWLANDS, OYNE

Lithic identification. Meta-volcaniclastic.
A faintly mottled volcaniclastic varying in colour from a dark greenish grey (5GY 4/1) to a light olive grey (5Y 6/1). The mottling may be due to inhomogeneities in the volcanic sediment and there is some limonite staining at one end of the artefact. Small, 0.5 mm diameter, limonite pseudomorphs after pyrite/pyrrhotite are present. The magnetic susceptibility is 0.06; this is low for the group but the bracer is thin.
Provenance. The rock is a meta-volcaniclastic. There are no meta-volcaniclastics in the local area, thus the bracer lithology is exotic with regard to the find spot. The bracer is similar in appearance to the Group VI axe head lithologies but is slightly atypical. The rock may be from the Langdale area of the English Lake District.

ID 92 ?SCOTLAND

Lithic identification. Jasper.
Description. A dusky red (10R 2/2) jasper cut by thin, very dark red veinlets. The jasper is slightly colour banded. The magnetic susceptibility is 0.02. Possibly an Irish jasper. See also Appendix 3.1.

ID 93 CRAWFORD

Lithic identification. A fine-grained, indurated sandstone.
Description. A dark yellowish brown (10YR 5/2), fine-grained, homogeneous rock with 0.2–0.4 mm diameter rounded grains but smooth to the touch. Broken areas show the rock to be very pale orange (10YR 8/2). The magnetic susceptibility is 0.10.
Provenance. Lower Palaeozoic Ordovician and Silurian sediments are very local to the find spot and clastic Permian sediments are local.

ID 94 DORNOCH NURSERY

Lithic identification. Jasper or fine-grained red siltstone.
Description. A greyish red (10R 4/2) jasper colour. The very fine-grained, homogeneous matrix carries 1 mm diameter, irregular, black patches. The magnetic susceptibility is 0.02.
Provenance. If an Irish jasper then it is exotic. A reddened siltstone could be local from the Devonian. See also Appendix 3.1.

ID 101 ARDIFFERY (Replica)

Description. The replica is of a dark green even colour and the form of the bracer resembles other curved examples which are made from Group VI rock.
Provenance. If the rock is a meta-volcaniclastic it is similar in appearance to the Group VI axe head lithologies. If this is correct then the original is from the English Lake District making it exotic.

ID 102 DUSTON

Lithic identification. A tremolite-bearing metamorphic rock. A ?nephrite jade.
Description. A fine-grained, homogeneous, greenish grey (5G 6/1) vitreous/saccharoidal, metamorphic rock that is very smooth to the touch. Where broken it shows a foliation. Thin, 1 mm wide, darker green amphibole-rich veinlets cross-cut the rock but the rock is poorly spotted, if at all. At higher power the rock shows itself to comprise compact, felted mafic crystals. The bracer has been thin sectioned and petrographically described as a 'tremolite fels' (sic) (Clough and Cummins 1988, 186).
Microscopical identification. Re-examination of the thin section shows the rock to be very fine-grained with a strong planar fabric. It comprises approximately equal amounts of acicular crystals of a colourless amphibole with low interference colours together with much fine-grained ?sphene (semi-opaque, high relief and high interference colours), not carbonate. Very thin quartz-rich streaks lie along the main fabric. At low magnification it is like Shorncote (ID 75). The magnetic susceptibility is 0.00.
Provenance. The bracer is exotic with regard to its find spot. Its petrography and macroscopical properties suggest that this may be a nephrite jade. If the bracer was nephrite jade then the nearest recognised sources are continental. Although amphibole-rich metasedimentary rocks are present in the NW Highlands of Scotland, fine-grained, dense, amphibole-rich rocks are rare in the rest of Britain.

ID 103 UPPER HEYFORD

Lithic identification. A spotted siliceous metamorphic rock. Fine-grained quartz-felted amphibole-rich rock.
Description. A fine-grained, homogeneous metasediment that is smooth to the touch. Although the main colour is a light greenish grey (5GY 7/1) very small, darker spots are present. The rock shows sedimentary features (flaser bedding/mudclasts) and the 1 mm thick bedding is at a high angle to the cleavage and the flat faces of the bracer. The rock has a very thin planar fabric/cleavage but is also saccharoidal at high magnification. The bracer has been thin sectioned and petrographically described as a rhyolite (Clough and Cummins 1988, 185).
Microscopical identification. Re-examination of the thin section shows the rock to comprise fine-grained quartz intergrown with acicular, often radiating, felted, colourless ?amphibole. Trace amounts of sphene and ?pyrrhotite are present and locally slightly coarser grained quartz-mosaics forms thin veinlets and patches. The rock is metamorphic, possibly a metasediment. The magnetic susceptibility is 0.01.
Provenance. The bracer is exotic with regard to its find spot. It shares many characteristics with the nephrite-jade bracers but is too quartz rich. Although amphibole-rich metasedimentary rocks are present in the NW Highlands of Scotland, fine-grained, dense, amphibole-rich rocks are rare in the rest of Britain. It possibly has a non-British origin.

ID 104 SCARBOROUGH

Lithic identification. A clean siltstone/fine-grained sandstone.
Description.A fine-grained, very light grey (N8), bleached?, homogeneous, clean, indurated siltstone/fine-grained sandstone (grain size <187μm). The siltstone is very thinly bedded/laminated, cut by thin stylolites and rough to the touch. Small, 0.2–0.5 mm diameter, irregular, black spots are present on the main surfaces. The magnetic susceptibility is 0.00.
Provenance. The rock is not sarsen but is a clean, siltstone/fine-grained sandstone. Similar sediments crop out in the local Mesozoic sequences of Yorkshire. If it were a seat-earth from the Coal Measures then it would be regional in origin, assuming that it was not taken from the float.

ID 105 MELTON QUARRY
Lithic identification. Meta-volcaniclastic.
Description.A greyish olive green (5GY 4/2), fine-grained, homogeneous, volcaniclastic rock. Locally the surfaces have pale patches (greyish yellow green 5GY 7/1) up to 17 mm in size. It shows soft sediment disruption of the very thin, 0.3 mm thick, bedding/laminae. Small, 0.5 mm diameter, limonite pseudomorphs after pyrite/pyrrhotite cubes occur. The magnetic susceptibility is 0.09. This is low for the group.
Provenance. The rock is a meta-volcaniclastic and is similar in appearance to the Group VI axe head lithologies. The rock may be from the Langdale area of the English Lake District and is exotic with regard to the find spot.

ID 106 HOCKWOLD
Lithic identification. A ?metasediment.
Description. A fine-grained, homogeneous metasediment. It is yellowish grey (5Y 8/1) and has faint spots. It has a poor planar fabric with very thin laminae and a non-conchoidal fracture. It feels slightly gritty and is rougher than typical flat bracer lithologies. The magnetic susceptibility is 0.03.
Provenance. The bracer is exotic with regard to its find spot. A metasiltstone rather than a metamudstone. However, XRF and reflectance spectroscopy analysis indicated that this bracer falls within the amphibole metamorphic group.

ID 107 ASTON
Lithic identification. A spotted, ?amphibole-rich metamorphic rock.
Description. A homogeneous, fine-grained, greenish grey (5G 7/1) rock with small, 2–4 mm diameter, irregular, darker greenish spots and thin, 1 mm wide, irregular, darker veinlets. The bracer is very smooth to the touch and where broken looks saccharoidal/vitreous. There is little fabric other than a major plane that has controlled breaks in the artefact. Original layering (?bedding) lies at very high angles to the flat surfaces of the bracer, like ID 103 (Upper Heyford). The magnetic susceptibility is 0.03.
Provenance. The bracer is exotic with regard to its find spot. Macroscopically it has a number of jade-like features. If the bracer was nephrite jade then the nearest recognised sources are continental. Although amphibole-rich metasedimentary rocks are present in the NW Highlands of Scotland, fine-grained, dense, amphibole-rich rocks are rare in the rest of Britain.

ID 108 BEN BRIDGE
Lithic identification. A fine-grained sediment/metasediment.
Description. A dark grey (N3), fine-grained, uniform, unweathered/unaltered rock that is smooth to the touch and has a conchoidal fracture. There is a little limonite-staining in the drill hole and fine-grained mica is absent. The magnetic susceptibility is 0.01.
Provenance. Fine-grained sediments/metasediments are common in highland Britain. No specific provenance is suggested but the artefact is probably exotic with regard to its find spot.

ID 111 LINDRIDGE
Lithic identification.A fine-grained laminated ?metamudstone.
Description. An olive black (5Y 2/1), fine-grained, homogeneous rock with very little fabric other than a very, very thin, planar fabric seen in oblique light. The magnetic susceptibility is 0.09.
Provenance. Fine-grained sediments/metasediments are common in highland Britain. Suitable rocks are present in central Wales so it could be regional but equally it could be from Cornubia and thus exotic.

ID 112 ALDINGTON
Lithic identification. Meta-volcaniclastic.
Description. A very fine-grained, uniform, olive grey (5Y 4/1) volcaniclastic with thin, sedimentary slumping and rare, sedimentary clasts and overall a very thin, planar fabric. Fresh breaks show the rock to be a dark greenish grey (5G 4/1) and to have a sub-conchoidal fracture. The concave surface has small limonite patches up to 4 mm in diameter and yellowish grey (5Y 6/2) areas; however, obvious limonite pseudomorphs after iron sulphides are absent. The magnetic susceptibility is 0.22.
Provenance. The rock is a meta-volcaniclastic but is slightly atypical. It is similar in appearance to the Group VI axe head lithologies. The rock may be from the Langdale area of the English Lake District and is exotic with regard to the find spot.

ID 113 LLANTRITHYD
Lithic identification. A spotted, ?amphibole-rich metamorphic rock.
Description. A greenish grey (5GY 6/1) 'spotted slate'. The rock has dark green (5G 6/1) spots and streaks and a very thin, planar fabric. It has a slight saccharoidal texture. The magnetic susceptibility is 0.03.
Provenance. A typical member of the spotted amphibole-rich bracers. Macroscopically it has a number of jade-like features. Its geochemistry suggests that it is too silica-rich to be nephrite and may be a calc-silicate; an actinolitic schist. Similar rocks are very rare in Wales only being recorded from Holy Island in Anglesey. This is exotic with regard to the find spot.

ID 114 DYFFRYN ARDUDWY
Lithic identification. Two fragments, both fine-grained laminated ?metamudstones/fine-grained volcanics.
Description. Smaller fragment. A homogeneous, yellowish grey (10Y 6/2), very laminated, very fine-grained, metasediment with a sub-conchoidal fracture and a slight vitreous look. Very slightly paler patches and 0.3–0.5 mm diameter limonite after pyrite are present on the surface.
Description. Larger fragment. A yellowish grey (5Y 7/2) surface but yellowish grey (5Y 7/1) where broken. The rock has a planar fabric, a sub-conchoidal fracture and carries abundant, small, 0.1–0.4 mm diameter, darker spots. The magnetic susceptibility is 0.00.
Provenance. A local/regional Welsh provenance is probable. The regional geology has abundant Palaeozoic metasediments and volcanics. Its geochemistry suggests that it might be an acid volcanic (rhyolite).

ID 115 SONNING
Lithic identification. Nephrite jade.
Description. A fine-grained, olive grey (5Y 4/1) rock with a strong foliation and 0.5 mm diameter, irregular, darker spots. It is very smooth to the touch and is vitreous. The bracer has been thin sectioned and petrographically described as a nephrite (fine-grained, felted tremolite-actinolite) with a low extinction angle and refractive indices of 1.62–1.636 (Clough and Cummins 1988, 143). Reflectance spectra suggest the presence of actinolitic amphibole. The magnetic susceptibility is 0.00.
Provenance. The bracer is exotic with regard to its find spot. Its petrography and macroscopical properties suggest that this may be a nephrite jade. If the bracer was nephrite jade then the nearest recognised sources are continental. Although amphibole-rich metasedimentary rocks are present in the NW Highlands of Scotland, fine-grained, dense, amphibole-rich rocks are rare in the rest of Britain.

ID 116 RAUNDS
Lithic identification. Meta-volcaniclastic.
Description. The rock is a fine-grained, greyish olive green (5GY 3/2) volcaniclastic and has broken along a thin, weathered, limonite-rich veinlet. Where freshly broken the rock is a medium bluish grey (5B 5/1). There is little internal fabric but a little sedimentary banding may be present. Pyrite/pyrrhotite and their pseudomorphs are rare. The magnetic susceptibility is 0.10; this is low for this group.
Provenance. The rock is a meta-volcaniclastic, if slightly atypical, and is similar in appearance to the Group VI axe head lithologies. The rock may be from the Langdale area of the English Lake District and is exotic with regard to the find spot.

ID 118 RAUCEBY
Lithic identification. Meta-volcaniclastic.
Description. A brownish grey (5YR 3/2) rock, but where broken the fresh rock is a pale blue (5B 6/2). The surface has 0.5 mm diameter, round black spots and has both faint, 5 mm diameter, yellow patches and streaks/banding. It is very smooth to the touch. The magnetic susceptibility is 0.05; this is low for this group.
Provenance. The rock is a meta-volcaniclastic and is similar in appearance to the Group VI axe head lithologies. The rock may be from the Langdale area of the English Lake District and is exotic with regard to the find spot.

ID 119 WINTERINGHAM
Lithic identification. Meta-volcaniclastic?
Description. A greyish olive (10Y 3/2) volcaniclastic. The surface is limonite-stained and shows no internal fabric but is cut by thin quartz veins. Limonite pseudomorphs after iron sulphides are absent. The magnetic susceptibility is 0.02; this is very low for the group and reflects the fragmentary nature of the artefact.
Provenance. The rock is a meta-volcaniclastic but is atypical. It shares similarities in its appearance to the Group VI axe head lithologies. The rock may be from the Langdale area of the English Lake District and is exotic with regard to the find spot.

ID 120 LITTLEPORT
Lithic identification. An indurated siltstone/fine-grained sandstone.
Description. A medium dark grey (N4), very indurated, siltstone/fine-grained sandstone (grain size is>187µm) lacking visible mica. The artefact is slightly gritty to the touch. The magnetic susceptibility is 0.02.
Provenance. Indurated fine-grained sediments/metasediments are widespread within highland Britain. However the lithology is exotic to the find spot.

ID 121 CALCEBY
Lithic identification. A spotted, ?amphibole-rich metamorphic rock.
Description. A pale olive (10Y 7/2), poorly spotted, metamorphic rock with a planar fabric Thin, 2 mm wide, dark green-grey (5G 6/2) veinlets lie at a high angle to the foliation and rare green spots are up to 2 mm in diameter. It is not as vitreous as some of the flat bracers but is smooth to the touch. The magnetic susceptibility is 0.01.
Provenance. The bracer is exotic with regard to its find spot. Macroscopically it has some jade-like features. If the bracer was nephrite jade then the nearest recognised sources are continental. Although amphibole-rich metasedimentary rocks are present in the NW Highlands of Scotland, fine-grained, dense, amphibole-rich rocks are rare in the rest of Britain.

ID 123 FERNIEGAIR
Lithic identification. A fine-grained, altered basic rock/?metabasalt.
Description (from photographs only). Photographs show a uniform, fine-grained, pale-coloured grey/red rock devoid of any fabric. ?Bands of limonite pseudomorphs after primary iron sulphide (SEM-EDAX confirmed the presence of limonite) have polished proud of the bracer surface. Slight mottling is a post manufacture patination. SEM backscatter photographs show the rock to be uniform and crystalline rather than clastic and to carry a fine-grained matrix with altered iron titanium oxide minerals that are now largely sphene (as suggested by the spectra obtained from the rock's matrix) together with ?chlorite and perhaps epidote group minerals. Limonite pseudomorphs after iron sulphides are present, as confirmed by SEM-EDAX.
Provenance. Possibly a local bracer as fine-grained altered basalts are nearby. It has little in common with Group VI.

ID 130 BOWERHAM BARRACKS
Lithic identification. A ?fine-grained altered volcanic.
Description (from photograph only). Photograph shows a fine-grained pale purple lithic with no fabric. The colour suggests a purple mudstone (?Devonian/Permo-Triassic) or a fine-grained altered volcanic. The paler areas appear to be variable, from pinkish-purple to orange rust. The variability of the grains and apparent granularity of the underlying surface suggest a fine-grained ferruginous sandstone.
Provenance. Unlikely to be local to find spot.

ID 133 ARCHERTON NEWTAKE
Lithic identification. Not a spotted or unspotted amphibole-rich metamorphic rock.
Description (FR). Visual inspection with a hand lens showed a grey, partly whitish, colour, although a circular patch where a label had been removed revealed a fresher, pale green rock. There are some darker veins (chloritic?) including some quite fine ones and the surface of the bracer is smooth. The fabric is fine-grained and may be fairly calcareous. No lamination is present.
Provenance. Unknown.

ID 134 FOX HOLE
Lithic identification. A spotted, ?amphibole-rich metamorphic rock.
Description (FR). Visual inspection with a hand lens showed a green-grey surface, although a fresh surface at a broken corner is blue/grey/green. It is of laminated stone and one diagonal crack may reflect the original cleavage. There are fairly faint spots of darker material visible on the upper face and a darker vein near one corner.
Provenance. As other amphibole-rich bracers.

ID 135 CASSINGTON
Lithological identification. Unspotted, ?felsite/ ?amphibole-rich metamorphic rock
Description. A fine-grained, light greenish grey (5GY 7/1) homogeneous rock. Where broken it has an irregular to sub-planar fracture. The homogeneity of the bracer is disturbed by short, thin, <0.1 mm wide, dark streaks and abundant, 0.1 mm diameter, limonite spots after sulphide but there is no real fabric. It is smooth to the touch.
Provenance. It is exotic with regard to its find spot.

ID 137 PYECOMBE
Lithic identification. An ?amphibole-rich metamorphic rock.
Description (AW). The bracer has a blue grey smooth surface with darker grey-green veinlets and mottling. A corner break reveals a fine-grained and laminated structure. There is a substantial calcareous deposit on the front face, derived from conditions in the grave. The rock seems very similar to that of the amphibole-rich bracers. Reflectance spectra suggest the presence of actinolitic amphibole.
Provenance. As other amphibole-rich bracers.

ID 139 MOLA
Lithic identification. A fine grained sandstone.
Description (from photographs only). A pinkish brown, slightly bleached, well-cemented sandstone.
Provenance. Possibly local to find spot.

ID 141 BROUGHTON-IN-CRAVEN
Lithic identification. The rock has been identified as a Group VI meta-vocaniclastic by M Boyd, geologist at Burton Constable Museum.
Description (AW). The bracer is dark olive green in colour and it is fine-grained with no apparent internal fabric.
Provenance. The rock is from the Langdale area of the English Lake District and exotic to the find spot.

ID 148 CARNEDDAU HENGWM
Lithic identification. A light red coarse siltstone.
Description (FR). The stone is light reddish, fairly fine-grained and micaceous and seems to be a coarse siltstone rather than sandstone. There are traces of lamination/bedding along the longer sides.
Provenance. Likely to be from the local Devonian Old Red Sandstone.

ID 149 THANET.
Lithic identification. A grey sandstone.
Description (FR). The bracer is made from a fine-grained grey sandstone, while the white flecks shown in the photograph are just surface adhesions of the local chalk.
Provenance. Not likely to be of local provenance.

ID 150 LOCKERBIE
Lithic identification. A weathered fine-grained dark-coloured ?lava.
Description (from photographs only). Photographs show a uniform, fine-grained rock weathered to a brown colour. The rock caries small limonite pseudomorphs after iron sulphides (SEM-EDAX at the NMS confirmed the presence of limonite) but has no fabric. A fractured corner shows a fine-grained grey green lithology. SEM photographs do not suggest that the rock is a volcaniclastic, but perhaps a very altered lava. There is however a faint planar preferred fabric.
Provenance. Unknown.

ID 153 CLIFFE
Lithic identification. Probably Kimmeridge shale.
Decsription (FR). Black laminated shale, the surface obscured by lacquer.
Provenance. Probably Kimmeridge, Dorset.

ID 154 MONKTON
Lithic identification. Amphibole-rich metamorphic.
Description. Grey-green (5GY /6/1) with very thin dark green veinlets. Very smooth to the touch; subconchoidal fracture with very poor foliation.
Provenance. The bracer is exotic with regard to its find spot. Macroscopically it has some jade-like features. If the bracer was nephrite jade then the nearest recognised sources are continental. Although amphibole-rich metasedimentary rocks are present in the NW Highlands of Scotland, fine-grained, dense, amphibole-rich rocks are rare in the rest of Britain.

4: MORPHOLOGY

David Bukach

This chapter considers aspects of bracer morphology, utilising recorded data on: colour; size; shape; the presence and shape of facet and flanges and perforations. These traits are examined separately in the following sections with a focus on the presentation of their occurrence on British bracers and their correlation with established rock types outlined in Chapter 3. The main emphasis here is to identify any patterns of similarity and/or variation which will help inform further interpretive discussion, although these patterns also hold wider implications for bracer classification generally (Chapter 10).

Not all of the 74 bracers studied could be included in each category of analysis as a result of their surviving condition: some were omitted as they were highly fragmentary, making accurate measurement and description of original characteristics impossible, and others were omitted as they had been modified from their original design (see Chapter 6.3). Bracers could only be included in the analyses below in circumstances where their state of survival was sufficiently complete to allow for measurements representative of original size or for other morphological aspects. Comparison is restricted to only those bracers with consistently comparable data.

4.1 COLOUR

Colour was recorded using general observation of overall colour in available light, and for purposes of analysis was simplified into seven colour groups ranging from green to grey to black, as well as red and brown. It may be noted that the stone used to make the bracers is not usually in fresh condition; alteration of the surface has occurred, depending on soil conditions, so that the colours recorded are not altogether the same as the fresh rock. In terms of the whole assemblage of bracers, discounting rock type initially, there is a clear preference towards bracers with light grey and green tones: these represent 80% of all bracers with recorded colour (Figure 4.1). This preference of colour is markedly different from observations of colour from continental bracers, which tend to be reddish or grey/black in colour (Chapter 9). A possible explanation could be that while colour had some significance, rock of a special type or from a special source was more important, leading to the choice in Britain of amphibolite with some resemblance to jade and Langdale stone from a distant mountain which had long been used to make stone axe heads. These Group VI bracers are almost exclusively dark green in colour, while amphibolite bracers tend to be green or light grey. The greatest variety of colours occurs in the remaining (miscellaneous) bracers; these also include the red/black examples (Figure 4.2).

4.2 SIZE

Although considerable emphasis has been placed on shape characteristics in past classification schemes, detailed comparison of metric data relating to size has not previously been attempted. For example, Atkinson's 1960 scheme (Clarke 1970) divided bracers solely by shape without any attempt to compare differences between larger versus smaller bracers. Data collected during the research here, however, provides an opportunity to compare some basic size characteristics among British bracers. Specifically, it is possible to test for relationships between length, width and maximum thickness, both in terms of absolute size and in terms of ratios between each measurement. These results can then be considered within the context of rock group and geographic distribution.

4.2.1 Length, width and maximum thickness

There is a notable difference in overall length within complete British bracers, varying in maximum length between 44.8 mm (Ben Bridge, ID 108) and 153.4 mm (Sturry, ID 6). Although there is a considerable overlap, bracers of amphibolite, Group VI and red/black types are longer than those of miscellaneous rock types (Table 4.1). Dividing all relevant bracers into groupings based on length from smallest to largest and comparing frequencies suggests a consistent trend towards longer bracers amongst amphibolites, red/black and Group VI types (Figure 4.3).

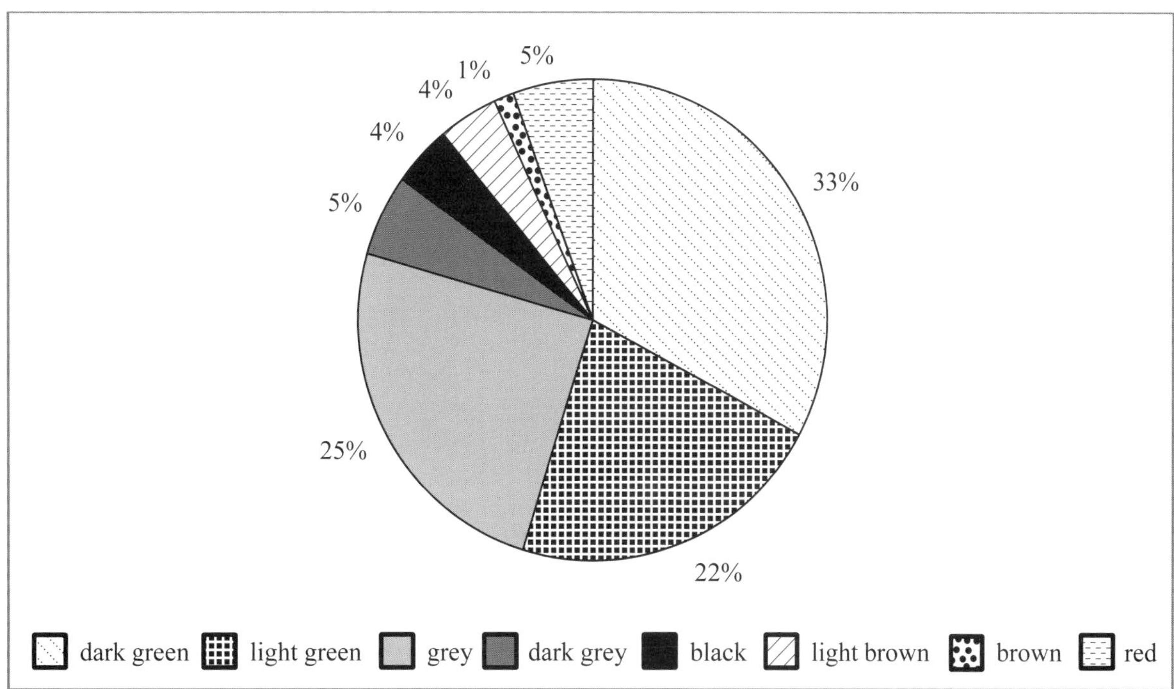

Figure 4.1. Bracer frequency, by colour (n=73).

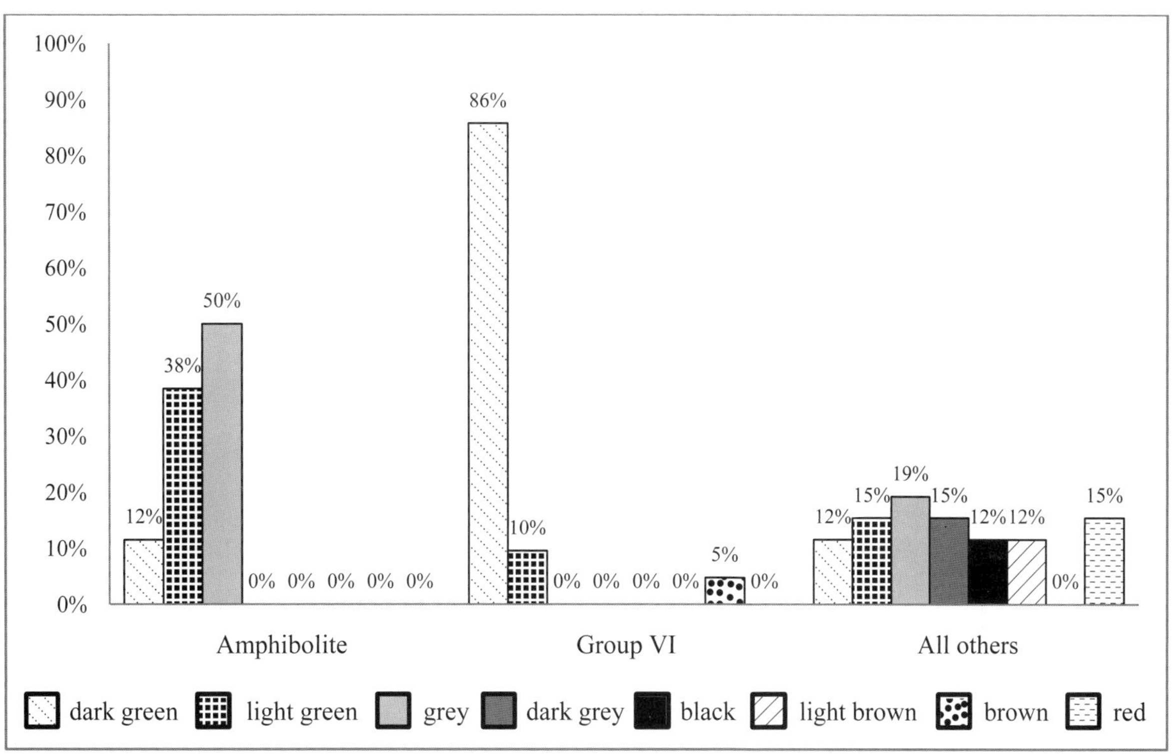

Figure 4.2. Bracer colour frequency, by rock type (n=73).

Although bracer width was measured both at mid- and end-point, analysis here emphasises mid-point measurements only. Mid-point measurements better define the overall size of the bracer than end measurements, which provide more insight into bracer shape. As with length, there is considerable variation in mid-point width measurements. Width values range from as little as 10.3 mm (Ben Bridge, ID 108) to 71.8 mm (Sutton Veny, ID 30). However, when viewed against rock type, some basic patterns emerge. Firstly, amphibolite bracer widths are more restricted in relation to other types, evidenced by: a slightly lower standard deviation than all but red/black bracers; the relatively few bracers under 25 mm in width, and the fact that over half fall between 30 to 40 mm (Table 4.2, Figure

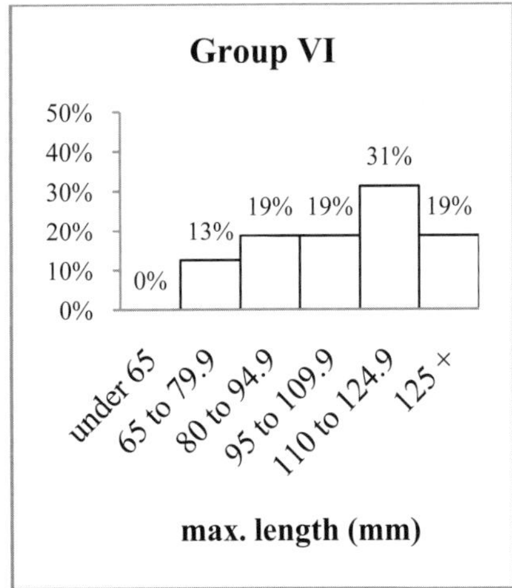

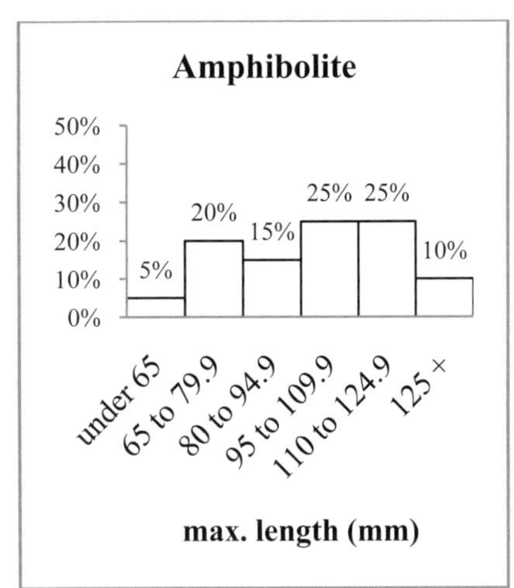

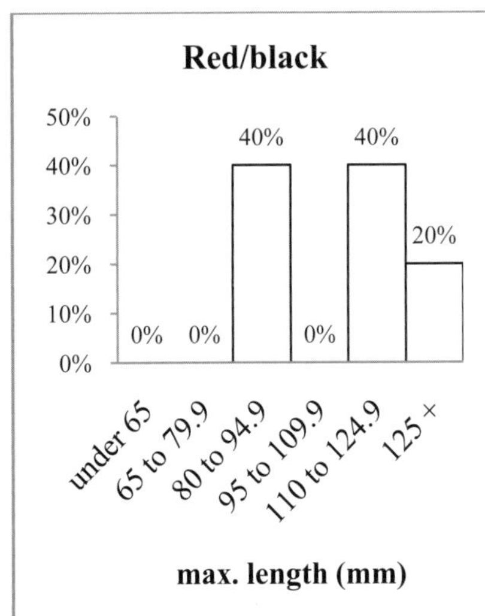

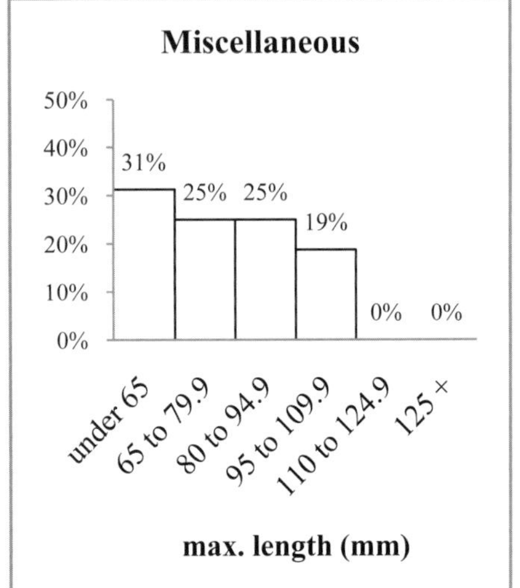

Figure 4.3. Frequency of bracer maximum lengths, by rock type (n=57).

	Average max. length	Std. dev.	No. of bracers
Amphibolite	99.1	22.3	20
Group VI	105.6	20	16
Red/black	109.5	6.9	5
Miscellaneous	76.7	18.1	16

Table 4.1. Average maximum length values for bracers, by rock type (n=57).

	Average width at midpoint	Std. dev.	No. of bracers
Amphibolite	36.1	11	20
Group VI	31.5	12.5	16
Red/black	26	6.9	5
Miscellaneous	26.6	12.1	16

Table 4.2. Average width at midpoint values for bracers, by rock type (n=57).

4.4). Bracers of amphibolite type are also more frequently wider than those of other types, with half measuring 35 mm or greater in width. Miscellaneous rock type bracers are frequently the narrowest, with nearly two thirds falling within the two smallest width ranges. Group VI bracers in general also have a restricted width range, with a large majority (69%) falling between 20 and 35 mm in width.

In viewing results for maximum thickness of bracer, there is a similarly wide range of observed thicknesses across all bracers, varying between 2.5 mm (Hartington, ID 152) to 10.5 mm (Newlands, Oyne, ID 90). If these results are compared against rock types, it is again apparent that there is less variability in amphibolite bracers than in the other types (Table 4.3). Amphibolite bracers are, on the whole thinner, and do not feature among the thickest bracers measured (Figure 4.5). Group VI bracers, and in particular red/black bracers, are the most robust, and again miscellaneous rock type bracers vary widely in terms of thickness. The thickest groupings are those of miscellaneous and red/black rock types, The red bracer from the Amesbury Archer grave (ID 56) is among the thickest of the miscellaneous group.

Thus, in examining each size characteristic in isolation and alongside rock type and colour, some patterns can be readily observed. Along all three dimensions, bracers of amphibolite rock type are comparatively more restricted in

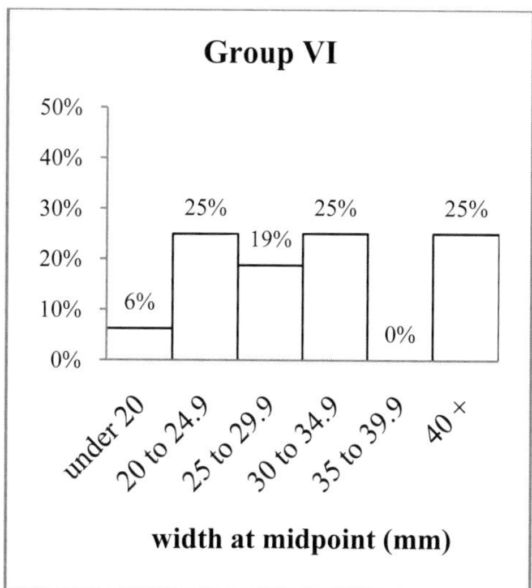

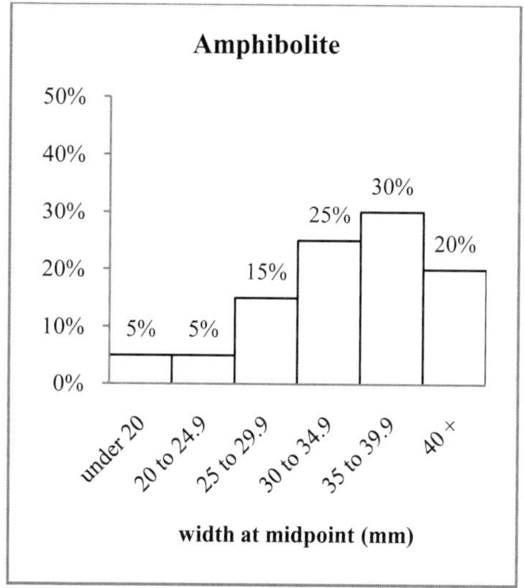

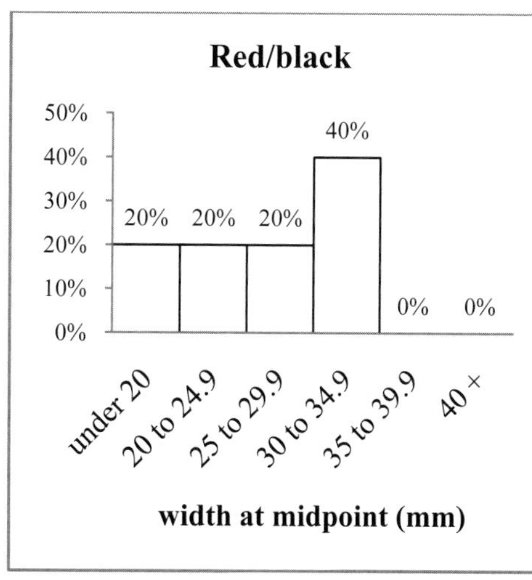

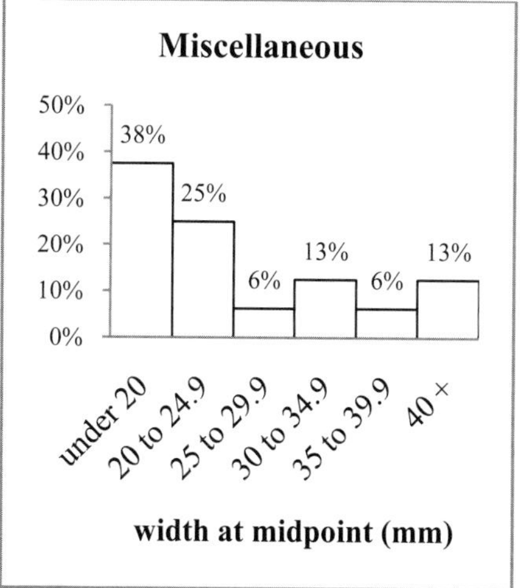

Figure 4.4. Frequency of bracer widths at midpoint, by rock type (n=57).

	Average max. thickness	Std. dev.	No. of bracers
Amphibolite	5.1	0.8	20
Group VI	6	1.3	16
Red/black	7.7	1.7	5
Miscellaneous	6.1	1.7	16

Table 4.3. Average maximum thickness values for bracers, by rock type (n=57).

variation than their non-amphibolite counterparts. Although only a few red/black rock type bracers exist, they tend to be relatively long and slender or short and thick. In addition, some miscellaneous rock type bracers which are similar in colour to amphibolite bracers are more likely also to share similar size characteristics. Four miscellaneous rock type bracers in particular stand out, namely Mildenhall (ID 9), Tytherington (ID 29), Ferniegair (ID 123) and Archerton Newtake (ID 133). Both Mildenhall (ID 9) and Tytherington (ID 29) are long and broad for miscellaneous rock type bracers, while Ferniegair (ID 123) and Archerton Newtake (ID 133) are amongst the widest. As a whole, these bracers are four of the five widest miscellaneous rock type bracers, the fifth being Cassington (ID 135). If we accept that many miscellaneous rock type bracers were made from locally procured stone, then these four bracers may represent an attempt to replicate those made from amphibolite but using local material. At the least it indicates the manufacture of some miscellaneous rock type bracers was made with reference to amphibolite types, and this pattern will deserve further attention using other morphological characteristics introduced below.

Graphically, the association suggested above can be seen when length and width are plotted together (Figure 4.6). As suggested by the data presented, amphibolite bracers tend to cluster around a hypothetical approximate size of 100 mm × 35 mm. Group VI bracers seem to have a fairly weak linear relationship with regards to length and width, with some sense of an appropriate length/width ratio in effect. This relationship will become much more significant when considered alongside shape characteristics below. Again, the small number of red/black rock type bracers make identifying a relationship between length and width difficult. Finally, miscellaneous rock type bracers are more widely scattered but are generally shorter in length.

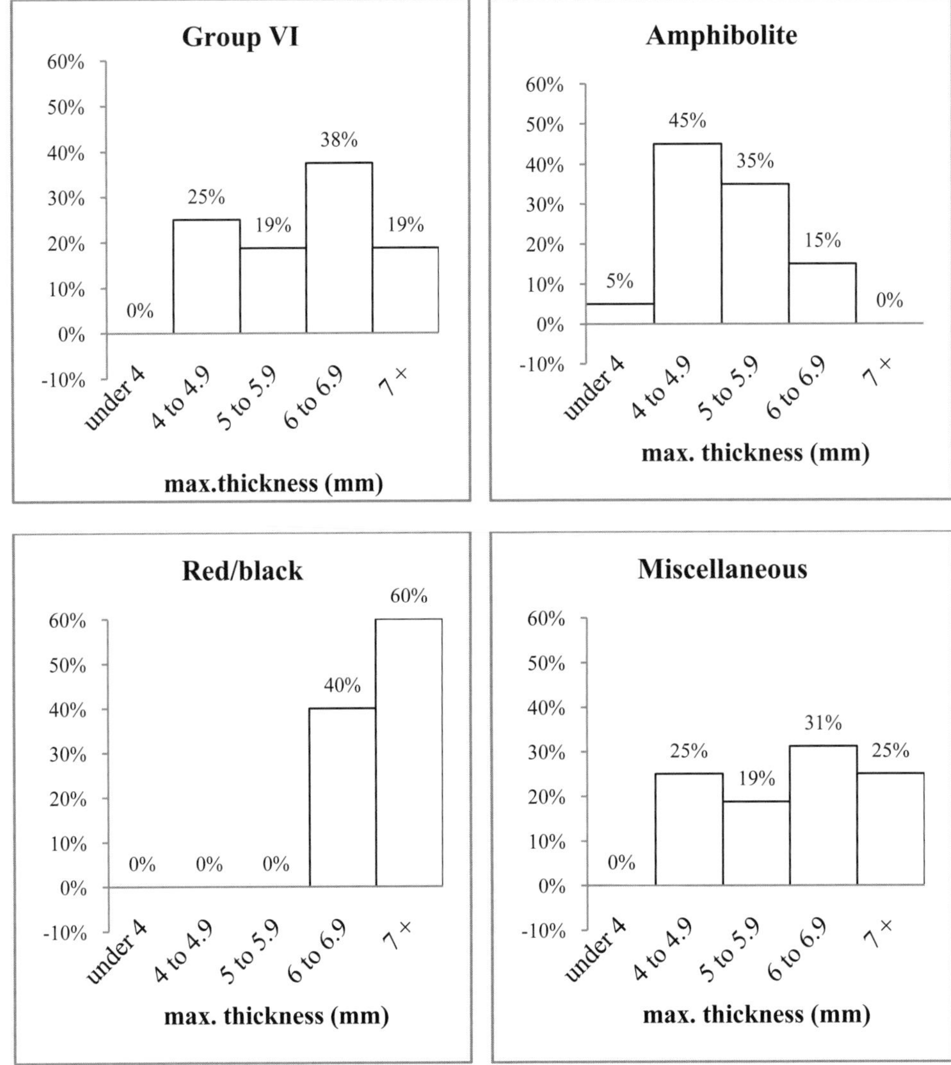

Figure 4.5. Frequency of bracer maximum thickness, by rock type (n=57).

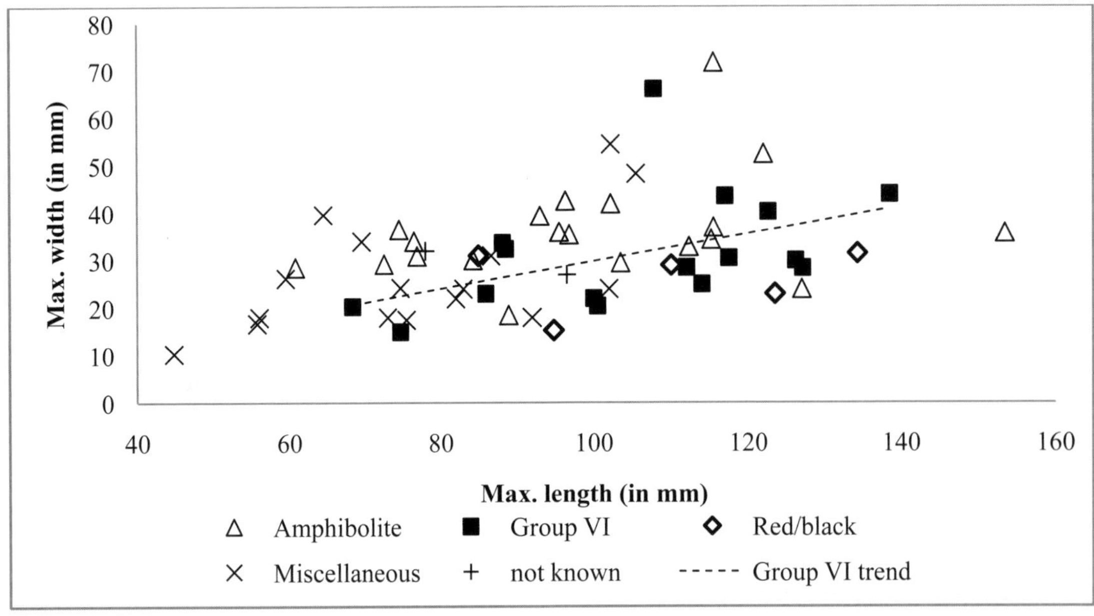

Figure 4.6. Comparison plot of bracer maximum length versus maximum width, by rock type (n=59).

4.3 SHAPE

Analysis of bracer shape was divided into four main parameters designed to classify shape characteristics of each bracer not only across the three dimensional planes, but also to define manufacturing choices which visually impacted overall shape, such as side, end and mid-point treatment. These characteristics consist of: outline shape; longitudinal profile; transverse profile; presence, location and characteristics of facets and/or flanges, and presence and extent of bracer mid-point waistedness. Several of these categories correspond to previous classification schemes such as that of Atkinson who divided British bracers on the basis of outline shape, transverse profile, waistedness and number of perforations. However, analysis presented here builds considerably on past schemes by incorporating new shape parameters (facets/flanges), as well as considerable metric, colour and rock type characteristics already explored. As with the examination of bracer size, individual parameters will be examined with relation to rock type before exploring ways of viewing the interrelatedness of shape data.

4.3.1 Outline shape and longitudinal/transverse profile

Bracers examined were divided into two principle outline shapes: rectangular or ovoid. Profile characteristics were also recorded along perpendicular planes, resulting in a transverse profile scheme (across the centre of each bracer) consisting of the following major categories (Figure 4.7):

- Flat – no curve on either long surface
- Plano-convex – rear surface flat, front surface convex
- Concavo-convex – rear surface concave, front surface convex
- Lentoid – both long surfaces not flat, side edges displaying a clear point (eye-lid shaped)
- Ovoid – both long surfaces not flat and overall oval or ellipsoid shape with no clear edge on sides

Waistedness, or the presence or absence of a thinner mid-point than end points was also recorded as an outline shape feature. Bracer longitudinal profile (along length of bracer) was similarly grouped into one of four main possibilities:

- Flat – no curve on either long surface
- Plano-convex – rear surface flat, front surface convex
- Lentoid – both long surfaces not flat, side edges displaying a clear point (eye-lid shaped)
- Dished on front – distinctive curve across length forming a dish or bowl profile

The frequency of different outline characteristics is summarised in the tables and diagrams below. The majority of all British bracers analysed are rectangular in shape (80%, 56 out of 70) rather than ovoid (20%, 14 out of 70), while nearly half (46%, 31 out of 67) were at least slightly waisted. In terms of transverse profile, only 15% were flat (10 out of 67), 41 (61%) displayed either plano- or concavo-convex features, while 12 (18%), three (4%) and one (1%) were lentoid, ovoid and rectangular respectively. With regards to longitudinal profile, a minority of 19 (of 65) were flat (29%), while 20 were plano-convex (31%), 12 lentoid (18%) and 11 dished (17%).

Exploring further, the relationship of these individual characteristics to rock types yields some important patterns. In terms of shape, both amphibolite and Group VI rock type bracers are much less variable than their miscellaneous and red/black rock type counterparts (Figure 4.8). Both amphibolite and Group VI rock type bracers are almost exclusively rectangular. Both tend to be waisted, although Group VI bracers are much more clearly so (Figure 4.9). In profile, amphibolite bracers show an affinity towards a plano-convex longitudinal and transverse profile (Figure 4.10 and 4.11). Group VI bracers, on the other hand, tend to be concavo-convex in transverse profile (65%) and have a dished longitudinal profile (53%). Red/black bracer types appear to be most frequently concavo-convex in transverse profile and plano-convex in longitudinal profile. Only miscellaneous rock type bracers have at least one instance of each longitudinal shape characteristic, and although they have some shape tendencies (ie. unwaisted, plano-convex longitudinal and transverse profiles), these are not nearly as strong as for the other types.

4.4 FACETS AND FLANGES

A key element not expressly considered in previous classification schemes is the presence, location and shape characteristics of faceting on British bracers. Thus, observations of facet location, either on bracer side or end,

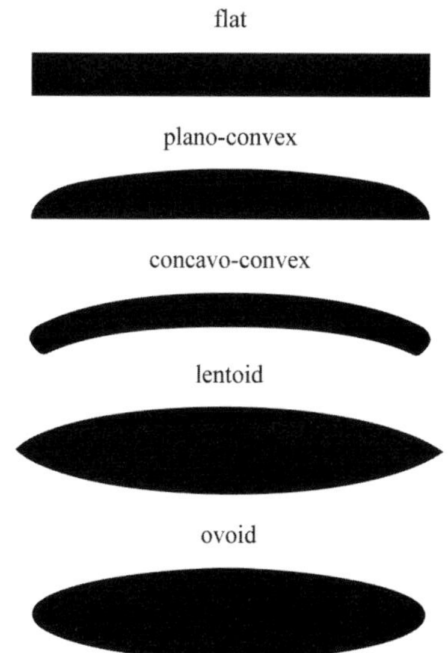

Figure 4.7. Illustration of bracer transverse and longitudinal profile classifications.

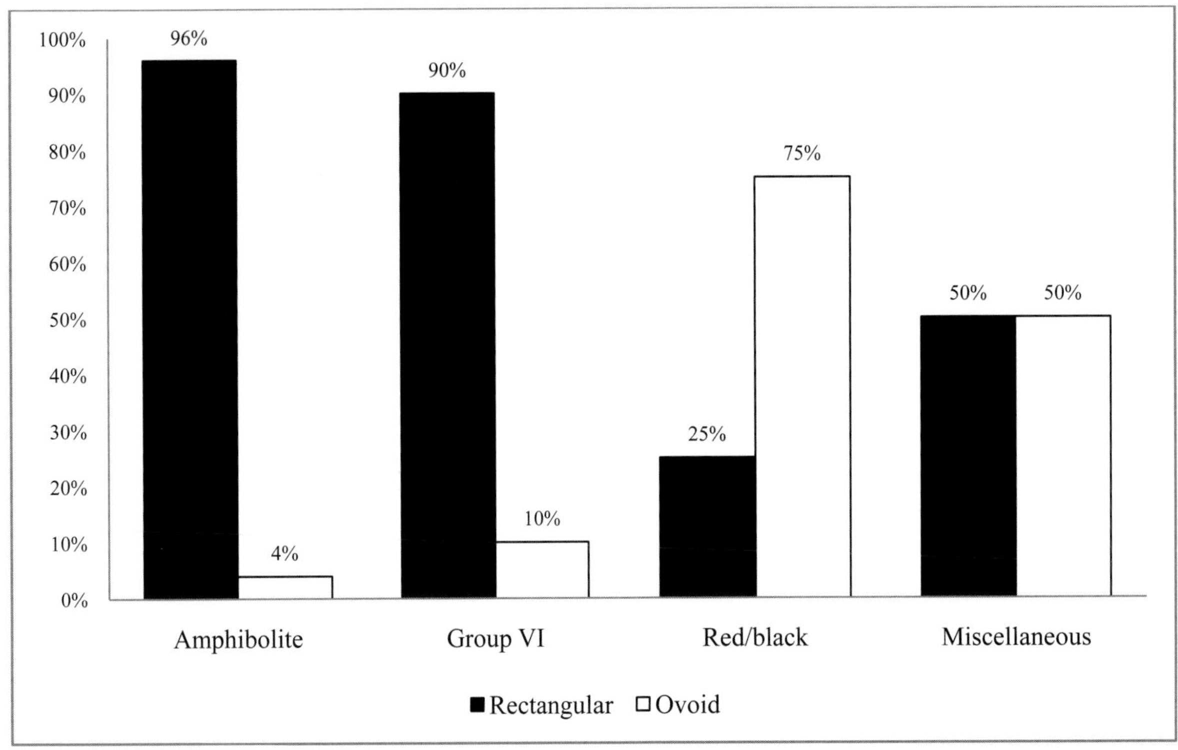

Figure 4.8. Frequency of overall outline shapes, by rock type (n=66).

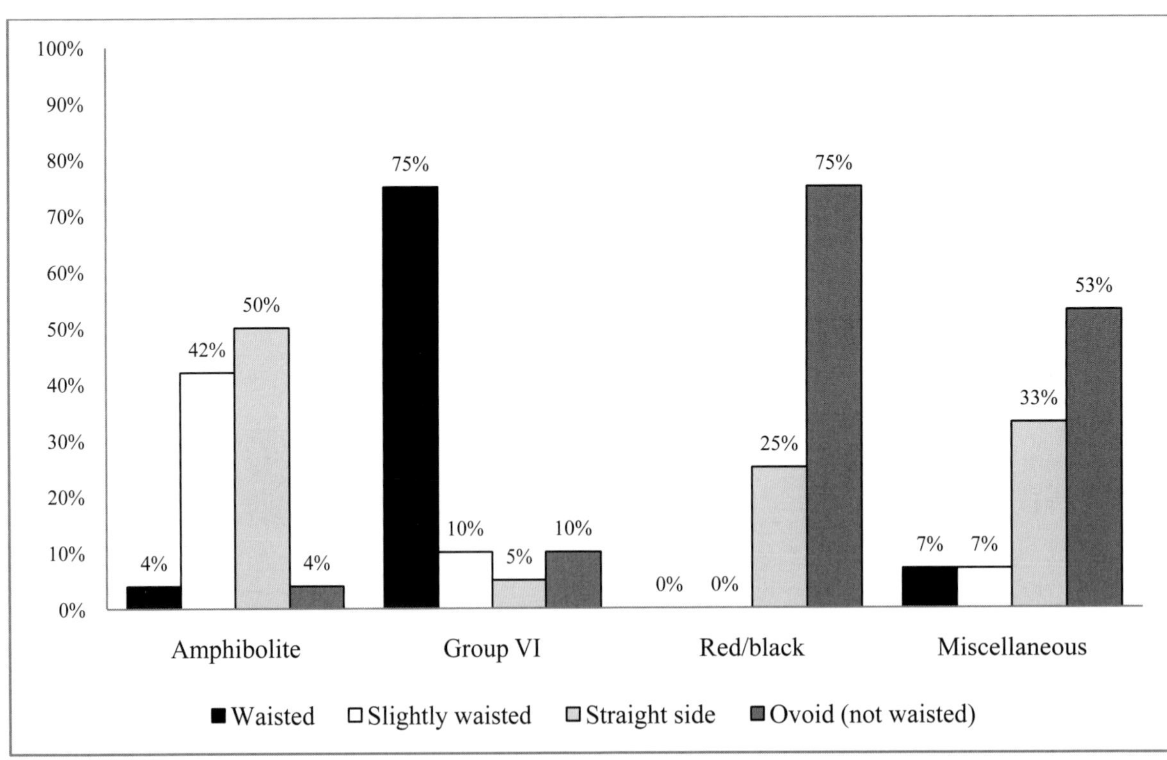

Figure 4.9. Frequency of bracer side outline shapes, by rock type (n=63).

were noted, as well as recording facet edge shape, with edges considered either sharp or rounded. In total, 41 of 67 bracers analysed were facetted (61%). When viewed alongside rock types, there is a relationship evident between material and the presence and location of faceting (Table 4.4). Amphibolite bracers were clearly not facetted as frequently as other bracers, with only 6 of 26 recording a facet (23%). Group VI bracers are nearly always facetted (90%), while both red/black and miscellaneous rock type bracers displayed high instances of faceting.

Across all bracers, when facets are present they occur most frequently at the ends or at both the ends and sides

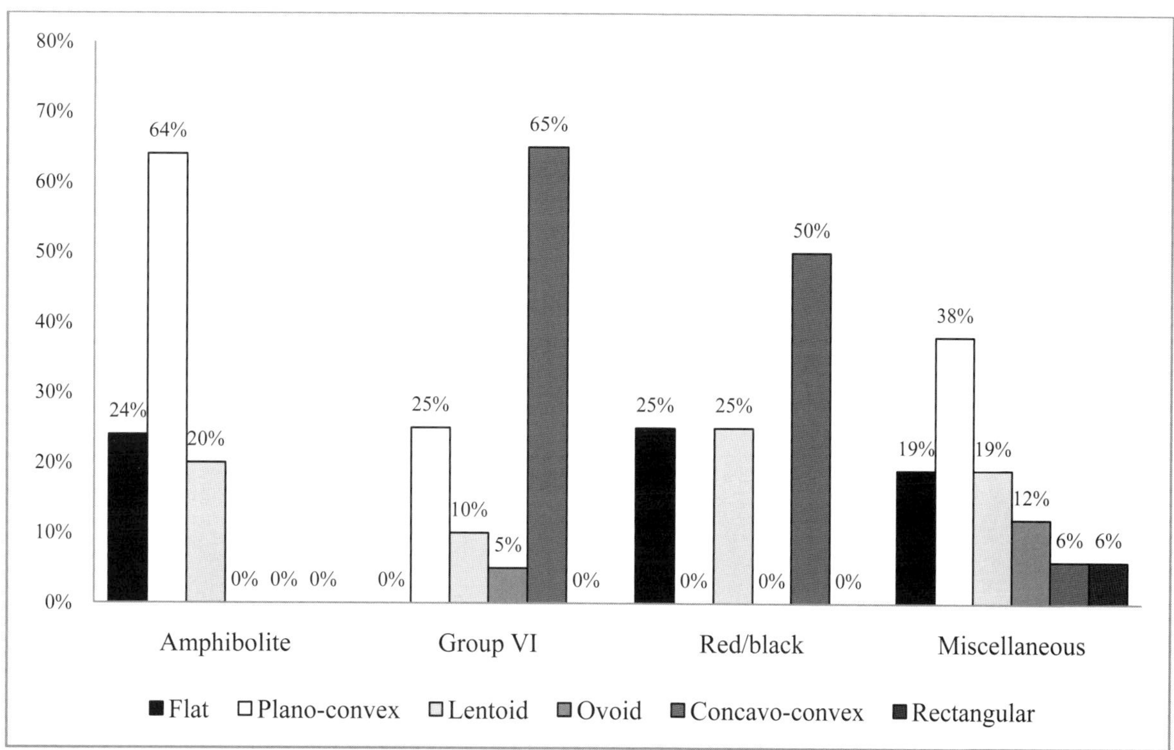

Figure 4.10. Frequency of bracer transverse profile shapes, by rock type (n=65).

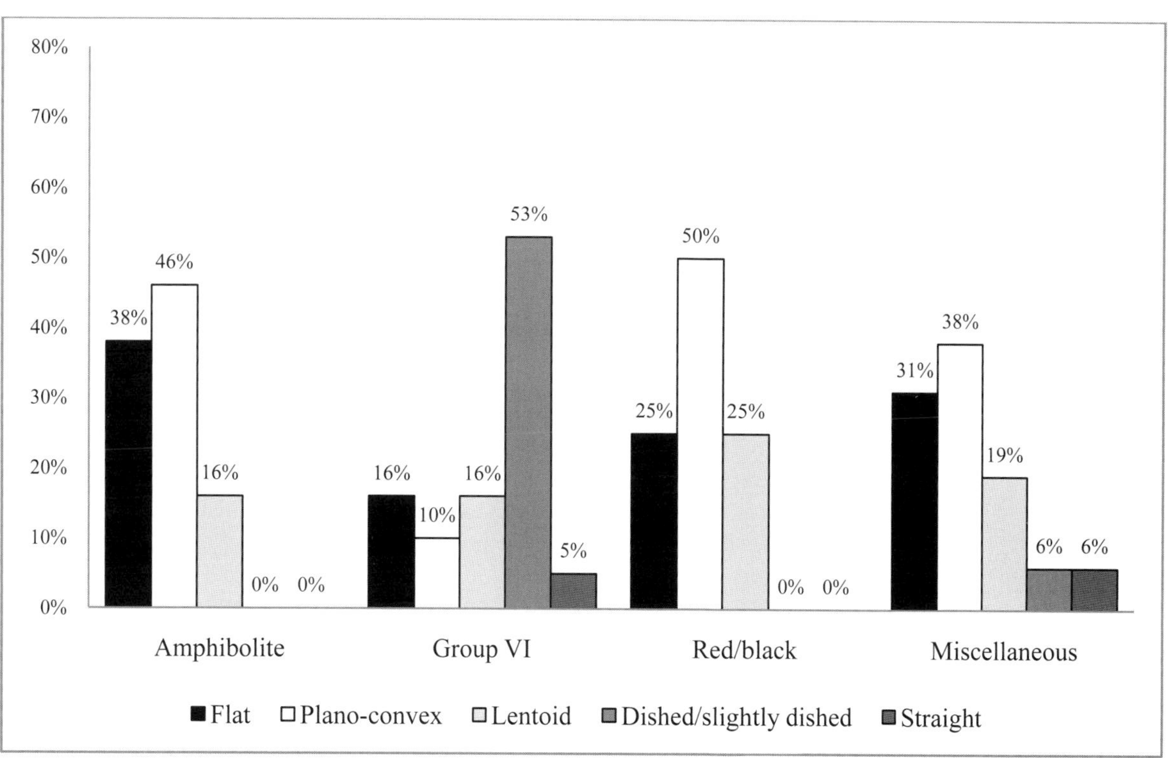

Figure 4.11. Frequency of bracer longitudinal profile shapes, by rock type (n=63).

(Figure 4.12). Only in a small number of instances do bracers occur with faceting on the side only. In the case of facet location on Group VI bracers, when side facets were present they always occurred alongside end facets. Amphibolite bracers, if faceted, tended to have end facets only. Bracers of miscellaneous rock type bracers tended also to be faceted, of which nearly half were faceted at both sides and ends (47%). Red/black rock type bracers were also commonly facetted, with most having facets on both sides and ends (67%). With regards to facet edges,

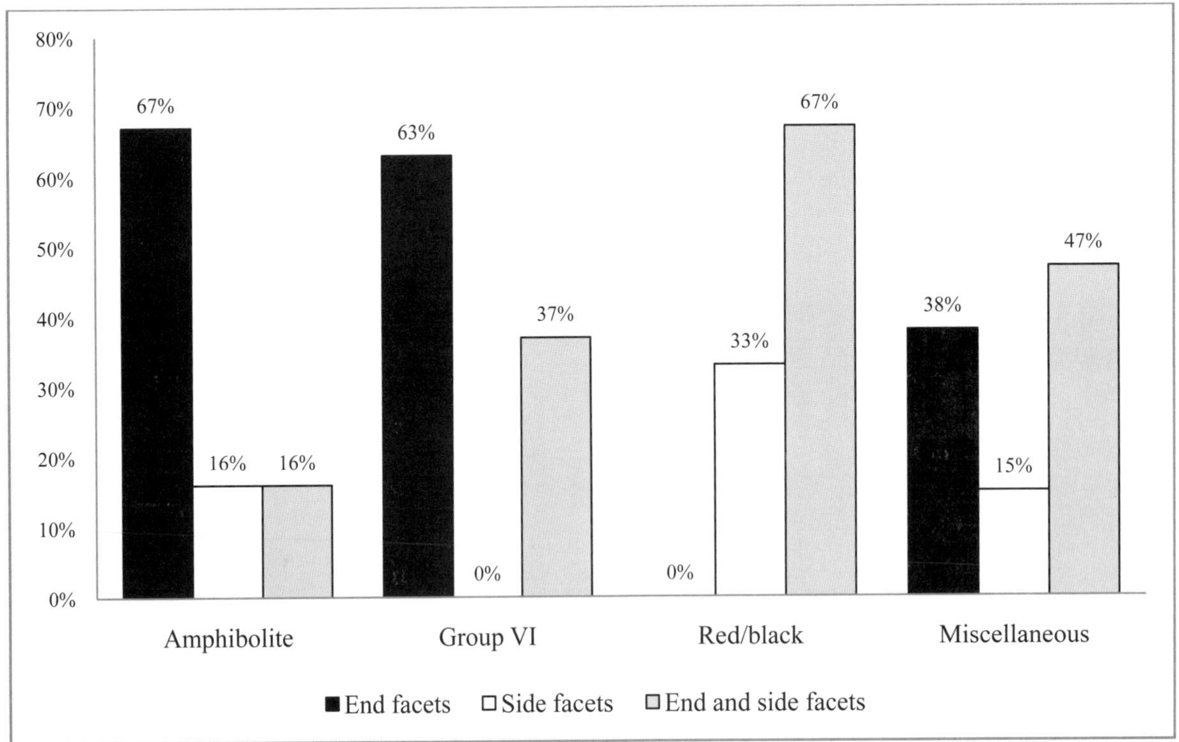

Figure 4.12. Frequency of facet types on faceted bracers, by rock type (n=41).

	End facets (a)	Side facets (b)	End and side facets (c)	Total faceted (a+b+c)
Amphibolite	4	1	1	6 (23%)
Group VI	12	0	7	19 (90%)
Red/black	0	1	2	3 (75%)
Miscellaneous	5	2	6	13 (81%)

Table 4.4. Frequency of faceting on bracers, by rock type (n=67).

only Group VI and red/black rock type bracers favour sharp facet edges. A total of 56% (10 of 18) of Group VI bracers have recorded instances of sharp end facet edges. Only red/black bracers frequently have sharp side (67%, or 2 of 3) as well as end facet edges (100%, or 2 of 2). Both amphibolites and miscellaneous rock type bracers tended to have rounded end facet edges (67%, or 3 of 5, and 55%, or 6 of 11 respectively). Flanges are recorded on only four bracers (ID 15, ID 73, ID 79 and ID 112), all on the ends and all unique to Group VI rock type bracers.

4.5 PERFORATIONS

Morphological examination of perforations consisted of classification on the basis of: number of perforations; shape of perforation; variation in maximum perforation size within and between bracers, and symmetry of perforation placement on the bracer.

4.5.1 Number and shape of perforations

A total of 72 bracers were compared, and either the actual number of perforations was recorded, or in the case of fragmentary bracers, the original number of perforations for each bracer was estimated on the basis of overall shape and amount of bracer remaining. Although most consist of either two or four perforations, aside from red/black bracers, each rock type can have few as well as many perforations (Figure 4.13). On the whole, Group VI bracers have four perforations (67%), while the majority of miscellaneous rock type bracers had only two (63%).

The overall shape of each individual perforation was classified into one of two dominant shapes (see also Chapter 5.4): funnel, having been drilled predominantly from one direction (either from the front or rear of the bracer), and hourglass, having been drilled from both sides. When viewed against rock type, over half of Group VI bracer perforations are funnel-shaped, while amphibolite, red/black and miscellaneous rock type bracer perforation shapes are overwhelmingly hourglass (Figure 4.14). In the case of the two miscellaneous rock type bracers with funnel-shaped perforations, both were Scottish examples (Glenluce, ID 77 and Newlands, Oyne, ID 90). Notably, Newlands, Oyne (ID 90) is also waisted, plano-convex in shape, similar to most Group VI bracers. Thus, the presence of funnel-shaped perforations may form part of

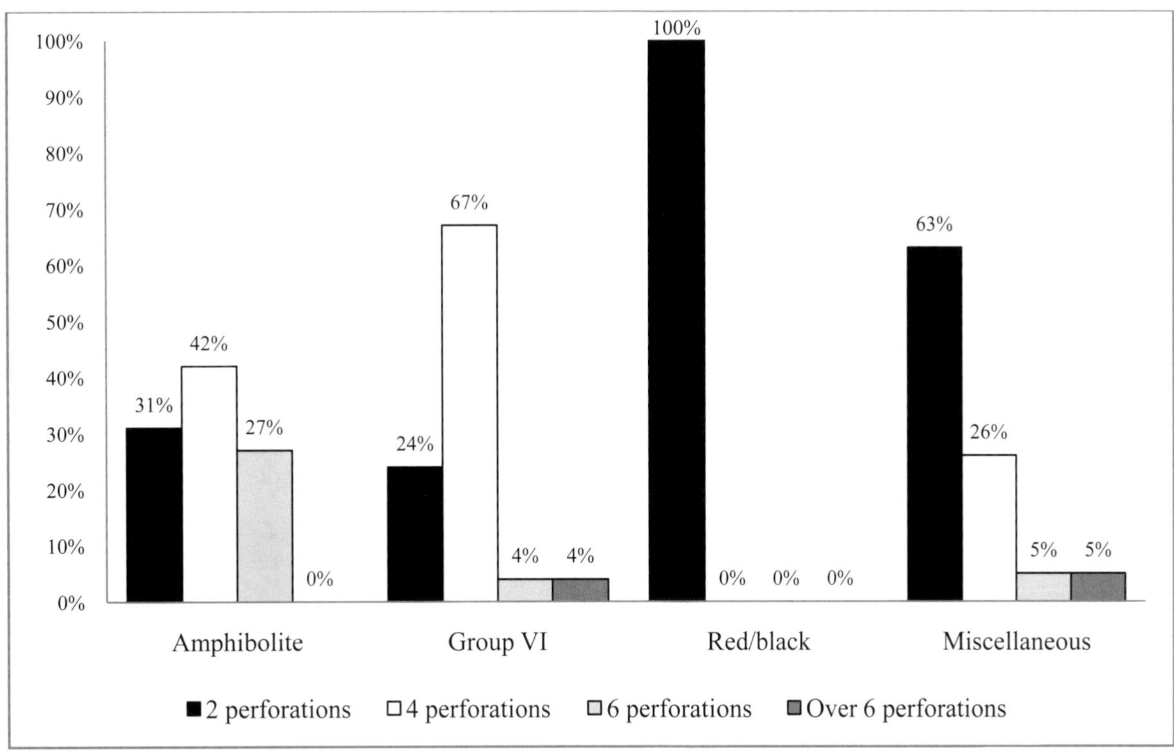

Figure 4.13. Frequency of estimated original number of perforations, by rock type (n=72).

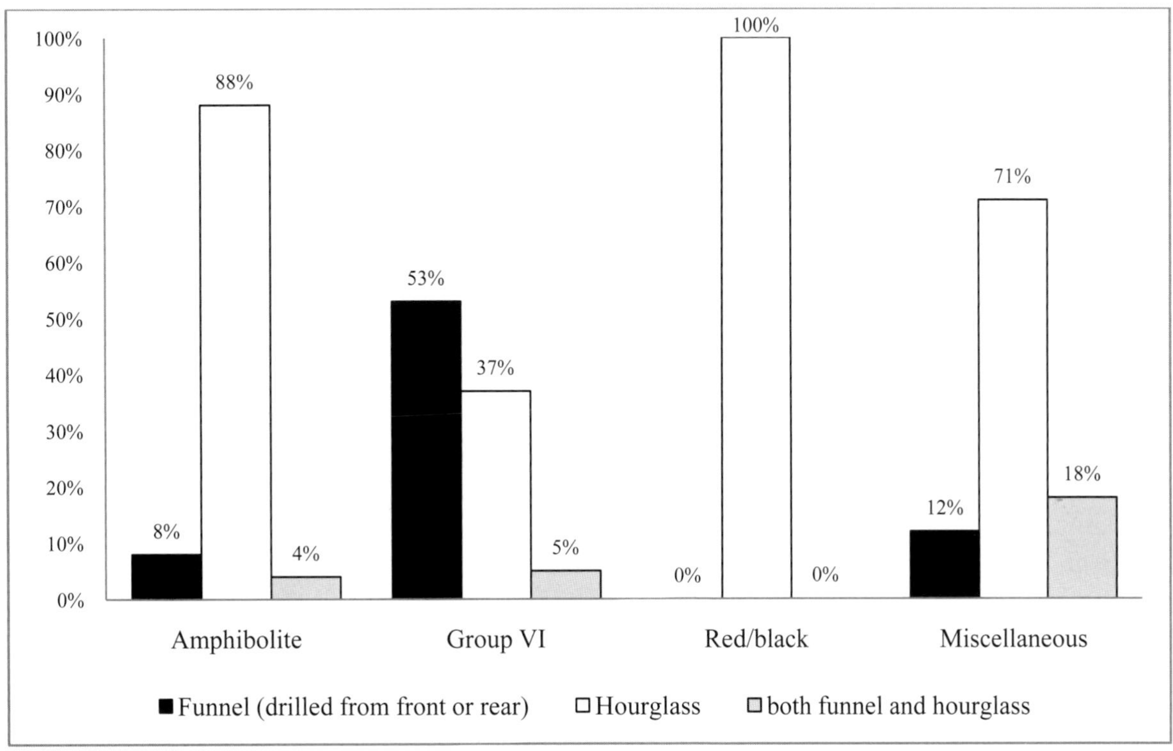

Figure 4.14. Frequency of bracer funnel versus hourglass perforation shapes, by rock type (n=63).

a design choice to replicate a Group VI bracer in local material. The presence of funnel-shaped perforations on the amphibolite bracer from Duston (ID 102), as well as the four bracers with multiple perforation types (ie. having both hourglass and funnel perforations on the same bracer; ID 11, ID 78, ID 87; ID 104) can be attributed to their fragmentary nature and their likely refashioning over time. Although this is discussed in much greater detail in Chapter 6, both the bracers from Corry Liveras (ID 87) and Scarborough (ID 104) show clear signs of having been

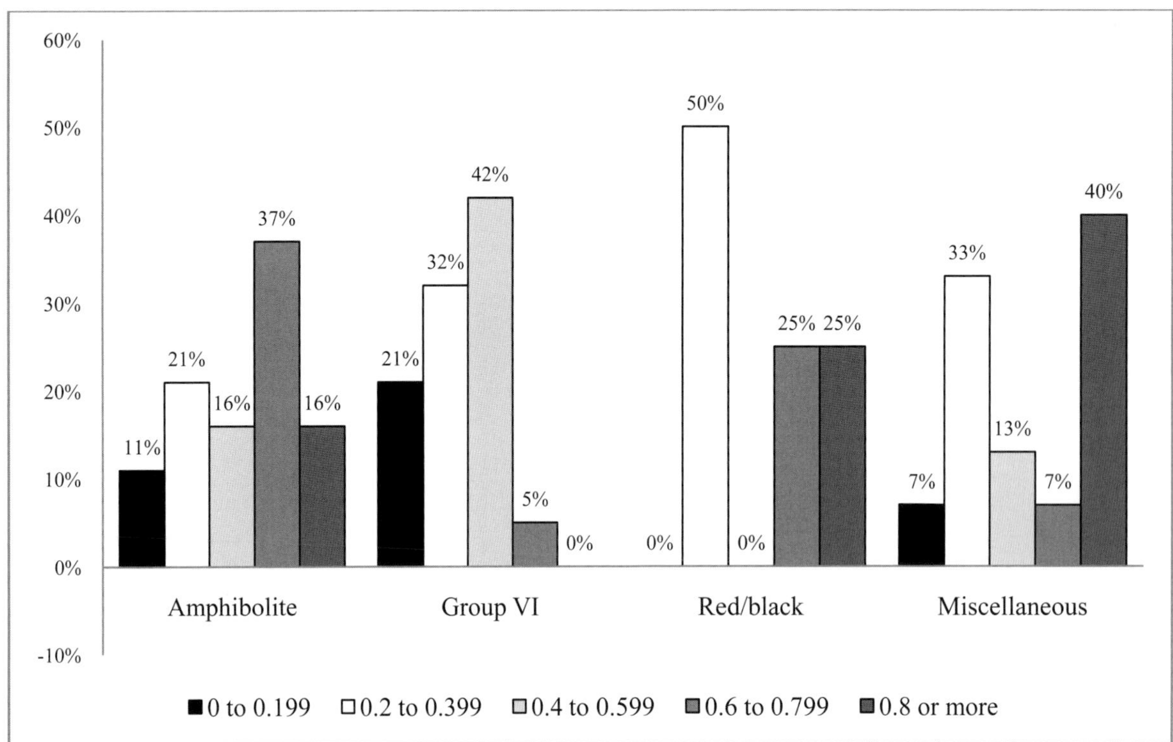

Figure 4.15. Comparison of frequency of perforation maximum diameter standard deviation values, by rock type (n=57).

	Average max. diam. (mm)	**Average Std.dev. (mm)**	**Avg. std.dev as % of avg. max. diam**	**Total**
Amphibolite	5.94	0.577	9.7%	**19**
Group VI	5.48	0.343	6.3%	**19**
Red/black	5.44	0.636	11.7%	**4**
Miscellaneous	6.73	0.634	9.4%	**15**

Table 4.5. Variation in bracer maximum perforation diameter, by rock type (n=57).

	Symmetric placement	**Asymmetric placement**	**Total**
Amphibolites	7 (32%)	15 (68%)	**22**
Group VI	13 (65%)	7 (35%)	**20**
Red/black	1 (25%)	3 (75%)	**4**
Miscellaneous	6 (38%)	10 (62%)	**16**

Table 4.6. Symmetry of bracer perforation location, by rock type (n=62).

broken and re-worked into a new bracer. Although the bracer from Brandon (ID 11) with six perforations (three at each end), is largely complete, the central perforations at each end are hourglass-shaped while the others are all funnel-shaped. In addition, the two central hourglass perforations are asymmetrically placed in relation to one another and to the remaining perforations, which suggests that these two perforations were added to the bracer at some later date. A similar configuration was noted on the bracer from Monkton (ID 154): two asymmetrically placed central holes appear to have been added later, possibly after the loss by breakage of one of the corner holes. The lone straight-shaped perforated bracer from Kelleythorpe (ID 13) coincides with the presence of rivets within the perforations, and would suggest that the perforations were drilled specifically for this purpose.

4.5.2 Perforation size, symmetry and variation

Perforation size against rock type was also considered, and maximum perforation diameter was also compared against different rock types. In addition, total variation in perforation size within individual bracers was also explored, with an eye to identifying the level of craftsmanship and standardisation inherent in each object. Although there is considerable variation in maximum perforation size across all bracers, Group VI bracers tended to have the least variation in perforation size when total variation was compared within each bracer. Put another way, on average, perforation size varied by less than 7% on each individual Group VI bracer, as compared to nearly 10% for amphibolite and miscellaneous rock type bracers (Table 4.5).

Variation in perforation size was measured by comparing the standard deviation of perforation maximum diameter amongst perforations within each individual bracer. Only bracers with two or more measurable perforations were compared. On the whole, Group VI bracers displayed the lowest standard deviation, with over half with a standard deviation under 0.4 and 95% under 0.6 (Figure 4.15). This is in contrast to the other rock types, whose standard deviation values more frequently exceeded 0.4 or greater. In the case of amphibolite rock type bracers it is difficult to see a clear pattern emerging: although there are some examples with a low variation in perforation size, there are also frequent examples with rather high variation as well. Similarly, the low total number of red/black bracers makes any conclusion regarding perforation size variation speculative.

Examining the symmetry of perforation placement on each bracer, or the extent to which perforations align along the horizontal and vertical axes of the bracer, provides similar results to perforation variation, with reduced asymmetry in Group VI versus other rock type bracers (Table 4.6). As with perforation variation, symmetrical placement could be the result of greater craftsmanship and standardisation, and points to a greater degree of care towards the manufacture of Group VI bracers. A note of caution should be made with regards to the link between perforation characteristics and craftsmanship, however, as it is also possible that variation in certain elements of perforation morphology may also be related to functional concerns, notably in relation to the method of fastening the bracer to the body. This issue is also pursued in Chapter 5.

4.6 DISCUSSION

Across many of the parameters considered above, there are significant relationships between some observed morphological characteristics and rock type. We can observe that several morphological characteristics, at least when considered individually, can be seen to be related to rock type. In order to express better the complex relationship between morphological characteristics as a whole, a cluster analysis was conducted (StatistiXL) using the criteria of maximum length, width at midpoint, maximum thickness, outline shape, transverse profile, longitudinal profile, and presence/absence of facets. The complexity and variation in perforation characteristics were not included in the final cluster analysis, as attempts at inclusion diffused the key morphological relationships listed. Colour was also excluded as it is potentially dependent on rock type.

A furthest neighbour cluster analysis was conducted which identified at least two highly significant bracer groups (Figure 4.16). In the case of groups A and B, rock type is a key determining characteristic (Figure 4.17). In the case of group A, 13 of 16 bracers (81%) are amphibolite, while the remaining three are of miscellaneous or red rock type. For group B, 15 of 20 bracers (75%) are Group VI, while three are amphibolite and a further two are miscellaneous. Additionally, distinct sub-clusters within both groups can also be identified which are even more strongly related to rock type (circled in Figure 4.16). Within group A there is a sub-cluster of nine bracers with the strongest similarities, all of which are amphibolite. Similarly, a distinct sub-cluster of ten strongly similar bracers are all of Group VI rock type. Thus, within both groups is a core of highly similar bracers whose similarity in morphology is strongly linked to the composition of the bracer itself.

Examining the results further, it is also significant that no Group VI rock type bracer is present in group A. Furthermore, the three amphibolite bracers within group B (Sittingbourne, ID 10, Thomas Hardye School, ID 67 and Hockwold, ID 106) themselves form a sub-cluster of long, thin bracers whose overall shape is very different from the more common wider amphibolite bracers which appear in group A. With regard to the four miscellaneous rock type bracers with colour characteristics similar to amphibolite identified earlier (Mildenhall, ID 9; Tytherington, ID 29; Ferniegair, ID 123, and Archerton Newtake, ID 133), only one falls within group A. It may be that although some reference to colour and shape might be made at a very basic level, other distinctive shape parameters were not carefully adhered to.

Lastly, two further clusters denoted as group C have also been suggested, although their coherence as distinct groups is unclear. Group C consists of a mix of all different rock types with weak similarities in morphological characteristics. Miscellaneous rock type bracers make up over half of this group, which, given the variation in individual morphological characteristics already outlined, is unsurprising. Although six red/black bracers fall within group C, they do not form a sub-cluster. A single amphibolite bracer (Sturry, ID 6) can be found in group C, and this bracer is distinctive due to its long, thin shape, presence of facets and lentoid transverse and longitudinal profiles. Two Group VI bracers in group C, namely the bracers from Glen Forsa (ID 86) and Rauceby (ID 118), are both ovoid in shape, unlike the waisted, rectangular forms common to Group VI bracers from group B. A small sub-cluster of bracers does not fall easily within any of these three groupings, namely the bracers from Winterslow (ID 4), Roundway (ID 28), Amesbury Archer (black) (ID 57)

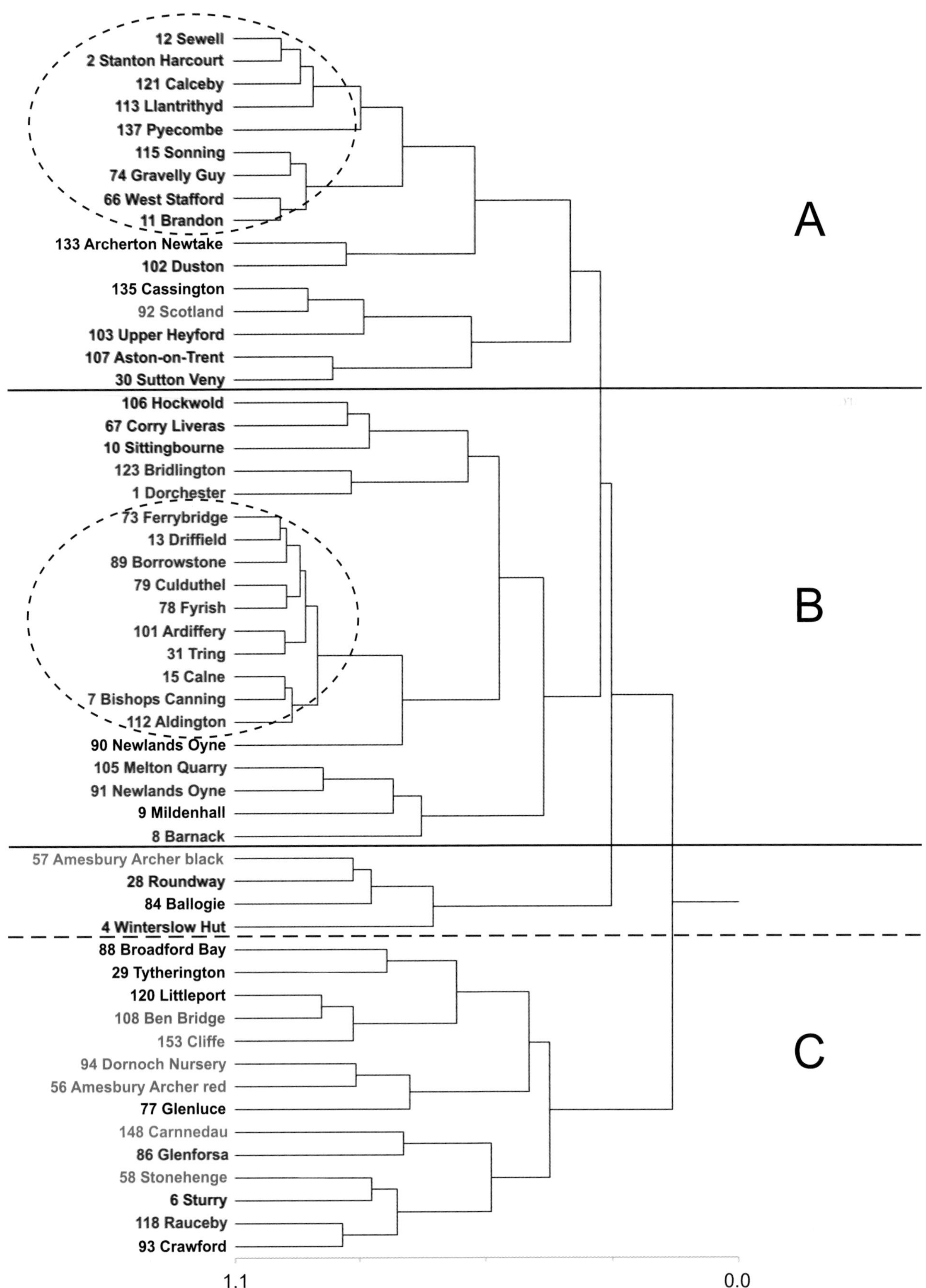

Figure 4.16. Results of cluster analysis illustrating main groups (A to C) and sub-clusters. Blue: amphibolite; green: Group VI; red: red/black; black: miscellaneous.

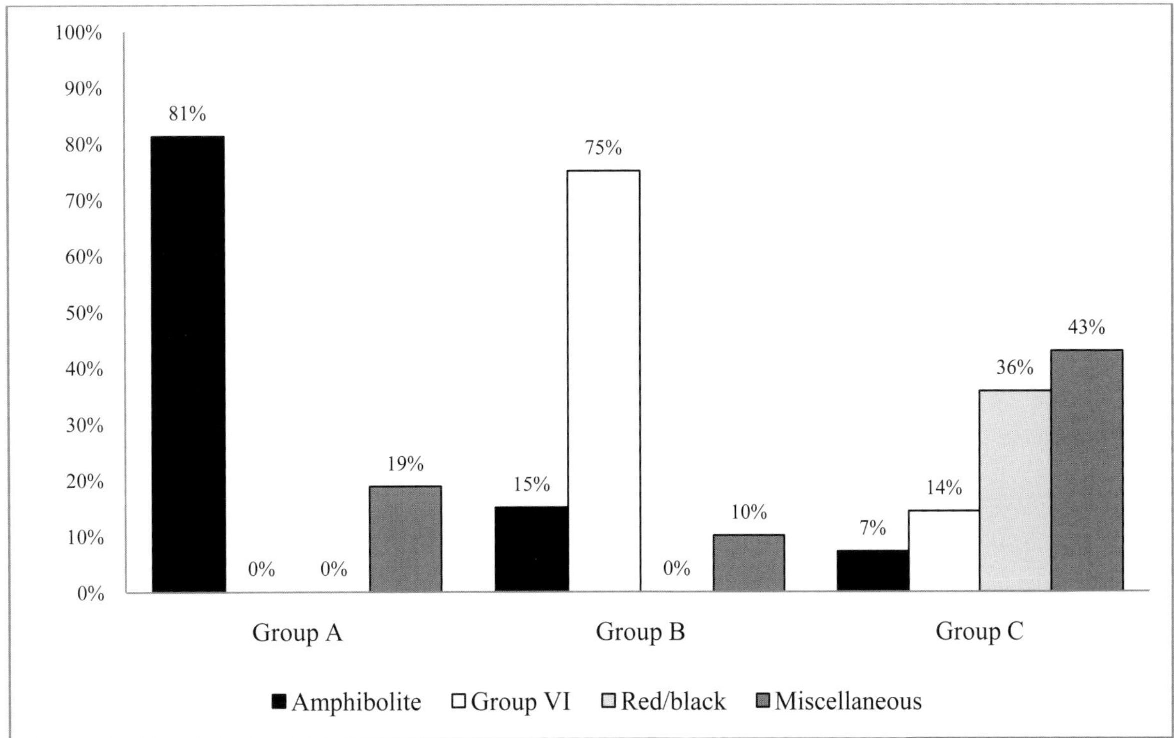

Figure 4.17. Frequency of rock types based on cluster analysis groupings (n=50).

and Ballogie (ID 84). Although all four bracers share a number of shape characteristics with both groups A and B, they are not distinctive as a unit and thus would seem to fit within the highly variable collection of bracers that make up group C.

Incorporating results from all analyses, it seems clear that rock type played an overarching role in establishing the final morphological characteristics of the finished bracer, and this is pursued in the following chapter. Given this, a summary description of bracer morphology on the basis of rock type can be presented which best incorporates all parameters examined here.

- *Amphibolite* bracers – dark green to light green/grey in colour; variable size, but some may coalesce around a hypothetical ideal size of 100 x 35 mm; variable thickness, but generally thinner for their size than other bracer types; frequently among the largest bracers, as measured by overall length, width and thickness; almost exclusively rectangular in outline; may or may not be slightly waisted, plano-convex in transverse profile; plano-convex or flat in longitudinal profile; unlikely to be faceted but if so, then likely on end only; have two or four perforations and no more than six; perforations will sometimes vary in size and are likely to be placed asymmetrically.
- *Group VI* bracers – dark green in colour; variable in size, but tend to follow a prescribed length/width ratio resulting in an overall long and thin shape; variable thickness, although frequently thicker than other types; very frequently among largest bracers, as measured by overall length, width and thickness; rectangular outline shape; waisted; concavo-convex in transverse profile; most frequently dished or flat in longitudinal profile; faceted, most commonly on ends or on both ends and sides; some are flanged on the ends; usually four perforations, but can have both fewer (two) and six or more; perforations tend to be more uniform in size and are generally placed symmetrically on the bracer.
- *Miscellaneous* bracers – highly variable in colour; highly variable length, width and thickness and perforation characteristics, although several are overall smaller than other types; less likely to be rectangular in outline shape than other types; generally flat or plano-convex in transverse profile; most likely flat or plano-convex in longitudinal profile; usually faceted, most often on ends and sides; normally only two perforations, although can have upwards of six or more; perforations will sometimes vary considerably in size and are likely to be placed asymmetrically.
  - *Red/black* bracers – these fall into two different groups, both of which contain items which are red and black. The first group are long, slender and more or less rectangular in outline, with flat facets on both ends and sides. The second group are short and relatively broad, with an ovoid outline and lentoid transverse profile. Members of both groups have two perforations of varying sizes, with hourglass profiles, and sometimes asymmetrically placed.

5: MANUFACTURING

John Hunter

5.1 BACKGROUND

Surface markings can appear on bracers as a consequence of both manufacture and wear. This section is concerned predominantly with processes of manufacture, and with evidence that gives some indication as to how the technology of bracer production might have taken place. In the first instance, it seems highly probable that selected sources were exploited to provide appropriately-shaped 'blanks' from the site in question for transport elsewhere. There are no published parallels to cite (but see Appendix 3.3), but useful analogies can be made with Neolithic axe manufacture and the removal of blocks of material from outcrops at Great Langdale (Bradley and Edmonds 1993, 102), or the removal of 'cushions' and 'rods' of dolerite for making tools in the Neolithic/Bronze Age on St Kilda (Fleming 1995, 31). Moreover, the collection and storage of 'virtually unworked raw [flint] material' awaiting manufacture found in pits at Titris Hoyuk, Turkey suggests how other contemporary material, albeit destined for utilitarian tools, might be processed (Hartenberger *et al.* 2000). With bracers, however, the sophisticated nature of the finished product suggests that all but the crudest level of working probably took place away from the outcrop site. Langdale tuff is one of the axe head materials that can be flaked (Coope 1979, 98), so that a rough out for a curved bracer could have been achieved by careful and skilled flaking, but persistent further chipping would have been needed to create the final shape. It may have been a lengthy and tedious business to make one of these elegant curved bracers. However, less effort was probably needed to produce a flat bracer, since experiments on slate showed that one of these could be completed in about two to three hours of work (Van der Vaart 2009b). With the amphibolite bracers there was a greater risk that breakage would occur across one of the holes. Production seems unlikely to have taken place at the exploitation site. Moreover, exploitation may also have been constrained by social or economic factors which may have influenced the extent to which the sources were in any way controlled, as might be realistically inferred from the limited locations of raw material identified in Chapter 3.

Several of the bracers show laminar flaws (below); presumably these may also have provided a natural fracture point for exploitation allowing slab-like pieces to be removed, particularly with amphibolites which possess a natural foliate structure; this would have to some extent defined the final shape. The Group VI rocks, on the other hand, are structurally isotropic and are more easily worked in any direction, hence allowing curved surfaces to be created. That said, however, the selection of material was one in which working properties, together with any constraints posed by local petrology, may have been less important than the perceived 'value' of the material or its source. Pieces seem to have been selected for their ability to be worked easily within a given size range (see Chapter 4.2.1).

5.2 STRIATIONS

A general overview of all the bracers examined here indicates that some evidence of working processes could still be identified, processes which lend themselves well to experimental research (Van der Vaart 2009a and b). The general shape of the object could be achieved by removing rough elements with a coarse granular stone or saw device, and then filing and chipping to trim the object down to its final size and profile. Most of the marks left by these processes were subsequently polished out, but a few have survived on examples that were being reworked. These included heavy diagonal reworking along the fractured edge of the bracer from Glenluce (ID 77) where a chisel may have been used, and intensive lateral working on one face of a broken bracer from Old Rayne (ID 82, Figure 5.4a). This latter piece also exhibited an unusually straight fracture which suggests that the surface may have been scored or cut in order to provide a clean break for ease of reworking. A small fragment from Winteringham (ID 119) might be interpreted similarly. The decorated curved bracer from Corry Liveras (ID 87) was clearly shortened from an original longer version, although any cut or saw marks have been polished out. Visual quality was evidently

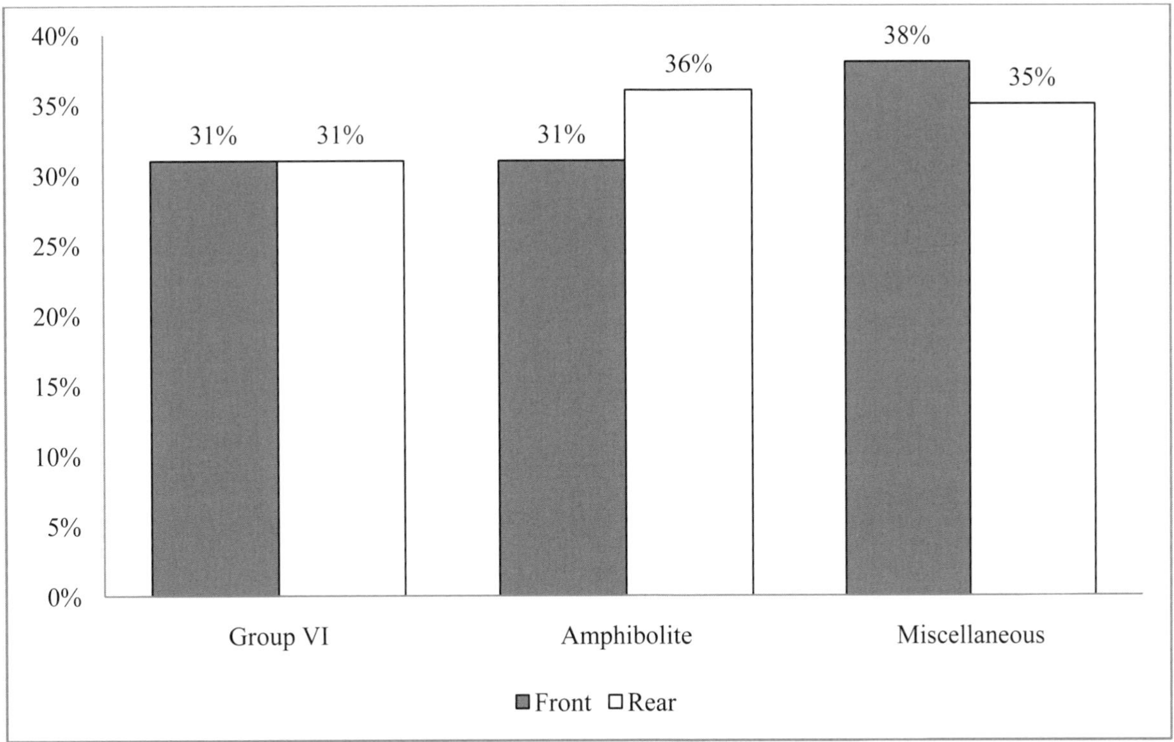

Figure 5.1. Percentage occurrence of striations according to rock type.

a key factor of final production. Quality appears to be not simply a matter of surface appearance, but also of symmetry of form in the creation of 'waisted' bracers (e.g. Barnack, ID 8; Mildenhall, ID 9; Aston, ID 107), elegantly curved examples (e.g. Tring, ID 31; Ferry Fryston, ID 73; Culduthel Mains, ID 79), and those with carefully shaped profiles (e.g. Calceby, ID 121, Figure 5.4b); all of these emphasise the extent of the quality of final shaping and finishing and, indirectly, the sophistication of process necessary to achieve this.

The amphibolite rocks have a hardness factor of 6.5 on the Mohs scale; the Group VI are not dissimilar with a mixture of feldspar (6–6.5), chlorite (2–2.5) and epidote. (7). Final polishing of both was probably undertaken by scouring with quartz sand (7 on the Mohs scale), one of the few available materials likely to have been hard enough, perhaps using a leather pad. Experiments have shown that wet clay may have been used, but may not have been particularly effective (Van der Vaart 2009b, 4). This finishing process could leave striations on the surface; the direction and intensity of these striations reflect the movement of the tools and/or abrasive used.

On the greater majority of the samples studied the striations were more evident on the flatter, less polished side of the object, presumably as this was the surface unlikely to be seen during use. It argues for a front and a back, the front generally being smooth, polished and with all but traces of the striations being polished out, and the rear, often rougher and matt with the striations more marked and representing the end of the coarse shaping process which would eventually be polished out on the final (front) surface. All of the bracers or part-bracers studied (with a small number excluded where possible striations were obscured by lacquering or showcase labels) exhibited striations of one form or another on either or both faces. Striations could be determined as being longitudinal, horizontal, or lateral, depending on the stroke direction used. The striations left by these processes can often be recognised by the naked eye, or more easily by the hand lens, and low level microscopy, under conditions of oblique lighting; they are better seen under magnification.

5.2.1. General trends

A general overview of the bracers indicated that the majority exhibited striations in one form or another on both surfaces with little difference showing between the different rock types (Figure 5.1). In 67% of bracers studied striations occurred on the front surface. Of these, those on Group VI items (31%) were predominantly diagonal, those on the amphibolites (31%) were predominantly longitudinal, and those in the miscellaneous group (38%) were a mixture of both. Figure 5.2 shows the extensive use of longitudinal striations on the amphibolite and miscellaneous groups in comparison to the Group VI group. The location of the striations tended to lie on the left and right sides of the front surface of the Group VI items (and is presumably a reflection of the curved geometry), whereas those of the other two groups tended towards one end of the object.

By contrast striations were identified on 92% of the rear (unseen) surfaces. Those on the Group VI bracers (31%) tended to be longitudinal, whereas those on the amphibolite bracers (36%) and bracers of the miscellaneous rocks group (33%) were mixed longitudinal and diagonal. This

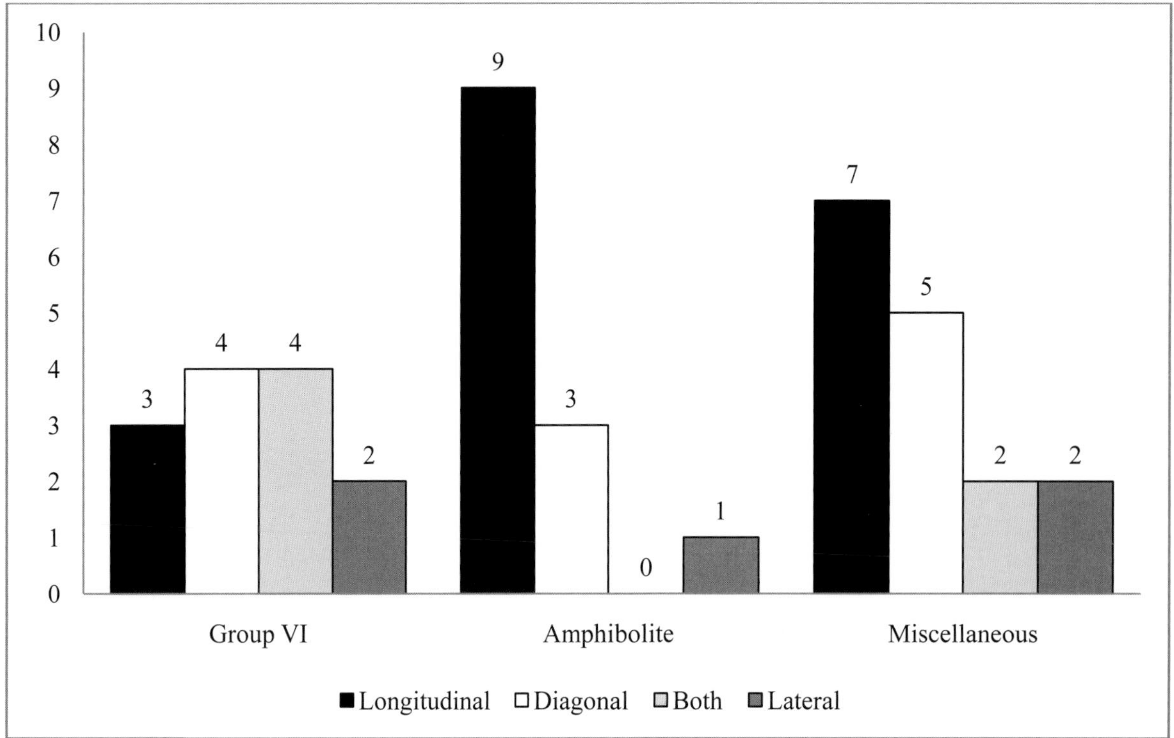

Figure 5.2. Front face, occurrence of striations by orientation.

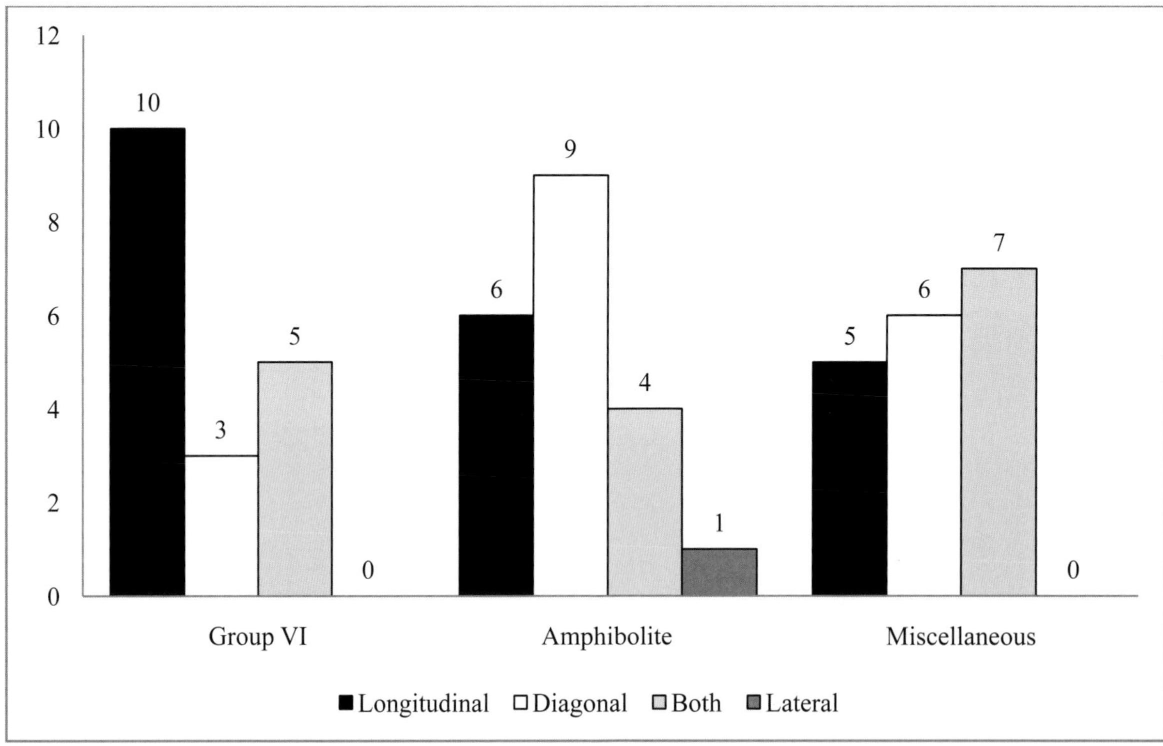

Figure 5.3. Rear face, occurrence of striations by orientation.

differs markedly from the orientations on the front faces, notably the extent of longitudinal striations on the Group VI types, presumably reflecting the only practical method of polishing the inside length of the curved profile, and the relatively high presence of diagonal striations on the amphibolite bracers (Figure 5.3). On these rear surfaces striations tended to occur across the full face as opposed to being confined to a specific area.

The majority of striations were very faint, but a number were marked and more clearly visible to the naked eye. The distinction between 'faint' and 'marked' is a subjective one; those recorded here as 'marked' were at the extreme

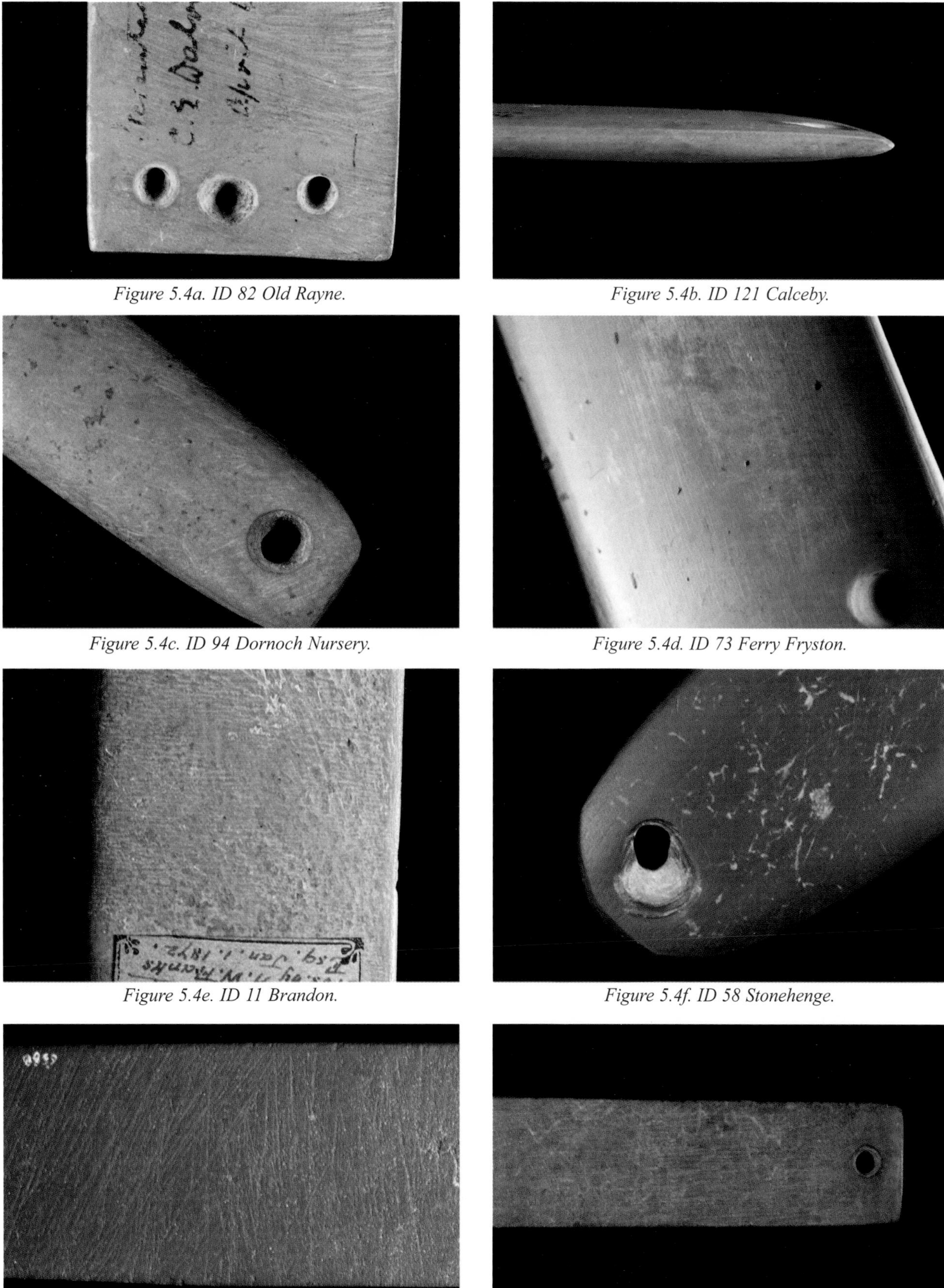

Figure 5.4a. ID 82 Old Rayne.

Figure 5.4b. ID 121 Calceby.

Figure 5.4c. ID 94 Dornoch Nursery.

Figure 5.4d. ID 73 Ferry Fryston.

Figure 5.4e. ID 11 Brandon.

Figure 5.4f. ID 58 Stonehenge.

Figure 5.4g. ID 56 Amesbury Archer.

Figure 5.4h. ID 57 Amesbury Archer.

Figure 5.4. Details of bracer features: 5.4a, lateral working on a fractured face; 5.4b, a carefully shaped profile; 5.4c, diagonal striations on rear; 5.4d, longitudinal striations on inside of curved bracer; 5.4e, lateral striations at end; 5.4f, lateral striations on front; 5.4g, diagonal and lateral striations on rear; 5.4h, longitudinal striations on rear.

of the range in order to minimise any ambiguity. Striations were also classified as either 'regular' or 'irregular', the difference being defined by specific and systematic strokes rather than by occasional and random strokes respectively. Here the comparison between the three geological groups also showed some distinctiveness: the Group VI examples had predominantly faint irregular striations on the front surfaces whereas the rear surfaces exhibited predominantly marked, regular striations. By contrast, the amphibolite items exhibited mostly faint and irregular striations on both surfaces, whereas the miscellaneous group showed mostly faint irregular striations on the front, but with a relatively high level of marked and regular striations on the rear.

Marked striations appeared typically towards the end and sides of the thicker pieces where finishing action was more pronounced; however, the greatest distinction was between the two main surfaces, the slightly rounded or curved surface (11% 'marked') and the flat surface (43% 'marked'), interpreted as the front and the rear faces respectively, presumably reflecting the fact that the rear surface was not intended to be seen. This was supported by the presence of regular/irregular striations. Overall 'regular' striations were in the minority: only 14% of the bracers exhibited regular striations on the front surface, whereas 49% exhibited regular striations on the rear surface. This was especially pronounced in the Group VI material where 66% of the rear surfaces showed regular striations, compared to 40% of the amphibolite bracers and 45% of the miscellaneous group respectively. Such characteristics may be reflections of working processes, namely that heavy regular stroke movements were necessary for coarser working, but that final polishing required a lighter, less regular, more multi-directional touch for finishing; this might explain the surviving coarseness of the rear (unseen) surfaces. However, the differences of character between bracers of the three geological types also suggests that structural characteristics may also have had a part to play. In addition there is the aspect of geometry, given the curvature of many of the Group VI pieces, which may have necessitated a finishing process different from that applied to the two groups of 'flat' bracers. There may also be a functional difference in the way that the rear of the curved Group VI bracers may have been fastened in comparison to fastening methods of flat bracers in the other groups.

Most of the bracer surfaces could be described as 'polished', although sometimes this was difficult to distinguish from occasional museum lacquering. Polishing appears to have occurred on both surfaces, although 10% of the surfaces could be described as 'rough' (ie unpolished). These were almost entirely restricted to the rear surface (92%) and support the view that the rear surface was not intended to be seen. Some surfaces could be described as 'highly polished' (17%) and attest to the high quality of the pieces. The fact that approximately one third of these (almost entirely within the amphibolite group) were polished on the reverse face indicates an adherence to overall quality, or even possibly to a different function. That apart, there appears to be no correlation between 'highly polished' and any particular geological types, or reworked examples.

5.2.2. Specific examples

Rear faces were thus arguably 'unfinished' by comparison to the more sophisticated front faces, striations occurring both diagonally (e.g. Dornoch Nursery, ID 94, Figure 5.4c) and longitudinally, often together and irrespective of profile (e.g. Barnack, ID 8; Amesbury Archer, ID 56). Nearly all the curved bracers also exhibited clear longitudinal striations inside the curved, unseen face, for example at Ferry Fryston (ID 73, Figure 5.4d) The sides of some rear surfaces also showed areas of more intense working, notably the piece from Newlands, Oyne (ID 90) which also showed the manufacturing marks for thong grooves. Diagonal markings were usually in a single direction although two examples, from Sewell (ID 12) and Melton Quarry (ID105) showed them in both directions.

There was some evidence to suggest that specific fields of the surface tended to receive working strokes in certain directions, presumably reflecting the way in which the object was held for working and the effort needed for shaping. The majority of bracers were relatively thin and may have been sufficiently fragile not to have been held in any form of vice. Working, therefore, was presumably a two handed, manual process, one hand being used to hold the object either freely so that both sides could be worked in the same grip, or pressed down against a flat firm surface where greater effort could be applied to a single face. The latter would minimise the risk of fractures and was no doubt used in the creation of perforations (see below). The two ends, top and bottom, tended to be worked diagonally, although a small number were worked laterally as well, for example the Amesbury Archer (ID 56) and Brandon (ID 11, Figure 5.4e) bracers. A small number also showed similar working on the front in addition, for example Old Rayne (ID 82), Broadford Bay (ID 88) and Stonehenge (ID 58, Figure 5.4f). It may be no coincidence that these three belonged to the miscellaneous group of rocks whose material characteristics may have required different directions of pressure for working. Reference to their morphology suggested that this could not necessarily be ascribed to factors of size (ie that only lateral strokes were possible when the object was held firm) but may reflect the method of creating bevelled or squared ends on certain types of rock. This certainly may have been the case for a fine-grained group of bracers which may have required, or allowed the craftsperson to work multi-directionally, for example on the two bracers from Amesbury (ID 56, diagonal and lateral on rear, Figure 5.4g; ID 57, longitudinal on rear, Figure 5.4h), and from Dornoch Nursery (ID 94, diagonal, longitudinal and lateral on rear and diagonal on sides, Figure 5.5a).

Little of this workmanship was evident on the front of the object where most of the deeper striations had been polished out. Where they did appear it was generally along the long or rounded sides of the front surface or at the ends

(29 examples, e.g. Amesbury Archer, ID 56; Glen Forsa, ID 86, Figure 5.5b) where specific shaping was necessary, for example, to produce facets or smooth rounded edges and where polishing may have been harder to undertake. These markings tended to be either longitudinal or diagonal presumably reflecting the relative ease or difficulty by which the object could be held secure. Only two examples exhibited both diagonal and longitudinal striations, at Ferry Fryston (ID 73) along the side of the face, and at Rauceby (ID 118) at the ends of the face. Much of the end working occurs in the vicinity of the perforations and seems likely to reflect the treatment necessary to 'clean up' after drilling, such as at Broadford Bay (ID 88) or Fyrish (ID 78, Figure 5.5c). In those instances where it was possible to determine it, it would seem that the perforations were drilled *after* the main polishing had taken place, and then finished separately. The curved bracer from Aldington (ID 112, Figure 5.5d) exhibited both longitudinal and lateral striations; the latter were located at the ends and presumably reflect the need to work the splayed profile as much as finish the perforations. Among the curved bracers this example was unusual in not having the striations polished out.

In a few instances the survival of manufacturing striations was inconsistent across the front polished face, for example at West Stafford (ID 66) and Rauceby (ID 118) where they occurred on one half only, at Ferry Fryston (ID 73) on one side only, and at Culbin Sands (ID 80) where they were sporadic. It seems unlikely that the polishing itself could have been variable given the relatively small surface area to be treated. Use wear is a possible cause for the inconsistency, but it is hard to see how this might have occurred (see Chapter 6.2).

The examples exhibiting faceted or bevelled edges would have required an additional element of workmanship and final polishing. On these faces most of the striations had been polished out although at Corry Liveras (ID 87) markings were evident on both the long edges (Figure 5.5e) and on the ends (Figure 5.5f). These varied in direction, presumably reflecting the need to address the narrow surface area from various directions in order to ensure a smooth and regular finish. The fine piece from Barnack (ID 8, Figure 5.5g) demonstrates from the striations how diagonal strokes were used to create the 'waisted' effect along the sides; similar strokes were used to form the bevelled ends on the bracer from Thomas Hardye School (ID 67). Several of the curved bracers exhibited diagonal striations in the formation of lipped flanges (e.g. at Calne, ID 5) and bevelled edges (e.g. Tring ID 31, Figure 5.5h).

5.3 FLAWS

Flaws were evident in approximately one-third of the items, and these were distributed across all three geological groups. Two main types of natural flaw occurred: the presence of small unsightly inclusions, and linear cracks or veins. The former could cause discolouration or even drop out during preparation leaving a small hole in the surface. Not all these holes have been fully polished out (e.g. Broadford Bay, ID 88, Figure 5.6a). Discolouration is the result of oxidation and was almost certainly evident at the time of manufacture; the bracer from Kelleythorpe (ID 13) provides a good example. By contrast, other types of discolouration such as the 'marble' effects on the objects from Gravelly Guy (ID 74) and Broadford Bay (ID 88) may have been the very features that made the rocks visually attractive in the first place. Several items exhibit linear flaws or dark veining, for example on Winterslow Hut (ID 4, Figure 5.6b), Brandon (ID 11) and Sutton Veny (ID 30). Such veining often occurs on the front face of amphibolite bracers and, along with mottling, may have been considered to add to the visual attraction of the bracers.

Some of these various flaws may have been largely unpredictable. The material may have been selected (or allocated) with major flaws inherent which may only have emerged as the object was being worked. This gave the craftsperson little opportunity to choose a 'good' and 'bad' side for the front and rear respectively. Some objects, for example the Amesbury Archer (ID 56) and Glenluce (ID 77) bracers may have been deliberately fashioned with the flaw on the reverse, but there are many others which exhibit highly visible flaws on the front surface too, for example at Sewell (ID 12), Aldbourne (ID 14) and Raunds (ID 116). These were presumably visible at the time of manufacture and perhaps further illustrate the importance of the material (and its source?) as an over-riding consideration. The piece from Mildenhall (ID 9) exhibits an awkwardly placed flaw which the craftsperson had to negotiate when creating a bevelled edge. The drilling of the Shorncote bracer (ID 75, Figure 5.6c) encountered a similar difficulty in having to execute a perforation across a linear flaw, whilst the Hemp Knoll (ID 7) piece suffered damage when a perforation ran through a flaw line and resulted in fracture. This seems to have occurred during manufacture as the perforation was unfinished. However, the notch created by the part-perforation seems to have been adequate for purpose (Figure 5.6d). While some veining and mottling may have been regarded as a decorative feature of the source rock, some linear or other flaws caused problems during manufacture. In spite of the existence of such flaws, the materials still seem to have been intrinsically valued in terms of their colour and, especially, their source.

5.4 PERFORATIONS

Perforations are one of the defining features of these objects. Current interpretation assumes that these would enable thongs or similar materials to secure the rear, usually unsmoothed, face of the bracer to the forearm, or to a sheath of leather or similar material wrapped around the forearm. The number of perforations required for this varied and possible underlying reasons for this are discussed in Chapter 4.5. A small number of bracers were difficult to interpret owing to breaks or reworking.

Drilling was probably undertaken using a bow drill, or device of similar design with a hard sharpened material such as flint providing the drill bit (Figure 5.7) although

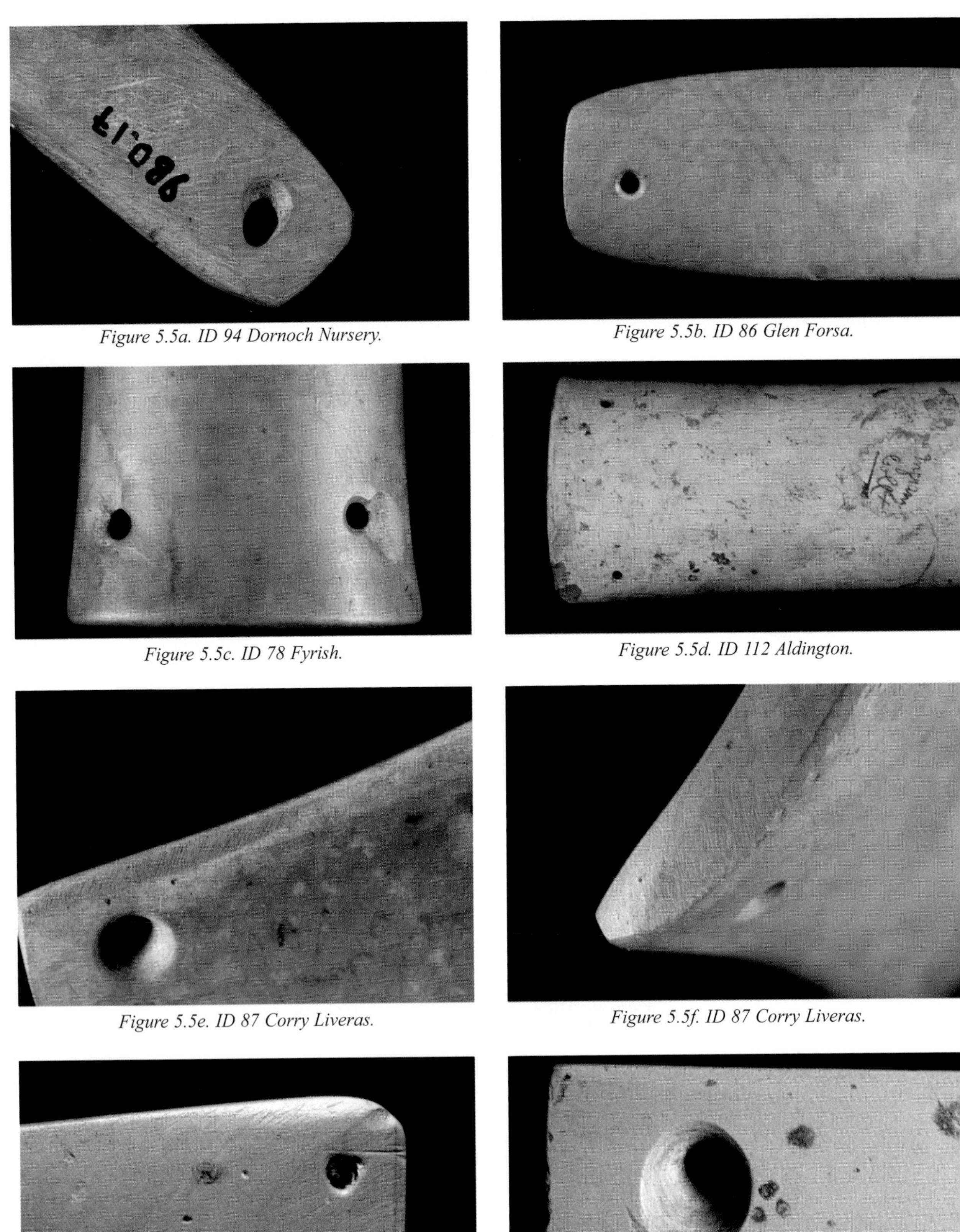

Figure 5.5a. ID 94 Dornoch Nursery.

Figure 5.5b. ID 86 Glen Forsa.

Figure 5.5c. ID 78 Fyrish.

Figure 5.5d. ID 112 Aldington.

Figure 5.5e. ID 87 Corry Liveras.

Figure 5.5f. ID 87 Corry Liveras.

Figure 5.5g. ID 8 Barnack.

Figure 5.5h. ID 31 Tring.

Figure 5.5. Details of bracer features: 5.5a, multi-directional striations; 5.5b, striations at the end of a front surface; 5.5c, markings from 'cleaning up' after drilling; 5.5d, longitudinal and lateral striations; 5.5e, striations on a long edge; 5.5f, striations on an end; 5.5g, diagonal striations forming a bevelled edge; 5.5h, diagonal striations on bevelled edge.

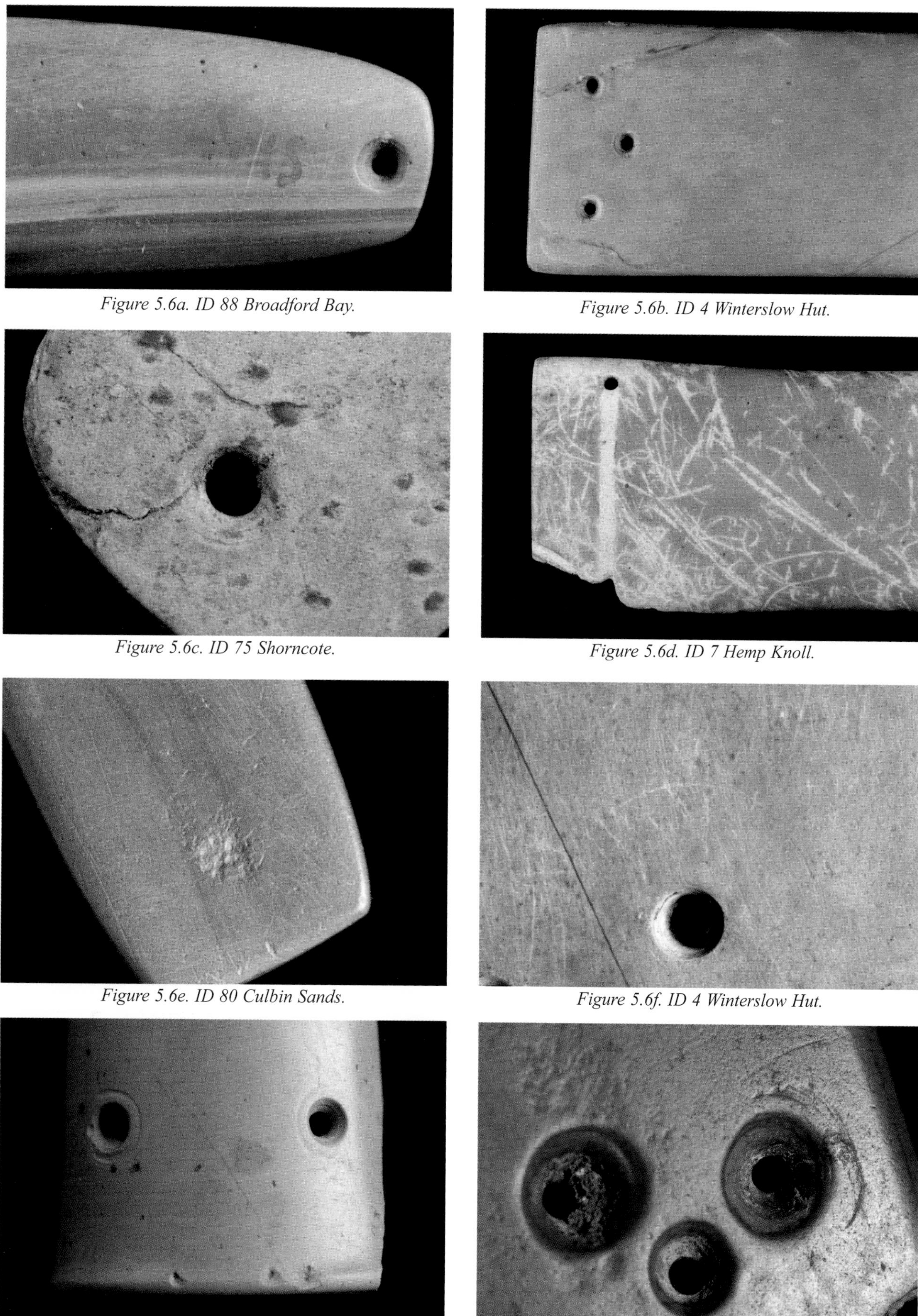

Figure 5.6a. ID 88 Broadford Bay.

Figure 5.6b. ID 4 Winterslow Hut.

Figure 5.6c. ID 75 Shorncote.

Figure 5.6d. ID 7 Hemp Knoll.

Figure 5.6e. ID 80 Culbin Sands.

Figure 5.6f. ID 4 Winterslow Hut.

Figure 5.6g. ID 73 Ferry Fryston.

Figure 5.6h. ID 115 Sonning.

Figure 5.6. Details of bracer features: 5.6a, a perforation not fully polished out; 5.6b, dark veining; 5.6c, a perforation across a flaw; 5.6d, a part perforation, but adequate for purpose, 5.6e, a possible reference point for a drill, 5.6f, a partial surface arc left from drilling, 5.6g, an almost complete circle left from drilling; 5.6h, broken arcs suggesting re-application of the drill.

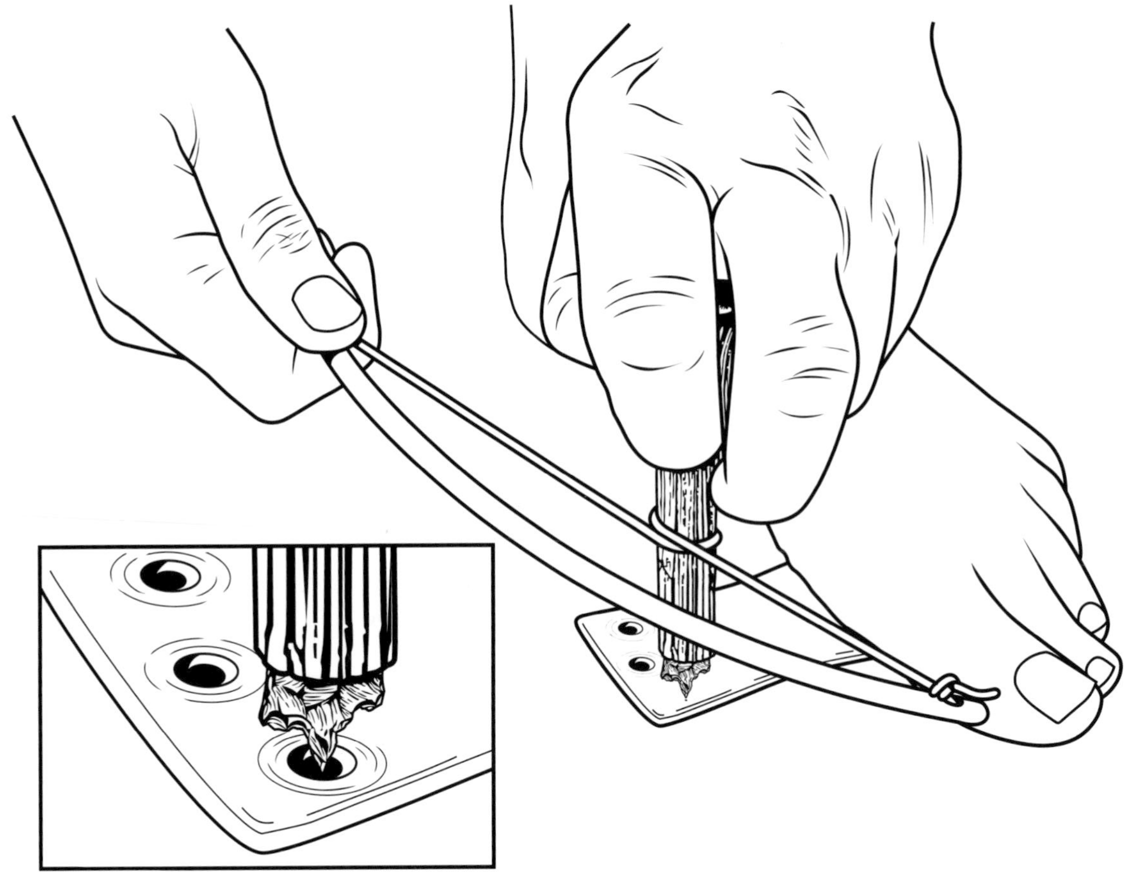

Figure 5.7. Reconstruction of bow drill and drilling point.

	2 perfs	4 perf	6 perfs	6 + perfs
Group VI	4	11	1	1
Amphibolite	6	7	5	-
Miscellaneous	13	5	1	1
Totals	**23**	**23**	**7**	**2**

Table 5.1. Number of perforations according to rock type (including all examples where at least one complete end had survived). See also Figure 4.13.

experimental work has shown that perforations can also be achieved with a hand-held flint (Van der Vaart 2009a and b). Several of the bracers provide clues as to how the perforations were created, drilling taking place *after* the piece had been fully shaped and polished. By the time the object was ready considerable effort had already been expended, and a fracture during drilling (to which some thinner bracers could be particularly vulnerable) must have been more than a little exasperating. Presumably the locations for perforations were marked up, although there is no evidence for 'laying out' a design as such, and then chipped away slightly in order to allow the drill bit a point of reference to prevent it slipping. This is evident on two examples, from Culbin Sands (ID 80, Figure 5.6e) and Duston (ID 102) both of which show reworking. The evidence suggests that there might have been at least two types of drill bit available (below); the commonest was probably of narrow triangular profile tapering to a point with the widest part of the triangle embedded or fastened into the vertical drill shaft (Figure 5.7) The widest part of the bit was likely to have been around 7 mm (the maximum perforation width measured). Triangularity of the bit profile effected a funnel shaped perforation in the bracer. This was normally undertaken from both faces to give an 'hour glass' profile (see Chapter 4.5.1).

The drill bit itself was probably no more than 4 to 5 mm in length; this can be interpreted from a number of examples where the bit has been allowed to penetrate too far causing the upper, unworked part of the bit (or indeed the shaft) to scar the surface of the bracer. This was evident either in the form of a partial ingrained arc in the bracer surface (e.g. Winterslow, ID 4, Figure 5.6f; Hemp Knoll, ID 7), almost a complete ingrained circle in the case of the bracer from Ferry Fryston (ID 73, Figure 5.6g), or as a series of broken arcs indicative of a drill being reapplied (e.g. Sonning, ID 115, Figure 5.6h; Calceby, ID 121). The process seems to have involved penetration of one side until the point of the bit had broken through the opposite face. The bracer could then be turned over and drilled down from the other surface to produce the 'hour glass' effect. Conversely, if the drill bit was allowed to complete the perforation from a single side, then the profile would be purely funnel-shaped (e.g. Dorchester XII, ID 1).

In either case, the vulnerable part of the process appears to have been the emergence of the drill bit on the second face; this could cause cracking or splitting, for example on the front of the Bishops Cannings bracer (ID 32, Figure 5.8a), or on the front of several curved bracers, for example from Fyrish (ID 78, Figure 5.5c) where attempts had been made to polish out the damage, and from Aldington (ID 112). There seems to have been little attempt to polish out any damage where it appeared on the rear unseen side of the bracer such as at Winterslow (ID 4) or Barnack (ID 8, Figure 5.8b).

The advantage of the 'hour glass' method was that it enabled any unevenness in the second surface to be tidied up, and possibly for this reason the majority of the bracers appear to have been drilled from the rear (unseen) side giving the perforation its widest diameter on that face as the triangular bit had the furthest to travel. Only six of the bracers examined appear to have had one or more of the perforations drilled initially from the front; these were spread across the three geological groups and showed no particular correlation with form. The average maximum diameter of the rear perforations was recorded as 4.9 mm. The perforation could be completed more delicately from the other face (normally the front), usually with a narrower diameter as the drill had less far to travel. The average maximum diameter of the front perforations was recorded as 4.5 mm. The rear diameter was wider than that on the front in 71% of the examples studied (in a percentage total of 184 available perforations, 130 were larger in the rear). This 'hour glass' effect also entailed a narrow 'waist' within the perforation. The diameter here was often less than 2 mm and rarely more than 3 mm and gives some limitations as to the type of thong or fastening used. Typical examples include those from West Stafford (ID 66) and Thomas Hardye School (ID 67) where the cruder, wider and deeper part of the 'hour glass' perforations at the rear contrasted sharply with the neater, narrower and shallower parts at the front. There are exceptions to this, for example the high quality Amesbury Archer pieces (ID 56 and ID 57) where the perforations are executed exquisitely from both faces, and the bracer from Stanton Harcourt (ID 2) where the front and rear faces both seem equally coarse.

The motion of the drill bit normally left circumferential marks on the inside of the perforation, described here as 'rilling'. These were evident in all but one bracer in both the Group VI and miscellaneous group respectively, but was less widespread in the amphibolite group where 12 bracers (50%) showed evidence for the rilling having been smoothed out. This may be a consequence of a less fine-grained material; alternatively it was noted that several of these bracers had been reworked, possibly involving smoothing as part of the reworking process.

The location of the individual perforations was generally symmetrical although there were significant exceptions (see also Chapter 4.5.2). Bracers with two perforations at each end were generally aligned with reasonable accuracy. Any variation lying within a few millimetres could be excused as lying within the range of acceptable practical error and was barely noticeable. Of the bracers with three perforations at each end, three exhibited the perforations spaced equidistantly in a straight line (e.g. Brandon, ID 11), while the other five had perforations spaced in a V-formation either with the point of the 'V' expressed towards the centre of the bracer (Winterslow Hut, ID 4, Figure 5.8c); Sutton Veny, ID 30; Bishops Canning, ID 32), or expressed towards the edge (Old Rayne, ID 82; Sonning, ID 115, Figure 5.8d). Exceptionally, the perforations on the Sutton Veny example (ID 30) were positioned much nearer the centre of the piece than any of the others. The current display of the Sutton Veny bracer in the Wiltshire Heritage Museum, Devizes (catalogue illustration below) shows how such a bracer might have been fastened.

The number of perforations, their positioning and their configuration must have had significant implications for the manner by which the object was fastened to the wrist, or other attachment. More ornate fastening methods will have been required for the Tytherington/Corton bracer (ID 29) with six perforations located (slightly unevenly) in a straight line at each end, and for the Barnack piece (ID 8) which exhibits nine perforations positioned in three sets of alternating V-formations. The Barnack perforations were capped with gold and therefore may not ultimately have been used for threading. However, in a possible primary function with open perforations any fastening is likely to have been complex. Use-wear (Chapter 6.2.1 and 6.2.4) suggests that the object was slightly worn from both primary and secondary roles. In addition, there are several examples where the perforations would appear to be deliberately asymmetrical (see also Chapter 4, Table 4.6), either with individual perforations at each end (e.g. Stonehenge, ID 58; Glen Forsa, ID 86; Crawford, ID 93; Littleport, ID 120), or with two perforations at each end (Roundway, ID 28). In these seven pieces the perforations are so significantly out of alignment that their positioning must be seen to be deliberate and possibly have fastening implications. This is pursued below.

A number of bracers are slightly concave on the rear to facilitate fastening to the wrist (e.g. Dorchester XII, ID 1), although many are flat (e.g. Tytherington/Corton, ID 29) or even plano-convex (e.g. Brandon, ID 11). The group of curved bracers would have fitted to the outside or inside of the wrist less comfortably and were perhaps more suited to the edge of the arm (Figure 5.8e); two of these, from Ferry Fryston (ID 73 and Aldington, ID 112), exhibit small nicks or grooves at the edges which may represent routes for thonging. This would indicate that the thong ran laterally outside the edge of the bracer. This contrasts with the piece from Hemp Knoll (ID 7) where weathering appears to have identified the route of the thong lying across the face of the bracer but not over the edges. By contrast again, the piece from Newlands, Oyne (ID 90) shows the thong running longitudinally in specially chased out grooves along the underside. These grooves appear to have been created before the perforations were drilled. Other than this, there is very little evidence as to how the thongs were attached and even less evidence of thong wear (but see Chapter 6.2.2) given (a) that bracers are made from hard materials and (b) that once strapped to the wrist the bracer is immobile (unlike objects such as pendants) with minimal opportunity for wear to occur within the perforations themselves.

By no means all the perforations were drilled vertically, in fact many were drilled at a slight angle. It was not always clear, however, whether this was a random factor or a deliberate exercise to route the thongs at specific angles through the perforations. The Group VI bracers are a case in point. The method of drilling these curved bracers was initially undertaken in the usual manner: it was initiated from the rear until the front surface was broken through, then the drill was applied to the newly created opening on the front and drilled through to the rear. Experimental work has demonstrated the difficulties of drilling on such curved surfaces (Van der Vaart 2009b, 5). In the flat (and mostly amphibolite) bracers this was drilled to make an 'hour glass' profile, but with the curved bracers showing four perforations (the majority of the four-holed type, see Table 5.1) drilling from the front was carried out with only a very light touch to finish off the perforation leaving a funnel-shaped rather than hour glass profile. The net effect was a wide, if fairly crude perforation from the (unseen) rear, but a very small and elegant perforation with a high degree of finesse seen from the front. However, it seems clear from analysis of the rear drilling that the angle of approach may have been significant, not so much for ensuring that the perforation appeared in the appropriate location on the front surface, but in order to route the thongs appropriately underneath. In most of the ten bracers where this could be studied the angle of the four perforations tended to be splayed inwards (e.g. Dorchester XII, ID 1, Figure 5.8f). This would suggest that the bracer was fastened in an even manner to an object of relatively consistent width, e.g. a forearm or staff. However, there were other bracers where the angles of the rear drilling lay in less consistent directions (e.g. Tring, ID 31) which may indicate that the object(s) to which they were attached were uneven or angular and required a different routing of the thongs in order to remain secure. It seems that the angle of drilling was also important on the flat Group VI bracers with two perforations; this configuration posed a different problem of fastening which appears to have been resolved by the two perforations being slightly offset, or by angling the drilling from opposite directions to route the thong accordingly, or both (e.g. Newlands, Oyne, ID 91). There is evidence of this among two-holed bracers in the other groups, for example at Stonehenge (ID 58). By comparison, there are examples from Ireland (Chapter 3, Appendix 3.1) where an assumed thong configuration required the perforations to be angled in opposite directions or to be routed through the end as opposed to the back of the bracer.

The majority of the bracers with two perforations occur within the miscellaneous group, with a smaller number in the amphibolite group (see Table 5.1). Without exception all of these exhibit inconsistency of drilling direction. Given that some of the perforations are true vertically (and sometimes in pairs, e.g. Broadford Bay, ID 88), this would suggest that the variation of the drilling angles may not be entirely accidental. Overall there appears to be no particular pattern in drilling direction: some perforations are drilled at opposing angles (e.g. Sturry, ID 6), but all give the impression of underlying significance. In some cases, perforations which appear to have been redrilled may in fact represent a secondary aspect of the primary manufacturing process necessary for ensuring that the thongs could be routed appropriately (e.g. Dornoch Nursery, ID 94). It seems likely, given the overall care manifestly taken in production, that these angled perforations were deliberate and offered fastening implications.

The same applies to the bracers with four perforations. About half of these belong to the Group VI curved type where the drilling appears to have been deliberately angled and splayed (above) whereas the others, a mixture of amphibolite and miscellaneous types, show no such consistency. In common with the two-holed bracers some drilling angles are aligned in pairs, or are alternate, or exhibit no obvious patterning at all. Consideration was given to the possibility that the differing angles of approach might be a reflection of the working position taken when the drilling took place, i.e. that the drill (if fixed) was not entirely perpendicular to the bracer, or conversely that the bracer was not bedded or held on an entirely flat plane. Hence when the bracer had been drilled from one side and turned over for redrilling, the same angle error would apply. The result would be a matching alignment between front and back on each perforation. There was some possible evidence for this, but insufficient to make a strong argument. Equally, in the case of bracers with four perforations, if each of the two perforations at a particular end were drilled one after the other, then any vertical error would be common to both. There is some modicum of support for this too, but inconsistently. Moreover, drilling was a slow process; any lack of true verticality would be both observable and remediable. It was also a difficult process effectively requiring three hands unless the object could be fastened in some type of clamp or vice. There is no evidence for this, and it is just as likely that the object could be held in place by a foot while two hands were used to operate the bow drill. It seems more likely that the angles of drilling were in the most part deliberate and represent some way of ensuring secure routing of thongs according to the shape and size of attachment.

The perforations of three items (Barnack, ID 8, Figure 5.8g; Kelleythorpe, ID 13; Culduthel, ID 79) were capped with gold on the outer surface and therefore could not be fastened by any thonging in the normal way; they may have been attached more rigidly using rivets instead. A further example from Borrowstone (ID 89) also contained the remains of bronze rivets on which gold may have been originally set, and at Sittingbourne (ID 10, Figure 5.8h) both perforations contained small traces of bronze suggesting a similar phenomenon. It is interesting to note

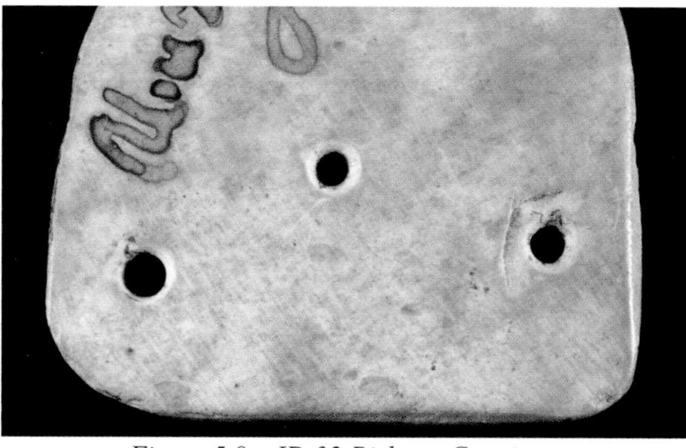

Figure 5.8a. ID 32 Bishops Cannings.

Figure 5.8b. ID 8 Barnack.

Figure 5.8c. ID 4 Winterslow Hut.

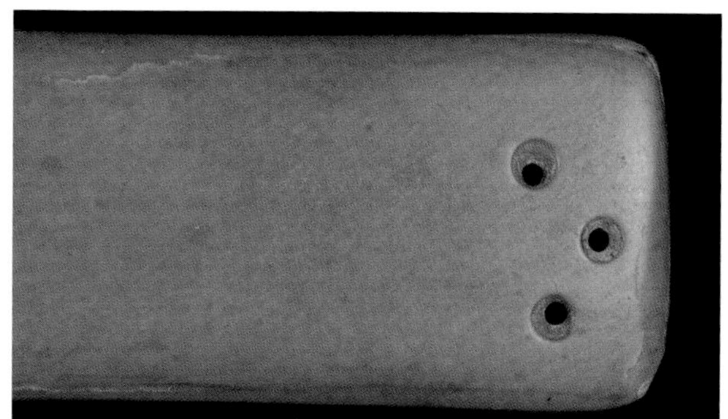

Figure 5.8d. ID 115 Sonning.

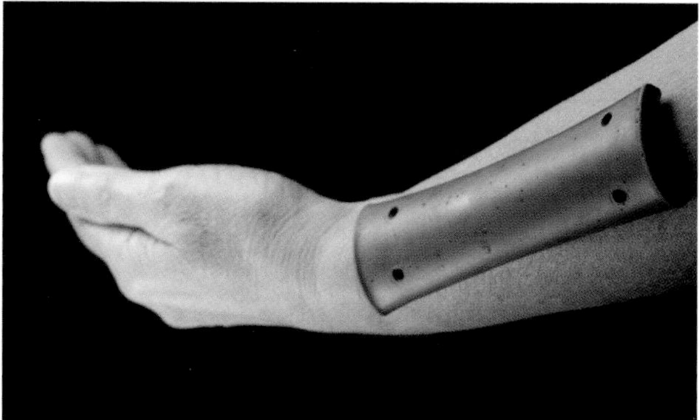

Figure 5.8e. ID 73 Ferry Fryston.

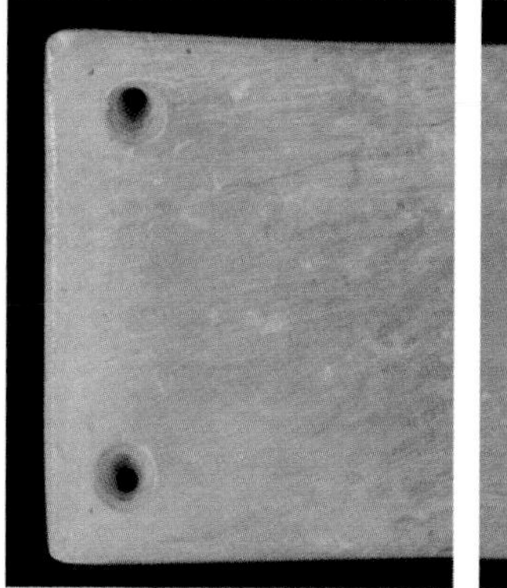

Figure 5.8f. ID 1 Dorchester.

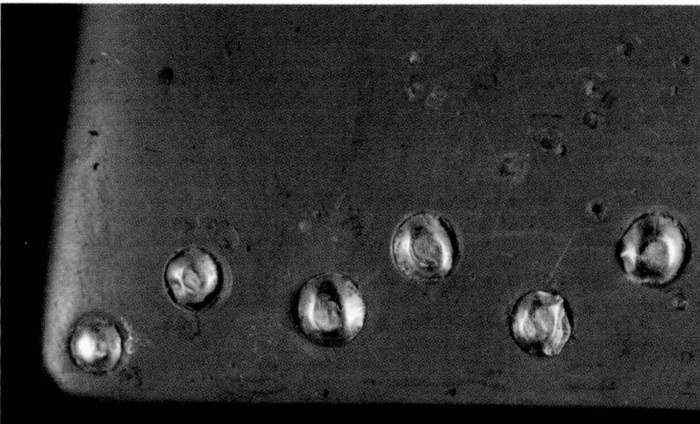

Figure 5.8g. ID 8 Barnack.

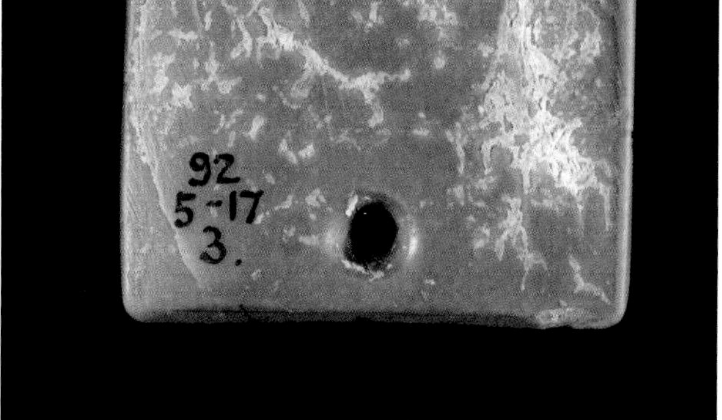

Figure 5.8h. ID 10 Sittingbourne.

Figure 5.8. Details of bracer features: 5.8a, splitting and cracking at exit point of drill; 5.8b, unpolished perforation exit at rear; 5.8c, 'V' formation of perforations expressed towards centre; 5.8d, 'V' formation of perforations expressed towards edge; 5.8e, curved bracer fitted to the front edge of the arm; 5.8f, angle of perforations splayed inwards; 5.8g, gold capped perforations; 5.8h, traces of bronze rivet in perforation.

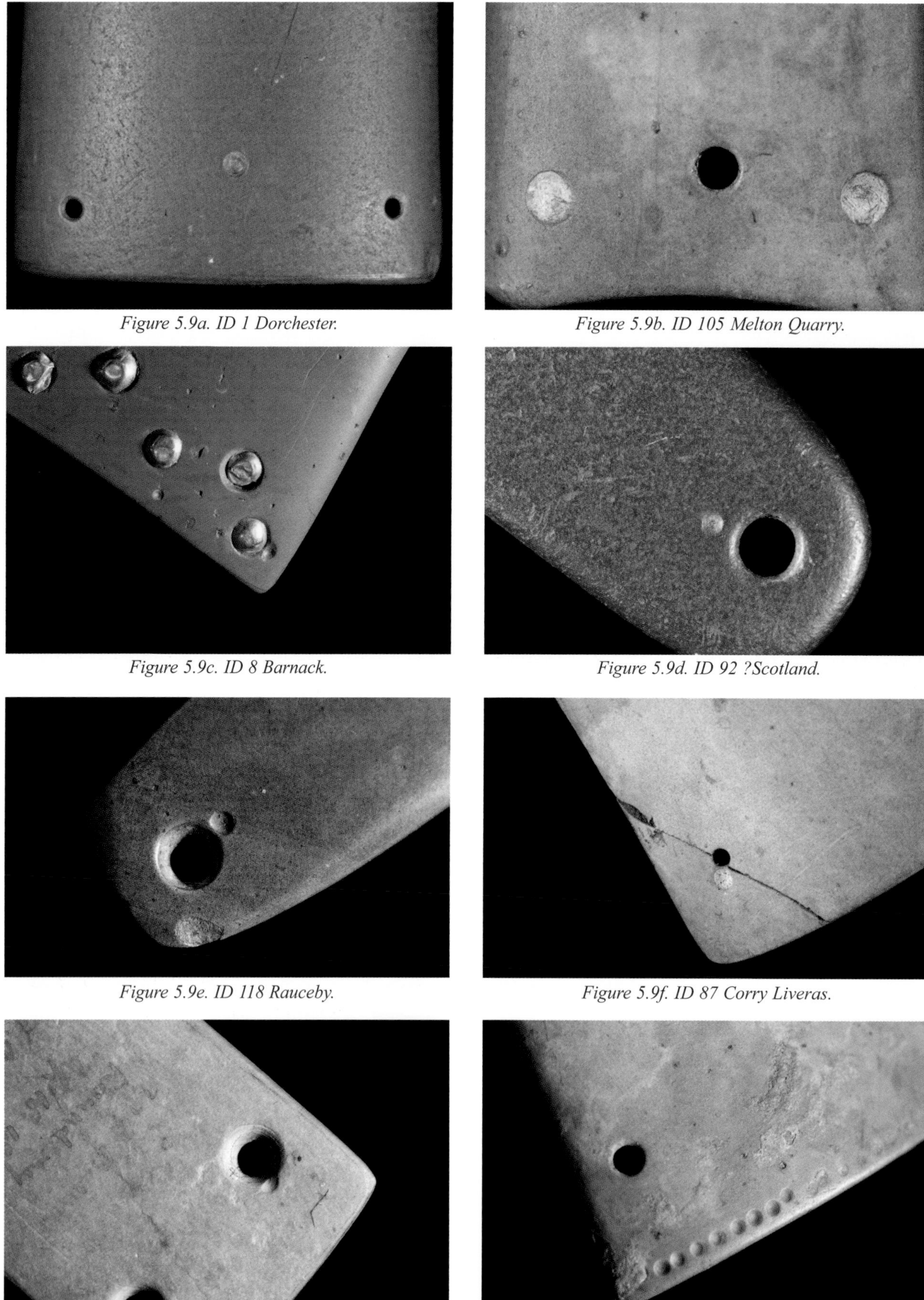

Figure 5.9a. ID 1 Dorchester.

Figure 5.9b. ID 105 Melton Quarry.

Figure 5.9c. ID 8 Barnack.

Figure 5.9d. ID 92 ?Scotland.

Figure 5.9e. ID 118 Rauceby.

Figure 5.9f. ID 87 Corry Liveras.

Figure 5.9g. ID 28 Roundway.

Figure 5.9h. ID 87 Corry Liveras.

Figure 5.9. Details of bracer features: 5.9a and 5.9b, part-perforations which may have been used for holding mounts; 5.9c–5.9g, possible 'starter' holes adjacent to full perforations; 5.9h, band of decorative depressions around lip.

that the perforation alignments of these bracers were either vertical or with only a slight angle. The three curved Group VI examples (ID 13; ID 79; ID 89) exhibited none of the pronounced splaying characteristics evident on the drillings of the other curved bracers. There is a strong argument here to propose that this lack of defined thonging route might indicate that these bracers were never intended to be fastened in the same way as the other bracers, and were manufactured accordingly.

These gold capped pieces exhibit exceptional workmanship; it suffices here to point to their ornamental rather than functional value and that they may not necessarily have been used as wristguards (see Appendix 10.1). That said, however, three further pieces, both of Group VI, from Dorchester XII (ID 1, Figure 5.9a), Melton Quarry (ID 105, Figure 5.9b) and Raunds (ID 116) exhibited complete perforations with symmetrical part-perforations which may have been used to hold some form of mount. In the case of the Dorchester XII example each end exhibited two complete perforations with a part-perforation creating a V-shape. The reverse was the case with the Melton Quarry piece where each end exhibited a single perforation with two part perforations also forming a V-shape. This may suggest that both pieces could have been worn functionally, yet still have been decorative.

The creation and shape of these part-perforations suggests that drilling must also have been undertaken with a more rounded drill bit, or using a different tool altogether. Here the effect was more of a circular shallow depression or pit with a slightly rounded base, typically less than *c.*1 mm in depth and less than 3 mm in diameter. In the examples cited above, their positions on the bracer surfaces were symmetrical and can be argued as decorative (see also Bartlett 1963), yet they also appear less symmetrically on other bracers, some twelve examples across all geological types, where they might be better interpreted as 'starter' holes – that is unfinished perforations such as on the fine bracers from Barnack (ID 8, Figure 5.9c), ?Scotland (ID 92, Figure 5.9d) or Rauceby (ID 118, Figure 5.9e). Here they could conceivably be argued as being part of an abandoned layout. It is, however, hard to accept this on the face of such fine pieces; nor does there seem to have been any attempt to polish them out. The piece from Aldbourne (ID 14) appears to be the reworking of a broken bracer and the two 'starter' holes are positioned at the corners in the appropriate sites for perforations, but neither were completed. A similar corner position is taken by the 'starter' on the bracer from Corry Liveras (ID 87, Figure 5.9f); this too must have been clearly visible when the completed bracer was in use. The bracers from Roundway (ID 28, Figure 5.9g), Glen Forsa (ID 86) and Littleport (ID 120) all exhibit traces of similar features but on the edge of full perforations. In none of these is it possible to say which was drilled first, the 'starter' or the full perforation. Here the 'starters' might be explained as either part of the layout or, less likely, as routing for thongs. Overall, these features are problematic. Some can be explained decoratively, indeed a band of smaller shallow rounded depressions was used to decorate the original end of the Corry Liveras bracer (ID 87, Figure 5.9h), others possibly as evidence of unfinished pieces. Equally plausible, however, given their visibility on objects which were highly valued, is that they represent some talismanic factor, or some significant marking reflecting use, achievement or even obsolescence.

6: FRAGMENTATION AND USE WEAR

Ann Woodward

6.1 FRAGMENTATION

A major aim of the project was to investigate to what degree individual bracers had been broken, where the various breaks occurred on the bracer, and to determine when the breakage had occurred. It was expected that some fragmentation may have occurred accidentally at the time of manufacture, other breaks during the use life, or use lives, of the bracer and yet others at the time of excavation or subsequently during the time of curation in museum collections. The methods used to describe the various breaks, and to assess the time at which fragmentation had occurred are outlined in Chapter 2.2.

6.1.1. Percentage present

The study of each bracer included an estimate of the percentage of the original artefact present. In the majority of cases (66%) the bracers were whole, or almost whole, at the 98–100% level, often with just one minor chip or flake. It is interesting to note that fragmentation of the remaining bracers formed an uneven pattern. Almost complete, and still functional as bracers, were a group of nine (13%) which survived at the 95 –96% level. Below this level there were three size groups: large fragments (three examples at 85–90%), five examples which were half-bracers, in the 50–60% range, and small fragments (six examples occurring at 33% or less of the original bracer).

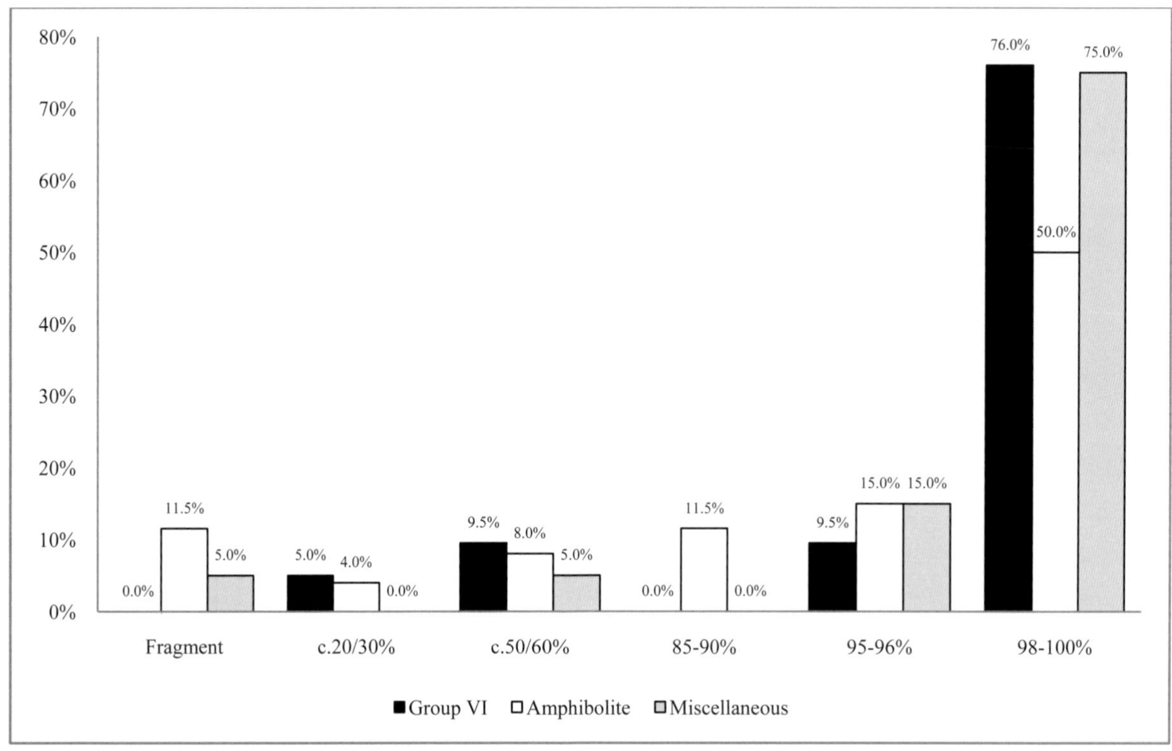

Figure 6.1. Percentage of bracers present according to rock type.

When these results are considered against the three rock groupings (Figure 6.1), some possible patterns emerge. The Group VI bracers tend to be either intact or near intact, or occur as significant fragments (half- or one third-bracers). In contrast, the amphibolite bracers seem to have been broken down more often into smaller fragments. This has interesting implications, given that the two rock types are structurally distinctive: the Group VI type rock is structurally isotropic and would have a tendency to fracture like glass, whereas amphibolites are planar in structure and more likely to fracture parallel to lines of foliation. The fragmentation of the two bracers types does not, therefore, fully match expected fracture patterns. Finally the bracers of the remaining miscellaneous rock group are nearly always found as whole or almost complete, usable, items, with fragments much less in evidence. This may indicate that these bracers were made from less valuable materials and/or were more robust as they tend to be thicker (see Chapter 4.2.1). They may have been everyday non-exotic items.

6.1.2. Age of breaks

The total number of breaks recorded on the sample of 67 bracers was 240 (see Table 6.1). On average they occurred at the rate of 3.5 per bracer. This approximate occurrence was also found for the amphibolite bracers (average 3.65 per bracer). However, breaks occurred more commonly on bracers made from Group VI rock (average 4.7 per bracer) and less commonly on bracers of the miscellanoeus rocks (average 2.3 per bracer). In terms of age, seven breaks were of indeterminate date and only a total of 27 were assessed to be modern in origin. The incidence of these occurred roughly equally amongst bracers of the three rock groups (Table 6.1). The greater majority (206), however, were considered to be ancient fractures. In the catalogue at the end of the volume this incidence is translated into *percentage present at deposition* in order to identify the level of completeness at the time of burial.

Of these ancient fractures 79 (38%) were assessed to have been related to the stage of manufacture, while 127 (62%) had been acquired during use. Breaks and irregularities formed at the time of manufacture consisted mainly of cracks or flaws present in the original piece of rock, which had been incompletely polished out, but occasionally more serious damage had occurred. The breaks acquired during the use life of the bracer were usually small chips or flakes, although larger breaks and missing portions also occurred at a significant level. The occurrence of breaks caused during manufacture and those acquired during use is summarised in Table 6.2.

It can be seen that the percentage of manufacturing fractures were more common on the amphibolite bracers. However this may relate to the natural foliate characteristics of the rock used rather than to a less refined process of manufacture. As far as breakage during use is concerned, an opposite pattern is apparent. The bracers of Group VI and of the miscellaneous rock group show high, and roughly equal incidences of use breaks, while the amphibolite examples seem to have been broken less. These statistics may relate to relative hardness of the rocks concerned, length of individual use lives for different bracers, or to the way in which bracers made from different rock were stored and used. However, if the bracers of Group VI and amphibolite rock were more prized as prestige items, with those of other rocks serving as more utilitarian everyday objects, then the latter group might be expected to display greater breakage. On the other hand, they tended to be both thicker and smaller which may have rendered them as overall less fragile.

Rock	**No. bracers**	**Indet**	**Modern**	**Ancient**	**Total breaks**
Group VI	21	3	10	86	99
Amphibolite	26	3	10	82	95
Miscellaneous	20	1	7	38	46
Totals	**67**	**7**	**27**	**206**	**240**
% of all breaks		3%	11%	86%	

Table 6.1. Breaks according to rock type and age of break.

Rock	**At manufacture**		**In use**	
	No. breaks	% breaks	No. Breaks	% breaks
Group VI	29	33%	57	67%
Amphibolite	38	46%	44	54%
Miscellaneous	12	31%	26	69%
Totals	**79**		**127 (+ 79= 206)**	

Table 6.2. Ancient breaks according to origin and rock type.

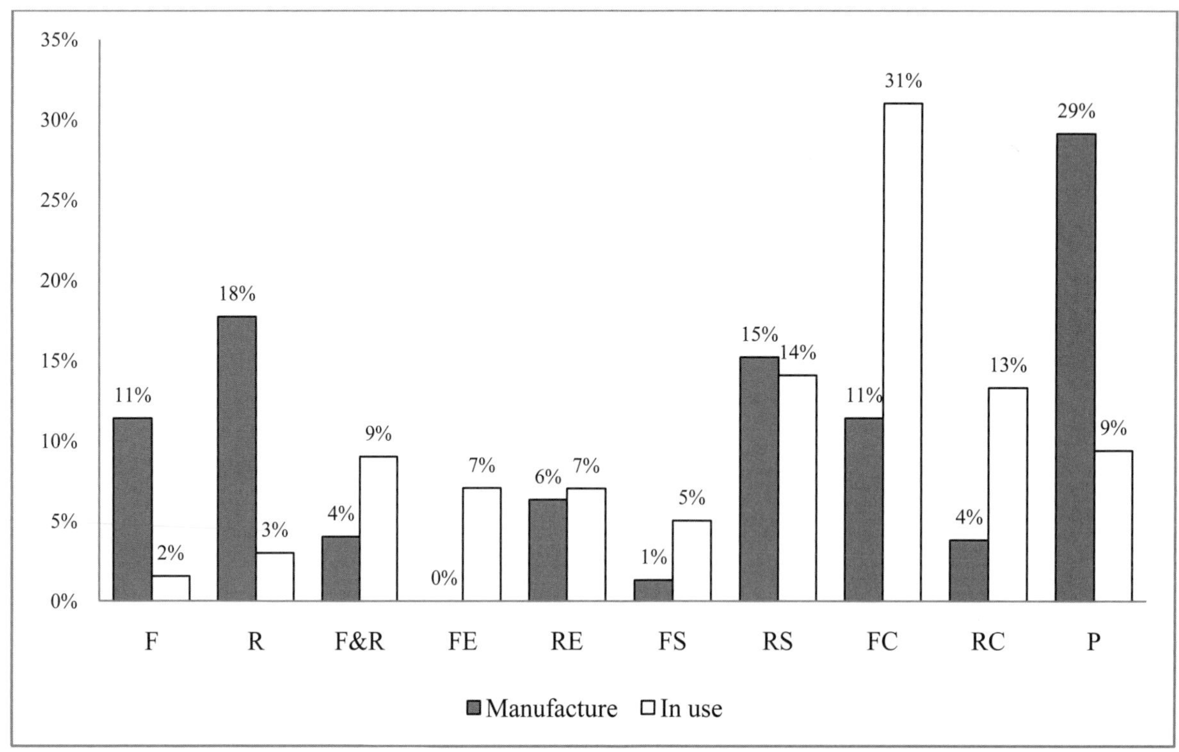

Figure 6.2. Incidence of ancient breaks according to location on bracer. Key: F front; R rear; F&R front and rear; FE front end; RE rear end; FS front side; RS rear side; FC front corner; RC rear corner; P at perforation.

6.1.3. Location of breaks

The location of each break was recorded according to its position on the front or rear of the bracer, and whether it occurred on the faces, sides or ends, or adjacent to one of the perforations. Breaks of different age origin tended to occur in different locations on the bracers (Figure 6.2). Those created during manufacture most commonly occurred on the front and rear faces (F, R, F&R), on rear side locations (RS) and, very particularly around perforations (P). This pattern reflects the positioning of flaws and flakes in the rock that could easily be polished out (see Chapter 5.3), as well as slight errors made during manufacture of the perforations (see Chapter 5.4). In contrast, although breaks that occurred during use show a wide pattern of locations on the bracer, the most common locations were at the corners (FC and RC), followed by rear side positioning, and then around perforations (Figure 6.2). Overall, breaks considered to have occurred at manufacture were much more often located on the rear of the bracer (64% of instances); in other words flaws and perforation errors were kept to the back wherever possible. However, the distribution of breaks in use, in relation to front and rear positioning, was much more even, with 54% of instances located on fronts and 46% occurring in rear locations.

The results can also be considered in relation to the three rock types employed. Taking firstly the breaks and irregularities caused during manufacture (Figure 6.3) it can be seen that such breaks on Group VI bracers were most often located around perforations. The amphibolite bracers displayed roughly equal quantities of breaks on the faces (usually flaws) and around perforations, with significant occurrences on the ends, sides and corners as well. The bracers made from the miscellaneous rocks also had high numbers of breaks or irregularities on the faces, but a much lower incidence of breaks on the sides, corners and at the perforations. Again, the high incidence of flaws on the faces of the amphibolite bracers may be related to the natural qualities of the rocks used. And it may be that the high numbers of breaks near the perforations on the Group VI bracers may be related to the difficulty of drilling holes in this particular type of rock.

Turning to breaks formed during use (Figure 6.4) it can be seen that bracers belonging to the three rock groups again display differing patterns. The overall patterning of location of breaks is generally more even than for breaks caused during manufacture, but with two significant exceptions: there is a high peak of chips on rear side locations for the Group VI bracers, and an even higher peak for front corner locations on bracers made from amphibolite.

Overall, most breaks tend to occur in corner locations (33% of all breaks incurred during use). It is important to consider which of these breaks were minor chipping on the corners, and which were so severe that they broke into a perforation. Such severe breaks would have seriously impeded the possibility of continuing to attach the bracer to a backing or directly to the arm. Of the 12 corner breaks that occurred during manufacture two had broken into one of the corner perforations, and might have rendered the bracer almost unusable as a wristguard from the outset. These are the bracers from Hemp Knoll (ID 7) and Mildenhall (ID 9; Figure 6.7a). However, if enough of the perforation survived the bracer could still have been

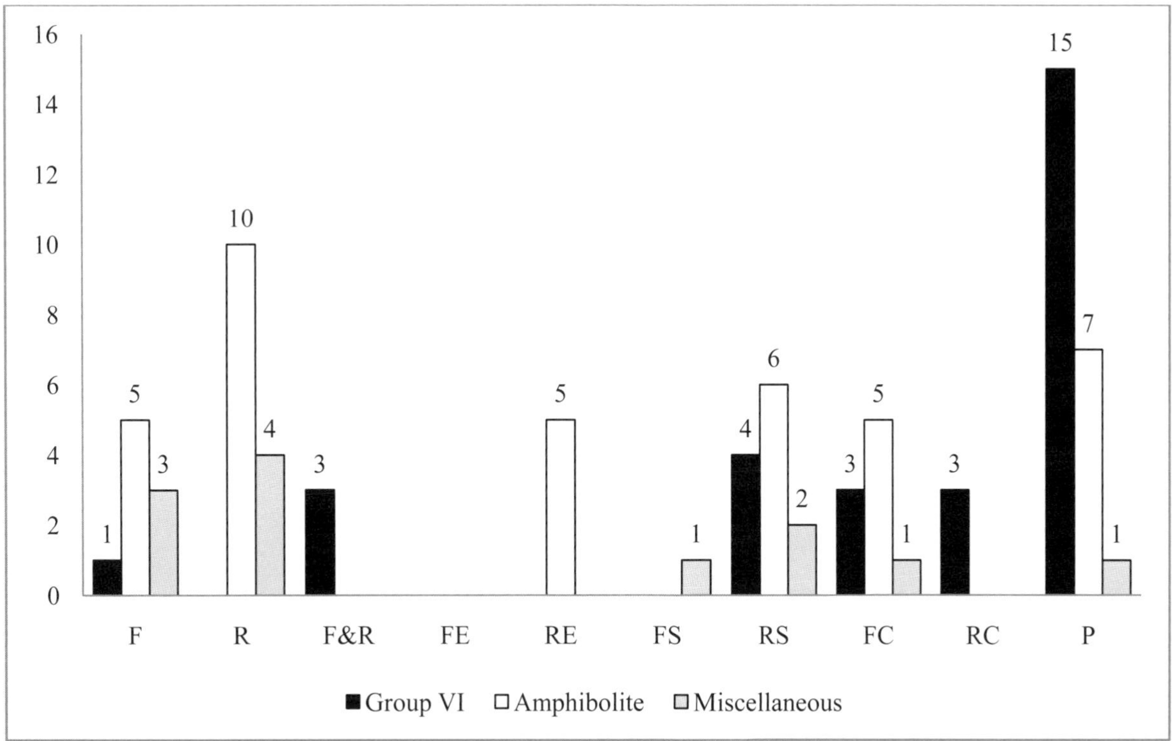

Figure 6.3. Location of breaks during manufacture (for key see Figure 6.2).

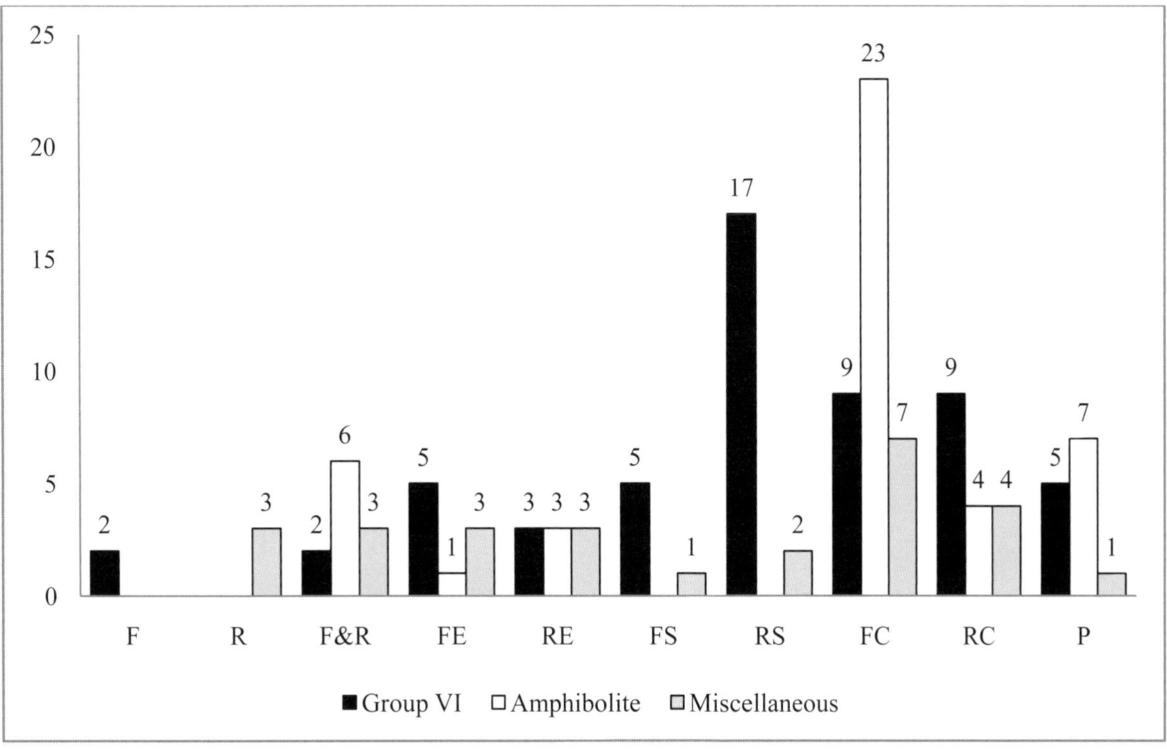

Figure 6.4. Location of breaks whilst in use (for key see Figure 6.2).

used, as is suggested by the thong marks on the Hemp Knoll (ID 7) bracer which will be discussed below. Corner breaks that ensued during use were far more numerous (a total of 56 instances), but in only four cases (7%) was the break catastrophic, with associated breakage into a corner perforation. Of these, three of the instances were on amphibolite items and one on a Group VI bracer. The three amphibolite examples were from Brandon (ID 11), Upper Heyford (ID 103) and Aston (ID 107). The bracer of Group VI rock from Winteringham (ID 119), with a

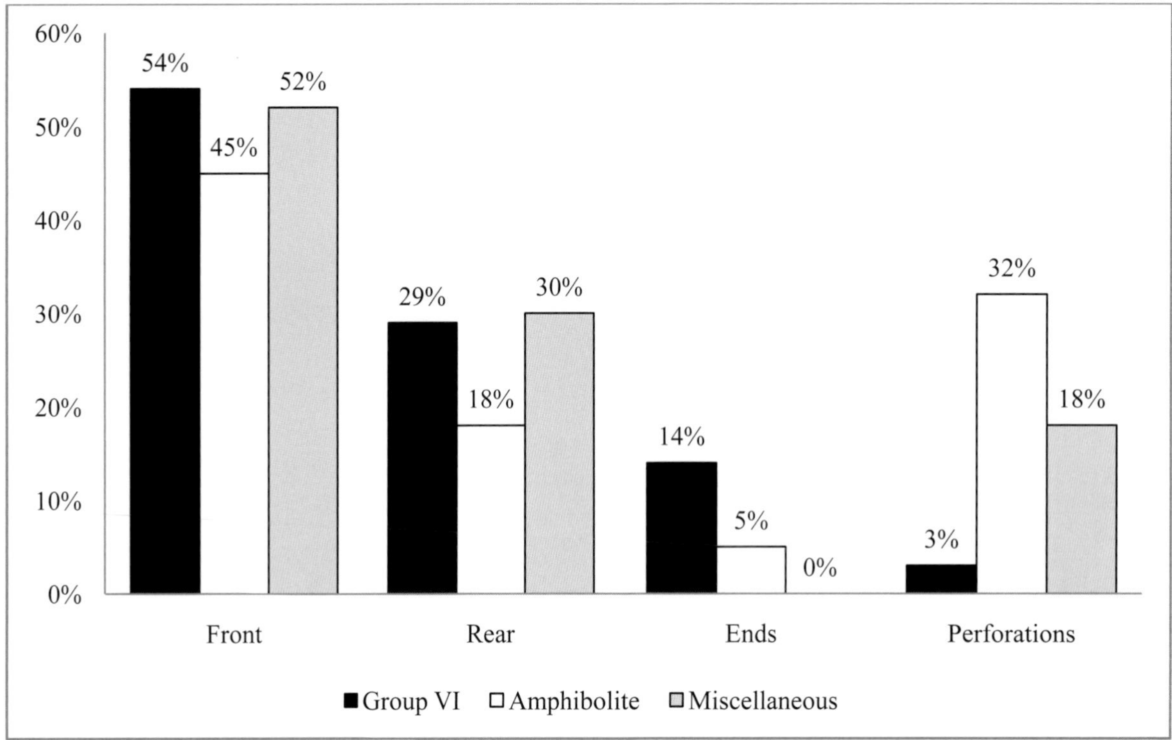

Figure 6.5. Incidence of wear in relation to location.

corner break extending into a perforation is a fragment, and will be discussed later.

6.2. USE WEAR

6.2.1. Surface wear

It proved very difficult to detect traces of use wear under the microscope, and to differentiate it from the striations resulting from manufacture (Chapter 5.2). The wear traces usually comprised scratches, often faint, which might be longitudinal, transverse, diagonal or multi-directional. They were often randomly distributed, but in a few cases the wear traces occurred in zones. In two cases front face wear occurred in occasional patches on bracers from Ferry Fryston (ID 73) and Offham (ID18), but in three cases the multi-directional wear scratches occurred in the central zone only, on examples from Barnack (ID 8), Brandon (ID 11) and Rauceby (ID 118). However, in the case of the bracer from Hemp Knoll (ID 7) the zones of multi-directional wear were located towards the perforations, leaving the central zone clear. Of these four bracers showing zonal wear, three are of Group VI rock and one of amphibolite. Occasionally there were thong grooves or marks (see below), and non-specific scuffing or abrasion was sometimes recorded.

Most of the wear traces occurred on the front face of the bracer. There were 39 instances of wear on the front compared with 20 on the rear i.e. almost twice as common. Wear on the ends of bracers was found to be very uncommon (five instances in total). The dominance of wear on the front surface was apparent in all three rock groupings (see Figure 6.5). That said, it should be emphasised that there are structural differences between the Group VI rocks and the amphibolites: the isotropic character of the Group VI rocks makes them much more susceptible to surface scratching than the amphibolites which are more prone to scratching along the fabric (i.e the thin sides) rather than on the top and bottom flat surfaces.

The lower incidence of wear on the rear faces was particularly marked for bracers in the amphibolite group; the bracers in the miscellaneous rocks group displayed no end wear. These results indicate that the front, more highly finished, face of each bracer was the face that received most wear and tear during use. However, the significant incidence of wear on the rear faces may indicate that, in these cases, part of each use life involved use of the bracer detached from any leather or other backing.

6.2.2. Wear at perforations

It had been expected that signs of wear around the perforations might have been widespread, but in fact there were only 13 instances overall. Wear around perforations was most prevalent on amphibolite bracers and may be a reflection of the relative softness of the section (as opposed to the surface) of its foliate structure. By contrast, wear around the perforations was very poorly represented amongst the Group VI bracers. Thong wear in the form of distinct smoothed grooves was detected on four bracers (see also Chapter 5.4). In three cases the wear indicated that thongs had been applied from perforation to perforation along the length of the bracer. In the case of the two two-holed bracers from Hockwold (ID 106) and Scarborough

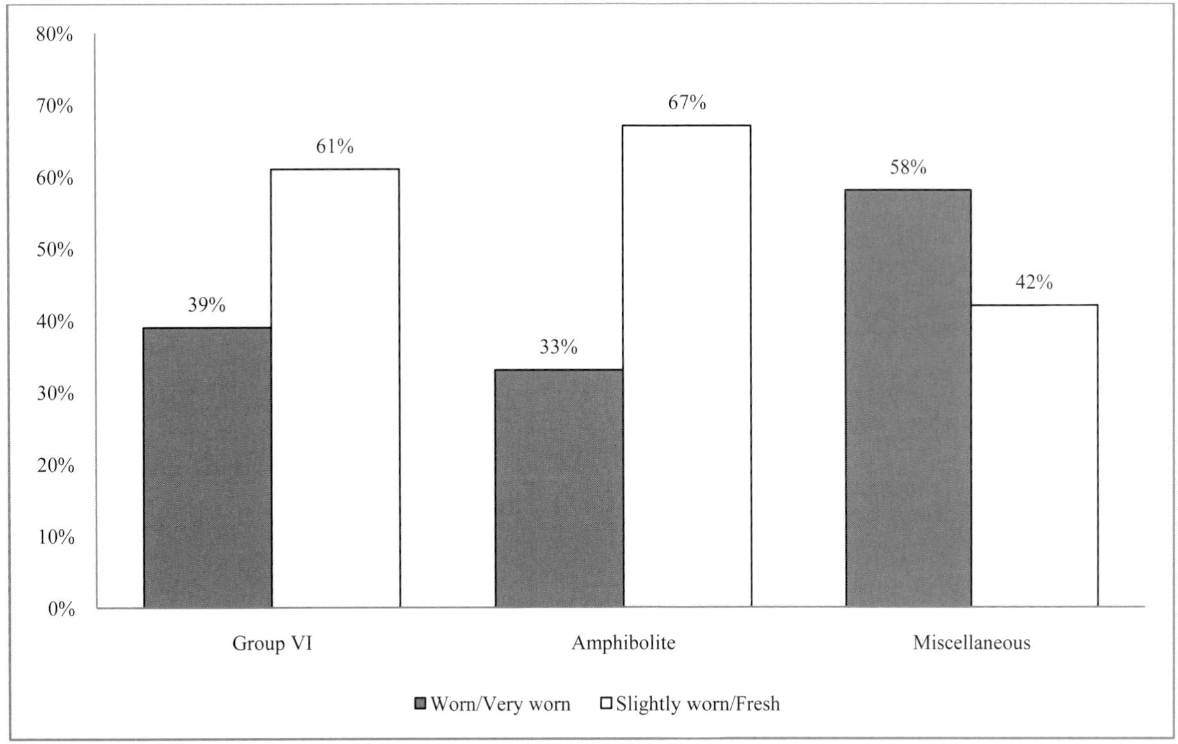

Figure 6.6. Wear categories by rock type.

Category	No. of bracers	No. of bracers	Percentage
Very worn	1	26	42%
Worn	25		
Slightly worn	32	35	56%
Fresh	3		
Indeterminate	1	1	2%
Totals	**62**	**62**	**(100%)**

Table 6.3. Overall wear categories for 62 bracers.

(ID 104, Figure 6.7b) the grooves were apparent on the front and rear of one perforation only in each case. On the third, four-holed example from Pyecombe (ID 137) grooves were present on all four perforations but only on the rear. In the final case, one outer perforation of the six-holed bracer from Sutton Veny (ID 30) displayed a diagonal groove towards the corner of the bracer. This was apparent on the rear surface, but the front surface could not be studied as this piece is firmly attached to a museum display mount. The longitudinal pattern of thong attachment suggested by these grooves is borne out by the remarkable bracer from Newlands, Oyne (ID 90, Figure 6.7c) which has two wide and parallel grooves, from 1.4 to 1.6 mm deep, running between, and beyond the two pairs of perforations on the rear (see also Chapter 5.4). However, an alternative and opposite system of thong attachment is indicated by the two linear marks, caused by differential erosion in the grave, which run transversely between the two end pairs of perforations on the front face of the bracer from Hemp Knoll (ID 7, Figure 6.7d). As noted above, this was also the only bracer that had zones of front face wear towards the perforations.

6.2.3. Overall wear category

At the time of record, the overall wear detected on each bracer was assessed using five categories: 'very worn', 'worn', 'slightly worn', 'fresh' or 'indeterminate'. Given the difficulties encountered in defining reference states, it was subsequently decided to combine the results to form two general categories: 'fresh to slightly worn' and 'worn' respectively. This effectively defined extremes of wear as opposed to gradations of wear and was felt to be more objective. However, the full results are summarised in Table 6.3.

The three 'fresh' bracers were all made from amphibolite. These include the two perfect examples from Dorset, from West Stafford (ID 66) and Thomas Hardye School (ID 67) which may never have been used, plus one which may have been unfinished, from Llantrithyd (ID 113). The incidence of the two general wear categories amongst the three rock groupings is plotted in Figure 6.6. This shows that, within the Group VI and amphibolite groups, slight wear was evidenced more often than heavy wear. This is particularly marked in the amphibolite group, which was the least worn group, although this may reflect the relative hardness of the planar surface. In contrast, the bracers made from other rocks displayed heavy wear rather more often. These results may indicate that the amphibolite bracers were the least used, and therefore perhaps the most valuable. On the other hand, the bracers made from the miscellaneous rocks group seem to have been the most used. These bracers are more variable in shape and were both smaller and thicker than those belonging to the other two groups; their greater wear may continue to suggest that they were designed for everyday use, rather than for display as exotic prestige items.

6.2.4. Wear on gold caps

Three bracers, all of Group VI rock, have rivet caps of gold surviving above the perforations on the front surface. On the Kelleythorpe (ID 13) bracer all four caps carried marked wear scratches and striations. These were sparse, but located all over each cap. Three had central dents or tiny holes and this may be damage caused as the ancient adhesive employed on the under sides decayed (Figure 6.7e). One cap also had a large nick extending from the apex to the margin. It was thought that such damage related to wear. However, some of the striations were circumferential and may have been polishing marks. These may have been from the original manufacture, although may equally have resulted from one or more episodes of repolishing. The four gold caps on the very similar bracer from Culduthel Mains (ID 79, Figure 6.7f) were also found to have small holes in the centre, and multidirectional scratches. Some of the caps also displayed radial linear depressions on their margins, but these would have been gouge marks from when the gold caps were originally pressed onto the bracer. The random scratches in all cases overlay original burnishing marks, thus indicating that the piece had been used. The eighteen gold caps covering the perforations on the bracer from Barnack (ID 8) did not have small holes at their apices, but eleven of them were slightly flattened at the top, and two carried slight indentations. Two had sunk down slightly into the perforation below and one was creased. Multidirectional scratching was again observed and the distortion of the shapes of the gold caps indicated wear (Figure 6.7g and Figure 5.9c).

6.3. RE-WORKING AND RE-USE

Remarkably, approximately one third of the corpus examined (19 examples) falls into the category of secondary working, either as broken or reused pieces, typically re-used as (smaller) bracers, pendants or tools (Table 6.4). It is also interesting to consider whether bracers made from particular rock types were selected for re-use. The data indicates that re-used items occur in all rock types, although the incidence of re-used or modified amphibolite bracers is highest. This may be a further reflection of the high value that seems to have been put on this particular rock type.

Type of re-use	Group VI	Amphibolite	Misc.	Total
As bracer	2	5	2	9
As pendant	1	5	2	8
As tool	1	0	1	2
Totals	**4**	**10**	**5**	**19**

Table 6.4. The occurrence of re-used bracers by rock type.

6.3.1 Bracers modified for continued use as bracers

Some bracers show signs of having been modified, following breakage or damage, for continued use as functional wristguards. In two cases such modifications were relatively minor. The smaller bracer from Newlands, Oyne (ID 91) possesses perforations which are located extremely close to the ends, and they seem to have been drilled after the ends themselves had been shaped. It seems likely that the original ends may have been damaged and then re-polished, with one end facet displaying faint and irregular diagonal striations. Moreover, the rounding of one of the ends appears to have encroached against the perforation itself (Figure 6.7h). The plough-damaged piece from Offham (ID 18) retains part of a re-worked edge near to the end where the perforations survive. Again the original bracer seems to have been damaged and then tidied up for continued use. At least one of the perforations may have encountered a bedding flaw during manufacture.

Sometimes bracers were cut down and/or modified by the drilling of new perforations, following major breakage. In one case, Brandon (ID 11), a new pair of centrally placed perforations was added following the breaking out of one of the original four corner perforations (Figure 6.8a) which had presumably made fastening either difficult or impossible. Two central perforations were subsequently added, one at each end and each of poorer execution than the existing perforations, presumably creating a new configuration for fastening. The fine long bracer from Sturry (ID 6), on the basis of the location of its thickest point, was possibly about 200 mm in length originally (now *c.*153 mm). Following a major break one end was re-worked and a new perforation, much more roughly executed than the original perforation at the other end, inserted. Similarly the *c.*55 mm long bracer from Glenluce (ID 77) had been cut down from a longer bracer of an estimated length of *c.*70 mm; the broken end was roughly re-bevelled, and a new, narrower perforation added (Figure 6.8b). The bracer from Calceby (ID 121) had been similarly shortened, presumably after breakage. Examination suggested that its original longitudinal profile was lentoid (Figure 6.8c), and that one end had been fractured and reworked. Two perforations had been added to the newly formed, shortened end, but these were of different character to the two original perforations at the other end. Another bracer which probably had been cut down after breakage is that from Ballogie (ID 84). This has one irregular, oblique end, which appears to have been re-worked. In the case of the bracer from Duston (ID 102), following severe ancient damage at both ends, there was a failed attempt to drill a new perforation at one end, and a break around the broken perforation at the other end had been re-polished (Figure 6.8d). Modification of this piece therefore appears to have failed, and this was also the case with the bracer from Aldbourne (ID 14) where, following a major break at one end, the broken surface was rounded off and roughly repolished (Figure 6.8e). One new corner perforation was attempted but then aborted. Modification as a new bracer seems to have been abandoned, but the piece remained in use as a potential pendant (see below).

The most successfully modified bracer studied was that from Corry Liveras (ID 87). This appears to have broken approximately across its mid point, and its original length would have been *c*.120 mm. The sides may have been 're-waisted' to make it symmetrical. The decorated end is original, while the broken surface was roughly cut, showing faint dense and regular diagonal striations which were not polished out (Figures 5.5e and 5.5f). Two new perforations were inserted, one of which may have been re-positioned after an abortive start.

6.3.2. Re-use as pendant or amulet

Eleven bracers were found as fragments which could not have functioned as bracers. The fragments may be large or small, but all have one or more perforations surviving at one end only. Some of these at least appear to have been modified for use as pendants. The re-worked bracer from Aldbourne (ID 14), a substantial fragment which retains two original perforations, has already been noted above. Another broken bracer, from Old Rayne (ID 82, Figures 6.8f and 6.8g), was fairly substantial and retained its full width. The main break is very neat, but not re-polished, and a secondary perforation had been inserted between the two original perforations at the other end. This central perforation which is of different character to the existing perforations lying on either side may have been related to the modification of the piece when it was still in use as a bracer, or may have been inserted to aid its suspension as a pendant. Another bracer, from Culbin Sands (ID 80), appears never to have been finished, as one of the terminal perforations was aborted, and may also have been used as a pendant. The still long, but cut down, bracer from Broughton-in-Craven (ID 141, Figure 6.8h) has a carefully polished broken surface and would have formed yet another example of a fine pendant. Other fragments do not exhibit any evidence of re-working or re-polishing of the broken edges, but nevertheless may have continued in use as pendants, using the surviving perforations as aids to suspension. One possible example is the fragment from Winteringham (ID 119, Figure 6.9a).

Three further bracer fragments are much smaller in size, but were found in sealed grave contexts. The broken end of one of these, from Shorncote (ID 75) was damaged during excavation so could not be studied in detail, but the broken edges of the fragments from Woodeaton (unstratified ID 3, Figure 6.9b) and Bishops Cannings (ID 32, Figure 6.9c) had been smoothed to varying extents. They may also have been re-used as pendants. However the perforated corner fragment form Wellington Quarry (ID 26) had not been re-worked and the broken edges are still fresh (Figure 6.9d). This means that it is unlikely to have been worn as a pendant as such; alternatively it may have functioned as a carefully curated un-strung amulet.

There are three more part-bracers which were not available for full detailed study, but which also probably functioned as pendants. These are the half-bracer from Fox Hole (ID 134 although there is a possibility that the unmodified fracture was modern), and two lost items: a half-bracer from Bridlington (ID 122), the broken edge of which had been 'rubbed down' (Sheppard 1930, 71–2) and another example from Dalmore (ID 127) where, again, the broken edge had been reworked (Jolly 1879). The last item was found with a set of 50 black stone disc beads, and the stone bracer-pendant may have been strung as a central ornament in this necklace, which, interestingly, was found in association with an adult male burial. Wear around perforations on the bracers as a whole was not commonly detected, but in one case, Culbin Sands (ID 80) wear at the upper edge of the surviving perforation, showed distinct wear on the front surface (Figure 6.9e). This would be in accord with usage as a pendant. The marked occurrence of half bracers has been noted. It is unlikely that bracers would have broken exactly across the centre if dropped accidentally, so this occurrence may indicate that sometimes bracers had been broken deliberately. Certainly the 'saw' marks on the part bracers from Aldbourne (ID 14) and Corry Liveras (ID 87) would lend support to such a hypothesis. The phenomenon is much more prevalent in Ireland, where a high proportion of the red jasper pendants were broken, apparently deliberately, and then re-used as pendants (Roe and Woodward 2009). It has been noted that some of the Iberian engraved stone plaques had been re-used in this way (Lillios 2002, 139 and fig 2a), so the idea may not have been a new one. Such deliberate breakage may have been associated with exchange and distribution of fragments within family and other social networks. Such a process has been termed social enchainment by Chapman (2000).

6.3.3. Re-use as tools

Only two examples of bracers show evidence of modification for re-use as tools. In the case of the bracer from Lindridge (ID 111) in the miscellaneous rocks group, a broken end had been bevelled on both sides to form an even sharp edge. However this edge, which appeared to have been designed as a cutting edge perhaps for a chisel, did not display much evidence of use-wear (Figure 6.9f). Neither was there any evidence for hafting, and with the added evidence of an attempt to bore a new central perforation at the other end, it may be that this piece was also intended to function as a pendant. A second modified Group VI bracer however did show signs of extensive usage as a tool. This was the half bracer from Raunds (ID 116), where the broken edge showed extensive wear polish, and pairs of nicks on the rear sides may have functioned as aids to the hafting of a handle (Figure 6.9g). The tool may have been used for burnishing leather (Healy and Harding 2004).

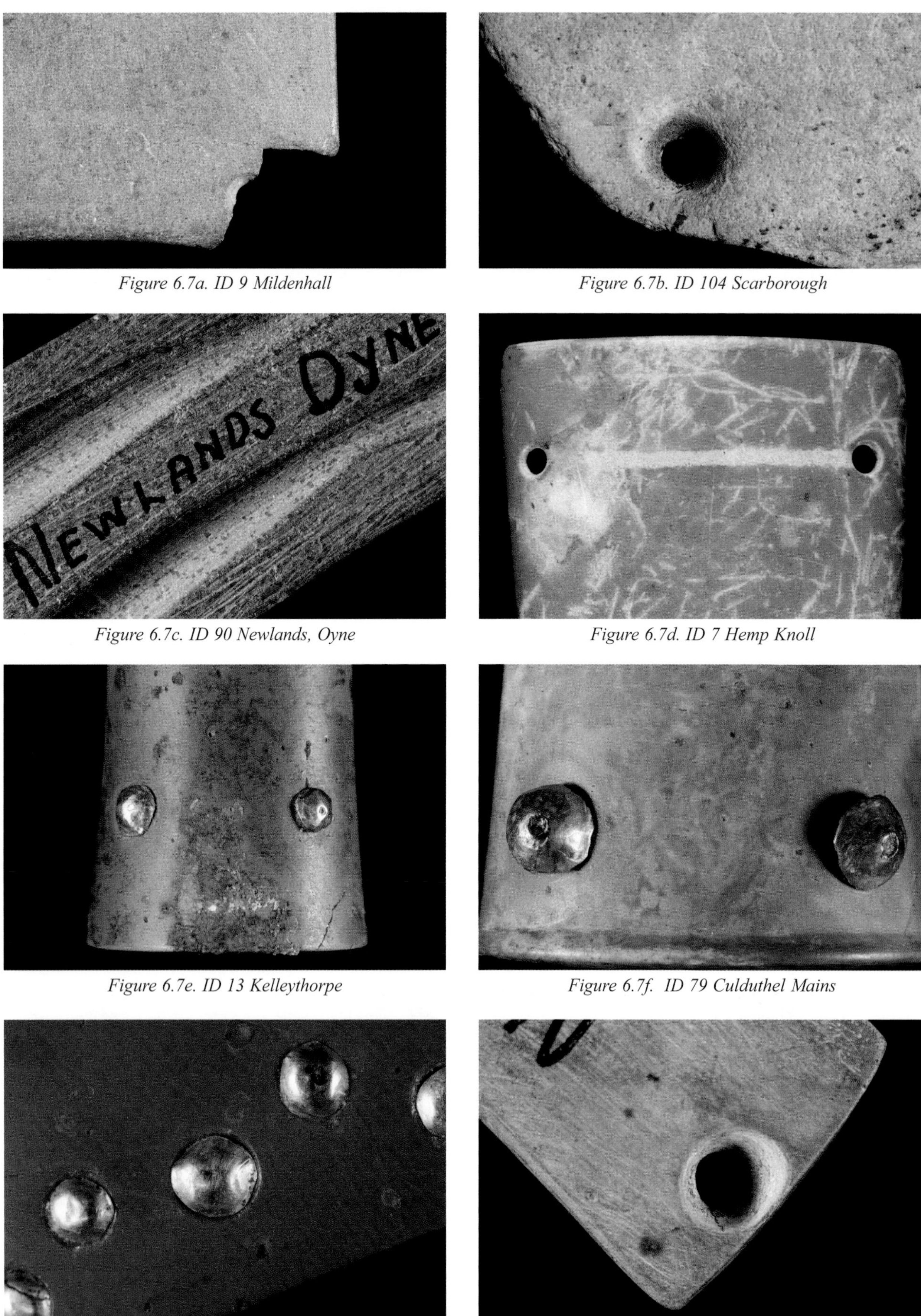

Figure 6.7a. ID 9 Mildenhall

Figure 6.7b. ID 104 Scarborough

Figure 6.7c. ID 90 Newlands, Oyne

Figure 6.7d. ID 7 Hemp Knoll

Figure 6.7e. ID 13 Kelleythorpe

Figure 6.7f. ID 79 Culduthel Mains

Figure 6.7g. ID 8 Barnack

Figure 6.7h. ID 91 Newlands, Oyne

Figure 6.7. Details of bracer features: 6.7a, a fracture probably rendering bracer useless; 6.7b, thong wear on front; 6.7c, thong groove on rear; 6.7d, shadow of thong across front; 6.7e, dents in gold caps; 6.7f, small perforations in gold caps; 6.7g, scratched wear marks on gold caps; 6.7h, perforation close to ?modified end.

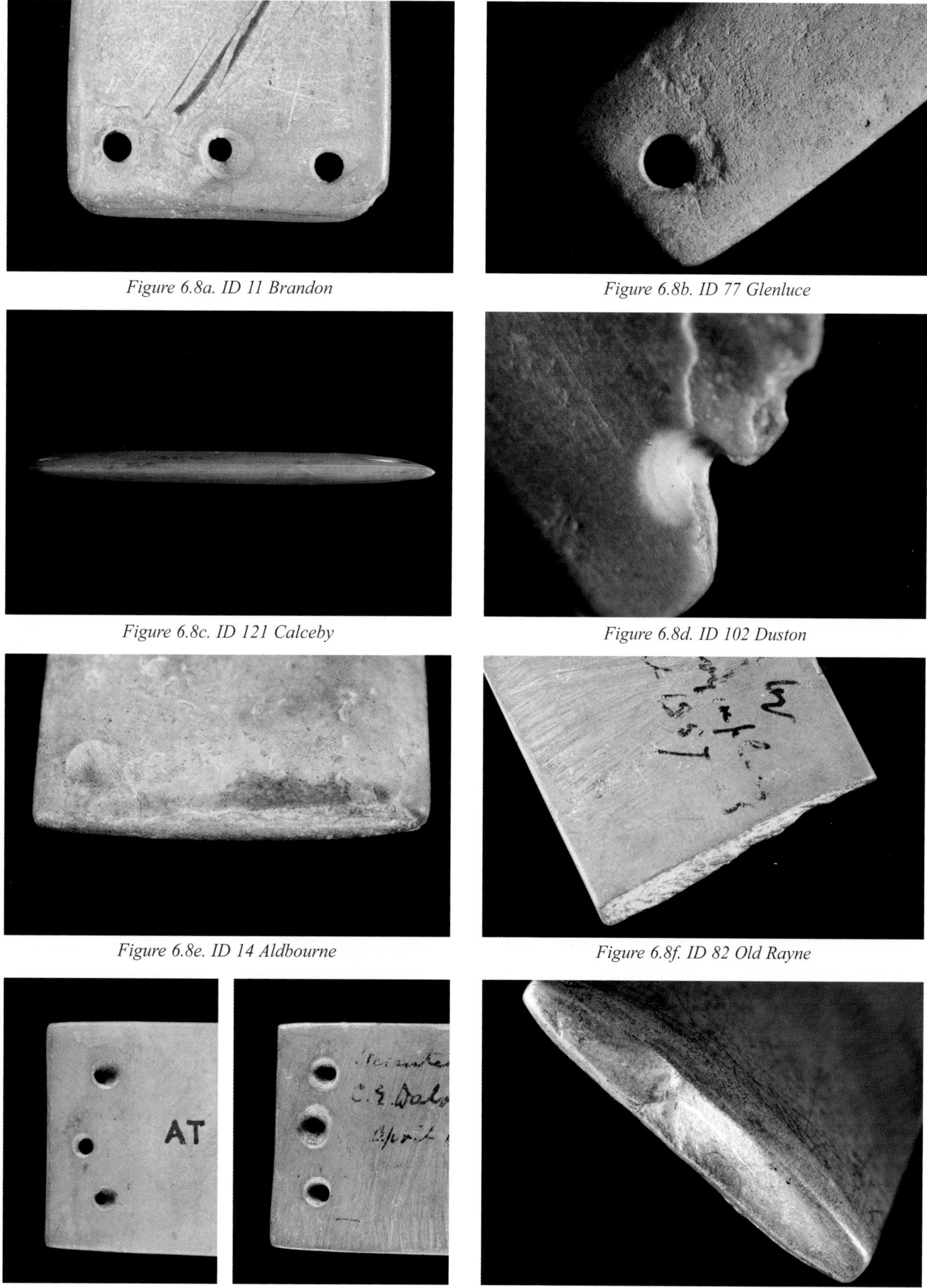

Figure 6.8a. ID 11 Brandon

Figure 6.8b. ID 77 Glenluce

Figure 6.8c. ID 121 Calceby

Figure 6.8d. ID 102 Duston

Figure 6.8e. ID 14 Aldbourne

Figure 6.8f. ID 82 Old Rayne

Figure 6.8g. ID 82 Old Rayne

Figure 6.8h. ID 141 Broughton-in-Craven

Figure 6.8. Details of bracer features: 6.8a, a new pair of centrally placed perforations (one shown); 6.8b, a new, narrower perforation in a cut down original bracer; 6.8c, the uneven profile of a original longer bracer; 6.8d, re-polishing of edge around broken perforation; 6.8e, a rounded and polished surface after fracturing; 6.8f and 6.8g, bracer showing fracture and secondary central perforation at original end; 6.8h, a polished, broken surface.

Figure 6.9a. ID 119 Winteringham

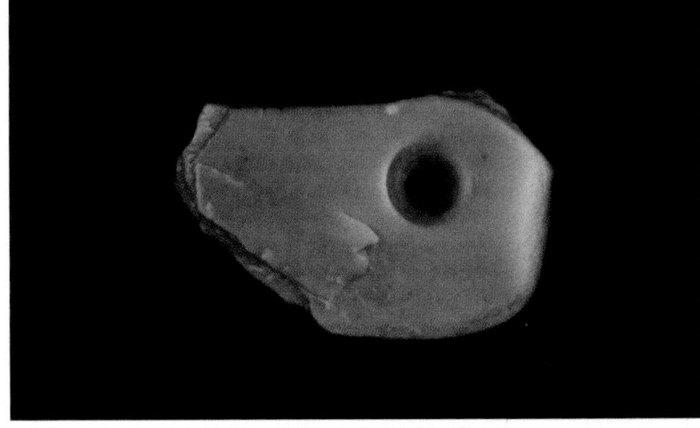

Figure 6.9b. ID 3 Woodeaton

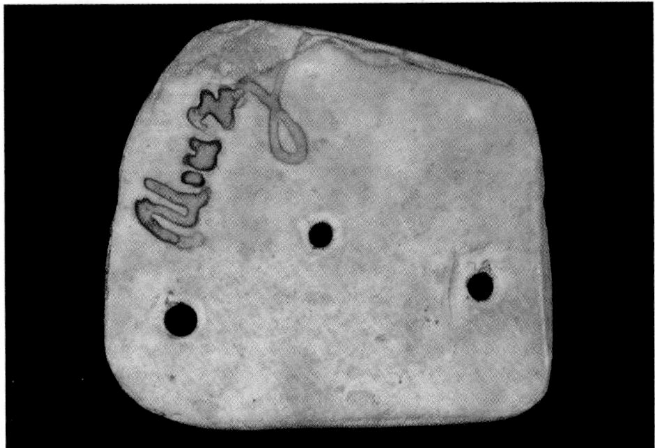

Figure 6.9c. ID 32 Bishops Cannings

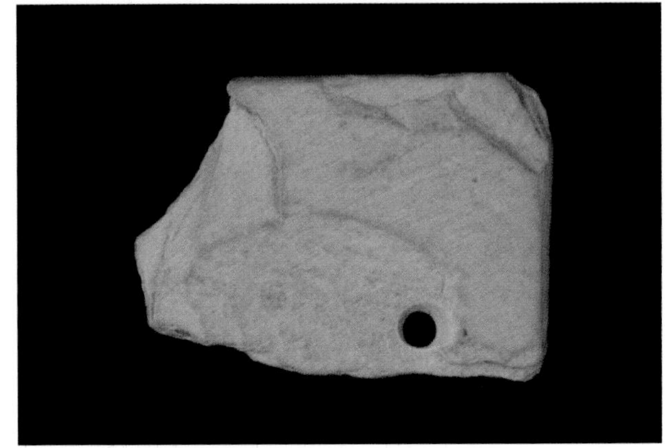

Figure 6.9d. ID 26 Wellington Quarry

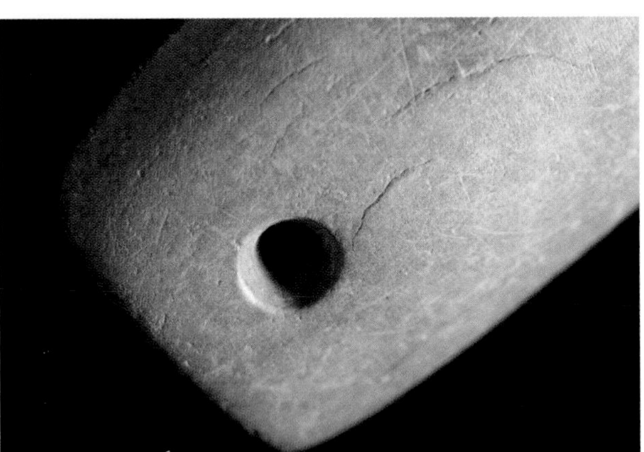

Figure 6.9e. ID 80 Culbin Sands

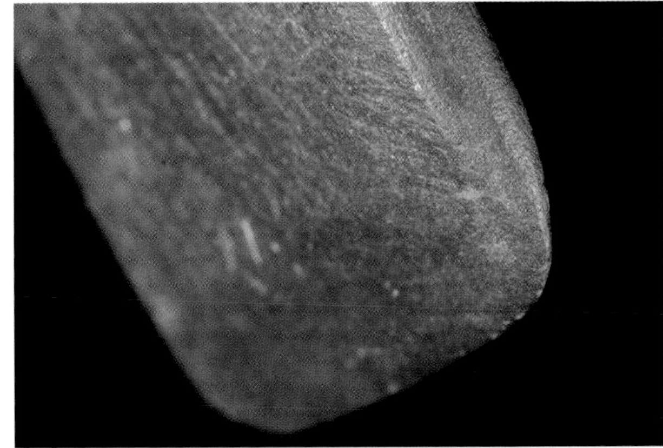

Figure 6.9f. ID 111 Lindridge

Figure 6.9g. ID 116 Raunds

Figure 6.9. Details of bracer features: 6.9a, broken bracer probably re-used as pendant, but broken edges unworked or re-polished; 6.9b and 6.9c, broken bracers probably re-used as pendant with smoothed broken edges; 6.9d, broken bracer probably re-used as pendant or amulet, but not re-worked or re-polished; 6.9e, wear on upper edge of perforation; 6.9f, broken bracer possibly re-worked as a tool; 6.9g, wear polish and possible hafting marks.

Type of re-use	Worn	Slightly worn	Indeterminate	Total
As bracer	6	4	0	10
As pendant	4	2	1	7
As tool	1	1	0	2
Bracers not re-used	15	28	0	43
All bracers	**26**	**35**	**1**	**62**

Table 6.5. The occurrence of wear on re-used bracers.

6.3.4. Overall wear category

It might be expected that bracers which had been re-used after breakage, either as refurbished bracers, or as tools or pendants, would exhibit more traces of wear than the general run of *de novo* bracers. A compilation of the totals for overall wear categories for the re-used items, set against the total dataset, is shown in Table 6.5. It can be seen that within the total dataset more bracers are slightly worn (56%) than worn. The items re-used as bracers, tools or pendants show more wear (58% of the re-used items), and if these are extracted from the main dataset, the non re-used bracers show a low incidence of wear at only 38% of the non re-used items. Thus the re-used items do indeed show more traces of wear, as originally postulated.

7: CHRONOLOGY

Ann Woodward

7.1 INTRODUCTION

In 1970 David Clarke was able to summarise the relative chronology of bracers which had been found in association with Beaker vessels up until the late 1960s. His results are embedded in a correlation chart within his Appendix 3 (Clarke 1970, 448). He concluded that flat bracers of Atkinson type B belonged mainly within his Middle Rhenish group, while the curved bracers of Atkinson type C1 and bracers of ovoid outline (type A) had a later currency, and were associated with Beakers of northern types only. Since 1970, the excavation of a significant number of new Beaker graves containing bracers has occurred and a series of associated radiocarbon determinations have been obtained. This allows a new appraisal of the dating of British bracers, although, as always, an increase in data and knowledge throws up several problems along with the desired answers.

There are two factors in particular which may affect the interpretation of absolute, or indeed relative, dates. Firstly this study has shown that bracers were often re-worked as new bracers, or to form new items such as pendants (Chapter 6). Also some of them display breakage, continued use and modification after minor breakage, and varying degrees of use wear. Thus an individual bracer may have had a long use life, possibly over several centuries. This means that the date of the grave, which usually has been obtained from the human bone, may not relate directly to the date of original manufacture of the bracer. Secondly, but linked to the first point, some of the bracers have been found in contexts of full Early Bronze Age date, usually in association with cremations. It seems likely that such pieces were heirlooms that had been in long circulation since their time of manufacture. Assessment of dating therefore needs to take into account the nature of the individual bracer concerned, including evidence for ancient breaks, re-working and use wear.

7.2 RADIOCARBON DATING

There are 26 radiocarbon determinations from 17 sites which relate to contexts containing bracers, and these are listed in detail in Table 7.1. Twenty-three of the dates apply to classic Beaker grave groups, while that from Old Rayne (ID 82) relates to a cremation found in a pit centrally placed within a recumbent stone circle, and that from Lockerbie (ID 150) is from an Early Bronze Age cremation burial. In the table the dates are arranged by rock type of the bracer (miscellaneous rocks, amphibolite and Group VI), and, within the three categories, in roughly chronological order.

The simplest issue to discuss is the question of the date of start of use. The earliest dates for bracers in Britain are for three that are red or black in colour and of unusually long and narrow form. Earliest of all is the well-known date for the Amesbury Archer burial (ID 56 and 57). The two bracers from this grave group are red and black, colours that are unusual in Britain, while the morphology of the two pieces is suggestive of a continental style of manufacture (Fitzpatrick 2011). The black bracer (ID 57) may be a direct continental import but the red one (ID 56) seems to owe more to Irish inspiration, although made by a continental hand (*ibid*). It may be bracers such as these which were associated with the first introduction of the artefact type to Britain. Falling not far behind chronologically is the burial from Dornoch Nursery (ID 94) with another red bracer, and the choice of red stone here may also be the result of contacts with Ireland. All three bracers are in near-pristine condition, although all had suffered some wear, particularly the black bracer with the Amesbury Archer burial (ID 57). Thus the radiocarbon dates may provide a reasonable guide to the likely time of manufacture.

However, there are dates for amphibolite bracers which are almost as early. These include the amphibolite bracer from Thomas Hardye School (ID 67) which is a near perfect piece with only one tiny ancient chip and which may have been never, or hardly ever, used. The other amphibolite bracer with an early date, from Sewell (ID 12), shows signs of slight wear, so may have been manufactured a little earlier than the radiocarbon date implies. Curved bracers made from Group VI rock may follow along just a bit later, as three further dates seem to suggest. An intact bracer from Borrowstone (ID 89) had also seen slight wear and so the bracer may have been made somewhat before the time of the burial to which the date relates. The same applies to the Fyrish example (ID 78), which again is just slightly worn. The new date for the Hemp Knoll burial (ID 7), again with a well-used Group VI bracer, also falls early. Thus the available dates suggest that all these types of bracer, made from red or black, Group VI or amphibolite materials were in use from, or soon after, the time of the earliest Beaker use in Britain, as currently understood. However, this general conclusion cannot be applied to the bracers of the miscellaneous rocks in general, because there is only one radiocarbon date which relates to the more common grey and brown bracers belonging to this morphological group. This is the date for the concavo-convex Newlands, Oyne (ID 90) bracer which was associated with another made from Group VI rock (ID 91) in a Beaker cist. This date lies considerably later than those for the earliest red and black bracers. The bracer from the Stonehenge burial (ID 58) is slightly different. It is almost black in colour but it is not of the long narrow and precise form characteristic of the other early red and black bracers. The date for this burial, derived from the mean of five determinations, is imprecise, with a probable range of 2400–2140 cal BC.

Apart from the early dates for the bracer burials at Thomas Hardye School (ID 67) and Sewell (ID 12) referred to above, the only other date available for an amphibolite bracer is that from Gravelly Guy (ID 74). In view of the other artefact types represented in this interesting grave group Needham has suggested that this grave belongs to a complex but limited time zone, falling around the time of his 'fission horizon' of 2250–2150 cal BC, a period when Beakers became more common and much diversification of styles took place (Needham 2005, 204–5). An alternative view for Gravelly Guy, suggested by Fiona Roe (pers. comm.), is that the bracer may itself be an heirloom, rather older than some of the other elements within the grave group. However, the bracer shows little damage and is only slightly worn.

Most of the radiocarbon dates still to be discussed relate to graves containing bracers made from Group VI rock, often in the distinctive form with concavo-convex profile. With the exception of the early date for Hemp Knoll (ID 7) (see above) there are four determinations which fall in roughly the same time span, occurring after the 'fission horizon' and within the Early Bronze Age period (see Needham 2005, fig. 13). Three of the bracers concerned are only slightly worn and display only a few ancient chips in each case, from Culduthel Mains (ID 79), Newlands, Oyne (ID 91) and Barnack (ID 8), and the dates may well relate approximately to the time of manufacture of the bracers. However the fourth bracer, from Raunds (ID 116) is a very worn piece, re-worked and re-used as a tool, and its date of manufacture may have been somewhat earlier. The latest reliable date therefore for the Group VI bracers as a whole is that for Ferry Fryston (ID 73). Slightly later than the group of bracers just discussed, this may be a good indicator of the extended currency of this class of bracer, lasting perhaps until around 2000 cal BC. The relatively late date for a Group VI bracer, from the Hemp Knoll burial (ID 7), falling well within the full Early Bronze Age, has been questioned by Needham in relation to the style of the associated Beaker vessel (Needham 2005, 195) and is further called into question by the new date obtained from the human bone (see above). In terms of the bracer, we may note that the piece was well worn, with many ancient chips and a broken perforation. It had, however, continued in use after breakage, and it may have possessed a very long use life. The bone toggle from this grave was also extremely worn, and had been re-used after significant breakage, and both items may have been heirlooms.

7.3 DATING BY ASSOCIATION WITH BEAKERS

The classic and innovative typological systems developed by Clarke (1970) and Lanting and Van der Waals (1972) were successively reassessed and simplified by Case (e.g. 1977 and 1993). However the disjunction between all the classificatory schemes and the available radiocarbon dates remained unresolved (Kinnes *et al.* 1991). More recently a radically new assessment of the entire Beaker sequence, based particularly on nuances of vessel profile, has been undertaken by Needham (2005), and this system fits much more neatly with the ever-increasing set of available radiocarbon dates.

There are 39 Beaker vessels which have been found in close association with 33 bracers, plus one group of sherds found in a pit with one bracer. These are listed in Table 7.2, where the various contexts are listed in order of the three bracer rock groups. Full references are given to the types as identified by Clarke (1970) and to the corpus and illustration numbers employed within that work. The classifications have been revised by Needham in relation to the novel scheme proposed by him in 2005. In instances where the Beakers concerned were illustrated in his seminal paper (Needham 2005) the figure number is shown in the table. Where no such figure number appears, the vessel has been assessed anew by Needham, using available published or unpublished illustrations (pers. comm.). The correlation between bracer finds belonging to the three main rock groups and the new Beaker types defined by Needham in 2005 is shown in Table 7.3.

The Needham category codes listed in the table are arranged in rough chronological order, from left to right. Low Carinated (LC) Beakers are the earliest, occurring mainly before the 'fission horizon', and some Mid Carinated (MC) vessels also begin early (see Needham 2005, fig. 13). Tall Mid Carinated (TMC) and Short-Necked (SN) forms were current mainly just after the 'fission horizon', although SN Beakers lasted longer. Long-Necked Beakers (LN) started after the 'fission horizon' and lasted well into the full (Wessex 1) Early Bronze Age, as did some varieties of the S-Profiled class (SP).

The figures shown in Table 7.3 serve to confirm the

Bracer ID	Rock type	Site name	Sample	Bkr type	Lab no	Date BP	cal BC 1 sigma	cal BC 2 sigma	
56/57	red/black	Amesbury Archer	human bone	LC	P-13852	3895±32	2460–2310	2470–2280	
94	red/black	Dornoch Nursery	cremation	LC	GrA-26515	3850±40	2410–2200	2460–2200	
82	misc	Old Rayne	cremation	urn	Gra-23982	3690±45	2140–1970	2200–1949	
58	red/black	Stonehenge	human bone	none	BM-1582, OxA-4886	mean of 5			
					OxA-5044 to 5046	3817±27		2400–2140	
90	misc	Newlands, Oyne		SN	V-2243-46	3757±29	2280–2060	2290–2040	Curtis *et al.* 2007
150	misc	Lockerbie	cremation	none	SUERC-19244	3635±25	2030–1955	2130–1920	
					(GU-16741)				
67	amphibolite	Thomas Hardye School		MC	R-29080/4	3856±30	2460–2190		Gardiner *et al.* 2007
12	amphibolite	Sewell	human bone	LC/MC	SUERC-26194	3830±30	2340–2200	2460–2150	Beaker People Project
74	amphibolite	Gravelly Guy	human bone	LN	UB-3122	3709±35	2190–2180	2200–1970	
89	Group VI	Borrowstone	human bone	SN	GrA-29082	3820±40	2340–2140	2460–2130	Shepherd 2005
			human bone		GrA-29083	3835±40	2400–2200	2460–2140	
78	Group VI	Fyrish	human bone	SN	OxA-13213	3816±29	2295–2200	2400–2140	
91	Group VI	Newlands, Oyne		SN	V-2243-46	3757±29	2280–2060	2290–2040	Curtis *et al.* 2007
8	Group VI	Barnack		TMC	BM-2956	3742±30	2200–2130	2280–2030	
					BM-1412		2080–2040		
79	Group VI	Culduthel Mains	human bone	SN	SUERC-26462	3735±35	2200–2040	2280–2020	National Museums Scotland
116	Group VI	Raunds	chamber sapwood	LN	OxA-7902	3775±45	2200–2030	2280–2250	
								2210–2020	
			human bone	LN	UB-3148	3681±47			
73	Group VI	Ferry Fryston	human bone	LN	SUERC-2263	3732±27	2200–2130	2210–2030	
							2090–2040		
7	Group VI	Hemp Knoll	charcoal	SN	NPL-139	3750±140	2030–1770	2140–1740	
					Har-2998	3540±70			
			human bone		OxA-2271-34	3834±29	2341–2206	2458–2200	Beaker People Project

Table 7.1. List of available radiocarbon dates from contexts containing bracers.

Bracer ID	Rock type	Site	County	DLC code	DLC no	DLC fig	SN code	SN sub-code	SN 2005
56	red/black	Amesbury Archer	Wilts	LC			LC x 2		table 1
57	red/black	Amesbury Archer					SP (low bellied), 2 x ?		
90	misc	Newlands, Oyne	Scotland	N4	1478	721	SN		
94	red/black	Dornoch Nursery	Scotland	AOC			LC		fig 5,13
108	misc	Ben Bridge	Somerset				diverse in form and decoration		
149	misc	Thanet	Kent	E Ang			MC		
153	red/black	Cliffe	Kent	E Ang			SP	Globular	
2	amphibolite	Stanton Harcourt	Oxon	AOC	774	not ill	TMC	all over cord	
4	amphibolite	Winterslow Hut	Wilts	W/MR	1204	134	TMC		fig 6,8
11	amphibolite	Brandon Fields	Suffolk	FN	852	429	SP	Globular	
				FN	853	430	MC		
12	amphibolite	Sewell	Beds	W/MR			LC/MC	Maritime-derived	fig 5,7
26	amphibolite	Wellington Quarry	Heref	E			LC	Maritime-derived	fig 5,3
28	amphibolite	Roundway	Wilts	W/MR	1135	132	LC	Maritime-derived	fig 5.5
66	amphibolite	West Stafford	Dorset				LC		
67	amphibolite	Thomas Hardye School	Dorset				MC		
74	amphibolite	Gravelly Guy	Oxon				LN	earlier series	fig 9,2
75	amphibolite	Shorncote	Gloucs				SP (lacking base and rim)		OxArch
107	amphibolite	Aston 1	Derbys				base lost ?LC/MC		
137	amphibolite	Pyecombe	W Sussex	E Ang			TMC		fig 6,6
144	amphibolite?	Mere	Wilts	W/MR	1125	130	LC	Maritime-derived	
154	amphibolite	Monkton	Kent				? (profile not yet reconstructed)		
1	Group VI	Dorchester XII	Oxon	W/MR	735	128	TMC		fig 6,7
7	Group VI	Hemp Knoll	Wilts	W/MR			SN		fig 8,10
8	Group VI	Barnack	Cambs	W/MR			TMC		fig 6,4
13	Group VI	Kelleythorpe	Yorks	N2(L)	1265	553	SN (neck angle indistinct)		fig 8,4
73	Group VI	Ferry Fryston	Yorks				LN		table 5
78	Group VI	Fyrish	Scotland	N4	1749	719	SN		fig 8,12
79	Group VI	Culduthel Mains	Scotland	N2(L)			SN (may be marginal to LN)		
86	Group VI	Glen Forsa	Scotland	N3	1531	676	SN		
				N2(L)	1532	677	Necked – rim lost		
89	Group VI	Borrowstone	Scotland	N2(L)			SN		
91	Group VI	Newlands, Oyne	Scotland	N4	1478	721	SN		
101	Group VI	Ardiffery	Scotland	N2(L)	1423	551	SN		
						552	SN		
105	Group VI	Melton Quarry	Yorks	AOC	1344	136	(Rim sherd only?)		
116	Group VI	Raunds 1	Northants				LN	earlier series	fig 9,5

Table 7.2. List of bracers (by rock type) found in Beaker contexts.

	Needham Beaker category						
Rock type	LC	LC/MC	MC	TMC	SN	LN	SP
Red or black	2						1
Amphibolite	4	2	2	3		1	2
Group VI				2	9	2	
Miscellaneous rock			1		1		

Table 7.3. The occurrence of bracers with Beakers classified according to Needham (2005) in rough chronological order. Key: LC = Low Carinated; MC = Mid Carinated; TMC = Tall Mid Carinated; SN = Short-Necked; LN = Long-Necked; SP = S-Profiled class.

information already derived from the available radiocarbon dates, and also to amplify the tentative conclusions. Firstly, the early occurrence of some red and black bracers is once again apparent. The pattern of dating for the Group VI bracers also is similar to that gained from the radiocarbon dates. Most of the associations (with TMC, SN and LN Beakers) would have dated from the period around and after the 'fission horizon'. The surprise comes with the consideration of the amphibolite bracers. The early currency suggested by the radiocarbon dates for Thomas Hardye School (ID 67) and Sewell (ID 12) is now strongly confirmed by four instances of amphibolite bracers occurring with Low Carinated Beakers, two with Mid Carinated vessels and two more with vessels of LC/MC form. Particularly interesting is the lack of Short-Necked Beakers with bracers of amphibolite. In part this may be influenced by the geographical distribution of these bracers. Most derive from southern England, and SN Beakers tend to display more northerly concentrations. However the only later context, which involves the LN Beaker from Gravelly Guy has already been questioned above. The amphibolite bracer from this grave might be an heirloom item.

The evidence of Beaker dating therefore seems to suggest that the long and slender red and black bracers may well have been primary. Bracers of amphibolite and Group VI rock all may have been in existence from fairly soon thereafter, but it can now be asserted that the amphibolite bracers were more prevalent in the earlier stages, before and during Needham's 'fission horizon', whilst the Group VI bracers were current from the 'fission horizon' onwards.

7.4 DATING BY ASSOCIATION WITH DAGGERS

Prior to the more extensive employment of radiocarbon dating, much discussion of final Neolithic and Early Bronze Age chronology has hinged upon detailed typological analysis of the morphology and contexts of metal daggers. The standard corpus and typological scheme is that devised by Gerloff (1975). Much of this scheme has stood the test of time, although due to the excavation of further dagger graves since the early 1970s, and to renewed research, some of the typology has been refined and some key chronological conclusions have been revised. Daggers which have been found in association with bracers belong mainly to the tanged copper series, with a few belonging to the flat riveted styles, and to the knife-dagger category. The tanged copper daggers (Gerloff 1975, nos. 1–19) are some of the earliest metal objects to be found in Britain, whilst the flat riveted category (*ibid*, nos. 20–105) represent the earliest use of bronze i.e. copper alloyed with tin. The main changes to the Gerloff scheme which relate to the period of bracer use are the sub-division of some of her categories (e.g. Needham 2004) and the back-dating of the flat riveted series. Gerloff originally envisaged that flat riveted daggers were roughly contemporary with the Wessex daggers of her Armorico-British types (Gerloff 1975, 47–9, 51–2, 56–7, 61–3, 65 and 67–8). However a series of new radiocarbon dates have shown that flat riveted daggers were being made much earlier than this, in the two centuries preceding 2000 cal BC (see Baker *et al.* 2003 and Needham 2007, 289 relating to the Rameldry and Ferry Fryston daggers respectively). Sheridan and Cowie supply a useful table of four radiocarbon dates for riveted flat daggers (Baker *et al.* 2003, 109, table 3), to which the date for Ferry Fryston may be added. A detailed discussion of this re-dating, and some of the implications, has been provided by Gerloff in her report relating to the dagger from the bracer grave at Gravelly Guy (Lambrick and Allen 2004, 82–87). Needham concluded that the important change from copper to bronze metallurgy occurred in the 22nd century cal BC, roughly contemporary with the 'fission horizon' which he defined in his new typo-chronological scheme for British Beakers (Needham 2005; Needham 2007, 288).

There are 14 sites where metal daggers have been found in association with bracers and a further dagger from Monkton, associated with bracer ID 154, awaits publication. These are listed in Table 7.4, where the classifications are summarised and the bracer rock types listed. In one of these the blade survived only as small fragments, but the bone pommel was present (Pyecombe ID 137). Six out of the seven amphibolite bracers found with identifiable daggers were associated with tanged copper daggers of the pre-'fission horizon' period. Most of these belong to Gerloff's simple Roundway or Mere groups, which were probably the earliest, with only one (Sittingbourne ID 10) falling into her group of slightly developed small blades with perforated tang, which may be a little later in date.

ID	Rock type	Site name	Type	Group	Gerloff	Notes
56 57	red and black	Amesbury Archer	Tanged copper			Three daggers
4	amphibolite	Winterslow	Tanged copper	Roundway	G4	
10	amphibolite	Sittingbourne	Tanged copper	Small		
26	amphibolite	Wellington Quarry	Tanged copper	Mere		Stain only
28	amphibolite	Roundway	Tanged copper	Roundway	G1	
67	amphibolite	T Hardye School	Tanged copper	Mere		Outline only
74	amphibolite	Gravelly Guy	Flat riveted	Butterwick		Tanged pommel
137	amphibolite	Pyecombe	Frags only			Tanged pommel
144	probably amphibolite	Mere	Tanged copper	Mere	G6	Bracer lost
1	Group VI	Dorchester XII	Tanged copper	Small	G10	
1	Group VI	Dorchester XII	Knife-dagger	With projecting butt	G239	
8	Group VI	Barnack	Tanged copper	Mere		
13	Group VI	Kelleythorpe	Knife-dagger	With projecting butt	G237	
73	Group VI	Ferry Fryston	Flat riveted	Milston		Needham type: Ferry Fryston
86	Group VI	Glen Forsa	Tanged copper	Very Small	G14	

Table 7.4 . Copper and bronze daggers associated with stone bracers.

One such dagger (not associated with a bracer) has a surviving tanged bone pommel (Shrewton 5k: Gerloff no. 12), which is identical in form to that from Pyecombe. This may indicate that the Pyecombe dagger was also of this small tanged copper type. The final amphibolite bracer is that from Gravelly Guy (ID 74) associated with a bronze flat riveted dagger of Butterwick type. However, Needham has suggested that this dagger may fall early within the flat riveted dagger series, and, as discussed above, the bracer might be an heirloom within this dated grave.

Three Group VI bracers also occur in association with tanged copper daggers. These belong to Gerloff's Mere, Small and Very Small groups respectively (see Table 7.4). These small-sized tanged copper daggers tend to have perforated tangs, and it is interesting therefore that the two knife-daggers associated with Group VI bracers are also of the fairly rare type with projecting and perforated butt. These are a sophisticated form of knife-dagger and were probably contemporary with the varieties of tanged copper dagger with perforated butts. All of these however may have been slightly later than the Mere type dagger from Barnack (ID 8). Latest of all was the dagger from Ferry Fryston. Similar to Gerloff's Milston type of flat riveted bronze dagger, this dagger has been grouped by Needham with a few others to make up his new Ferry Fryston type (Needham 2007, table 30). He sees this new dagger type as being a little earlier in date than the Milston type (*ibid*, 288), so possibly earlier than the Type Butterwick flat riveted dagger from the Gravelly Guy amphibolite bracer grave.

It can be concluded from the foregoing discussion that current thinking on the dating of dagger types shows that the range of daggers associated with amphibolite bracers tends to be somewhat earlier than those associated with bracers made from Group VI rock. However, both types of bracer do have single associations with bronze flat riveted daggers dating from around or after the 'fission horizon'. This might suggest that both types of bracer had long currencies. However, if the Gravelly Guy bracer is accepted to be an heirloom, then the tendency for amphibolite bracers to be earlier is amplified. In general these conclusions concur with the results of the analysis of Beaker associations discussed above.

7.5 DATING BY ASSOCIATION WITH FLINT ARROWHEADS

Flint arrowheads were not included in Needham's diagram, but in the light of the typological scheme and associated patterns of dating devised by Green (1980) some useful information may be gained. In Table 7.5 the types of arrowhead found in association with bracers, according to Green's nomenclature, are listed. It is interesting to note that about half of the sites involved have been excavated since the publication of Green's corpus in 1980.

Most of the arrowheads are of Sutton type, with a few examples of the fancy versions: the Ballyclare, Conygar and Green Lowe types. The Sutton and Conygar types are found throughout the chronological span of barbed and tanged arrowheads (Green 1980, 129–30), whilst those

Site	Bracer ID	Rock	Arrowheads	Green type	Reference
Winterslow 3	4	Amphibolite	2	Ballyclare	Green no.254
Wellington Quarry	26	Amphibolite	4 + 3 blanks	Sutton a x 1 Sutton b x 2 Conygar x 1	Harrison *et al.* 1999, fig. 6
Roundway 8	28	Amphibolite	1	Sutton b	Green no.206
Tring	31	Group VI	3	?Green Low	Green no.182
Amesbury Archer	57	Red and black	17	Sutton b x 12 Sutton c x 1 Green Low x 1 Conygar x 2 Sutton b/ Conygar x 1	Fitzpatrick 2003, 149
Stonehenge	58	Misc	3	Sutton x 1 Conygar x 2	Evans 1984, 20-21
T. Hardye School	67	Amphibolite	3	Sutton	Gardiner *et al.* 2007, fig. 9b
Culduthel Mains	79	Group VI	8	Sutton x 1 Conygar x 6 Green Low x 1	Clarke *et al.* 1985, fig.4.16
Newlands, Oyne	90 and 91	Group VI Misc	1	?Sutton b	Green no.21
Dornoch Nursery	94	Red	5	Sutton	Ashmore 1989, 69-70
Ardiffery	101	Group VI	7	Sutton b	Green no.27
Aston 1	107	Amphibolite	1	Sutton b	Green no.152

Table 7.5. Flint arrowheads from bracer graves. Notes: the arrowheads from the Stonehenge burial were in the body, not grave goods; the Culduthel Mains arrowheads were identified by Alan Saville; Amesbury Archer data from forthcoming report by Phil Harding, courtesy of Andrew Fitzpatrick.

of Green Low type tend to occur in late Beaker contexts only (see Green 1980, tables VI, 8 and VI, 9). Moreover, this pattern is neatly confirmed by the association of five Green Low arrowheads with the S4 Beaker from ring ditch 201, grave 203 at Barrow Hills, Radley, Oxon (Barclay and Halpin 1999, fig. 4.78). It is interesting therefore to note that Green Low arrowheads were found with the Group VI bracer from Culduthel Mains (ID 79) and in the grave from Tring which also included two Group VI bracers (ID 31 and 146) and a jet pulley ring. The latter is also a late Beaker type (see below), and so this association adds weight to the hypothesis that the Group VI bracers tended to occur late in the overall Beaker sequence. However, it should be noted that one Green Low arrowhead was found amongst the group of 17 in the early grave of the Amesbury Archer (ID 56 and 57).

7.6 DATING BY ASSOCIATION WITH OTHER ARTEFACTS

There are various other categories of artefact which can be used, on the basis of repeated associations with other dated objects or radiocarbon dates, to provide chronological information in relation to bracers. Many of these were discussed systematically by Clarke (1970: see his summary diagram on page 448), and the general principles of time spans and potential overlaps between artefact types have been depicted in diagrammatic form by Needham (2005, figs. 11 and 12). The types can be grouped into two main chronological zones which fall before and after the 'fission horizon' of 2250–2150 cal BC, although most of them occupy an area of intense overlap in the period immediately following that horizon. The remaining discussion will consider artefact types in these two chronological zones, which are for simplicity referred to as 'early' and 'late' types.

7.6.1. Early types

The spectacle-shaped bone belt ring found with the Group VI bracer from Melton Quarry (ID 105) is matched by similar items from Folkton 245, Burial 8, Yorkshire (Kinnes and Longworth 1985, 116), associated with an LC Beaker, one from Stanton Harcourt XXI, 1a, also with an LC Beaker (Barclay *et al.* 1995, fig. 53) and another from a pit just outside Wilsford G1, Wilts (ID 1073), associated with two Beakers of early type and an early radiocarbon date of 3878±20 BP, 2460–2290 cal BC at 2 sigma; NZA-29534 (Leivers and Moore 2008, 25–30). These are related morphologically to simple circular belt rings such as that from Wilsford G1 (Clarke 1970, fig. 138) once again associated with an early (LC) Beaker burial. The more complex belt ring from Sittingbourne, found with an amphibolite bracer (ID 10), may be related to this series, although it was also associated with a dagger with a riveted tang which may date rather later (see above).

Spatulae of bone or antler occur in four bracer graves, where they are associated with Beakers of LC form, at Boscombe Down (Amesbury Archer ID 56 and 57) and Mere (ID 144) and with the later LN type, at Gravelly Guy (ID 74) and Raunds (ID 116). Other graves containing spatulae have mainly been associated with Beakers of developed (especially LN) types (Green Low, Bakewell, Mouse Low, Smerrill Moor, West Overton 6b and Amesbury 51 (Clarke 1970, figs. 776, 757, 862, 846 and nos. 139, 1131, not ill, also Radley grave 203, see above). There is only one other association with an early LC Beaker, from Stanton Harcourt XV, grave 1/1 (*ibid*, fig. 191). These associations suggest that spatulae were in use throughout the currency of Beakers. Although present in some of the earliest graves, they appear to have been more prevalent after the 'fission horizon' than may be indicated in Needham's diagram (Needham 2005, fig. 12).

Gold tress rings are not included in Needham's diagram, but are consistently associated with Beaker groups of early date. A pair of tress rings occurs with two bracers from the Amesbury Archer grave (ID 56 and 57), while radiocarbon dates for the pairs from Chilbolton and the 'Amesbury Archer's Companion' also fall early in the sequence (Needham 2005, 185, table 1).

Two dress pins made from copper and bronze have previously been compared to typologically dated forms in Europe. Thus the broken pin from Roundway 8 was once compared to the racquet-headed pins of Reinecke A1 origin (Clarke 1970, 95; Gerloff 1975, 32). Its association with a copper dagger would now indicate a pre-Migdale tradition date (before *c*.2200 cal BC) and this predated continental A1 (O'Connor 2010). The double spiral-headed pin from Sewell is not matched in the ornaments belonging to the Adlerberg, Singen and Straubing groups, and, like the Roundway pin, is probably earlier than these European groups, and represents a pre-Migdale insular type (*ibid*). However, a different interpretation is offered in Chapter 9.3.3.

The set of disc beads, along with the associated re-worked bracer from Dalmore (ID 127) unfortunately have not survived for study. These beads, described in the original antiquarian report as 'albertite' were probably made from jet or a jet-like substance. Disc beads have been found in some very early Beaker graves such as Chilbolton, Hants (made from Kimmeridge shale; Russel 1990, fig. 4) and Folkton 245, Burial 8 (also with a spectacle-shaped bone belt ring, see above). The Folkton beads, analysed within the Leverhulme project (ID 366(N)) were shown to be made from Whitby jet, and a similar result was obtained for the beads from Beggars Haven, East Sussex, which were associated with an MC Beaker (Kinnes 1985, A10). Thus most of the known Beaker associations for disc beads appear to be early. However such beads are commonly found in unaccompanied graves of later Beaker date (just before and around 2000 cal BC) and in graves of the full Early Bronze Age, and hence their value for dating purposes is slim.

7.6.2. Later types

Sponge finger stones are a specialised and finely-made type of smoothing or polishing tool. Their occurrence was listed by Smith and Simpson (1966) and the main examples were illustrated by them (*ibid*, fig. 6). They sometimes occur as pairs and, when found with a Beakers, the vessels belong to the later series of Long Necked forms (*ibid*, Appendix VI). In four cases they are also associated with jet V-perforated buttons and/or pulley rings, which are discussed below. Of the three sponge finger stones to have been found in association with bracers two are from Raunds (ID 116), one made from a mudstone or shale, and, in the same grave, a similar object made from chalk, which appears to have been provided as a non-functional copy. These relatively late stone items were found with the Group VI bracer portion which had been reworked as a tool. The third sponge finger stone derives from the Gravelly Guy group, where it was associated with a flat riveted dagger, bronze awl and antler spatula as well as the amphibolite bracer (ID 74).

Specialised items made from jet and jet-like substances include V-perforated buttons and the so-called pulley belt rings. These occur consistently with later types of Beaker only (see Clarke 1970, 448). There is only one pulley ring from a bracer grave, a large example made from jet (ID jet 483, identified by A Sheridan *contra* Bussell) found with the two bracers at Tring (IDs 31 and 146). The only bracer-associated V-perforated buttons are the set of five jet ones from Raunds (bracer ID 116; button set: Harding and Healy 2007, fig. 4.6). Both items are associated with Group VI bracers, thus confirming the pattern of a relatively late continuing currency for bracers of this material. The only other button set found with a Beaker is that from Kirkaldy, Fife, associated with a late Southern style Beaker (Clarke 1970, fig. 1014). The simple shale ring from the Amesbury Archer grave (IDs 56 and 57) is related stylistically to the simple bone belt rings discussed above, and is not out of place in this early dated grave. Of particular interest is the apparently unique sub-square flat button with two through perforations from Cassington (ID 135), which is apparently unique in the British Isles. This may relate to the through-perforated bone button from Airlie, Angus, associated with a late Northern style Beaker (N3) and an early radiocarbon date of 2310–2140 cal BC (Baker *et al*. 2003, 103). This may indicate that the Cassington bracer burial (ID 135) lies early in the sequence. Unfortunately the rock type of this bracer has not been exactly determined. Of interest is the unique use of shale, most probably from Kimmeridge, for the bracer from Cliffe (ID 153). The style of the Beaker suggests that this too is a later type.

Another component of Needham's later Beaker assemblages is the flint dagger. Only one bracer grave contained such a dagger, that from Raunds (ID 116). They occur elsewhere mainly with Beakers of Southern type, sometimes as the sole accompanying grave good, or in association with jet buttons and/or pulley rings. It can be seen once more that the Raunds grave group fits well within the established chronological pattern.

Finally consideration should be given to the few items of amber found within bracer graves. These include a belt ring with traces of a V-perforation from Raunds (Harding and Healy 2007, fig. 4.6) and a segment from a second ring, rather poorly preserved, from Ferry Fryston (Brown *et al.* 2007, fig. 170). There are also chunky beads or V-perforated buttons from Kelleythorpe (ID 13) and Culduthel Mains (ID 79). It is interesting to note that all these finds of amber were associated with finely-made curved bracers manufactured from Group VI rock. This suggests that the use of amber may have been more widespread in later Beaker times. However there are a few earlier instances, such as the amber disc bead associated with the early style Beaker from Brampton, Cambs. (Clarke 1970, no. 363; Needham form LC, but with possible sinuous profile, pers. comm.).

7.6.3. Other Early Bronze Age grave assemblages

Five bracers were found in association with other grave goods of Early Bronze Age date, contemporary with the Wessex Series graves (*c.*1950–1400 cal BC), and four of these are known to have been accompanying human cremation burials. The primary cremation at Aldbourne contained three artefacts in addition to the reworked amphibolite bracer (ID 14): an oval perforated stone pendant, a perforated bone pin and a set of bone 'tweezers'. Such a grave group is typical of the later stage of the Wessex Series, *c.*1750–1400 cal BC. A second late Wessex Series group derives from the early antiquarian find from Broughton-in-Craven where the reworked Group VI bracer (ID 141) was found with an urn of unknown type, a Class IB bronze razor (Manby 2000, 9) and a Developed Series battle-axe (Roe 1966, no.317, stage V). The bracer from Bishops Cannings (ID 32) probably came from a burial in a barrow. It is a fragment reworked as a pendant, and was found with a bone toggle with expanded ends. This type of toggle appears to imitate faience beads in form, and may again date from the later part of the Early Bronze Age (Piggott 1958). Two further bracers were found entire, but associated with cremation burials and urns. At Bowerham Barracks (ID 130) the vessel was a Collared Urn, while at Ferniegair (ID 123) it was a Cordoned Urn. According to the recent appraisal of all available radiocarbon dates for Wales and the north of England, Collared Urns date from 1900 to 1700 cal BC and Cordoned Urns between 1750 and 1500 cal BC (Brindley 2007, 321, table 67).

7.7. CONCLUSIONS

This chapter has presented a detailed consideration of the direct dating of bracer graves, through radiocarbon dating of the human remains concerned, and of the typology and accepted date ranges for associated grave goods made from various different raw materials.

The available radiocarbon dates suggest that narrow bracers made from red or black rock were being made from the time of the earliest Beaker use in Britain, while those of Group VI or amphibolite materials were initiated a little later. There are three dates for bracers made from the miscellaneous rocks group, one of them relatively early and two relatively late. For Group VI bracer graves, some determinations fall around or after the 'fission horizon' and others extend into the Early Bronze Age period.

The evidence from the most recent systems of dating different styles of associated Beaker vessels suggests that the narrow red and black bracers may well have been primary. Bracers of amphibolite and Group VI rock may all have been in existence from an early period of Beaker use in Britain, but it can now be asserted that the amphibolite bracers were more prevalent in the earlier stages, before and during Needham's 'fission horizon', whilst the Group VI bracers were current mainly from the 'fission horizon' onwards. A discussion of the current thinking on the dating of dagger types shows that the range of daggers associated with amphibolite bracers tends to be somewhat earlier than those associated with bracers made from Group VI rock. In general these conclusions concur with the results of the analysis of Beaker associations summarised above. Only one type of barbed and tanged flint arrowhead can be closely dated within the Beaker period. This is the Green Low type, of later Beaker times, which occurs almost entirely with curved bracers of Group VI rock.

Amongst other types of grave good thought to occur early in the Beaker sequence, gold tress rings are from graves with early radiocarbon dates, including the Amesbury Archer grave with its red and black bracers. The two pins, one of copper and one of bronze, probably pre-2200 cal BC in date, were found in association with amphibolite bracers only. Simple bone belt rings occur generally with early Beakers but were found once each with bracers of amphibolite and Group VI rock. Antler or bone spatulae have been found three times with amphibolite bracers and once with a bracer of Group VI rock. However their associations overall suggest that spatulae were in use throughout the currency of Beakers. Most of the known Beaker associations for disc beads of jet and jet-like materials appear to be early. However such beads are commonly found in unaccompanied graves of later Beaker date and in graves of the full Early Bronze Age.

Finally, there is a group of artefact categories which recur in grave groups containing later style Beakers, and which occur mainly with Group VI bracers. This group includes sponge finger stones (the exception being the association with an amphibolite bracer at Gravelly Guy (ID 74)), jet V-perforated buttons and pulley rings, most of the amber items and flint daggers. The occurrence of such items in bracer graves is rare, but it does serve to amplify the general conclusion that bracers of Group VI rock, although apparently made from early Beaker times, were most commonly deposited during the late Beaker period. On the other hand, bracers of amphibolite tend to have been made and used mainly in early Beaker times, not long after the long bracers made from distinctive red and black rocks. No conclusion concerning the dating of the smaller bracers made from other rock types can be advanced, mainly as they were never deposited as grave goods. The only date available is the radiocarbon determination from the Stonehenge burial, where the bracer happened to be attached to the body of the murdered victim.

Five very long-lived bracers, three of them reworked into alternative artefacts, were found with objects of Early Bronze Age (Wessex Series) date. These were probably heirlooms. They may originally have been made as early as *c.*2300 cal BC and may have been still in use as late as the end of the Early Bronze Age, *c.*1400 cal BC. Thus their use lives may have been as long as 700 years, or 28 human generations.

8: CONTEXTS AND ASSOCIATIONS

Ann Woodward

8.1 GENERAL CONTEXTS

8.1.1 Distribution

The total number of bracer find spots that could be considered in detail is 84. Of these, 28 (33%) are stray finds and 56 (67%) are from recorded contexts. The stray finds are listed in Table 8.1 where any details of the location are shown. Some were found on the surface of ploughed fields, several were chance finds in gravel pits, and others were found during building works such as pipe laying. One item, the bracer from Sonning (ID 115) was found in the River Thames. This may have been deliberately deposited in the river in prehistoric times, or may have eroded from a site near to the ancient riverbank. The overall distribution of these stray finds in relation to the finds of bracers from recorded contexts shows that they are distributed particularly in the midland counties and north-east England (Figure 8.1). The reason for this slight concentration is not immediately apparent. Strays also occur both in the south-eastern zone and in the same

ID	Site name	Details	Reference
3	Woodeaton	Surface find: Manning Collection	Unpublished
9	Mildenhall	Stray find: no details in Sturge Register at BM	Smith 1937
18	Offham	Metal detector find	Unpublished
77	Glenluce	Found at Mid Torrs	Wilson 1876
80	Culbin Sands	Stray find	Walker 1967
84	Ballogie	Stray find	Anon 1893
92	?Scotland	Unlocated	?Unpublished
93	Crawford	Stray find	RCAHMS 1978
102	Duston	On surface at Duston Gravel Pits, 1973	Museum record
103	Upper Heyford	In pipe trench SE of village, 1949 (museum records)	Kennett 1969
104	Nr. Scarborough	No details	Unpublished
111	Lindridge	6 feet down in gravel deposit	Allies 1849
112	Aldington	5 feet down in gravel pit on Parks Farm	Ingram 1867
113	Llantrithyd	Stray on medieval site, but location probably uncertain	Savory 1980
115	Sonning	Stray find in River Thames	Salzman 1939
118	Rauceby	No details	Petch 1958
119	Winteringham	In sand pit at junction of Ermine Street and the Winteringham-Ferriby road	Dudley 1949
120	Littleport	Stray find	Salzman 1938
121	Calceby	Stray find; no trace of any barrow	Petch 1958
122	Bridlington	In a field near Bridlington	Sheppard 1930
124	Thoresway	'Close to a known Beaker period burial mound'	Everatt 1971
126	Lanarkshire	Unlocated	
128	Nr. Gainsborough	No details	?Unpublished
129	High Dalby	No details	?Unpublished
134	Fox Hole	Stray find near Fox Hole	Unpublished
136	Black Knoll	No details	Chitty 1967
139	Mola	Carmarthen Museum	?Unpublished
147	Sandy	No details	Evans 1897

Table 8.1. Bracer contexts: stray finds.

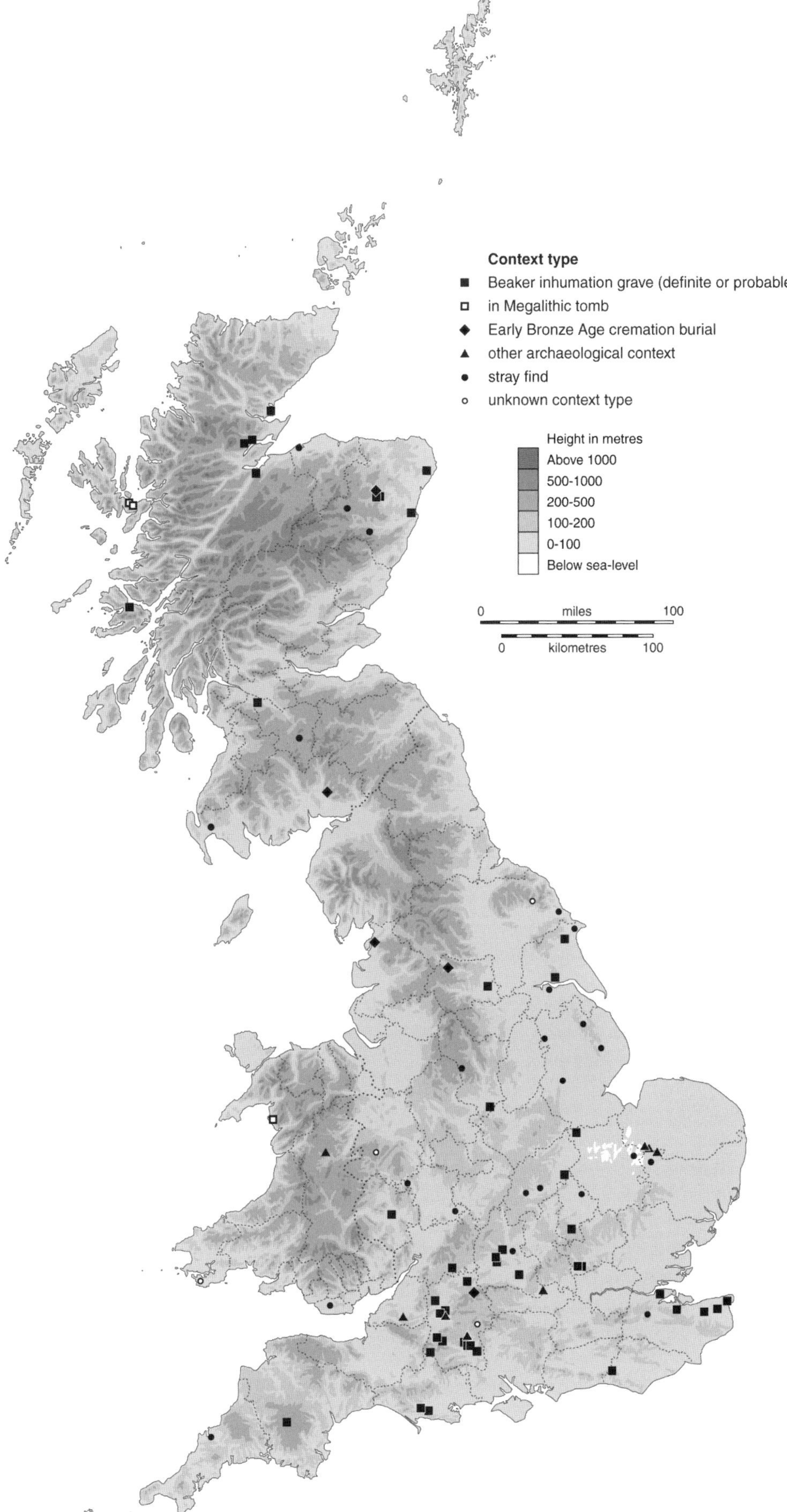

Figure 8.1. Distribution of bracers according to context type.

Context	Amphibolite	Group VI	Red/black	Misc
Stray finds	8	3	-	9
Beaker graves	16	16	2	7
EBA graves	2	1	-	3

Table 8.2. The occurrence of bracers by type of context and rock group.

Breakage	Amphibolite	Group VI	Misc
Entire	3	2	8
Severe break	3		1
Half only	1		
Fragment only	1	1	
Totals	**8**	**3**	**9**

Table 8.3. The degree of fragmentation amongst stray bracers.

two regions of Scotland where bracers from archaeological contexts occur. Most bracers from funerary contexts are from Beaker age inhumation graves. These are distributed mainly in south-east England and in north-east Scotland; both these areas are characterised by particular dense concentrations of Beaker activity (see Clarke 1970, Maps 1–10). There are also a few examples of bracers from Beaker occupation sites, one in Somerset and one in Norfolk, one from a recumbent stone circle in Scotland, and two or three from the chambers of megalithic tombs (in north-west Wales and the Isle of Skye). Finally there is a wide but sparse distribution of bracers associated with cremation burials of full Early Bronze Age date.

Most of the stray finds were made during the early 20th century, while some date from antiquarian activity and collecting in the 19th century: four of these are from England and three from Scotland. The occurrence of the three different rock groups amongst the stray bracers, and those from graves, is shown in Table 8.2. These figures relate only to the bracers that were available for chemical analysis during the project.

It can be seen that, whilst the majority of bracers found in Beaker graves were made from amphibolite or Group VI rock, bracers made from the miscellaneous rocks group were much more common among the stray finds. Among the latter, simple narrow bracers with only two perforations were also much more common than those deposited as grave goods. Moreover, these simple 'stray' bracers tended to be whole and virtually undamaged, while the stray finds of bracers made from amphibolite or Group VI rock were more often broken (see Table 8.3). Furthermore several made from the latter rocks only survived as fragments.

8.1.2 Burials

The details of recorded archaeological contexts relating to bracers are summarised in Table 8.4 and full information may be found on the CD-ROM. Most of the well provenanced bracers derive from inhumation burials in Beaker-age round barrows or flat graves. A total of 19 bracers were found with burials in round barrows, or ring ditches, with 15 of them having been in central and primary locations. The only exception is the burial from Thomas Hardye School (bracer ID 67) which was located eccentrically in a square enclosure which joined two adjacent round mounds both of which also contained Beaker-age graves, as well as later interments (Gardiner *et al.* 2007, 31–42). In addition 12 of the bracer burials were found in flat graves, and nine in stone cists. All except one of the latter are located in Scotland, with the ninth situated on Dartmoor. There are also a few bracer finds groups from gravel sites which probably came from flat graves, although no human remains were preserved, and finally, an unlocated findspot of a bracer found with 'an interment' which probably denotes an inhumation at Calne (bracer ID 15).

Six bracers were found with human cremation burials, and in five cases these were associated with other artefacts which can be dated to the full Early Bronze Age (see Chapter 7). The contexts of the bracer found inside a Collared Urn at Bowerham Barracks (ID 130) and of that found with an urn and other Early Bronze Age grave goods at Broughton-in-Craven (ID 141) are not known, but the one associated with a Cordoned Urn at Ferniegair (ID 123) was excavated from a cist. The bracer from Aldbourne (ID 14) was found with other Early Bronze Age grave goods in association with the primary cremation at the centre of a round barrow. Another example was located in a pit at the centre of the recumbent stone circle at Old Rayne (ID 82). This is the only example of a bracer found in association with an earth or stone monument, apart from the Beaker grave found in the ditch at Stonehenge (ID 58). The sixth bracer was found on top of a small heap of stones overlying a double cremation burial in a pit (Lockerbie ID 150). With the cremation burials there were an antler pin and flint items, including a plano-convex knife.

There are two bracers which were found during the

excavation of megalithic cairns, sites which are primarily of Neolithic date. In both cases the original contexts for the bracers had been lost, but they may have been associated with secondary Beaker burials placed within the stone chambers. At Dyffryn Ardudwy the bracer (ID 114) was found in two pieces and originally interpreted as a pair of pendants. The bracer may have been broken at its time of first discovery when the East Chamber was emptied by antiquarian activity or earlier. The Corry Liveras chambered cairn on Skye in which ID 87 was found was excavated in the early 19th century (Henshall 1972, 484–5). This was probably a secondary Beaker-age stone cist. A second bracer (ID 88) was found on the seashore nearby, and may well have been thrown out at the time of the early excavation.

8.1.3. Other contexts

A few bracers have been found in prehistoric contexts which are non-funerary in nature. At Ben Bridge, the bracer (ID 108) was recovered from a Beaker pit. The pit was almost one metre in diameter and contained a substantial assemblage of flint items, including 12 scrapers, 8 cores and 92 flakes, many of which were burnt. There were also 100 sherds from a minimum of six Beaker vessels and four sherds from Neolithic vessels. The bracer had been carefully placed at the top of the pit fill. The excavator considered that the finds assemblage might have indicated that the pit had contained a cremation burial, but no traces of burnt bone survived. It seems unlikely that all the cremated bone would have been totally destroyed, and the mixed sherd assemblage would be an unusual accompaniment for a Beaker-age burial. It may be that the pit was a domestic one, albeit with the deliberately placed stone bracer at the top. Deposits of bracers within pits on Beaker settlement sites elsewhere in Europe are fairly well known (see Chapter 1). Two bracers have been found on a well-known Beaker settlement at Hockwold in East Anglia (ID 106 and 132). They were found as surface finds in the vicinity of Site 49, which produced sherds from Southern and rusticated Beakers, worked flints and animal bone (Bamford 1982, 18). The final, possibly domestic context for a bracer comprises the finding of a broken and abraded bracer in a hearth within the stone burial cairn at Carneddau (ID 148). The hearth (context 16) was located in the north-east sector of the cairn next to cist 5. The excavator felt that this burnt feature was probably not a pyre, but it may have been associated with ritual or funerary activities.

8.2. ASSOCIATIONS

8.2.1 Bodies

Of the 26 Beaker inhumations recorded, all but one was a crouched burial (see Table 8.4). The only exception is the extended burial at Tring (ID 31); this seems an unlikely attitude for a Beaker burial, but the late 18th-century account specifically mentions that both the arms and legs of the skeleton were extended. In the 17 cases where it could be determined on which side of the body the bracer had been laid, it was laid on the left. However, the orientation of the burials was more variable: in 13 cases the head was positioned between north and east, with a slight preference for north-east; in the other seven recorded cases, heads were placed at the west, south and north-west twice each, and at the south-west once. This pattern of orientation is very similar to that obtained for all the Beaker burials analysed by Clarke (1970, 456). Nor is any particular correlation between orientation and bracer rock type apparent.

The sex of the body could be determined in 21 cases. Of these instances, 19 were male and two probably male. Age of the individual could be assessed in a few more cases, although the age categories recorded in the various excavation reports are not easily comparable. Also it must be borne in mind that the relevant anatomical reports have been undertaken by a wide range of specialists, and over a very wide time range. The first point to make is that no children (boys) are represented at all. In 11 cases the age is recorded merely as 'adult', but in 18 cases a closer estimate of age has been made. It is possible to group the various age estimations or terms used in four major groups, as listed in Table 8.5. This demonstrates that a wide range of age groupings are present amongst the Beaker bracer graves. No overall estimates of age ranges for Beaker graves as a whole have been attempted, but it seems possible that the relatively large number of senior and elderly individuals represented may be significantly high. The question of whether age of the people buried relates to the type of bracer involved, or the number of grave goods associated with each individual, will be considered below.

In five cases the reports on the human remains also provide statements concerning stature. In each case the male involved was described as being particularly tall or robust. The body buried at Roundway (bracer ID 28) would have been over 6 feet (1.83m) tall and the femur of the Kelleythorpe burial (bracer ID 13) was particularly long, at 19 inches (0.48m). The archer buried in the ditch at Stonehenge (bracer ID 58) is estimated to have been between 1.76–1.78m in height, and the skeleton at Stanton Harcourt (bracer ID 2) is recorded as being robust. The man buried at Monkton (bracer ID 154) was large and about 5 feet 11 inches tall (1.80m). The exceptional extended burial from Tring (bracer ID 31) has already been mentioned, but in this case the skeleton was described as being of 'common size' only. The Stonehenge archer was aged between 25 and 30 when he was killed, and the Kelleythorpe burial is recorded only as 'adult'. However the other tall individuals belonged in the older age groups: the 'mature' body at Stanton Harcourt (bracer ID 2), and the 70 to 80 year old individual at Roundway (bracer ID 28). There is thus a hint that the men buried with bracers were particularly tall, robust and long-lived members of the populations concerned.

8.2.2 Grave goods

The pattern of association of grave goods of various categories found in bracer graves, and in relation to the

ID number	Site	Location	Position	Type	Body	Attitude	Side	Head at	Sex	Age	Notes
1	Dorchester XII	n/a	in henge XII		inhum	crouched	on L	NE	prob M	20–30	
2	Stanton Harcourt	primary	central	pit grave	inhum	not known			?M	mature	robust skeleton
4	Winterslow Hut	primary			inhum	crouched	?	NE	?	adult	
6	Sturry				no survival						found with Beaker pottery
7	Hemp Knoll	primary	central		inhum	crouched	on L	N	M	35–45	
8	Barnack	primary	central		inhum	crouched	on L	NE	M	35–45	
10	Sittingbourne			flat grave	inhum	crouched	on L	S	?	adult	
11	Brandon Fields			probable flat grave	no survival						no barrow or bones found
12	Sewell			flat grave	inhum	crouched	on L	N/NE	M	adult	
13	Kelleythorpe			cist	inhum	crouched	on L	E	?	adult	femur L 19ins
14	Aldbourne	primary	central		crem				M	adult	
15	Calne			interment	prob inhum						
26	Wellington Quarry			flat grave	inhum	indet					scraps of bone only
28	Roundway	primary			inhum	crouched	on L	N	M	70–80	>6 ft tall
29	Tytherington/Corton	primary			inhum	crouched		N			
30	Sutton Veny	no details			crem						'in a barrow'
31	Tring			?flat grave	inhum	extended	not recorded				of common size; legs and arms extended
32	Bishops Cannings				no record						probably EBA group
56	Amesbury Archer			flat grave	inhum	crouched	on L	W	M	35–45	
57	Amesbury Archer										
58	Stonehenge			flat grave	inhum	crouched	on L	N	M	25–30	176–178m tall
66	West Stafford	unknown			inhum	unknown					
67	Thomas Hardye School	eccentric	square enclosure		inhum	crouched	on L	NW	M	15–21	subadult/adult
73	Ferry Fryston			flat grave	inhum	crouched	on L	E	M	40–50	
74	Gravelly Guy	primary	central		inhum	crouched	on L	NE	M	45+	
75	Shorncote			flat grave	inhum	crouched		W	?	adult	
78	Fyrish			cist	inhum				M	elderly	
79	Culduthel Mains			cist	inhum	crouched			M	adult	
82	Old Rayne			pit in stone circle	crem						
86	Glen Forsa			cist	inhum						
87	Corry Liveras			chamber in meg cairn	none						
88	Broadford Bay			from meg cairn	none						

89	Borrowstone			cist	inhum	crouched	on L	E	M	25–35	
90	Newlands, Oyne	primary		cist	inhum	crouched	on L	NE	M	35–40	
91	Newlands, Oyne										
94	Dornoch Nursery			cist	inhum			?S	indet	17–25	
101	Ardiffery			cist	inhum					youth	incomplete inhum + dog
105	Melton Quarry			grave	no survival						
106	Hockwold		settlement	u/s on settlement							
107	Aston	primary	central	old ground surface	no survival						
108	Ben Bridge			pit	none						
114	Dyffryn Ardudwy		East Chamber	disturbed, 2 findspots	robbed						
116	Raunds	primary			inhum	crouched	on L	SW	M	adult	
123	Ferniegair			cist	crem						
127	Dalmore			cist	inhum	crouched			M	senior adult	
130	Bowerham Barracks			no details	crem						
132	Hockwold		settlement	u/s on settlement	none						
133	Archerton Newtake		in cairn	cist	robbed						
135	Cassington			pit, probably grave	none						
137	Pyecombe	primary			inhum	crouched	on L	NW	M	mature	
141	Broughton-in-Craven	unknown			crem						
142	Bulford			in a barrow	no mention						
144	Mere				inhum	crouched			M	adult	
					inhum	crouched				young	to R of male
148	Carneddau	secondary	NE sector	hearth 16	none						
149	Thanet	primary			inhum	crouched	on side				
150	Lockerbie	secondary		enhanced knoll	crem				M	adult	
									–	youth	
154	Monkton	primary			inhum	crouched	on L		M	adult	5ft 10ins tall

Table 8.4. List of bracers discovered within burial contexts.

Age group	Range in years	Published categories	Number of burials
Young	Up to 25/30	Youth; young; 15–21; 17–25; 20–30	5
Adult	25/30–45	25–35; 25–30; 35–45; 35–40; mature	9
Senior	45+	40–50; 45+; senior adult	3
Elderly	70-80	70–80; elderly	2
Total			**18**

Table 8.5. Age groupings for Beaker burials with bracers.

Artefact type	Red/black	Amphibolite	Group VI	Misc	Total
Beaker	2	14	13	4	33
Dagger	1	9	4	-	14
B&t arrowheads	2	5	4	1	12
Bone toggle		2	3		5
Amber			5		5
Bone/antler spatula	1	2	1		4
Gold	1	1	2		4
Jet/shale	1		1	1	3
Bone ring		1	2		3
Tusk	1		1	1	3
Fire kit	2				2
Copper alloy pin		2			2
Sponge finger stone		1	1		2
Jet/shale pulley			1		1
Copper alloy awl		1			1
Bone pin	1				1
Metalworker's stone	1				1
Flint dagger			1		1
Totals	**13**	**38**	**39**	**7**	**97**
EBA urn			1 or 2	3	4 or 5
EBA objects		2	1	1	4

Table 8.6. Number of sites containing categories of artefact found in association with bracers of differing rock type.

rock type of the bracers concerned is summarised in Table 8.6. The total incidence of artefact types varies from 33 sites where Beakers were found in bracer graves, and 14 where such graves included copper or copper alloy daggers to single instances of a jet/shale pulley ring, a copper alloy awl, bone pin, metalworker's cushion stone and flint dagger. The chronological range of some of these various classes of artefact has been discussed in the previous chapter. The distribution of the different grave good types amongst graves producing bracers made from the different rock types can be seen to be fairly even. Daggers, copper or bronze pins and fancy flint arrowheads are more commonly associated with amphibolite bracers, while amber objects occur only with bracers made from Group VI rock. This patterning is mainly due to chronological factors which have been already been discussed in Chapter 7.

In order to assess whether this profile of object associations reflects a particularly unusual or rich range of artefacts, it is useful to compare the totals with those for other Beaker graves which contain items in addition to the Beaker, but not including a bracer. Such a comparison is presented in Table 8.7, where an estimation of grave good occurrences in non-bracer Beaker graves has been attempted using the list of associations in Clarke's corpus

Artefact type	Bracer graves	Non-bracer graves	Sex associations
Dagger	14	11	Male
B&t arrowheads	12	11	Male
Bone toggle	6	-	
Amber	5	2	Male
Bone/antler spatula	4	3	Male
Gold	4	3	Male
Jet/shale	3	2	
Bone ring	3	3	Male
Tusk	3	1	
Fire kit	2	3	Male
Copper alloy pin	2	-	
Sponge finger stone	2	1	Male
Jet/shale pulley or button	1	14	Mainly male
Copper alloy awl	1	3	Mainly female
Bone pin/awl	1	3	Mainly male
Metalworker's stone	1	2	
Flint dagger	1	12	Male
Bone pulley	-	2	Male
Copper alloy earring	-	1	Male or female
Decorated bronze bracelet	-	1	
Battle-axe	-	2	
Totals	**64**	**80**	

Table 8.7. Categories of artefact found in bracer and non-bracer Beaker graves (number of graves). Data for non-bracer graves and sex associations taken from Clarke (1970) Appendices 3.1 and 3.3.

(Clarke 1970, 438–447, Appendix 3.1). This clearly does not include data relating to burials excavated since the late 1960s, but it may serve as a general summary of the overall picture. The table also includes a statement of associations with sexed burials, as known before 1970 (taken from Clarke 1970, Appendix 3.3).

It is immediately apparent from the table that the overall pattern of grave goods associated with bracer graves does not differ in any general way from the pattern associated with Beaker graves that do not contain bracers. Metal daggers and fancy flint arrowheads occur evenly between the two groups of graves, as do various other less commonly occurring artefact categories such as bone or antler spatulae, items of gold and bone belt rings. Thus it cannot be deduced that bracer graves are particularly richer or less rich that other Beaker graves containing grave goods. There are, however, two categories of object that occur almost exclusively in bracer graves: the two metal pins and the bone toggles.

The bone toggles are quite different from the bone belt rings, which have been considered separately in the tables. The toggles are variable in form, but all possess one or more side perforations. These items may have held a special function in association with bracers, possibly in relation to activities involving falconry (below, see Appendix 10.1). The two pins are rare and probably special items. They may not be related to continental forms (see Chapter 7.6.1 and for an alternative suggestion see Chapter 9.3.3) but instead could be innovative forms of dress ornament which are found only with finely-made amphibolite bracers.

As the bracer graves have often been interpreted as the graves of archers, it is instructive to consider other Beaker graves which contain barbed-and-tanged arrowheads, but no stone bracer. There are 11 such graves, and in seven of these the grave goods also include other fancy items: gold tress rings at Radley 4A, a gold cap and bone belt ring at Farleigh Wick, further bone belt rings at Stanton Harcourt and Clinterty, spatulae at Alsop Moor and Mouse Low, a flint dagger at Alsop Moor and a jet button at Lambourn 31 (Clarke 1970, figs. 63, 259, 261, 661, 776, 862 and 867 respectively). Additionally, the Boscombe Bowmen burial included a boar's tusk and a rare type of bone toggle amongst the grave goods (Fitzpatrick 2004, 13). This suggests that these fancy arrowheads were a valuable item in general terms.

Some groups of artefact appear to occur more often in non-bracer graves. These are mainly the flint daggers and jet buttons and pulley objects and also a couple of metal smithing stones. These categories, plus the rare occurrence of battle-axe associations, tend to occur with Late Beaker types (see Chapter 7), when the deposition of bracers in inhumation graves was becoming much less common. Two special ornament types, the bronze earring and decorated bronze bracelet also occur only in graves which did not contain bracers. In both these cases, the only other object in the grave was the Beaker itself.

8.2.3. Location of objects in relation to the body

The location of grave goods in relation to the layout of the inhumation is an important factor. Such details are recorded for 24 burials out of the total of 37 inhumations found with bracers. The locations may inform how objects were worn on the body and how tools or weapons were attached. In addition the position of the Beaker itself may be found to relate to other parameters such as the age or sex of the body. However, one of the most interesting points to have arisen from the careful excavation of bracer graves in recent years has been the recognition that some of the grave goods had in fact been buried as distinct groups. These were placed near to the body, in various locations, and may originally have been contained in bags or pouches made from organic materials such as cloth, fur or leather. Whilst it can be postulated that items found in particular positions *upon* the body probably were the possessions of the individual concerned, the nature of the groups of objects found in these discrete caches is more problematic. It may be that the contents of a cache were further belongings of the person buried but, alternatively, these groups of items may have been deposited by one of the mourners, or even as a collection of individual items contributed by a group of family or community members. The contents of these caches will be considered in more detail below, but firstly the available evidence for the placement of selected object categories on the bodies themselves should be summarised.

Most bracers have been found in relation to the lower arm or wrist bones, and it is this factor that has contributed most to their overall interpretation as archers' wristguards. For functional use as a wristguard, the bracer would need to be positioned on the inside of the left wrist for a right-handed archer, or on the inside of the right wrist for a left-handed archer. However, the detailed descriptions of the location of bracers indicates that they were often placed on the lower arm, but in a higher position than the wrist itself. Also, in a fair number of cases the bracer was undoubtedly mounted on the *outside* of the arm, not the inside. This fact has been noted independently and fully discussed by Fokkens *et al.* (2008), who have recorded the incidence of this placing of bracers throughout Europe. They suggest that such bracers were not functional items serving as archers' wristguards, but were exotic ornaments mounted on the outside of the arm where they would have been highly visible during displays, parades or ritual gatherings. Nine British bracer graves are included in the list published by Fokkens (Fokkens *et al.* 2008, 136–140), and here we can add some details for a further 12 graves. Key bracer positions are as follows:

- *Outside left forearm.* Dorchester XII (ID 1), Hemp Knoll (ID 7), Barnack (ID 8), Amesbury Archer black bracer (ID 57), Thomas Hardye School (ID 67)
- *Outside right forearm.* Kelleythorpe (ID 13)
- *Inside left forearm.* Sewell (ID 12), probably Roundway (ID 28), Borrowstone (ID 89)
- *Inside right wrist.* Probably Tytherington/Corton (ID 29)
- *Under right arm.* Winterslow (ID 4)
- *Under left arm.* Monkton (ID 154)
- *Mid-body or at level of waist (where no/minimal survival of bones).* Wellington Quarry (ID 26), Dornoch Nursery (ID 94)
- *Near left side of body.* Mere (ID 144)
- *At or beyond feet.* Tring (ID 31), possibly Shorncote (ID 75)
- *In cache at or near feet.* Ferry Fryston (ID 73), Gravelly Guy (ID 74), Raunds (ID 116)
- *In cache at knees.* Amesbury Archer red bracer (ID 56)

Of the 12 bracer positions recorded as being related to the lower arm, six were on the outside of the arm and four inside. This confirms the general conclusion made by Fokkens *et al.* (2008) that more bracers were located on the outside of the arm than inside. Moreover, the fact that the majority were found on the left arm (nine out of 12) tends to suggest that most of the individuals concerned were right-handed. Particular placements do not relate to the different rock types from which the bracers were made, nor do bracer positions on the right or left of the arm, or on the inside or outside of the arm, correlate with any of the known age groupings of the associated burials.

The placement of the Beaker vessel is recorded for 19 graves. Most were positioned at the feet (12 examples: ID numbers 7, 8, 12, 13, 28, 57, 67, 73, 75, 116, 154 and probably 94). However, in three cases these Beakers were associated with the deposition of caches of objects in this location. Four Beakers had been placed at the head (ID numbers 57, 89, 91 and 144), but in only one case (ID 89) was the exact position – behind the head – noted. Other positions for the Beaker comprise: in front of the body (IDs 1, 4, 29), and behind the body (IDs 57, 74 and 137). There is no obvious correlation between the position of the Beaker and the age of the burial, or the rock type of the associated bracer.

The position of Beakers deposited with inhumations has previously been listed and considered by David Clarke (1970, 454–5). He categorised the positions into four groups: in front of skull; behind skull or shoulders; in front of feet and behind the legs or feet. These categories are not easily comparable with the information gained for bracer burials, as summarised above. By preparing summations from the lists published by Clarke, it is possible to calculate that in female burials Beakers were more often located in front of the skull or body, and that Beakers in male burials were much more likely to be placed behind the head or shoulders. Occurrences behind the legs or feet were roughly equal. The bracer grave data does not fall obviously into the male pattern deduced from Clarke's figures, but the dataset is very small and the records highly variable. Also it is important to note that several of the 'at feet' locations are directly related to caches of objects placed at or near the feet of bracer burials. This detail is only known certainly for burials excavated under modern conditions, and it may be that some of the Beakers recorded by Clarke were also part of object caches.

The position of a copper or bronze dagger in the grave does not seem to have been standardised. There are thirteen recorded instances from eleven graves, with two instances each in the Amesbury Archer (ID 56 and 57) and Dorchester XII (ID 1) graves. Three relate to the hands (ID 1, knife-dagger, in front of hands; ID 28, knife dagger at left hand, tip down; ID 73, knife dagger in hands, tip down). A further three daggers were placed in front of the face (ID numbers 57, 67, 74). Other positions include beneath the right elbow (ID 1), at the left elbow (ID 8), near the arm (ID 4), below the right shoulder (ID 154), near the left side (ID 144), near the waist (ID 26) and, in two cases, behind the back (ID 13, 56/57). Where two daggers were present, as in the graves which contained bracers ID 1 and ID 57, they were located in different positions in relation to the body. No daggers were found in caches, although the only flint dagger from a bracer grave, that from Raunds (ID 116) was included within the cache.

Of the 11 bracer graves that contained barbed-and-tanged arrowheads, the position of the arrowheads was recorded in seven cases. The largest number were found with the Amesbury Archer bracers (ID 56 and 57) where 17 arrowheads were found mainly in the area between the waist and the legs. However, record of their alignment and orientation did not indicate that they had been contained in a quiver, and six of them had probably been added to the grave later than the main group of nine (Harding and Fitzpatrick pers. comm.). Other smaller numbers of arrowheads were found in similar body positions in three other cases: between the legs at Tring (bracer ID 31), behind the feet at Thomas Hardye School (bracer ID 67), and at the other end of the cist from the skull at Dornoch Nursery (bracer ID 94). The two Winterslow arrowheads (bracer ID 4) were also found between the knees and the feet of the skeleton, but in this case they were found beneath the inverted Beaker and so may not have been mounted. In contrast, at Roundway 8 (bracer ID 28) a single arrowhead was found near the skull. And at Wellington Quarry (bracer ID 26) the arrowheads and arrowhead roughouts were found scattered within the grave where almost no bones had survived. In several cases, the arrowheads appeared to have been in mint condition at the time of their deposition in the grave.

Turning to the types of ornament found within bracer graves we may consider items made from gold, bronze, amber and bone. The tress rings found with the Amesbury Archer red bracer (ID 56) were found within a cache of objects, but elsewhere, as at Chilbolton, Hants, Radley 4A, Oxon and Boscombe Down, Wilts with the Amesbury Archer's Companion such ornaments have been found in the vicinity of the skull (Russel 1990, 156; Barclay and Halpin 1999, 154; Fitzpatrick 2003, 150). The exact location of the Mere gold caps (ID 144) was not recorded, and the other instances of gold ornamentation are the rivet caps on three Group VI bracers (IDs 8, 13 and 79). The two dress pins were found at the left upper arm in the case of the grave at Sewell (bracer ID 12) and adhering to the bracer at Roundway (ID 28). The excavator thought that the Roundway pin had probably been placed on the breast of the body, but functional associations of the pins with the bracers themselves, as argued for the bone toggles and fancy bone pin below, cannot be ruled out.

The amber beads and button found at Kelleythorpe (bracer ID 13) were around the neck of the skeleton, and were undoubtedly part of a necklace, but the position of the bead at Culduthel Mains (ID 79) is unknown. The fragmentary ring from Ferry Fryston (bracer ID 73) was found near the shoulder of the body, but the V-perforated probably amber pulley ring from Raunds (bracer ID 116) was part of the cache of objects found at the foot of the inhumation. As noted previously, all the amber items were found with Group VI bracers.

Of particular interest is the varied set of perforated toggles made from animal bone and these will be discussed in more detail in a later Leverhulme volume. These are highly variable in terms of size, overall morphology and the location of side perforations, but they seem to form a functional group of items which are found almost exclusively in graves that also contain bracers. Of the six examples known, the position in relation to the body was recorded in five cases. On three occasions the toggle was placed on the left side of the body: at the thigh at Hemp Knoll (bracer ID 7), at the left elbow at Barnack (bracer ID 8), and at the left arm at Thomas Hardye School (bracer ID 67). Others were positioned on the chest at Sewell (bracer ID 12) and in front of the pelvis at Borrowstone (bracer ID 89). The Borrowstone object, which is unpublished, may have been a belt ring, but the other items were all situated in a zone that would have been close to the bracer, which in all these cases was situated on the left lower arm. It seems possible therefore that the toggles may have possessed a specific function related to the use of the stone bracers (see also Appendix 10.1.6) It is equally possible that the extremely unusual hammer-headed bone pin which was found next to the black bracer on the left forearm of the Amesbury Archer (ID 57) may have held an associated function.

8.2.4. Composition of caches

The important recognition of caches of objects within certain bracer graves has already been mentioned. This has resulted from careful modern techniques of excavation and recording. In order to demonstrate the variation and size of such caches the main examples found within bracer graves are listed in Table 8.8.

It can be seen that the contents of caches very often contain flint items. Other objects include a mixture of apparently valuable items such as the gold tress rings, flint dagger, jet button set and sponge finger stones. In addition to the caches listed in Table 8.8 it is also relevant to note that the objects found at the foot of the only bracer grave which is known to have held an extended individual, from Tring (ID 31), may also have been deposited as a cache. The description of the find was made in the late 18th century, but the record is very specific, and states that the two Group VI bracers, one on them never perforated, and the very large jet pulley ring, were found at the feet of the skeleton.

8.2.5. Early Bronze Age associations

In eight cases, stone bracers have been found in association with objects of full Early Bronze Age date, usually forming grave goods for human cremation burials. At Aldbourne

Site	Bracer ID	Stone	Metal	Jet/ Shale	Flint	Amber	Bone
Amesbury Archer (at knees)	56	Red bracer	Dagger Gold tress rings	Ring			
Amesbury Archer (behind back)					Tools		
Amesbury Archer (in front of arms)					Tools		
Gravelly Guy	74	Bracer Sponge finger			Scraper × 2		Spatula
Ferry Fryston	73	Bracer			Borer Flake		
Raunds	116	Bracer Sponge finger Chalk finger		Button × 5	Dagger Scraper × 3 Knife & flakes	Ring	Spatula × 3 Tusk

Table 8.8. The composition of caches of artefacts found in bracer graves.

(bracer ID 14) the cremation of an adult male was found at the centre of a round barrow. The grave goods comprise the bracer itself, which was reworked and reused, an oval pendant, also of stone, a perforated bone point and a pair of bone 'tweezers'. A second diverse group of grave goods accompanied the reworked bracer from Broughton-in-Craven (ID 141). The human remains and some of the objects have been lost, but the group originally comprised an urn of unknown type, a bronze razor knife, a stone battle-axe and a group of perforated bone points. Both these graves are rich burials of Early Bronze Age date. And in both cases the bracers, which had been reworked to form secondary artefact types (pendants), must have been heirloom items with long life histories. The same was probably the case with the fragment of a bracer, which may also have been reused as a pendant, found probably in a barrow at Bishops Cannings (ID 32). This was from a less lavish grave group, but was associated with a bone toggle of typical Early Bronze Age type, with expanded terminals (cf Piggott 1958, and not to be confused with the special type of toggles found in Beaker bracer graves). At Lockerbie (ID 150) the bracer was placed over a double cremation burial which also included an antler pin, a plano-convex knife and further items of flint. Two more bracers were found as complete and unburnt items, in association with urns, but in the absence of any further grave goods. These are the bracers from Bowerham Barracks (ID 130), found inside a Collared Urn and that from Ferniegair (ID 123) which was found with a cremation in a cist, associated with a Cordoned Urn. Finally, the broken bracer from Carneddau (ID 148) was recovered from a hearth within the make-up of a Bronze Age cairn. There were no other associated artefacts. The hearth was located near to a burial cist, but was not thought to have been a pyre area.

8.3. CONCLUSIONS

Although the majority (56) of the bracers studied were found in recorded archaeological contexts, a further 28 (33%) are stray finds. In Bronze Age grave contexts the bracers are mainly those made from amphibolite or Group VI rock. In contrast, amongst the stray finds, many more are made from rocks of miscellaneous types.

Most of the grave finds were associated with primary Beaker inhumations in round barrows or ring ditches, or flat Beaker graves. However, two derive from megalithic cairns. These were probably from secondary cist burials in monuments which were originally constructed in the Neolithic period. There are also five bracers found with Early Bronze Age cremation burials, and a few from domestic contexts. The bodies in the inhumation graves were virtually all crouched, lying on the left side and with the head orientated mostly between north and east. Where the sex of the skeleton could be determined it was always male. No children are represented, but a wide age range, from *c.*15 to *c.*80 years is evident.

The bracer graves also contain a wide range of other associated artefact types, most commonly Beaker vessels, copper or bronze daggers and flint barbed-and-tanged arrowheads. The numbers of goods per grave are not substantially different from those found in other Beaker graves with grave goods, but without bracers. Daggers and fancy flint arrowheads occur roughly equally between accompanied graves with and without bracers.

Stone bracers were usually found in relation to the lower arm bones: six instances on the outside of the arm, and four times on the inside. Nine out of the 12 well-recorded instances were found on the left arm, indicating that most archers may have been right-handed. Beakers were found mainly at the feet (12 instances) with four at the head, and a few in front of the body, or behind it. The position of metal daggers does not seem to have been standardised. Three were in the hands, three in front of the face, and other positions include two behind the back. The positioning of some barbed-and-tanged arrowheads between the waist and feet suggests that some of the arrowheads may have been deposited within a quiver made from perishable materials. However others occupied different positions in the grave and sometimes were pristine and probably never mounted or used. Ornaments for adorning the hair were found either side of the head, and others were placed around the neck, or in upper body positions suggesting that here they were associated with longer hair, perhaps plaited, or else with garments. An interesting group of bone toggles appear to occur almost exclusively in bracer graves. These regularly occur on the left side, in a mid-body position, and they may even represent a specialised item of equipment used alongside the bracers in activities other than archery, possibly falconry (Appendix 10.1).

The whole topic of placement of objects with the body is complicated by the fact that groups of items sometimes occur in tight groupings or caches. The existence of such caches has only recently been appreciated as a result of a series of meticulous modern excavations. The caches were placed most commonly at the feet, and may contain bracers, sponge finger stones and a flint dagger as well as dress ornaments of jet/shale and amber. Such groups of objects may not have been the possessions of the person buried, and may have been offered by one or more of the mourners present at the burial ceremony. Finally, the associated finds in five Early Bronze Age cremation burials indicate that some bracers, often reworked into different artefact types, may have continued in use over many centuries.

9: CONTINENTAL LINKS

Fiona Roe

9.1 PREVIOUS WORK

No study of British bracers would be complete without turning to the continental examples, both to review the range of forms found across the Channel, together with their distributions, and to consider possible antecedents for those found in the UK. The main sources of information are in two seminal papers by Edward Sangmeister. In the first of these (1964) he provided an overall survey of European bracers, together with indispensable maps showing the distribution of the different varieties of bracer and a catalogue of 379 finds, both of which, in the absence of further such comprehensive surveys, are still useful today. In the second paper (1974) he looked in more detail at central European bracers, again with an invaluable catalogue and further distribution maps. Sangmeister commented on the contrasting distributions of flat and curved bracers, noting that the main concentration of flat bracers with two perforations lay in southern and western Europe (1964, 95), while by contrast the curved bracers were mainly to be found in eastern Europe, and especially in Bohemia and Moravia (1964, 93 and abb. 7). Both these main varieties of bracer occur in the British Isles, so that the areas where the two distributions overlap may be of relevance in providing clues as to some precursors for the British series.

Three German regional studies, which followed on from Sangmeister's work, filled in more detail for the Rhineland (Köster 1966; Bantelmann 1982; Gebers 1978 and 1984), while in 1970, in her review of French Beakers, Françoise Treinen usefully included mention of a number of bracers found in France, together with thumbnail illustrations (Treinen 1970). A more recent paper described bracers from around Trier, on the river Moselle (Jacobs 1991) but none of these works addressed the question of the sources of stone used to make the bracers. It is in the Czech Republic that a start has been made with investigations into the lithic materials that were selected for bracers and their possible sources (Turek 2004), and this is a line of enquiry that holds much further potential.

Since 1974 much of interest has been written on the subject of European Beakers, in which bracers often merit a mention, but usually without any further attempt at analysis. There have also been individual reports of Beaker burials with bracers amongst the grave goods (e.g. Husty 2004; Weinig 1991), but there has been no further comprehensive study of the European situation as regards bracers, although a number were illustrated in 1980 by Richard Harrison. It would be a daunting prospect to survey the present volume of finds over Europe, with an estimated total of 1000–1500 (Heyd 2000, 283). There are as many as about 50 bracers now known from southern Germany alone (Heyd 2007, 348 and fig.12) and over 350 from Spain (Harrison, pers. comm.). For an overall survey it is therefore necessary to return to Sangmeister's two original publications for a review of the main varieties of bracer found in Europe.

9.2 BASIC TYPES AND DISTRIBUTIONS

In 1974 Sangmeister outlined seven different types of bracer (116, abb. 8) in a scheme that remains relevant today (Figure 9.1). Four of his types are for flat bracers and three are for examples that are curved, as seen in cross-section. Not all of these types relate directly to British forms but some compare well and so this scheme can be applied without too much difficulty to the British series. The flat bracers will be discussed here first, followed by the more elaborate curved examples.

9.2.1 Flat bracers

The most basic variety of bracer, flat, and with two perforations, corresponding to Atkinson's B1 and A1 types (Clarke 1970, 570), equates with Sangmeister's type G (1974, 118 and abb. 8, G). Turning to Sangmeister's maps showing the distribution of his bracer types in central Europe, further clues can be obtained as to possible correlations between these and the British forms. His distribution shows concentrations of flat bracers with two perforations on the middle Rhine and the Moselle and also,

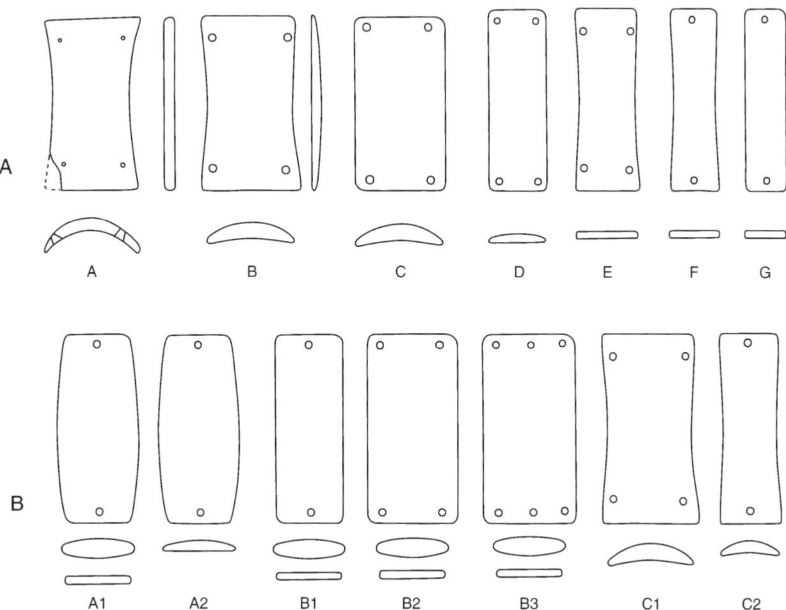

Figure 9.1. Summary of bracer classification systems (after Fokkens et al. *2008): top (A), Sangmeister 1974; bottom (B), Atkinson (Clarke 1970).*

closer to our own shores, on the lower Rhine (1974, 128 abb. 9). He had earlier recorded a concentration of similar bracers, again not so far from UK shores in Brittany, and the distribution of these and other more distant examples found in Portugal, Spain and southern France are to be found in his 1964 paper (1964, 95, abb. 2 and 3). It is clear that this particular variety of flat bracer was a common one in certain areas, amounting to 75% of the flat bracers listed in the earlier paper (*ibid*, 94). Amongst flat bracers recorded in the UK, there is a lower proportion of this variety, those having two perforations accounting for 54% of the total, with the remainder possessing four or more perforations.

Flat bracers with four perforations and straight sides, which correspond to Atkinson's B2 form, feature in Sangmeister's scheme as his type D (1974, 117 and abb. 8, D4). These seem to be of less frequent occurrence on the continent than the variety with a single boring at each end. They appear barely to have been recorded in Iberia (Sangmeister 1964, 96 and abb. 6) and only amount to some 25% of the flat bracers found in central Europe, but Sangmeister was able to demonstrate a scatter of finds which include some from the Rhineland (1974, 128 abb. 9). In the UK the situation is somewhat different, since here flat bracers may have four, six or even, in one case, twelve perforations (ID 29, Tytherington/Corton); these, taken together, amount to some 46% of the flat bracers. One slightly curved bracer from Barnack (ID 8, form C1) even has eighteen perforations, an insular design that incorporates gold capped rivets. Some eleven British bracers with six perforations are now known, amounting to 17% of the flat examples, a detail that is pertinent to comparisons with the continental evidence, since Sangmeister was originally only able to list 8 examples (2.1 %) from the whole of Europe (1964, 94 and abb. 5).

Sangmeister put forward two further types of flat bracer, E and F (1974, 117–8 and abb. 8, E, F), both of which had long sides that were noticeably concave, a detail that is of rare occurrence amongst flat bracers in the UK and so does not feature in the Atkinson scheme. Neither of Sangmeister's concave-sided flat types appears to be especially common in central Europe either (Sangmeister 1974, 129, abb. 10). His type F (1974, 118) is a variety with two perforations and these seem to be known mainly from Spain, Portugal and north Italy (1964, 95 and abb. 4), as for example finds from Beaker contexts at El Cerro de la Virgen, Granada (Schüle and Pellicer 1966, 29, fig.19) and Mejorada del Campo, near Madrid (Garrido-Pena 1997, 192 and fig. 4). There only appears to be one British bracer of this particular variety, from Newlands, Oyne (ID 91). Apart from this one exception, the British bracers with two perforations are divided between those that have a rounded outline and markedly convex sides, Atkinson's A1 form (see also Sangmeister 1964, abb. 3) , and those of more frequent occurrence that are approximately rectangular, with near straight or just slightly convex sides, Atkinson's B1 form (see also Sangmeister 1964, abb. 2). It has been concluded that on the whole the Type F continental bracers contributed little towards the design of those found in Britain.

Sangmeister's type E bracers (1974, 117 and abb. 8, E) differ from type F in having four perforations but otherwise have similar long sides that are markedly incurved. Again this variety is relatively uncommon in central Europe (1974, 129 abb. 10), but they appear to be more typical of finds from Spain (1964, 114, 118 and abb. 5). Most British bracers with four perforations have long sides that are straight or just slightly concave, and there is only one that approximates to type E, from Mildenhall (ID 9). However the occurrence on the continent of bracers of type E with six perforations is of interest. They appear again to be concentrated in Spain (Sangmeister 1964, 118 and abb. 5), although there is one from the river Rhine at Mainz (Gebers 1984, 53 No 86b and taf. 24, 42). Sangmeister was able to quote another three bracers of varying types with six perforations from central Europe (1974, tabelle 4b, 4c and 4d). There have since inevitably been further finds, as for example from Altenmarkt in southern Germany and Tvořihráz in Moravia (Heyd 2000, figs. 4, 16). It seems entirely possible that the idea for the British bracers with six perforations could have come from the continent but was further developed in Britain.

Other features recorded on bracers from Britain can also be traced to continental examples, such as the presence of dimples or incomplete perforations, apparently only partially bored. Finds of type E bracers from Henzing, Austria (Neugebauer C and J-W 1998, 314 and abb. 9, 8) and Předmostí, Czechoslovakia (Jacobs 1991, 102, abb. 6, 2) have this detail, while such part perforations are known from four British bracers (Dorchester XII, ID 1; Melton Quarry, ID 105; Lindridge, ID 111 and Raunds, ID 116; see also Chapter 5.4). Another feature, noted by Sangmeister on three of his type G bracers (1974, 118) as well as on two type E ones, is the occurrence of nicks in the sides of a bracer. This particular detail was noted on a couple of British bracers (Ferry Fryston, ID 73 and Aldington, ID 112; see also Chapter 5.4).

9.2.2 Curved bracers

Turning to the second main grouping of bracers, those that are curved in cross-section and have four perforations, Sangmeister divided these between three types, his A, B and C (1974, 115–7 and abb. 8, A,B,C; Figure 9.1). There is a clear correlation between his type B and the British curved bracers, Atkinson's form C1, which, unlike the flat ones, have concave long sides, along with mainly straight short sides and a moderate amount of curvature. Type B bracers are most common in eastern Europe, but examples have also been recorded from the Netherlands, the Rhineland and southern Germany (Sangmeister 1974, abb. 10). Bracers of Type A (Sangmeister 1974, 115), which are also most frequently found in eastern Europe, are those with extreme curvature, which is often accompanied by incised decoration at either end, and at first sight these ones would appear to have little in common with the British series. However these type A bracers, which were often made from red or reddish stone, are the ones which may also have a raised lip or moulding at either end, a sophisticated feature seen for instance on the beautifully crafted examples from Kornwestheim, Baden-Württemberg (Sangmeister 1974, 105 abb. 2) and Worms (Rheingewann), Rheinland-Pfalz, (Gebers 1984, taf. 52, 10). This particular design feature occurs on four of the British C1 bracers (Calne, ID 15; Ferry Fryston, ID 73; Culduthel Mains, ID 79 and Aldington, ID 112; see also Chapter 4.4) and seems sufficiently striking to have been copied from elsewhere. Another less common detail is a decorative feature seen on the bracer from Corry Liveras (ID 87), which has 28 small indentations at the unbroken end. A similar form of decoration has been recorded on a bracer of Sangmeister's type B from Mikulov/Nikolsburg, Moravia (Freising 1938, 52 and abb. 3).

Thus it can be seen that, in addition to some basic bracer types, the presence in Britain of certain design details such as a larger than usual number of perforations, part-perforations, nicks in the side, rows of indentations and ends with raised flanges, may also represent incoming ideas from the continent. Some continental bracer forms, however, barely relate to the British series, such as the flat types with markedly concave sides that seem to be typical of Iberia. Such Iberian bracers appear to include ones that are later in date, often being contemporary with Argaric sites, as for example at El Quintanar (Martín *et al.* 1993, 38). Likewise the bracers with extreme curvature and incised decoration seem to be typical of eastern Europe but as a type are not found in Britain, even if the end flanges were copied. It has been concluded that neither eastern Europe nor the Iberian peninsular played a large part in the possible links between British and continental burials with bracers. Thus the search for continental parallels for British bracers can be simplified by leaving aside both the Iberian and east European examples. The areas that have yielded finds of bracers similar to those found in the United Kingdom include Brittany and the lower and middle Rhine and these are considered in more detail below, together with northern France, a region that hardly featured in Sangmeister's analyses.

9.3 AREAS OF CONTINENTAL INTEREST

9.3.1 France

It has been possible to pinpoint areas of the continent that are of potential interest for tracing the likely origins of British bracers, though admittedly by reference to research carried out some 40 to 50 years ago, in papers now deserving of some radical updating. Two such areas are Brittany and other parts of northern France (Figure 9.2). The finds of Beaker pottery from France have an uneven distribution, but there is a particular concentration in Brittany as well as another in the South of France (Vander Linden 2006, fig.1) and these groupings are echoed in the numbers of bracers found in the same areas (Figure 9.2). The greatest number of bracers has been recorded in southern France, where at least 30 examples are known, mainly with two perforations (Guilaine *et al.* 2001, 238), coming predominantly from caves (*grottes*) and megalithic tombs with just a few from tumuli. Brittany comes next in importance, and here 20 bracers from old excavations are relatively well known and in seven cases are recorded in association with Beaker pottery (Treinen 1970, 70; Salanova 2000). There are another two finds from the Channel Islands (Hawkes 1937, 68). Many of these bracers are from megalithic tombs, including six examples from allées couvertes, while there is just one from a tumulus.

Brittany needs to be brought into closer focus, since

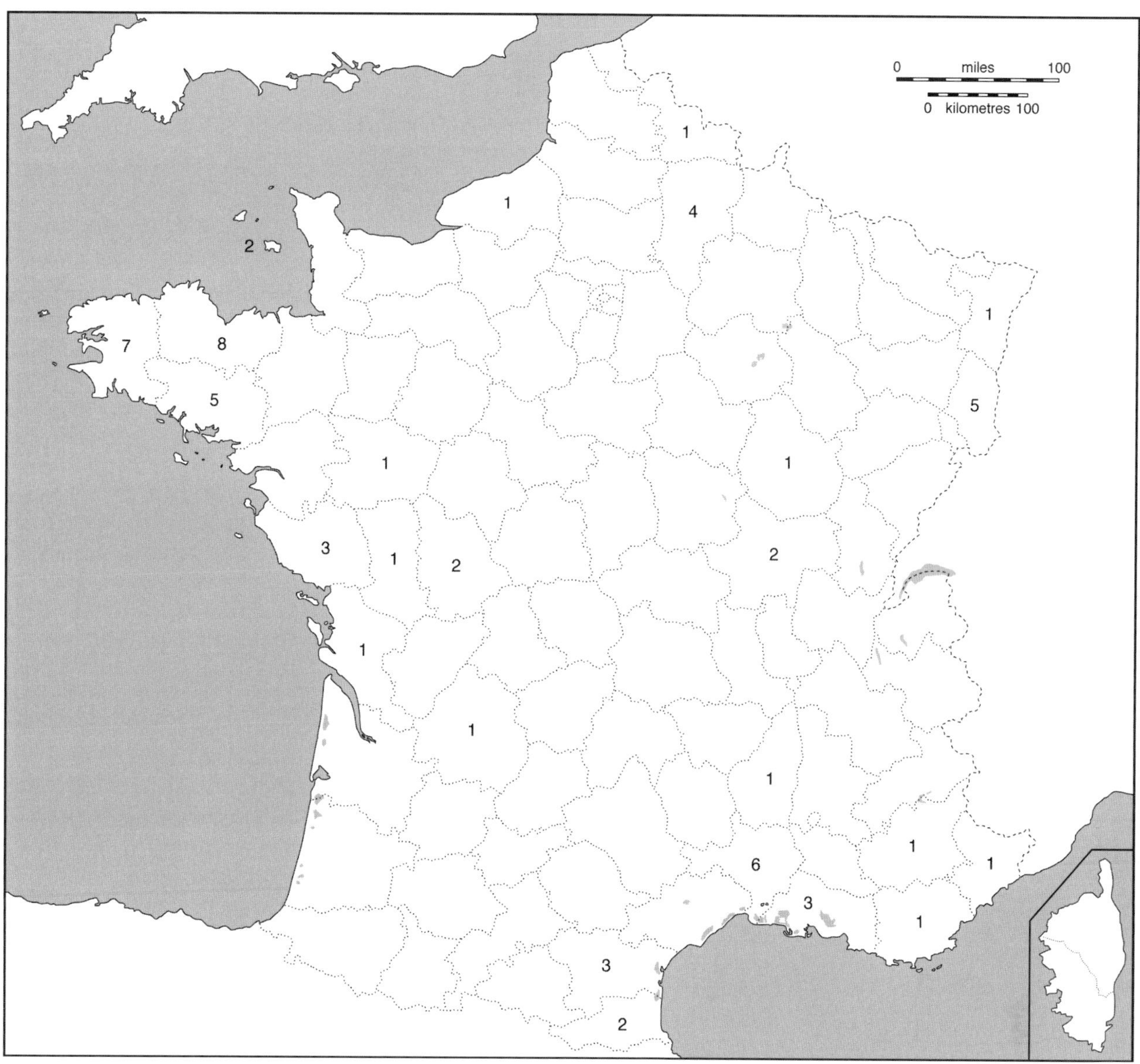

Figure 9.2: distribution of bracers in France (numbers in each Département).

it had recognized links with the United Kingdom during the Bronze Age (Briard 1993; Needham 2000, 176), while at least four Neolithic stone axe heads made from the Breton Type A dolerite found their way into southern Britain (Le Roux 1979, 50). The bracers from Brittany are nearly all flat, narrow examples with two perforations, the single exception being a flat bracer of red stone with four perforations from the tumulus de Lothéa, Fôret de Carnoët, Finistère (Briard and Mohen 1974, 49). This bracer has concave long sides and is less like the British ones, but most of those with two perforations resemble Atkinson's B1 variety and would not be out of place in a British context. Significantly though, Needham, in his analysis of British Beakers, did not consider that there were particular links between Brittany and south-west England, because of differences in Beaker styles and burial practices between the two regions (Needham 2005, 179 and fig. 3). The evidence provided by the bracers seems to be in agreement with this theory. Only two bracers have been recorded from south-west England and both are flat with four perforations (Archerton Newtake, ID 133 and Fox Hole, ID 134) and so are unlike the series of Breton bracers with two perforations.

At this time Brittany was adhering to the megalithic tradition, which stands in contrast to the Single Graves tradition of nearly all the British Beaker burials, including those found with bracers. However the Irish bracers predominantly have two perforations (Harbison 1976), as do the Breton ones. Beaker pottery has also been recorded from Irish megalithic tombs and although only one probable example of an associated bracer is known, at least three more have occurred in proximity to these tombs (Neil Carlin pers. comm.; Roe and Woodward 2009). Overall it seems likely that the Breton links were mainly with Ireland rather than with the United Kingdom. One or possibly two sites on the west coast of Britain have yielded bracers with two perforations from megalithic contexts. A broken, bracer with two perforations came from the disturbed chamber of a portal tomb at Dyffryn Ardudwy (ID 114) (Powell 1963). On the island of Skye a bracer with two perforations was found near a cairn of the Hebridean group at Broadford Bay (ID 88), and it is thought that it may have been thrown out of the chamber during some early investigations (Henshall 1972, 485). This bracer looks like an Atlantic type but a second one of the Group VI rock type, which was found in the chamber at Broadford Bay (Corry Liveras, ID 87), is of the curved C1 variety and seems more likely to have been a later insertion. The form A1 bracer, also made from Group VI rock type, from Glen Forsa (ID 86) may have been one of those that introduced the use of this stone for bracers into northern Britain. Other, non associated bracers which might relate to routes up the western seaways, as illuminated by Cunliffe (2001, 211) include two bracers each with two perforations from Dumfries and Galloway, one from Glenluce (ID 77), the other from near the head of the Solway Firth at Lockerbie (ID 150). These provide a suggestion of contacts emanating from Brittany or indeed even from further south down the Atlantic seaboard. Such contacts, apart from the likely ones with Ireland, may have been restricted to just a few connections with the western coasts of Wales and Scotland.

Leaving Brittany aside, the rest of northern France facing the English Channel is likely to be of relevance when considering precursors for the British bracers. This part of France has, however, traditionally been a region without much evidence for Beaker activity, a matter that is partially being resolved by further archaeological work (Salanova 2000). Here six bracers have been traced, from the Départements of Aisne, Nord and Seine-Maritime (Bailloud 1964, 347; Blanchet 1984, 75–99; Felix and Hantute 1969; Billard *et al* 1998, 362). Only one is from a burial, while two others came from surface flint scatters. Illustrations of four of these bracers demonstrate that they are of the flat variety. Two have four perforations, resembling Atkinson's B2 form; one has two perforations and compares with Atkinson's B1 form, while the fourth recorded example has two perforations and markedly concave long sides. The distribution of this group of bracers falls within Needham's 'Fusion Corridor', his area of cultural interaction with Britain (2005, 182 and fig. 3). Of particular interest is the grave group from Aremberg, Wallers, Nord (Felix and Hantute 1969), a single grave under a small mound, where a flat bracer with four perforations, seemingly very like British ones, was found with two Beakers, five barbed and tanged arrowheads and a tanged copper dagger. Comparisons have been drawn between these Beakers and British ones (Vander Linden 2006, 79) and Needham has commented that the appearance of these Beakers, as shown in the published illustrations, indicates close relationships with the British series, although perhaps also reflecting a local tradition (pers. comm.*)*. Another flat bracer with four perforations from Oulchy-la-Ville, Aisne (Parent 1975) also compares well with British examples with four perforations. Thus the bracers add to the potential interest of the Beakers from this part of France.

9.3.2 The Netherlands

The Netherlands is another key area at the north-east end of Needham's Poitou-lower Rhine axis (2005, 177). The bracers from here are once again mainly old finds and reasonably well known (van Giffen 1930; Bursch 1933; Butler and Van der Waals 1966; Sangmeister 1974; Lanting and Van der Waals 1976) and some 50 are known to the present writer, while no doubt more exist. A high proportion have been recorded from the province of Gelderland. Where details are available the Dutch bracers have almost invariably been retrieved from single burials beneath barrows. These bracers are more varied in shape than those so far discussed from France, with both flat and curved examples, and, as the pottery also shows, other influences have been in action here. In fact only three bracers of the curved variety are known, from Ginkelse Heide, Noorderheide and Stroeërzand (Barneveld), all in Gelderland (Butler and Van der Waals 1966, 49 and 124; Clarke 1970, 171) but these are of interest since in form they compare with the British C1 variety. The majority of the flat bracers recorded from the Netherlands have two perforations, one of which, a red one from Garderen, Gelderland, was found with a Beaker compared by David Clarke to his Short Necked Northern series (1970, 186 and fig. 681). Most of these bracers approximate to Atkinson's B1 group, with straight or slightly convex long sides (Sangmeister Type G; 1974, 118). Only four known flat examples have four perforations and these compare with Atkinson's B2 bracers (Sangmeister Type D; 1974, 117). There are however, another seven flat bracers with concave long sides (Sangmeister Types E and F; 1974, 117–8) which seem to be less like most British examples, although they could have inspired a comparable bracer from Newlands, Oyne (ID 91).

A small, but useful study of 15 Dutch bracers conducted by van der Vaart (2009a) provides detailed descriptions, together with both line drawings and photographs. Examination by this author of eleven of these bracers held at Leiden demonstrated that these Dutch ones differed from the UK bracers both in colour and in choice of stone. In the Netherlands the continental preference for both black (or grey) and red bracers seems to have been followed. The bracers with two perforations appear to have been mainly dark coloured and were sometimes made from lydite but more frequently from a near black, fine-grained sandstone, which apparently weathers to shades of grey-brown. It was noted that these bracers all had flat sides and ends, comparable to the two Amesbury Archer pieces (ID 56 and ID 57) but unlike other British examples which had more rounded sides. Two curved bracers with four perforations were examined; one, from Stroeëzand, was thought to be made from a dark red Permian or Triassic sandstone with very small, pale green reduction spots, while the other, from Ginkelse Heide, was made from a yellowish, fine-grained sandstone, possibly also Permian or Triassic, and then apparently coated with iron oxides to achieve the desired red effect. Morphologically these two bracers resemble British ones of the C1 variety, and so have potential for links with the UK, especially northern

England and Scotland, and these suggested links can be further substantiated by taking the pottery, burial customs and other associated finds into account.

As far as the pottery is concerned, Needham has recognized various Low Carinated Beakers from the Netherlands and also Belgium (2005, 179, figs. 4a and b). Links between the pottery of northern Britain and the Netherlands have long been considered (Sheridan 2008, 247), as for instance mapped by Clarke (1970, 158, fig. XI). Such links now seem re-affirmed by the most recent discoveries at Upper Largie, Argyll, a site which in addition to Beakers and burial customs that can be paralleled in the Netherlands, has early dates (Sheridan 2008, 251–2). Connections between southern England and the Netherlands appear more tenuous, but the Short-Necked Beaker from Shrewton 5K, Wiltshire has been compared with one from Ede, Gelderland (Needham 2005, 191). A change of burial customs in Scotland, specifically the adoption of burials in wooden cists, with palisaded ring-ditches, as seen at Upper Largie, can be attributed to influence from the Netherlands (Sheridan 2008), and similar changes elsewhere in Britain were noted by David Clarke (1970). Bone has a poor survival rate in the Netherlands (Butler and Van der Waals 1966, 100), so that the bone belt rings discussed by Clarke (1970, 113) cannot be compared. However, the amber objects from some northern British bracer burials may be of relevance here, while some metal objects such as single tongued daggers also have potential for links across the North Sea (Needham 2002, 112; Sheridan 2008, 257). Metal smithing stones are a further innovative item with some well known Dutch finds (Butler and Van der Waals 1966; Freudenberg 2009).

9.3.3 Germany (former BRD)

Although Germany is not immediately adjacent to the British Isles, David Clarke noted that the fast flowing current of the Rhine would enable an easy boat passage to the North Sea, with only a day and a night needed for a journey from the middle Rhine (1970, 92). He commented on groups of Beaker finds concentrated on the Rhine around Koblenz and Mainz which compared with others from southern England, his Wessex/Middle Rhine group (1970, 92 and fig. IX), and he was able to list six English bracers found in association with this variety of Beaker (1970, 98), five flat and one slightly curved, with two, four or six perforations (IDs 1, 4, 12, 28, 30 and 144). Needham has also seen stylistic links between British Lower Carinated Beakers with All Over Cord decoration and ones from the middle Rhine, as well as some from the Netherlands (2005, 179 and fig. 4b). By no means all Beaker burials included bracers amongst the grave goods and it has been estimated that in southern Germany only 8.9% of the graves contained them (Heyd 2007, 348). However bracers are of relatively frequent occurrence in Germany generally, including ones from the middle Rhine area and southern Germany (Sangmeister 1964 and 1974; Heyd 2007, 348), and a closer focus is needed on these particular finds.

Colour is a relevant factor, since available records suggest a marked preference in Germany for stone that is either reddish or black/grey (Sangmeister 1974, 114). This is in marked contrast to the British preference for two particular varieties of blue-green stone. There are very few bracers from Britain that could be described as either red or black, but these include the two from the Amesbury Archer grave-group (IDs 56 and 57), found with the inhumation of a man who is thought to have come from central Europe, perhaps from close to the Alps (Fitzpatrick 2003). This could mean that he came, if not from Bavaria itself, at least from that general area (Fitzpatrick 2011).

As with the Beakers, comparisons can be made between the varieties of British bracers and ones from the middle Rhineland. Good details are available for these German ones, from find spots mainly in Rheinland-Pfalz and Hessen (Gebers 1984, karte 23). Here flat bracers are the predominant type, but nearly a third consists of the curved variety, a contrast with both France and the Netherlands. In France curved bracers only occur in the east of the country, with two examples known from Alsace (Sangmeister 1974, 132, nos. 64, 72) and it seems as though the Rhine was a boundary to the west of which curved bracers were not being made. In the Netherlands just three examples of curved bracers are known. Flat bracers with two perforations account for half of those recorded from the middle Rhine area. Associated finds for these include two from Mülheim, Kr. Mayen-Koblenz, one found with a Beaker of Needham's Low Carinated variety (2005, fig. 4b, 27), the other with a Beaker of Clarke's Barbed Wire variety (1970, fig. 358). Flat bracers with four perforations are less common and have not always been found in associated contexts, but one such was found with a Beaker with zoned ornament at Friedbach-Fauerbach, Stadt Friedberg (Gebers 1978, 159 and taf. 35, 8–9). There may well be some more recent finds. It is notable that only four flat bracers listed from this area have concave long sides, a point that coincides with the lack of popularity of this variety in Britain.

A number of the middle Rhine bracers approximate to the British curved variety (C1) and these include a quite strongly curved one found with a Beaker of Needham's Low Carinated form at Monsheim, Kr. Worms (Gebers 1978, 64 and taf. 30, 3, 4; Needham 2005, fig. 4b, 36), while others associated with Beakers include finds from Bodenheim (Gebers 1978, 24 and taf. 43, 8,9), Ilvesheim (Gebers 1978, 129 and taf. 29, 10,11) and Worms-Hochheim (Gebers 1978, 105 and taf. 30, 1,2). A further mildly curved bracer illustrated by Clarke, from Darmstadt Waterworks, was found with a footed bowl (1970, fig. 198). The middle Rhine repertoire also includes a few of the more strongly curved bracers, Sangmeister type A, the variety more typical of Eastern Europe, which includes bracers that may have incised lines at either end and also moulded lips at the short sides.

Bone toggles, of a variety rarely found in the UK, provide another point of comparison. One is known from Barnack, Cambridgeshire (ID 8) and another, which came from the Boscombe Bowmen burial in Wiltshire (Fitzpatrick 2004, 13), appears very similar to others from the Rhineland (Gebers 1978, taf. 30, 6 and 10). So-called arrowshaft smoothers may provide another link between Britain and the continent. Although these artefacts have not in fact been recorded in association with any British Beakers, they are known from some Early Bronze Age contexts (Annable and Simpson, 1964; Woodward *et al* .in prep.). On the continent however they have been quite frequently found in Beaker contexts, as for instance from Löbnitz, eastern Germany (Harrison 1980, fig. 26) and from grave 9 at Bruck, eastern Bavaria, where the grave goods included a flat bracer with four perforations (Schmotz 1992, 66 and abb. 14). The burial rite in the middle Rhine area relates to the Single Grave tradition. As has been found for other areas, the middle Rhine bracers tend to belong to old finds with limited records, but at least half are known to have come from flat graves in small cemeteries (Gebers 1984).

The situation in southern Germany is altogether different, since, in addition to the older finds (Sangmeister 1974), recent excavations are providing details of new bracer discoveries from a number of cemeteries (Heyd 2007, 336, fig. 6). The bracers from this area are varied in character, with shapes that can in many cases be compared with British examples (Heyd 2000, 285 and taf. 76). The burial rite in cemeteries may seem far distant from the British Beaker burial customs but there are other points of interest. Possible continental links for the copper raquet-headed pin from Roundway, Wiltshire (ID 28; Clarke 1970, 95) and bronze spiral-headed pin from Sewell, Bedfordshire (ID 12) have been called into question (Brendan O'Connor, 2010 and pers. comm.), but to counteract this it appears that the Sewell pin was made of metal from a far distant source (Needham, pers. comm.). The Roundway dagger is also thought to be made of copper from a continental source (Clarke 1970, 98). It could be that these two pins from early Beaker burials are in fact of continental origin and that it is mainly the later Early Bronze Age pins that are insular versions (Needham 2000, 178). It has long been suggested that the best parallels for the riveted knife-dagger from Dorchester XII (bracer ID 1) could lie in the Upper Rhineland or Bavaria (Case 1965). Heyd has pointed out that in southern Germany there is a correlation between occurrences of copper daggers and gold objects in graves, and also with bracers (2007, 348), and these are all items that were found together in the Amesbury Archer's grave along with a metal smithing stone, an item found in craftsman's graves (2007, 360); stone tools of this kind are increasingly being recognised from German and other assemblages (Freudenberg 2009).

9.4 DISCUSSION

It has been possible to identify specific areas of Europe likely to have been most relevant for the transmission of the Beaker/bracer combination to the UK. This is a complex issue, but a study of only those Beaker grave groups that also contained bracers provides some distinct clues as to the origins of the British Beaker series. A marked contrast can be seen between the Atlantic tradition of collective burial in megalithic tombs, which left some traces up the west coast of Britain, and the Single Graves tradition, which seems to have been responsible for most of the British burials with Beakers and bracers. It has been concluded that Brittany was not a key area for the transmission of the bracer idea to Britain, although it may have had an important role in the movement of the same idea to Ireland, where a strong tradition of bracers with two perforations arose (Harbison 1976). The rest of the French Channel coast may have had some connections with southern England, but the modest number of known finds in northern France, both of Beaker pottery and of bracers, suggests that such links could only have been limited in extent. Altogether stronger Beaker/bracer traditions existed in parts of Germany, and the middle Rhine area appears a good candidate for links with southern England, while it is the lower Rhine area that can be seen to connect in particular with northern England and Scotland but also with Wessex. The Rhine was an important prehistoric highway and some additional links with the vibrant Beaker communities of the upper Rhine and Bavaria need not be entirely discounted.

The present study has not come up with any clear instances of actual bracers that may have been brought across the Channel, although three possibilities exist. The bracer that seems most likely to have been directly imported is the Amesbury Archer's black one (ID 57). Two further *possibly* imported bracers in the miscellaneous group are both made from non local rock. The one from Mildenhall (ID 9) has incurved long sides in the style of Sangmeister's Type E (Figure 9.1), while a damaged bracer from Thanet (ID 149) has long sides that are flat in the continental style. The red/black colour preferences were not ones that gained currency in Britain, perhaps partly because colour was of less importance than a rock from a special source, and perhaps partly because suitable red and black materials, especially good red stone, were not easily found. Instead the amphibolite, a rock close to nephrite in composition and one that bears some resemblance to jade was selected, perhaps because there was still knowledge of the prized jade axes. Not long after, a special stone axe head material, the Langdale stone, which is also greenish-grey in colour, was adopted for the manufacture of curved bracers. This might explain why only three certain finds of red bracers are known from the UK, all with two perforations. The one from the Amesbury Archer's grave group (ID 56) is most probably made from red mudstone possibly from Pembrokeshire, while the other two, from Dornoch Nursery (ID 94) and Carneddau (ID 148) were both made from reddish, local Old Red Sandstone. Two of these finds have early radiocarbon dates that are remarkably similar, with those of 2460–2310 cal BC at 1σ (3895 ± 32 BP: OxA-13541) for the Amesbury Archer (Needham 2005, 185) close to those of 2450–2200 at 1σ (3850 ± 40 BP; GrA-26515) for the Dornoch cist burial (Sheridan 2007, 109). These dates indicate that the bracers concerned may not be the earliest from Britain but would still be well up amongst early Beaker associations in the Needham scheme (2005, fig. 13). It may be noted that although the red Amesbury Archer bracer (ID 56) appears to be made from a Welsh stone, the technique of manufacture, with flattened long sides, is more typical of continental bracers and the same detail can be seen on the black Amesbury Archer bracer (ID 57). Black bracers from Britain are also few in number. It has not been possible to locate a source for the stone used to make the Amesbury Archer's black bracer but a European source would not be entirely out of the question. This black stone differs quite markedly from the materials used for the A1 style black bracers from Ben Bridge (ID 108) and Stonehenge (ID 58), as shown by the plot of chemical compositions (see Chapter 3, Figures 3.1 and 3.4). However black bracers of Sangmeister's type G/Atkinson's form B1 are common enough on the continent. A classic example is the bracer from an inhumation burial (Grab 1) in a small cemetery with Maritime Beakers at Trieching, lower Bavaria, found with a Beaker with zoned decoration, a tanged copper dagger and flint arrowheads (Heyd 2000, 82 and taf. 83). There is a relatively early date range for this burial, of 3915 ± 28, 2460–2340 cal BC at 1 σ (Heyd 2000, 472), which suggests that it could have been a little earlier than that of the Amesbury Archer.

It was originally suggested by Sangmeister, operating without the benefit of radiocarbon dates, that the form of bracer with two perforations could be the earliest variety (1964, 96). Heyd, aided by only a few dates, proposed for southern Germany a simple progression from flat bracers with two perforations through to mildly curved ones with four perforations (2000, 472; 2007, 332 and fig. 4). This scheme is now supported by radiocarbon dates from Scotland (Sheridan 2007, 109, Appendix 1), which show Dornoch Nursery (ID 94), with a red bracer with two perforations, as one of the earliest Beaker sites in Scotland, while Fyrish (ID 78), with a curved bracer of Group VI rock type with four perforations, was maybe two or three generations later (see also Chapter 7, Table 7.1). It was left to Case to suggest that the stone bracer was an Iberian innovation (2004a, 207), while at the same time advocating the primacy of Beaker pottery in the Iberian peninsular (2004b). Here bracers have been recorded from many different types of site, including Argaric ones of Bronze Age date. However they also occur in rock cut tombs and megalithic monuments, together with Beaker pottery, as for example at the hypogeum of São Pedro do Estoril (Brandherm 2009, 174, fig 2) and the megalithic tombs at Lorca de Seixas (Brandherm 2009, 175, fig 3) and Pedra Branca (Ferreira *et al.* 1975, 168). Such associations may be amongst the earliest occurrences of bracers in Iberia. Some confirmation for this comes from a fragmentary bracer of unknown type but likely to have had two perforations from the settlement at Porto Torrão, Ferreira do Alentejo, (Cardoso and Soares 1992, 219), which has one of the earliest radiocarbon dates for Beaker sites in Portugal (ICEN 61: 4230 ± 60 BP; Müller and van Willigen 2001, 64, fig. 7).

Further dates for the intervening stages of movement between Iberia and the Channel would be an advantage, since none too many were available from Müller and Van Willigen's Region III in their recent survey (2001, 64 and fig. 9). Nevertheless the general picture is clear enough, with maritime movement from Iberia northwards up the Atlantic coast (Cunliffe 2001, 197, 211), involving the re-use of megalithic tombs in Brittany and most probably also in Ireland. There was also traffic to southern France, where the megalithic tradition was again part of the story. Routes northward from here, up the rivers Rhône and Rhine, had long been traditional. It may have been along the upper Rhine, or perhaps in Bavaria that innovative forms of curved bracers were developed, which were to lead ultimately to finely crafted, decorated varieties, including the ones of Group VI rock type with gold rivet caps (IDs 8, 13 and 79).

There are precedents for the dissemination of valued objects across Europe, such as jade axe heads (Petrequin *et al.* 1998, fig. 1), daggers of Grand Pressigny flint (Cunliffe 2001, 218–20) and Breton dolerite Type A axes (Le Roux 1979), and it would be no surprise if groups of bracers made from specific materials were also found to have been widely distributed. The British survey has shown that two main lithic materials were selected for bracers and there must be other instances of such selection on the continent, though currently just a few hints of this can be gleaned from the literature and also from a modest number of bracers examined in continental museums. People were moving around during the Beaker period (Price *et al.* 2004), some no doubt more than others, and bracers made from identifiable materials must sometimes have moved with them, providing potential for further research into the Beaker enigma.

10: DISCUSSION

John Hunter, Ann Woodward, David Bukach and Fiona Roe

10.1 BRACER GEOLOGY

Very early on in the process of examining this corpus of stone bracers it became apparent that one of the key characterising features of the objects was their geological origin. Many of them could be divided into two well-defined petrographical types. One of these types was derived from a Langdale tuff and known as the *Group VI* type – a definition employed by the Implement Petrology Group (IPG) for Neolithic axe heads manufactured from the same source (Keiller *et al.* 1941), and the term adopted here. The other type was an actinolite-bearing amphibole-rich rock of less precise geographical origin, known here as the *amphibolite* type. There was also a third group comprising various other geologies known here as the *miscellaneous* type which included a sub-set of bracers which are distinctively red or black in colour. The use of both compositional and petrographical analysis identifed the first two of these types as clearly defined geological entities. Additionally, there is some evidence to suggest that the use of magnetic susceptibility could also be used as a discriminating factor, although with less confidence. Colour too could also be used to define the two types, but in a more limited way (below). Of those bracers known in Britain and either examined or analysed during the research (n = 74) 24% were of the Group VI type, 38% were of the amphibolite type, and 38% were of the miscellaneous type. The first two types merit some initial discussion here; the miscellaneous types will be reviewed subsequently. The distribution of bracers made from the three main rock groupings is shown in Figure 10.1.

To some extent the geological nature of the two raw material types has considerable implications for the manner by which the respective bracers can be procured and worked; it also poses significant impositions on shape and, thus, could indirectly affect function. In turn this may also have a bearing on context, distribution and date. These factors are discussed in some detail below, but the initial part of this synthesis must necessarily establish the individual underlying geological characteristics.

The Group VI bracers all appear to belong to a tuff exploited in the Langdale part of the English Lake District. This was a source already prized in the Neolithic and one that clearly held a greater embedded social value than one simply offering the practicalities of suitable stone. This is emphasised by its restricted outcropping and relative inaccessibility. The material is a light, dull green colour often exhibiting small characteristic surface rust coloured 'spots' which tend to be indicative of the most fine-grained tuffs (see Appendix 3.3). An important feature of the tuff, however, lies in its isotropic structure which allows it to be worked in any direction without splitting, although it shows a relatively high number of minor fractures around the perforations. These may represent particular difficulties in drilling holes in tuff, or indeed in addressing a drill to a curved surface. Its qualities otherwise enable it to be fashioned into the distinctive curved form of bracer which constitutes the majority of the Group VI bracers studied here. The finishing process has a tendency to leave diagonal striations on the front surface; this reflects the characteristics of the rock as well as the curved nature of many of objects produced.

By contrast the amphibolite bracers are laminar and naturally foliate; they cannot be worked into curved shapes, but their fine-grained structure allows them to be precisely formed, often very thinly, with polished surfaces. Fractures are relatively common due to the vulnerability of working the thin foliate structure. The working striations tend to lie longitudinally on the front surface as a result and these bracers tend to be a greenish or bluish grey pastel shade. The source of origin for the amphibolite group is still open to debate. Although amphibole-rich rocks do occur in south-west Britain (south Wales or Cornwall) the best known matches are rocks in the Highlands of Scotland (see Chapter 3). It is also feasible, from a geological point of view at least, that the exploitation occurred in continental Europe, possibly in the Alpine region or in Spain, although no known matches to continental artefacts or sources have been established so far. However, the concentration of amphibolite bracers in middle and southern England, and the current absence of identification of any bracers made

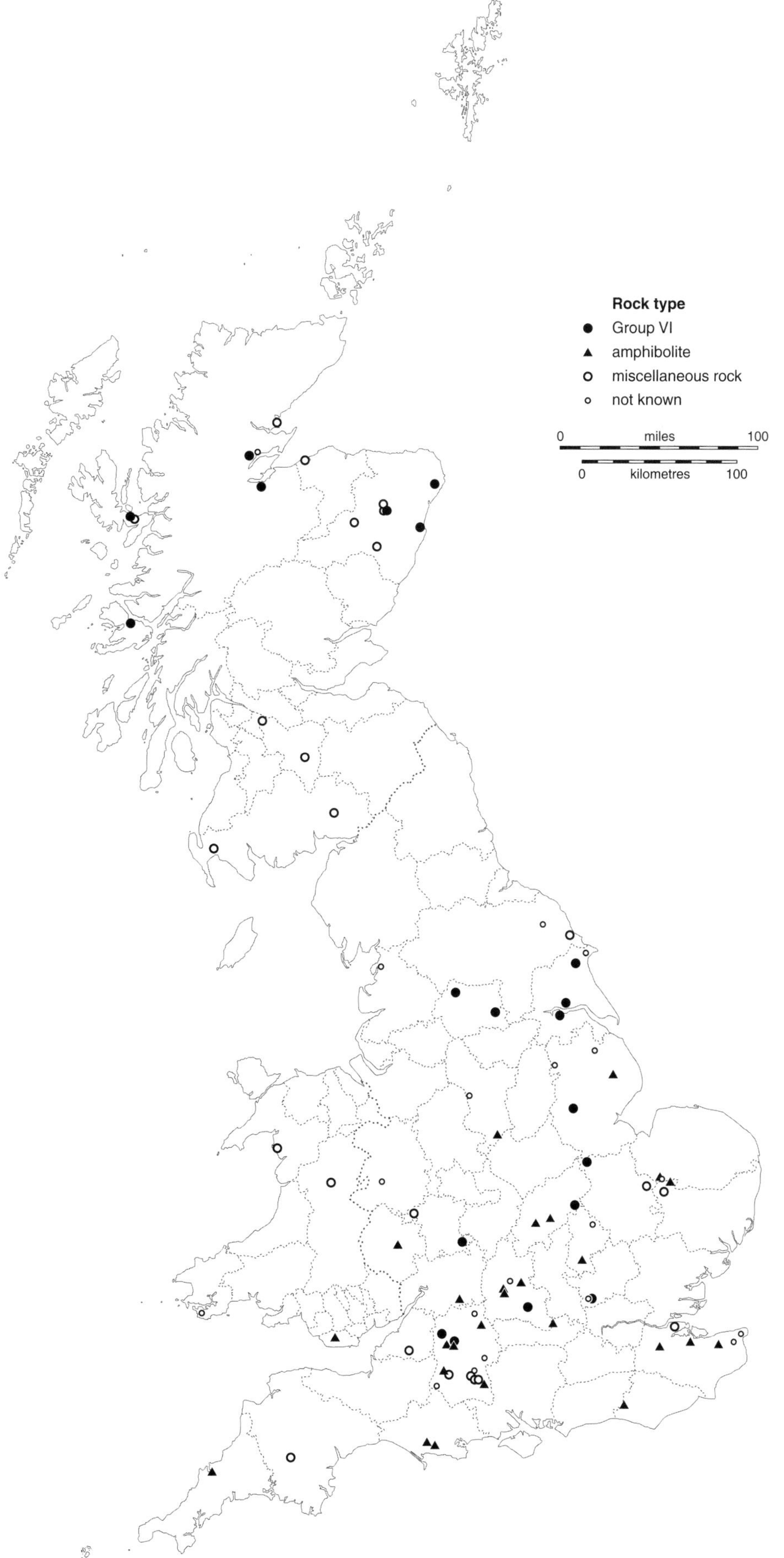

Figure 10.1. Distribution of bracers according to rock type.

from this material in Europe, does seem to indicate that the rock derives from an English (or possibly Welsh) source.

The distribution of the bracers made from Group VI rock is concentrated in eastern England and Scotland (Figure 10.2), and in the midlands as far south as north Wiltshire. None are known from the region which contains the rock source (Cumbria), and there are none known from the most northern counties of England, or from southern Scotland. The slight cluster of Group VI bracers in Yorkshire is highly reminiscent of the marked concentration of Neolithic Group VI axe heads in this region, and it is instructive to consider this parallel further. In overall terms the distribution of Group VI axe heads extends further south in England than that of the bracers, embracing the central Wessex region, and reaching the southern coast in the Solent Basin area (Clough and Cummins 1988, map 6; Field 2008, fig. 5.6, b). Group VI axe heads also occur in Wales (Darvill 1989, fig. 4) while no known bracers made from this rock occur west of Worcestershire. And the distribution of Group VI axe heads in Scotland, albeit sparse, does reflect the eastern bias of the Scottish Group VI bracers distribution. Thus the distribution of bracers mirrors that of the earlier axe heads in general, but it is much more restricted in its extent.

The distribution pattern of bracers made from amphibole-rich rock is totally different from that of the Group VI examples, and is almost complementary (Figure 10.2). Amphibolite bracers are concentrated in the southern counties and the Thames valley, with a few outliers as far north as Lincolnshire, in East Anglia and in south Wales. There are none known from any location in northern England, and none at all from Scotland. This distribution only overlaps with the Group VI findspots in Lincolnshire, Northamptonshire, Oxfordshire and north Wiltshire. The main concentration of amphibolite bracers lies in Wiltshire, Oxfordshire and Kent. This might not immediately appear to support the idea that the raw material was sourced from the south-west or from south Wales (see above). However, once again it is useful to consider the distribution of Neolithic axe heads, this time those from known Cornish sources. For instance the distribution of Group I axe heads, with a source located at the south-western tip of Cornwall shows marked concentrations in Wessex and the midlands, and not in Devon and Cornwall, except around the source itself (Clough and Cummins 1988, map 2), and they also occur in Wales (Darvill 1989, fig. 8). There are also a number of Neolithic axe heads, and a few battle-axes, which are made from amphibolite or related rock types. Checking through the thin sections made from these axe heads might reveal whether any of the rocks relate to the amphibolite used to make the bracers. However the laminated structure of the bracer material would have made it unsuitable for the manufacture of axe heads, so that little correspondence can be expected. It is not always possible to demonstrate continuity in the exploitation of sources for axe head materials from Early Neolithic times through to the Bronze Age. The end date for the production or circulation of axe heads is not clearly known, though there is evidence that some axe head materials were still current during the Bronze Age, in particular Cornish greenstone. This has been recorded in association with Deverel-Rimbury pottery on the Perry Oaks site at Heathrow and also at Cotswold Community in Gloucestershire (Shaffrey and Roe 2010, 78), so it seems that the long standing interest in lithic supplies from the south-west was maintained.

What is most important is that the distributions of the amphibolite and Group VI bracers are almost mutually exclusive. The amphibolite types may have been in use first (see Chapter 7), but certainly some of the Group VI items were also being deposited not long thereafter, so the distributions are certainly in part contemporary.

Amongst the bracers of miscellaneous rock type it is useful to separate out three examples of marked slender, elongated and sub-rectangular shapes made from distinctive rocks which are red or black. These three bracers came from two early Beaker graves (Amesbury Archer, ID 56 and 57 and Dornoch Nursery, ID 94) and are quite different from all other bracers from England, Wales and Scotland. The red colour of two of these bracers suggests Irish influence, a factor now emphasized by the discovery that the man buried at Culduthel (ID 79), though admittedly at a later date, came from Northern Ireland (A. Sheridan, pers. comm.) A number of axe heads made from the Irish Group IX porcellanite have been found in England and Scotland (Clough and Cummins 1988, 273, Map 9) and so indicate some earlier contacts between Ireland and the UK. These contacts continued with the later importation into Scotland of goods that included pottery and flat axes of Irish copper (Cressey and Sheridan 2003), while Irish gold would have been sought after, more especially in England. Thus a couple of red bracers that seem to imitate the Irish jasper, another special material, need come as no surprise. The black Amesbury Archer bracer (ID 57) does not fit into this scenario and a possible continental origin is proposed. Four other red or black bracers are shorter and more thick-set with rounded outlines. There are radiocarbon dates for one of these, from Stonehenge (ID 58), but the wide range of between 2400 and 2140 cal BC (see Table 7.1) is unhelpful. These four too stand out as being somewhat different in character from other bracers recorded from the UK.

The rest of the bracers made from miscellaneous rock types tend to occur in non-burial contexts, or are stray finds Unfortunately the two available dates again do little to show where they stand chronologically. One is for a bracer (ID 90) associated with a Group VI one at Newlands, Oyne and suggests a middle of the range chronological position, while the other is for an Early Bronze Age cremation burial at Lockerbie (ID 150). In terms of shape and size they are generally smaller, with only two perforations and with slightly tapered ends. In terms of overall distribution these miscellaneous examples are concentrated especially in Scotland, and otherwise quite widely scattered across mid Wales, East Anglia and the south-west, including south Wiltshire (Figure 10.2). Thus they overlap with the distributions of both the Group VI and amphibolite bracers, whilst also appearing to fill in some of the gaps in those distributions: notably in Wales, and in southern Scotland.

10.2 THE BROADER PICTURE

Given the ubiquity of bracers throughout most parts of Europe it seems appropriate to discuss these British bracers within their wider continental setting. Chapter 9 provides a context in which the British bracers can be placed; it also reviews the varied health of bracer studies throughout Europe and the different typologies established by previous scholars in attempts to categorise and track bracer development. Interpretation has traditionally been based on morphological characteristics and the number of perforations per item. The picture is a confusing one, and geological study is only beginning to be drawn in as a complementary measure (e.g. Turek 1998). Moreover, no concerted large-scale survey has been carried out, even at a basic level, and the likely total of known European bracers can only be estimated at somewhere between 1000–1500 items. A digital database for Europe as a whole is however currently in preparation (Fokkens *et al.* 2008, 125; www.surfgroepen.nl/sites/beakernetwork).

Apart from basic similarity of intrinsic form, British and continental bracers have a number of features in common (e.g. nicks and possible mount settings) which reinforce the likelihood of a common cultural tradition, but there are also differences, and to some extent this explains why there is no single defined typology. Reference to the schematic typologies in Figure 1.2 (Chapter 1) illustrates the extent to which Sangmeister's (continental) types differ from Atkinson's (British) types: there are significant, if subtle, morphological distinctions between the two geographical groups. The discussion in Chapter 9 pursues this further: it demonstrates that bracer morphology can vary widely across Europe noting, for example, that flat, two-holed bracers are ubiquitous although more common in western Europe, while curved ones occur in certain areas only. It is also noted that not all continental types can be paralleled in Britain. It is less clear, however, as to the relative importance of cultural influence and typological development in this variation, or whether differences might be more firmly based on geological or functional factors.

There are a range of broad morphological types (e.g. curved, flat, waisted etc.), several perforational variants (notably the two-perforation and four-perforation types), and often a colour distinction. In short the term 'bracer' has been used as a collective term to describe a group of similar stone objects whose single common feature is the presence of one or more perforations at either end. One might justifiably question whether such a range of known shapes and styles can represent typological development, whether it simply reflects variations on a theme, or whether it should be viewed on a different basis altogether, perhaps as an indication of the differing constraints of the materials used. It may be conceivable, for example, that the occurrence of flat bracers with four and six perforations, which tend to be found in Britain rather than elsewhere, may reflect local geologies offering relative ease of drilling compared to other geologies abroad. In his study of Moravian bracers, Turek (pers. comm.) has noted that bracers were fashioned from softer rocks than those used in Britain. In the same way, the squarer profiles of continental examples (as opposed to the rounder profiles of British bracers) may reflect geologies which present different working challenges. The regional distinctiveness identified in Chapter 9 may have as much to do with the characteristic geological resources as with the more traditional assumptions of social preference and assumed typological development.

The analysis of manufacturing traits undertaken here demonstrates the extent to which geological factors might be at play in bracer production. In general it appears that Group VI tuff was selected from particular beds which provided the finest-grained working material. This high quality rock is visually evident in view of its distinctive 'spotting', a feature which marks it out from other lesser fine-grained tuff outcrops which are harder to fashion. It is interesting to note that this was not the typical outcrop material exploited in the production of the earlier Neolithic axe heads (Chapter 3, Appendix 3.4) where the working of tight curvature and fine detail was not as critical. It is possible, therefore, that these tuff outcrops were specifically targeted in view of their working properties, while the presence of iron sulphide inclusions, which when freshly worked would have shone like gold, could have been an additional attraction. The same might be argued for the amphibolite bracers where the aim appears to have been the creation of elegant, flat, thin objects, often with carefully fashioned lentoid profiles, waists, or rounded edges. Many of the amphibolite bracers exhibit fault lines which would have made working (and drilling in particular) awkward in an already time-consuming and tedious fashioning process. These flaws must have been apparent at the time of procurement and during working yet were accepted nonetheless, perhaps because to a prehistoric eye the darker veins and streaks added to the character and attraction of a special rock. Several of these bracers fractured or split during the manufacturing process (Chapter 5), yet still appear to have been used. These 'flaws' in both bracer types might be interpreted in one of two ways: either that the source (i.e. the material) used was carefully selected on the basis of its working qualities irrespective of visual impairment or, conversely, that the selection of material was beyond the control of the craftspersons concerned who were only allowed to use material available to them. Whether any restricted availability was a product of social inhibition and controlled filtering of resources, or one of simple accessibility remains open to question. In any eventuality, and in one way or another, both sources of materials were demonstrably 'special'.

There is now growing evidence to suggest that there are some continental bracer groups which also have distinctive geological pedigrees, notably the red curved bracers with a distribution in central and Eastern Europe (Sangmeister 1964, 93, abb. 7), and the grey/black bracers

Figure 10.2. Distribution of bracers separately according to rock type.

ID	Site	Perfs	Colour	Likely imitation of
9	Mildenhall	4	Olive grey	Amphibolite
29	Tytherington/Corton	12	Light olive	Amphibolite
90	Newlands, Oyne	4	Dark grey	Group VI
123	Ferniegair	4	Pale grey/red?	Group VI
133	Archerton Newtake	4	Whitish grey	Amphibolite
135	Cassington	2	Light greenish grey	Amphibolite
148	Carneddau	2	Red	Red
150	Lockerbie	2	Brown	Group VI
153	Cliffe	2	Black shale	Black

Table 10.1. Bracers of miscellaneous rock type possibly mimicking defined geological types or distinct colours.

which characterise parts of the Rhineland (Sangmeister 1974, 114). Roe has also identified likely commonality of source among the collection at Leiden (pers. comm.). In other words, as in Britain, there is also evidence of procurement through specific sources (possibly also involving colour). However, it remains open to question as to whether these broad regional distributions reflect zones of cultural influence or, more simply, the practical routes through which specific geologies could be sourced. In Britain, the Group VI bracers are predominantly found in the far north, and the south midlands, but not in southern England, whereas the amphibolite types appear to belong (with slight overlap) to central and southern England (see above). Other social or cultural factors may also be implicit and possibly underlie the overall distribution which shows a range of highland and river valley find spots distinctly focused on eastern England and eastern Scotland. Firstly we may postulate that the bracers, or raw materials for their production, may have been distributed mainly by sea or river. However it is also interesting to note that the overall distribution of bracers, with its eastern bias, coincides closely with the distributions and concentrations of early and middle style Beakers (*sensu* Case 1977, roughly equivalent to Clarke's 1970 types: AOC, E, W/MR, N/MR, and to the Needham 2005 types that occur before and around the 'fission horizon'). A glance at the relevant distribution maps in Clarke's corpus (Clarke 1970, maps 1 to 3) reveals a distribution of Beakers, mainly from graves, which occurs particularly in eastern England and Scotland, Wessex and the Thames valley, associated with occasional outliers in Wales and the south-west peninsula. This tallies almost exactly with the overall distribution of bracers from graves, and confirms their very distinct cultural context.

At this point the nature of the British bracers made from miscellaneous rocks – the third group identified – and the sources of their raw material needs to be discussed further. These bracers fall into several common geologies, mostly siltstones, mudstones, slates or fine-grained sediments the chief characteristic of which is a laminar structure which allows them to be worked in much the same way as the amphibolite. Moreover, some of them also appear to mimic the amphibolite bracers in terms of colour (e.g. olive grey or greenish grey). Interestingly, unlike most bracers of miscellaneous rock type which have two perforations, these particular items were wider, and possess four or more perforations. However, unlike their amphibolite cousins, their sourcing is more likely to have been local. These are listed together with probable red/black and Group VI copies in Table 10.1.

The miscellaneous group includes eight or so red and black bracers. All have two perforations but nevertheless exhibit considerable variations in form and have different affinities. Some of the geological sources are far distant while others seem to be local. The black Amesbury Archer bracer (ID 57) with its early date is visually very similar to the grey/black continental types and chemically is unlike other British bracers. It has been postulated that it may well come from the continent and research to follow up further clues continues. By contrast, two other bracers with early dates, the Amesbury Archer red example (ID 56) and the Dornoch Nursery reddish one (ID 94), may represent attempts to replicate 'authentic' red jasper bracers. Possibly the same could be true of the pink/red Carneddau bracer (ID 148). The Amesbury Archer's red bracer was probably obtained from a distant source in Pembrokeshire, but the other two paler red ones seem to be made from local stone. It is interesting to note that Harbison has already observed the likelihood of attempts to replicate the red jaspers within Ireland itself in his study of the Irish bracers (1976, 31–3, Appendix C). In other words, there is affirmation here of 'special' sources if the Irish jaspers were being deemed worthy of imitation.

An interpretation of a couple of black bracers, from Stonehenge (ID 58) and Ben Bridge (ID 108), both made from rocks non local to their findspots, could be that they represent attempts to replicate the porcellanite source used for small number of the Irish bracers. This black stone, interestingly, is also a known source for Group IX Neolithic axe heads and may again have been revered as a special material from a sacred mountain. The Amesbury Archer's black bracer (ID 57) does not closely resemble the porcellanite ones, so that a continental source for it may be more likely. If the black bracer from Cliffe, on the estuarine coast of Kent, is made from Kimmeridge shale, as seems likely, it was deposited under a Beaker some 211km (131 miles) from the source area in Dorset but somewhat further if carried by a sea journey. The Amesbury Archer's grave goods included a shale ring and once again we seem to have evidence for a valued material. The idea of special materials is reinforced by a further bracer in the group (Newlands, Oyne ID 90) which appears to represent a direct copy of a Group VI curved bracer but using a local geological source which does not lend itself well to curved workmanship. As a result it has a flat, as opposed to a concave underside which necessitated the crude chasing of wide grooves to carry the thongs. There are also potential Group VI 'copies' in Ireland (ID 95 and ID 97; see Chapter 3, Appendix 3.1). These are both flat with two perforations each with a colour similar to that of the Group VI types, but with different geologies. Interestingly a number of Group VI Neolithic axe heads have been discovered in Ireland (Cooney and Mandal 1998, 11); this might suggest that the 'genuine' material was known but that imitation was possible from more local sources.

10.3 THE BRACER IN CONTEXT

Contextually, apart from valuable research by Heyd (2007), little continental work has been carried out, although there is some correlation between bracers and their deposition in single graves containing Beakers. This is particularly evident in northern France (excluding Brittany) and in the Rhineland, but only in as much as current research has been undertaken. The same limited research also provides an inferred relationship with "arrow straighteners", bone toggles, pins, metal smithing stones and knife daggers, and this is pursued below. Bracers from Brittany, nearly all with two perforations, mostly appear from chambered tombs and so seem to belong to an Atlantic tradition which links Iberia with Brittany and, in a more limited way, with the western coasts of Britain. Bracers found in southern France have also mainly been found in megalithic tombs. Use of the Atlantic route could satisfactorily explain the presence in Ireland of bracers with two perforations, though here special local materials, jasper and porcellanite were chosen for making many of them (Chapter 3, Appendix 3.1). Two bracers, one from Wales and one from western Scotland, may relate to the same Atlantic tradition. Each has two perforations and is made from miscellaneous rock. The two fragments from Dyffryn Ardudwy (ID 114) are from a chambered tomb, while that from Broadford Bay (ID 88) is thought to have been thrown out of the chambered tomb there.

The study of the British contexts undertaken here provides more detailed analysis. Approximately two-thirds of the British bracers have recorded contexts, mostly in burials from the late Neolithic and Early Bronze Ages. These bracers are predominantly of the Group VI and amphibolite types and occur almost entirely in Beaker-related burials in south-east England and north-east Scotland, in inhumations, cremations and secondary burial contexts. There are also a small number from pits. Chronologically, they appear to occupy a fairly tight range of dates within the latter part of the third millennium BC on the basis of a growing number of radiocarbon measurements based on associated materials. These show the presence of bracers from the earliest period of known use through until the latest dated Beaker example (Ferry Fryston, ID 73) at approximately 2000 BC. There are some interesting observations to be made on the distribution of rock types throughout this range. The earliest dated examples belong to the two red bracers from Amesbury (the Archer burial) and Dornoch (ID 56 and ID 94 respectively) and the black bracer from Amesbury (ID 57). All three are morphologically similar with two perforations and belong to the 'miscellaneous' group. There are some amphibolite and Group VI examples which are also dated quite early, but insufficient amphibolite pieces from dated contexts to confirm any trends. Moreover, there are also factors involving possible heirloom items, re-working or length of use life which have the potential to blight more detailed analysis of these dates. Nevertheless, Clarke's original (1970) hypothesis that flat bracers occurred with early Beakers and predated curved bracers largely holds good in that the eight dated Group VI (curved) examples are all generally dated later, and can be refined further through Needham's review of Beaker typology (2005). Reference to his new seriation confirms the early position taken by three red/black bracers but also suggests an early appearance for the amphibolite examples. It reaffirms the position of the Group VI bracers as being concentrated in the later part of the period. This appears to be a chronological trend which is supported by association with other artefacts with defined typologies such as daggers or arrowheads, or with artefacts known to lie early or late within the overall Late Neolithic and earlier Early Bronze Age periods.

This chronology, however, omits reference to the other third of the bracers studied which, in common with many of the examples studied in Ireland, are classified as stray finds in that they had no secure archaeological context. Interestingly, these strays are predominantly bracers of the miscellaneous rock types, and with a distribution largely peripheral to the other two groups, in the midlands and north-east England.

A breakdown of the types of context in which bracers of miscellaneous rock type have been found is provided in Table 10.2. Interestingly, all the miscellaneous bracers found in Beaker graves are those which are red/black or those which have been argued to be imitations of red/black, amphibolite or Group VI bracer types; and these eight bracers include most of the miscellaneous bracers that possess four or more perforations. A large number of the remainder are stray finds. Only one derives from a context of undoubted Beaker age (Ben Bridge, ID 108) while those from chamber tombs may have belonged originally to Beaker or Early Bronze Age graves, and the stone circle may have been of Bronze Age rather than Beaker date. There is also one example from an Early Bronze Age cremation. Thus it could be argued that the miscellaneous

Type	Perforations	Beaker grave	EBA context	Other	Stray find	ID numbers
Red/black and red/black copies	2	4	1		1	56, 57, 92, 94, 148, 153
Amphibolite copies	4 (one with 12)	3	1			9, 29, 133, 135
Group VI copies	one with 2; two with 4	1	2			90, 123, 150
Miscellaneous	2			Chamber tomb 2		88, 114
	6			Stone circle 1		82
	2			Beaker pit 1		108
	2		1			130
	six with 2; one with 4; one with ?4				8	77, 80, 84, 93, 104, 111, 120, 139
Totals		**8**	**5**	**4**	**9**	

Table 10.2. Bracers of miscellaneous rock type: context types.

bracers that are not copies of red/black, amphibolite or Group VI bracers may have had a rather later currency than those types. Future radiocarbon determinations might serve to further discussion of this point.

There is, it seems, an emerging distinction in both distribution and depositional context: on the one hand the Group VI and amphibolite types, and copies of them would both appear to belong to a distinctive Beaker cultural milieu, while on the other hand the miscellaneous types tend to occupy a discrete geography, possibly on the grounds that the other two rock types were (for whatever reason) unobtainable, and occupy a context which was rarely funereal. These miscellaneous bracers, most of which exhibit two perforations might, by typological analogy with the three elongated red/black dated bracers, be considered to appear early in the sequence. On the other hand, some may be derivative imitations of the bracers found in Beaker graves, manufactured from various local or regional rock types, and in areas outside the main concentrations of Beaker activity. In which case, these may have had a currency which was predominantly later than that of the amphibolite and Group VI bracers.

10.4 THE BRACER AND THE INDIVIDUAL

Many of the bracers discussed here were excavated in antiquity according to accepted methodologies of the day, and although some of these may fall short of expected modern standards, a number of observations can nevertheless be made. The majority of bracers with recorded contexts appear in burials and therefore are likely to represent items of personal adornment associated with, or donated to, the particular deceased individual concerned. However, a small number of bracers appear in pits without associated human remains; these are divorced from individualisation and represent anonymous depositions. This phenomenon is pursued below. Bracers which occur in inhumation graves are normally found lying on the left-hand side of the body, usually on the lower arm and often on the outside of the forearm. According to interpretation, archers' wristguards would be located on the inside of the lower left arm in order protect the wrist from the rebounding string of a bow drawn by the right hand. In other words, the presence of bracers on the left forearm would indicate a right-handed archer. In several cases it is more likely that the bracer had in fact been worn on the leading edge of the forearm, rather than the outer face of the arm. This applies particularly to the curved bracers, the diameter of which is too small to fit on the wider part of even a small female arm (see Figure 5.8e). Similar problems apply to the interpretation of bracers recorded lying adjacent to the lower body (seven examples), as well as those which seem likely to have been deposited in caches in various positions in the grave. There are four specific examples of this, including that of the cache located near the feet in the Amesbury Archer (ID 56) burial. Are we to assume, as we assume with regard to the bracers recovered from pits, that these were depositions of anonymous character – they were not a reflection of the occupation or status of the individual, but talismanic of the society members/mourners that presented them within the funeral ceremony?

Examination of the human remains in these burials suggests that the typical burial incumbent was male, probably older rather than younger, and robust in stature, although this interpretation should be treated with some caution, given the variation in the osteological techniques used and the (early) date of some of the anthropological observations. Nevertheless, there is a sense of consistency, and it is exciting to believe that the status implied by the quality of the bracers might be mirrored in both the social and physical stature of the 'archer' to whom the bracer belonged. That said, in those graves where the bracer lies in obvious association with the body, it is difficult to identify other trappings which might suggest that the incumbent was indeed an archer. The most obvious associations, barbed and tanged arrowheads, are recorded in only 12 of the 31 Beaker inhumations which contain bracers; they also occur in inhumations without bracers and are not therefore exclusively bracer-related. There is some slight relationship between inhumations containing bracers and the presence of objects of amber, or bone toggles and rings, or metal pins. Their presences are interesting, but not sufficiently consistent to be meaningful, although the presence of bone toggles is also known from continental bracer burials (above). However, study of the wider Beaker context suggests that the metal pins and bone toggles almost always occur with bracers and therefore may be significant even although the numbers are small. Within the burials they all occur in close proximity to the bracer itself.

10.5 FUNCTION OR DECORATION?

The bracer or 'wristguard' is traditionally seen as being specific to the practice of archery and is applied to the inside of the forearm or wrist to ensure protection of the wrist. There are plenty of ethnographic and modern analogies for this, although bracers are usually fashioned from leather or some similar flexible material which additionally provides protection for the forearm itself. The bracers discussed here are very different: they are inflexible, are found in a range of different shapes and sizes and possess a variety of fastening configurations according to their respective number and arrangement of perforations. In order for a bracer also to be functionally effective in allowing an arrow to fly smoothly, it would need to possess a smooth, flat surface that presented no impediment to either string or fletching when the arrow was released. Most of the bracers are shaped to facilitate this, but those Group VI curved bracers which splay out slightly at the ends, and those bracers which bear gold caps, certainly do not. In fact they would offer the opposite of the required qualities. Moreover, it would seem that the fastening of any of these stone bracers to the wrist using thongs or even thin cording passed through the perforations would also impair the smoothness of the surface. It is not clear how bracers were attached although there are clues from the alignment of some of the perforations, from the directions of drilling, and from small nicks cut into the edge of some bracers to route the fastenings (e.g. Ferry Fryston, ID 73). For example, those with two perforations often exhibit the perforations lying offset and/or with alternate angles of drilling suggesting that the thonging was specifically routed in a certain direction. Those with four or six perforations sometimes show similar angled directions of drilling, although many appear to be random. Either way the fastening would have necessitated the thongs lying on the outer surface of the bracer in a manner that would have impeded the smoothness of the arrow's flight. One example shows this routing quite clearly (Hemp Knoll, ID 7). The curved Group VI examples mostly exhibit a high degree of symmetry and consistency in the way the perforations were drilled from the rear but in all cases the thong must have crossed the outer surface in order to be fastened securely. Reference to the position of those bracers found within inhumation burials shows that only a proportion were located inside the wrist of the individual; this does much to support growing opinion (e.g. Case 2004a, 207; Fokkens *et al.* 2008) that bracers were more likely to be worn on the outside of the arm rather than on the inside. Such factors raise the question as to whether all bracers can be ascribed an archery function. One alternative possibility is an association with the art of falconry: some 'bracers' may have been used as decorative elements on the upper leading edge (as opposed to the inside or outside) of the arm. Falconry, like archery, has traditionally been viewed as a high status activity and the accompanying grave goods are commensurate with both. Moreover, there are also some objects found in association (notably bone toggles) which may also have possessed a falconry function. This possibility of some bracers being used in falconry is explored in detail in Appendix 10.1.

Some bracers may simply have been emblematic, a manifestation of status, power or achievement through which the individual, possibly an archer or falconer, might be recognised in death as well as in life. The fastening, for which the perforations were clearly intended, may have been to a leather wristguard or gauntlet, or even to clothing on a different part of the arm. Evidence for the existence of some form of backing material is to be found on a bracer from El Quintanar, Albacete, Spain; a clear gap can be seen between the bracer and the well preserved long silver rivets (Martin *et al.* 1993, 34 and Fig. 12b). Another clue comes from Borrowstone, Aberdeenshire (ID 89), where the bracer was found " lying on the right forearm, on a pad of organic material" (Shepherd 1984, 14). The position and direction of the drillings might offer some indication as to the shape or proportions of the part of the body or object to which the bracer was attached. Proximity to the body suggests that the bracers were a special part of personal adornment, that they were worn as part of uniform, regalia or costume; this is reflected in the choice of material, and care in manufacture and finishing. The idea of costume may help explain the 'unfinished' perforations which adorn a small number of bracers (e.g. Melton Quarry, ID 105) where symmetrically located depressions or dimples may have originally housed circular decorative mounts or pastes. The discovery of ochre on Dutch examples may further support the original existence of surface decoration (Van der Vaart 2009a, 40). It does not, however, explain the other part-perforations which lie adjacent to full perforations and which appear to represent unsuccessful attempts at drilling leaving unsightly blemishes on even the finest examples (e.g. Barnack, ID 8).

It is also clear from the way the bracers were finished that only one face was intended to be viewed. There is ample evidence to demonstrate that in nearly all instances the two faces were treated differently. Both were smoothed, often leaving working striations. One surface was almost always better smoothed and polished than the other leaving only faint striations (or no striations at all), and this is assumed to be the front (seen) face. Less effort was expended on the other face where almost every example still exhibited coarse working marks that had not been fully polished out. This face was intended to be secured against another surface, possibly leather, when the object was worn. Very few bracers can be argued to be reversible and evidence of use wear tends to confirm this. Bracers were fixed objects, unlike pendants or tools which could move or be manipulated. In instances where use wear can be identified, usually in the form of scratching or scuffing, it is heaviest on bracers from the miscellaneous group. These are in general thicker and ostensibly more durable than the other two groups, but there is no evidence to indicate that they may have been used any differently. On all geological groups use wear appears on the front surface and less frequently on the rear. Although both Group VI and amphibolite rocks are of similar hardness, the Group VI tuff is more susceptible to surface scratching, whereas the planar nature of the amphibolites make the sides more likely to show wear than the flat surfaces. There is, however, some chipping on the underside of some of the Group VI curved bracers suggesting that they were not permanently fixed, perhaps being taken off and stored between wearing. This may also explain why fracturing during use, especially among the amphibolite bracers, mostly occurred at the corners, and might indicate vulnerability during attachment and detachment processes.

Some of the Group VI bracers may have been permanently fastened; these are the examples exhibiting gold caps to the perforations through which bronze rivets appear to have been used to fix the bracer to a setting. This would have been a permanent arrangement and likely to have utilised materials more rigid than leather, such as wood or bone. It indicates accoutrements rather than costume itself, possibly involving attachment to a staff, standard or rod of office. Moreover, the angles of drilling for the perforations in these gold-capped examples are almost entirely vertical or near-vertical; this suggests that the objects were produced for permanent fixture, that the need to undertake angled drilling for routing the thong was unnecessary, and that the gold capping represented a primary rather than a secondary function. The presence of use wear markings on the gold caps themselves is probably indicative of a long life before deposition.

The Group VI curved bracers deserve particular mention at this point in view of their unusual concavo-convex shape. This is an inappropriate bracer shape for application to the forearm, particularly those with extreme curvature (e.g. Kelleythorpe, ID 13). The symmetrical way in which the perforations tend to be carefully angled and splayed seems to be significant; it suggests that the bracers may have been fastened around an object of regular thickness, such as a staff, or even the handgrip of the bow itself rather than on the forearm. Attachment in this way would have suitably obscured the rear coarse surface leaving only the better-finished front face and bevelled edges visible. There is, unfortunately, insufficient data available regarding the precise location of these objects within the burial to pursue this theory further. The only curved bracer likely to be exceptional to this is the example from Newlands, Oyne (ID 90) where the routing of the thong has been chased through the flat rear face. However, this is not a Group VI example but a probable copy (above) produced from a local source. It effectively mimics the curvature and the splayed ends, but has been made to be fixed to a flat rather than to a curved surface.

10.6 VALUE

The phenomenon of fragments (i.e. incomplete bracers) holds an important place in this study. Sangmeister has already noted an unexpectedly high proportion (12%) of continental bracers appearing as fragments, including those in funerary contexts, and there are three examples here in Britain (e.g. Bishops Cannings, ID 32). This not only attests to the intrinsic or symbolic value of the material, but it also provokes some discussion regarding the nature of fracturing. Additionally, Harbison's study records that some one-third of all the bracers in his Irish corpus were broken, an observation since supported by more recent work (Roe and Woodward 2009). Different geologies present different fracture vulnerability, and here the isotropic nature of the Group VI tuff produces the tendency to shatter rather like glass. However, these bracers tended to be mostly intact, whereas the majority of the broken amphibolite bracers were fractured *across* the plane rather than more natural splitting *along* the planar lines. It is conceivable that at least part of this fracturing may have been deliberate and undertaken using types of knife or saw which have left the characteristic tools marks recorded here. Approximately one third of all the bracers studied exhibit some form of re-working or re-use and this is an astonishingly high proportion; many of these belong to the amphibolite group. Several bracers have been resurrected from fractured larger bracers and are re-perforated, but not always in a manner, or at a size, that makes them functionally effective as wristguards (e.g. Corry Liveras, ID 87). Others were re-fashioned into pendants or amulets (e.g. Old Rayne, ID 82) or shaped into tools (e.g. Raunds, ID 116). Some also suffered corner damage during manufacture to the extent to which they were virtually unusable as bracers *per se* (e.g. Hemp Knoll, ID 7), yet they still found their way into both inhumations and cremations as somehow being deemed worthy of deposition.

The extent of the re-working that took place would appear to be an implicit reflection of the contemporary value placed on the material, irrespective of its final condition. As far as the Group VI and amphibolite bracers are concerned, perhaps it was the nature, or the source of the respective rocks that was important, that they held an intrinsic quality of which we have little modern-day comprehension – something perhaps, in the case of the Group VI examples, to do with the continuity of powers held by original axe heads, and in the case of the amphibolite examples, perhaps a perceived link with treasured Neolithic axe heads made from jade – or it may have had to do with symmetry, visual quality and a connection with ancestry. Both Group VI and amphibolite fragments are more common than those of the miscellaneous bracers; perhaps the fragmentation reflects some form of social 'currency' by which individual elements of a complete object were shared amongst groups or family members on the basis of their intrinsic value (see Chapter 6 and Chapman 2000). This is no more than conjecture, but conjecture well founded on the basis of the research conducted here.

We can assert, with some conviction, that the Group VI and the amphibolite bracers were 'special' as a result of targeted procurement, and were fashioned to a high standard by craftspersons who knew exactly what they were doing in adherence to a long-standing tradition. This seems likely to have been a common procedure throughout Europe and is perhaps a dimension of Early Bronze Age society that has not been fully recognised. Specific rock sources have been exploited, and zones of distribution established, although we have little understanding of the geographical and cultural parameters involved, other than their ostensible relationship with Beaker culture. But the role and high status of the archer as perceived by Clark (1963), Case (2004a, 202) and others remains intact. The archer was a person of rank with whom these special rocks were associated, although the strict role of the wristguard had long since become symbolic; it had become emblematic, ornamental and fixed in memory rather than being functional. Ironically, many of these objects may not be 'bracers' at all. There is growing evidence to suggest that many may have been worn symbolically on the outside or front edge of the arm as an indication of status or achievement, rather than on the inside of the arm as a functioning wristguard; equally, some may have been used in falconry. Others may have been attached to wooden staffs, to other ceremonial objects, or even to the bow itself. The tuff and the amphibolite items were of value in their own right, even as fragments when they continued to hold a significant funereal position. We have perhaps been inadvertently led astray by an emphasis on typology, on dimensions, shape and numbers of perforations, when these artefacts are essentially ceremonial and part of regalia. We know little of the objects or materials to which they were attached: some may indeed belong to the forearm, others perhaps to outer garments, shoulder straps, or perhaps independent objects. These are not bracers *per se* used by the archer of the day, but finer points of ceremonial dress whose origins, perhaps once archery-based, had since evolved into a more symbolic role. The Group VI and the amphibolite examples seem to belong to 'core' Beaker culture; many of the bracers of the miscellaneous rock types, despite their early appearance, may well be copies and also occur in Beaker graves. But the other examples made from the miscellaneous rock types occur in areas where Beaker culture was less dominant, where procurement access may have been restricted, and where utilitarian or ceremonial activities required these objects to be of more robust type and character. Also there is a hint that these items, many of them found as stray finds, may have been rather later in date than the bracers found in Beaker graves.

APPENDIX 10.1: ASSOCIATIONS WITH FALCONRY?

10.1.1 INTRODUCTION

Falconry or hawking is a human pastime which involves the use of trained birds of prey (raptors) to hunt or pursue other birds or small animals. Now mainly practised as a sport, in the past it was also employed as a means of acquiring meat for food. Furthermore it was generally associated with particular sectors of society, often those of high status. Hawks cannot be domesticated and will not breed in captivity, so each bird must be captured in the wild. A trained bird would therefore have been of great worth.

A key connection between birds of prey and Beaker graves accompanied by stone bracers is provided by the contents of one of the earliest Beaker graves to be excavated and recorded in the north of England. This is the burial found in a barrow at Kelleythorpe, Driffield, East Yorkshire (Londesborough 1851, pl. XX, 2; Kinnes and Longworth 1985, 145; bracer ID 13). It contained a very fine curved bracer made from Group VI rock, and embellished with gold studs. It is notable that 'in front of the body was the upper part of a hawk's head and beak' (Mortimer 1905, 275). This find has led to informal discussions of the possibility of a connection between bracers and falconry, as at the Prehistoric Society conference *Is there a British Chalcolithic?* in 2008, but the idea has not previously been fully aired in print.

Interestingly the occurrence of hawk remains in Early Bronze Age barrows was also noted by Thomas Bateman in relation to his extensive investigations in the Peak District. For instance, on Stakor Hill (Hartington Upper, Derbyshire), between two inhumations (one crouched and accompanied by two bone points), were 'two instruments of flint, and the lower mandible of a hawk, supplying the third instance in which we have observed the remains of this bird in tumuli' (Bateman 1861, 80, footnote). Furthermore his *Appendix on animal remains found in the tumuli* lists under 'Falconidae': 'two species, unrecognisable from the remains, but one rather large' (*ibid*, 299). Also, in discussion of the half bracer found in a field near Bridlington, East Yorkshire (ID 122), Sheppard drew attention to the burial from Kelleythorpe which has already been mentioned above. Following brief description of the finding by Lord Londesborough of a bracer similar to the Bridlington example, but curved, on the wrist of the body at Kelleythorpe, he made the following observation:

'As the remains of a hawk occurred in the same cist, it is possible in this case the bracer was to protect the flesh from the claws of the bird' (Sheppard 1930). This appears to be the only previously published mention of this potentially interesting functional connection.

10.1.2 FALCONRY IN HISTORY

Falconry is known to have been one of the most popular field sports of the medieval world, and is thought to have been introduced into Europe from Asia in late Roman or immediately post-Roman times (Cherryson 2002, 307). One important source is a book by Emperor Frederick II *Concerning the art of hunting with birds* first written in the 11th century AD, and further details of the association of different birds with varying scales of social status were provided in the 15th-century *Boke of St Albans* (Grant 1988, 180). Evidence of hawking equipment from medieval sites is rare, but finds of the skeletons of birds possibly used in falconry are much more common. The occurrence of short winged and long winged hawks on a series of 19 archaeological sites was listed by Cherryson (2002, table 1). It seems likely that many of the birds represented were trained raptors. This is because several species were of foreign derivation, or would have naturally inhabited habitats which were far removed from the urban, and even some rural, sites within which they were found. Also, in northern Europe, some of the bird remains were found in association with human burials of later Saxon date, and appear to have been trained hawks that were buried with their owners. Many of the English sets of bird remains studied comprised entire skeletons, which again tends to suggest that the birds were intentionally, and respectfully, buried by human agency (*ibid*, 311). Additional evidence is provided by the evidence of pathological changes to the leg bones of two hawks from a site in Hampshire; injuries which were probably caused by the tethering of the birds (*ibid*, 312). A final factor in favour of the identification of trained birds of prey is that the skeletal remains tend to be found on high status sites such as castles and manor houses, or on rich properties within urban contexts. Leather or wooden falconry equipment is not likely to survive, but there are finds of metal hawk rings from a few medieval sites in England (Serjeantson 2009, 322).

In a study of 27 faunal assemblages from Anglo-Saxon England only five produced remains of traditional falconry birds (Goshawk or Peregrine Falcon), and only one of these sites was of high status (Dobney and Jaques 2002, 16). However the incidence of such birds on urban sites may reflect the purchase or exchange of such birds in these commercial locations. Dobney and Jaques further suggest that the remains of buzzards, present on 13 of the 27 sites studies, may suggest that these birds may have been trained to take live prey, especially as they tend to occur on high status estate centres. And the remains of red kite may reflect the practice of kite-hawking, the hunting of red kites with other more traditional birds of prey (*ibid*, 17–18). Thus, 'some of the high status sporting pastimes, traditionally associated with high and later medieval times, may actually have their roots in England during the Saxon period' (*ibid*, 19). A clear falconry scene is depicted on the October scene from the 10th-century AD Cotton Tiberius Calendar (reproduced in Strutt 1810) and further pictorial evidence is provided by the occurrence of mounted high status falconers on a series of 9th-century AD Pictish sculptures from Scotland (Carrington 1996). Probable representation of a falconer occurs also on the Bewcastle Cross, dating from the late 7th or 8th century AD (Kitzinger 1993, 10–11), while literary reference to Welsh falconry occurs in the 10th-century AD *Laws of Hywel Dda*, including mentions of the specific equipment employed: mews, jesses and gloves (Jenkins 1986, 14–15).

10.1.3 FALCONRY IN ANCIENT HISTORY AND PREHISTORY

It is also possible to find evidence for falconry having existed before the Saxon and medieval periods. Although there is no definite evidence for hawking having been practised in Roman Britain (Parker 2007), the remains of a sparrowhawk were found in a late Roman villa ar Boreham, Essex (Serjeantson 2009, 321). The sport is depicted on a late Roman floor mosaic at Argos in Greece, and the earliest literary evidence also comes from Greece. Passages from Xenophon and Aristotle suggest that falconry was practised by the Persians (Carrington 1996, 462). In Hittite documents from the second millennium BC onwards, and in sculptures from the first millennium BC there are mentions and depictions of a god which holds a raptor perched on the left fist (Canby 2002, and Serjeantson 2009, fig. 13.2). It is thought that the activity may have been developed first in the Asiatic steppes (Dobney and Jaques 2002).

It may be that the origins of the sport date from a very much earlier era than this. Dobney has drawn attention to the occurrence of a 'remarkably consistent presence of the bones of birds of prey (raptors)' on sites of later Palaeolithic and proto/early Neolithic date *c.*10,000 to 8,000 BC, in Israel, Jordan, Syria, Iraq and Iran (Dobney 2002, 76 and table 1). Some of these same sites also produced significant quantities of remains from small mammals and game birds, indicating that hunting skills were both varied and highly developed. Although such faunal evidence cannot be used as proof, it can be suggested that maybe one of the new hunting strategies was the art of falconry (*ibid*, 76). Most of the birds found on these early sites are not those of the falcons traditionally used in falconry (*Falconiformes*) but eagles, buzzards, vultures and the eagle owl. Although these birds are not favoured by modern falconers, there is much evidence that a very wide range of species was trained to fly to the fist and to hunt in recent and modern Central Asia, India and even Europe. In Russia the golden eagle was employed to catch wolves, foxes, deer and hares, for both meat and furs. And in 17th century AD Persia such birds are recorded as also taking cranes, ducks and geese, partridges and quails. Vultures are carrion feeders and will not hunt and kill live prey in the wild. However there are literary sources from the 5th century BC which record the training of vultures. Although they may not have been used for hunting they could have been used as lures in the training of smaller birds of prey. Also from the early Near Eastern sites there are many bones from the eagle owl. Although not popular with falconers today this bird can also be trained to take prey, and it is particularly effective at night (*ibid*, 77–81). Raptors are also commonly associated with ritual activities, and in Central Asia especially with shamanism. For instance, the birds may have been totemic icons or viewed as ancestral to a shaman. Thus the birds evidenced by the raptor remains on these early sites may have fulfilled a ritual role, alongside their economic importance (*ibid*, 81). This interesting study not only extends the practice of the art of falconry far back into deep prehistory, to the very beginnings of the Neolithic period in the Near East, but also emphasises that the art may have embraced both spiritual and basic economic overtones. Also birds of prey may, along with the dog, have been one of the earliest tamed and trained animals in the world.

10.1.4 EVIDENCE FOR FALCONRY IN PREHISTORIC BRITAIN

Apart from the raptor remains from Beaker and Early Bronze Age graves mentioned at the beginning of this discussion, is there any other possible evidence for the practice of falconry from prehistoric sites in this country? Such evidence might include the presence of the bones of either raptors or their dedicated prey within relevant species lists from excavated sites. Some of the most extensive lists of bird species represented on prehistoric British sites relate to the Iron Age 'lake villages' of the Somerset Levels. Amongst the birds listed from Glastonbury and Meare are a series of birds of prey: the white-tailed sea eagle, possible golden eagle, goshawk, peregrine falcon, an unidentified large falcon, and buzzard (Gray 1966, 409; Coles and Minnitt 1995, 195). Moving back in time to the Bronze Age and Neolithic periods, information is harder to come by. This is mainly because settlement sites dating from these periods are relatively rare, so few faunal assemblages are available for study. However there is a little data that may contribute to the question. Bones from hawks were recovered from Late Bronze Age Unit 4 layers at Brean Down, Somerset (Bell 1990, 231) and, also of Late Bronze date are remains of buzzard and white-tailed sea eagle from Potterne, Wiltshire. The sea eagle item here was a claw which had been perforated as an ornament or charm (Lawson 2000, 108–9, 239 and fig. 93, 61). For the Late Neolithic and Early Bronze Age period, there are the finds of hawk remains from barrows, as described at the beginning of this discussion. Large birds of prey have also been found on Late Neolithic henge monuments including kite at Durrington Walls, Wiltshire (Harcourt 1971, 346) and the articulated wing of a sea eagle from Coneybury, Wiltshire (Richards 1990, 153). From sites throughout all these periods possible examples of prey: duck, fox, deer and wolf as well as smaller furry mammals are well represented. As in the case of the species lists from the early Neolithic Near Eastern sites, such evidence cannot be used as firm proof that falconry was being practised, but it is highly suggestive. The white-tailed sea eagle appears to have been of particular importance in earlier prehistory, as its tail feathers were the preferred material for the fletching of arrows. These birds seem to have had a magical role, with the fletched arrows taking on the power and keenness of vision of the eagle itself. And a grave from south Sweden contained a special deposit of four eagle claws (Clark 1952, 39). The eagle wing from Coneybury may also have been a ritual deposit, as it was found in the basal layers of the ditch of the henge monument (Richards 1990, 153, table 80 and fig. 100). Further evidence of the ritual significance of raptors includes a Chalcolithic flute from France, which was made from the leg bone of a black or Griffon vulture (Scothern 1989, pl. 36).

10.1.5 FALCONRY EQUIPMENT

The range of equipment associated with the art of falconry is relatively standardised, and similar devices may have been in use for many centuries. Details of the basic components are described in modern treatises on the art of falconry (e.g. Ford 1992) and are illustrated on many commercial websites (Figure Appendix 10.1). The pieces of equipment are designed in order that the hawk may perch on the leading edge and lower thumb joint of the left hand, and then be released when the selected prey is in sight. Thus the basic accoutrement is a strong glove or gauntlet, made from leather, with a long body which covers and protects the wrist area. The glove has a projection on the lower edge which is perforated to hold the falconer's leash. This is a thin rope or cord which is attached to the bird by means of a special slipknot known as a falconer's knot. When pulled the rapid release of the knot allow the bird to fly free.

The leash is often attached to a decorative tassel which is fixed through the perforations in the lower edge of the glove. The outer end of the leash is attached to a pair of jesses, narrow strips of leather which are in turn attached through eyelets to aylmeri anklets, again of leather, which surround each leg of the hawk. Immediately above each anklet there may also be a second encircling leather band (a bewit) to which a bell, traditionally of silver, is attached. A third bell may also be attached to the tail feathers by means of a soft leather strip passed through a heart-shaped plectrum made from stiff leather. The near ends of the jesses may be attached to the leash by means of a swivel, which ensures smooth running of the leash at the moment of release. Modern swivels are most often made from stainless steel and comprise a large hoop to hold the jesses, with a smaller ring for the leash attached through a hole in the base of the large hoop.

Other key equipment comprises the lure and the hood. Lures consist of an animal skin attached to a solid base or fresh pieces of meat, attached to a long cord or string. The cord is wound round a rod, usually made from wood, which is held in the right hand. The lure is swung and

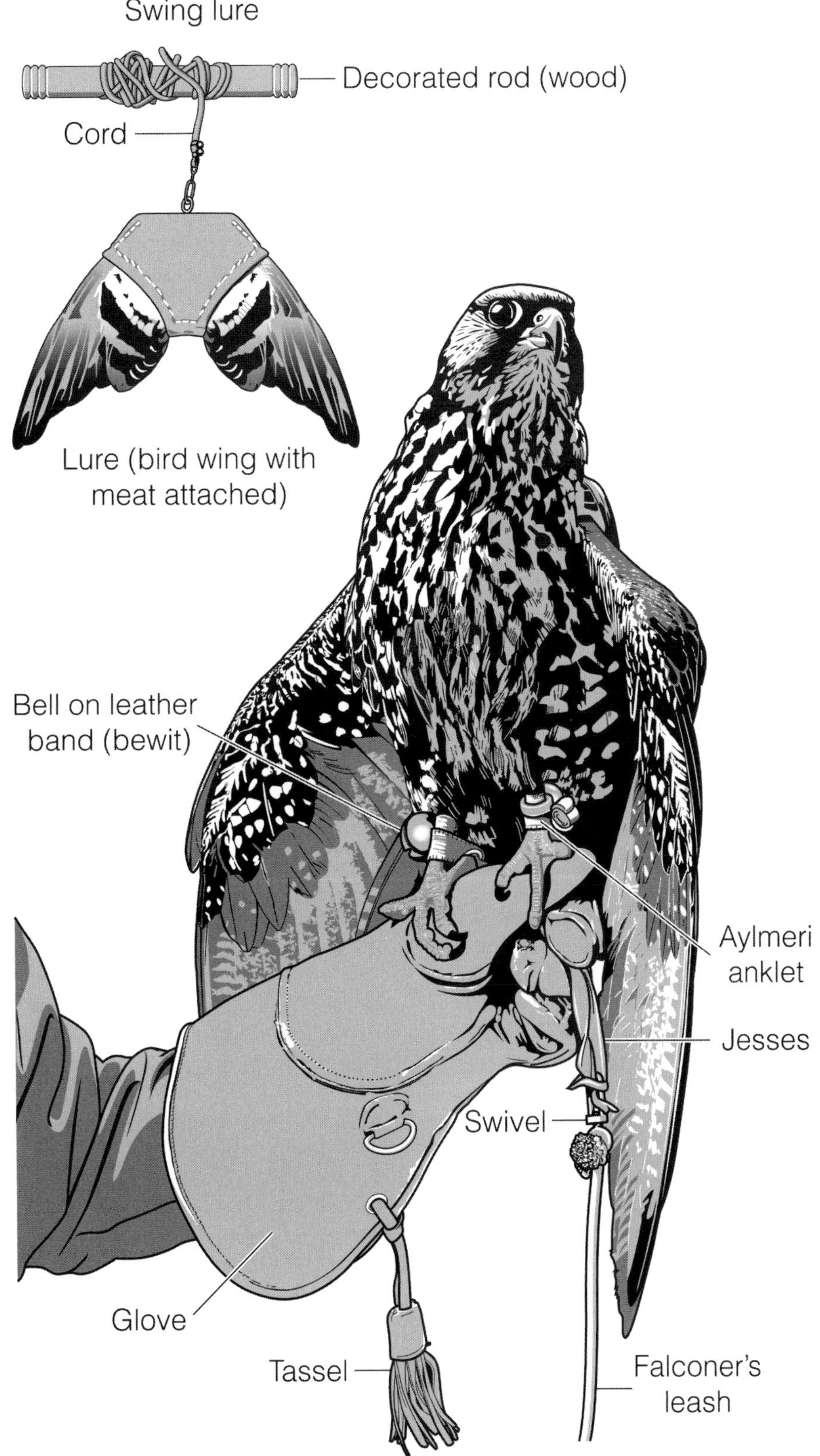

Figure Appendix 10.1. Falconry equipment and terminology (after Ford 1992).

gradually extended until the correct moment for the bird to be released is reached. Lures are mainly employed in the training of birds, and the skin or meat used will relate to the kind of prey that is to be hunted in due course. Another device used in training is a long cord attached to the bird known as a creance. This is in effect a long extension of the basic leash, and is wound round a rod in a similar way to the lure line. The rods are often decorated. Hoods are a form of blindfold, which serve to prevent the bird from being distracted prior to the chosen time of flight. They are usually made from leather, and often are decorated, with a marked top knot which enables to falconer to remove the hood with a rapid flourish at the appropriate moment. It can be concluded that falconry equipment was both varied and highly specific. However nearly all the devices, even in modern times, are made from perishable materials (especially leather) and such items are unlikely to have survived in archaeological contexts.

10.1.6 POSSIBLE FALCONRY EQUIPMENT IN BEAKER GRAVES

It has been argued in the present volume that stone bracers may not have been primarily designed as functional wristguards for use in the practise of archery. The lack of use wear, presence of upstanding studs, positioning of some examples well above the wrist, fineness of the raw materials selected and the tightly curved morphology of some of them all argue against this simple interpretation. It has further been postulated that the bracers were valuable items, worn by mature men, possibly as part of ceremonial outfits. Another practise which involves the lifting of the arm, such that a bracer attached to the lower arm would be highly visible, is falconry. The bracer could have been attached to the cuff of a leather glove or gauntlet, or just above it, with the bird perching on the leading edge of the hand. As the bird was set free, or was in the process of landing, movement of the arm would have enhanced the flashy and colourful appearance of the attached stone arm ornament. Most of the falconry equipment described in the last section would have been made from perishable materials such as leather, sinew, fur or textile, and such materials do not normally survive in Early Bronze Age graves. However, it has been noted that a class of artefact that regularly occurs with bracers, and sometimes in a similar relation to the left of right arm, is the bone toggle. Body placement suggests that these toggles were not intended as fasteners for cloaks or other costume, and it may be that they were used as simple reels for fastening and winding the string for a lure, or for a training string or creance. Further interest is supplied by the record of the equipment used in modern Eurasia for the support of golden eagles, which are rather heavy to carry on the hand. This equipment comprises a crutch of bent wood which rests against a girdle, supported by a leather strap over the left shoulder, or on a perch fixed to the saddle (Dobney 2002, 77). Prominent amongst the equipment that survives in British Beaker graves is the series of special 'belt rings', made from bone, jet or shale and which are often highly decorated. These may not all have functioned as fasteners on belts or girdles, but may have been employed on other straps, perhaps higher on the body where the ring would have been more highly visible. A functional connection with the strappage needed for the support of an eagle used in falconry is thus possible.

Special 'belt rings' were found in six bracer graves of Beaker date as follows: in shale with the Amesbury Archer (bracer ID 56 and ID 57), in jet at Tring (ID 31 and ID 146), in amber at Ferry Fryston (ID 73) and Raunds (ID 116) and bone at Sittingbourne (ID 10) and Melton Quarry (ID 105).

10.1.7 CONCLUSIONS

The practise of falconry, well documented from medieval and Saxon times, can be traced back in literary and archaeological sources to the 2nd millennium BC in Anatolia. It probably developed on the steppes of Eurasia, from whence it spread westwards into Europe. There is circumstantial evidence that falconry may have first developed many millennia ago, at the very beginning of the Neolithic period in the Near East, and from the outset the art may have encompassed both ritual and economic functions. Within this framework it can certainly be postulated that the art of falconry may have been well known in the Neolithic and Bronze Age periods as far west at the British Isles. As in the Near East, there is circumstantial evidence from prehistoric Britain that suggests that falconry was being practised. This takes the form of the faunal remains of raptors and of small mammals and other birds that may have been their prey.

Most falconry equipment would have been made from perishable materials such as leather or wood, and cords made from sinew or textile. Such items do not survive well in archaeological contexts, and no prehistoric examples have been identified in the literature. However, the association of the hawk skull and a stone bracer in the Beaker grave from Kelleythorpe has inspired the idea that stone bracers, now interpreted as valuable and ornamental attachments for the lower arm, and not as functional archers' wristguards, may have been worn to enhance the status of falconers. With the left arm raised to support the hawk, such an ornament would have been highly visible for considerable periods of time. It can also be suggested that a series of varied bone toggles, which were sometimes placed in Beaker graves near to a stone bracer and next to the lower arm may also have been used in falconry, as winders or reels for the cord for a lure, or for a training string or creance. The so-called 'belt rings' of jet, shale or bone, also found in Beaker graves, are another group of decorative and valuable items. Usually interpreted as belt rings, it may be that they were used in a more general sense in relation to leather or textile straps, located more visibly on the upper body, and possible connected also with the ancient art of falconry. In recorded history falconry has always been the sport and pastime of high status men: the finding of possible falconry equipment in a series of well-furnished Beaker graves belonging to mature males may indicate that the same applied in the Late Neolithic and Early Bronze Age Britain. Also, as in ancient Eurasia, falconry may then have been associated with ritual and magical activities as well as with the excitement of the hunt.

ILLUSTRATED CATALOGUE OF BRACERS

Key: each entry contains the following basic data (where available) under the heading of object ID number and identifying name:

- Context (burial, stray etc; 'G' denotes Grinsell barrow number)
- Closest find address (parish, county)

- Holding museum/owner and accession number
- Reference(s); usually a single reference is included, often the primary account

- Maximum dimensions (length × breadth × thickness)
- Geological type and general colour
- Estimated percentage present at deposition
- Possible reworking
- Manufacturing marks (striations/polishing)
- Number of perforations
- Points of special interest (*e.g.* decoration)
- General condition or wear

In order to maintain consistency for comparative purposes the scale of the images is approximately two-thirds of original size throughout.

ID 1: Dorchester XII

Beaker inhumation grave, Dorchester-on-Thames, Oxfordshire.

Ashmolean Museum 1950.395; Case 1965; Whittle *et al.* 1992, fig. 25, 4; 88.2 × 35.3 × 5.0mm; Group VI type, greenish grey (5G 5/1); 98% present at deposition; evidence of striations and polishing; four perforations; two locations of possible mounts; slightly worn.

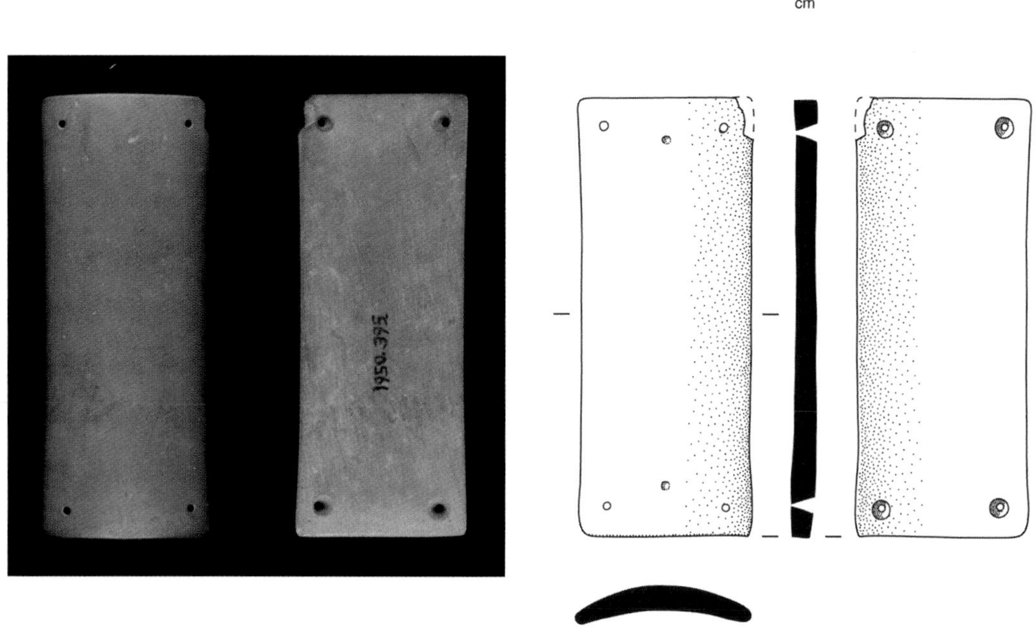

ID 2: Stanton Harcourt

Beaker inhumation grave, Stanton Harcourt, barrow XV, 5, Oxfordshire.

Ashmolean Museum 1964.451; Case 1963, fig. 82; Barclay *et al.* 1995, fig. 51, 8; 96.3 × 43.7 × 5.7mm; amphibolite type, light greenish grey (5GY 8/1); 95% present at deposition; evidence of striations and polishing; six perforations; slightly worn.

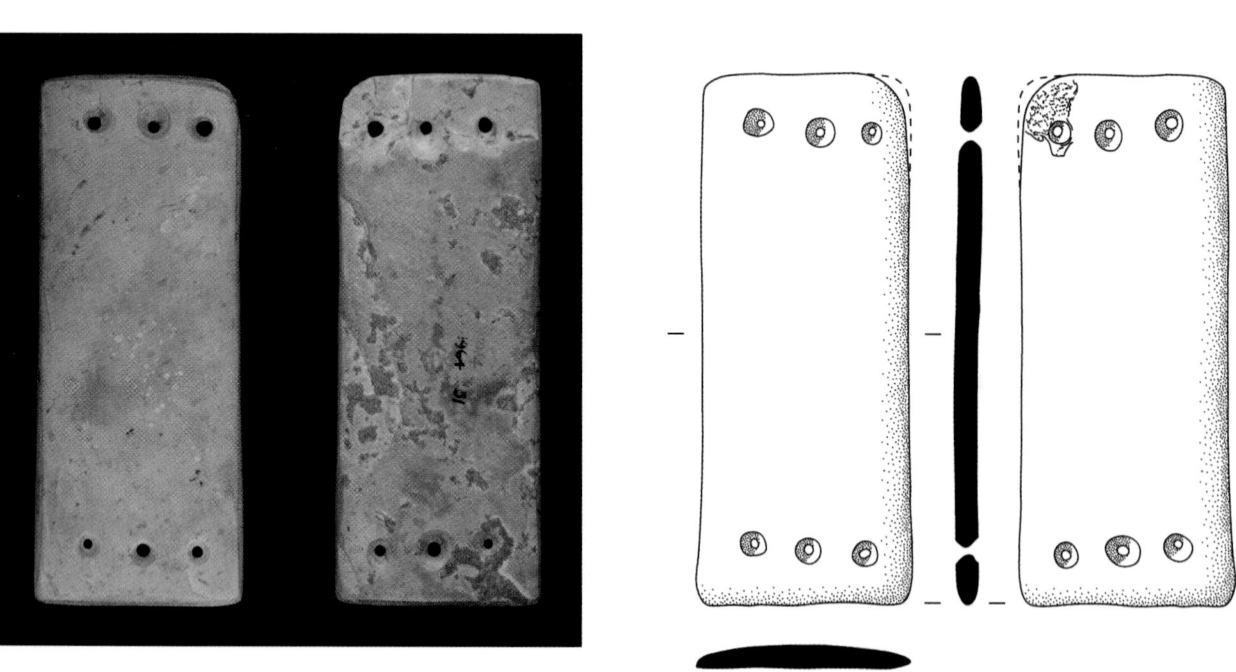

ID 3: Woodeaton

Stray surface find, Woodeaton, Oxfordshire.

Ashmolean Museum 1921.162. Manning Collection; unpublished; fragment 22.6 × 14.6mm; amphibolite type, greenish grey (5GY 5/1); fragment only; reworked as pendant; evidence of polishing; one perforation surviving, probably four originally; worn (as pendant).

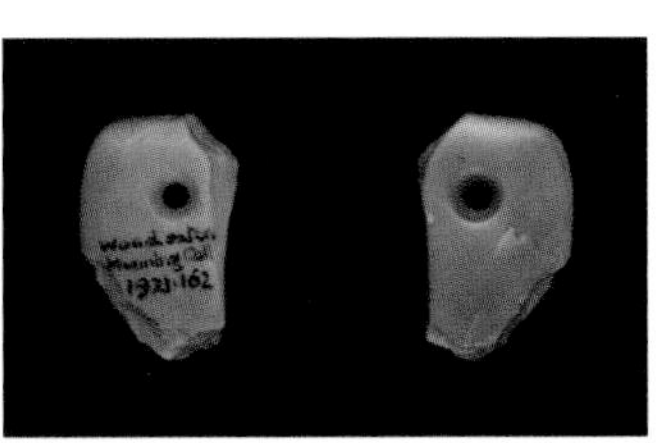

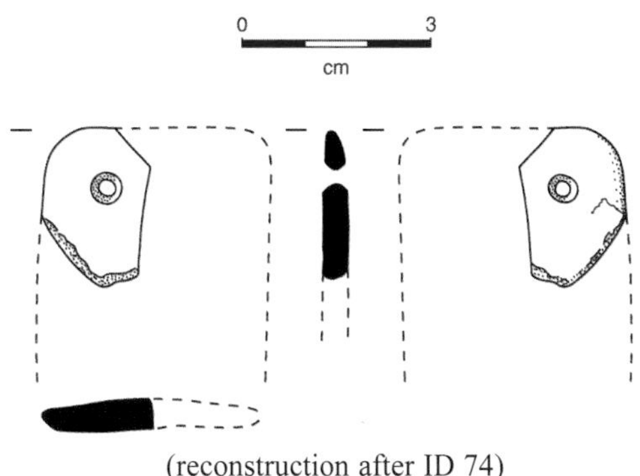

(reconstruction after ID 74)

ID 4: Winterslow Hut

Beaker inhumation grave, Winterslow G3, Wiltshire.

Ashmolean Museum NC.461; Stevens and Stone 1939, 174–182, pl. V, c; 122.0 × 52.5 × 5.9mm; amphibolite type, greenish grey (5G 5/1); 100% present at deposition; evidence of striations and polishing; six perforations; slightly worn.

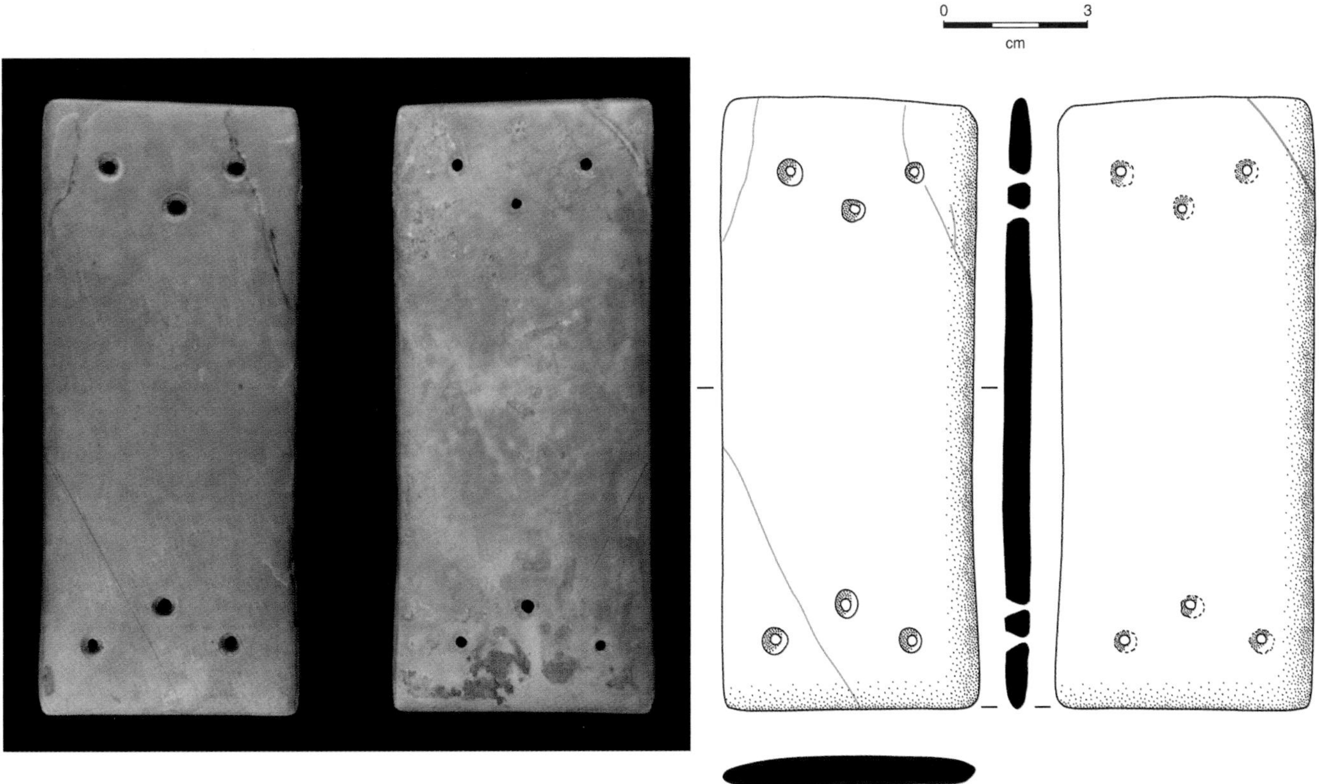

ID 6: Sturry

Beaker inhumation grave, Sturry, Kent.

British Museum 1977 5–1 3; Jessup1933,174–178;153.4 × 35.9 × 6.7mm; amphibolite type, light olive green (5Y 6/1); 95% present at deposition; evidence of polishing; two perforations; slightly worn.

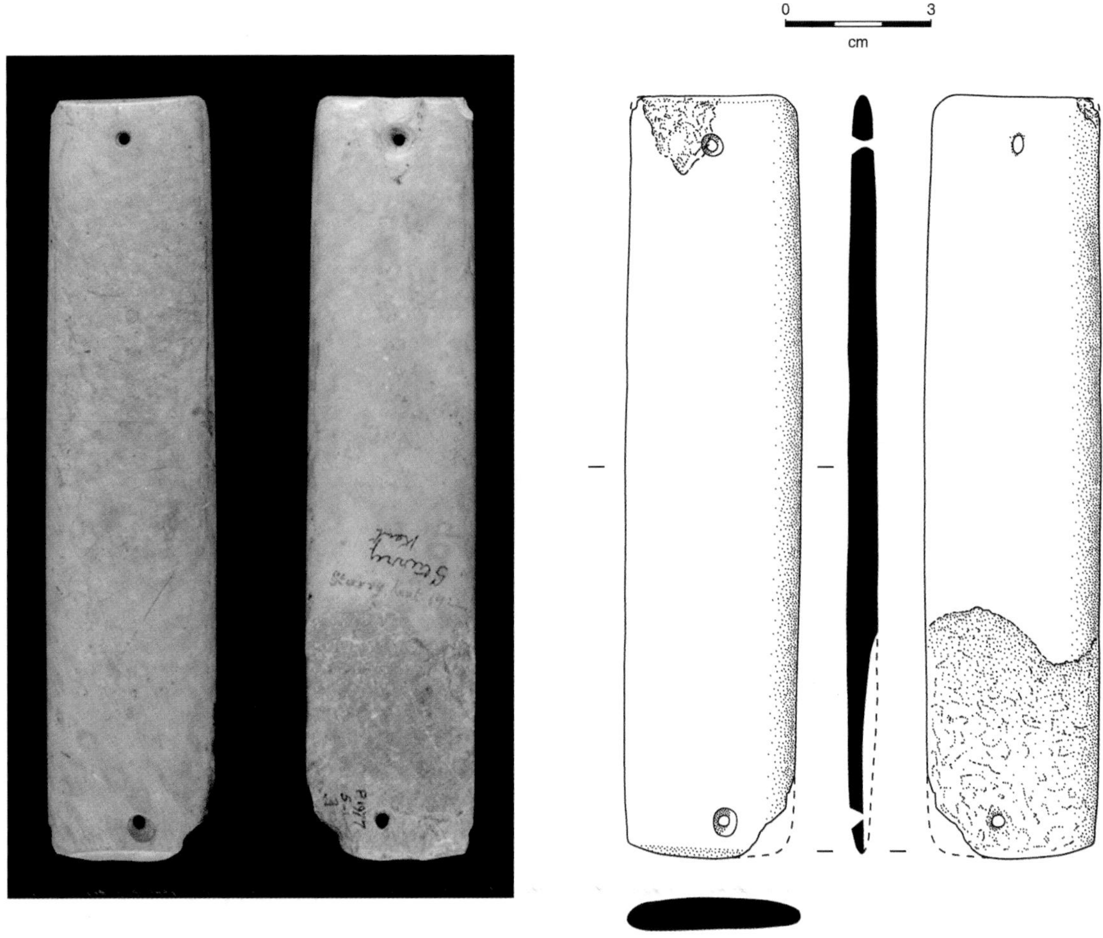

ID 7: Hemp Knoll

Beaker inhumation grave, Bishops Cannings G81, Wiltshire.

British Museum 1981 3–1 2; Robertson-Mackay 1980, fig. 11, 1; 117.0 × 47.7 × 6.7mm; Group VI type, medium bluish grey (5B 6/1); 95% present at deposition; evidence of striations and polishing; four perforations; possible thong markings; worn.

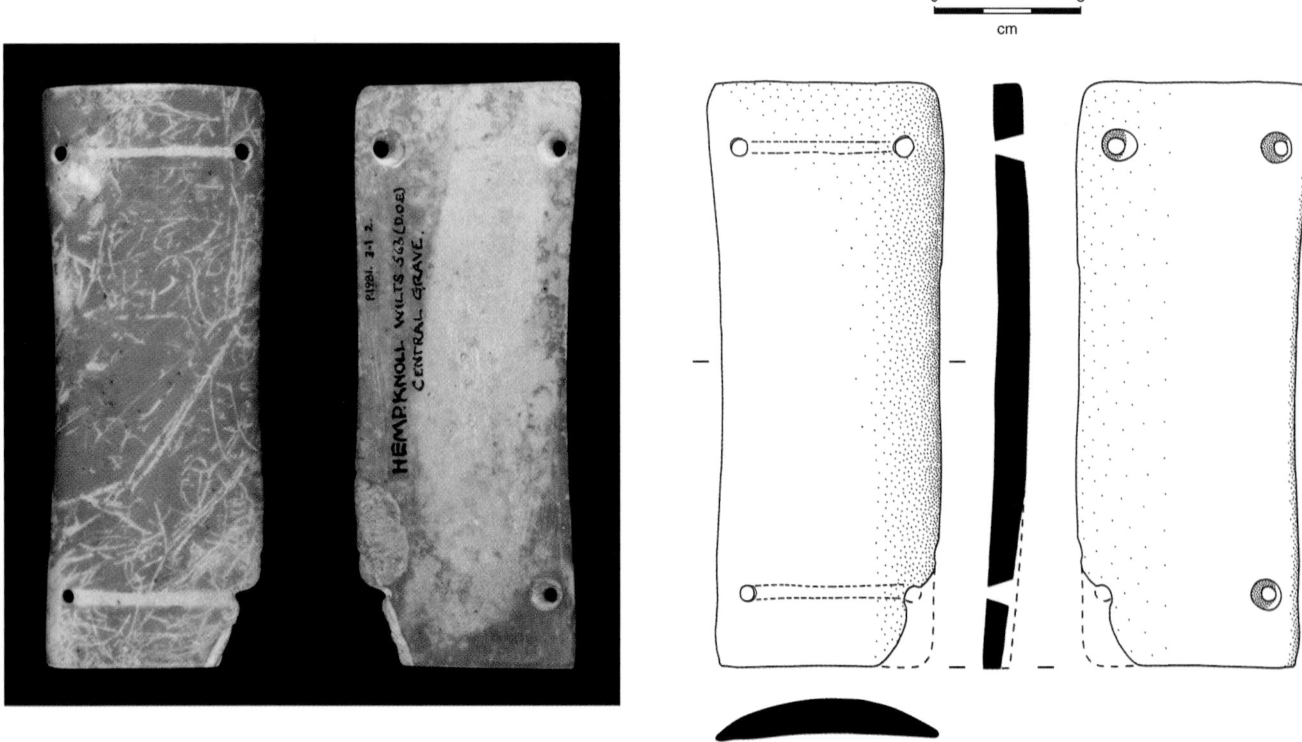

ID 8: Barnack

Beaker inhumation grave, Barnack burial 28, Cambridgeshire.

British Museum 1975 9–1 3; Kinnes 1985, A7, 3; 107.8 × 71.5 × 4.15mm; Group VI type, grey olive green (5GY 4/2); 99% present at deposition; evidence of striations and polishing; eighteen perforations with gold caps; slightly worn.

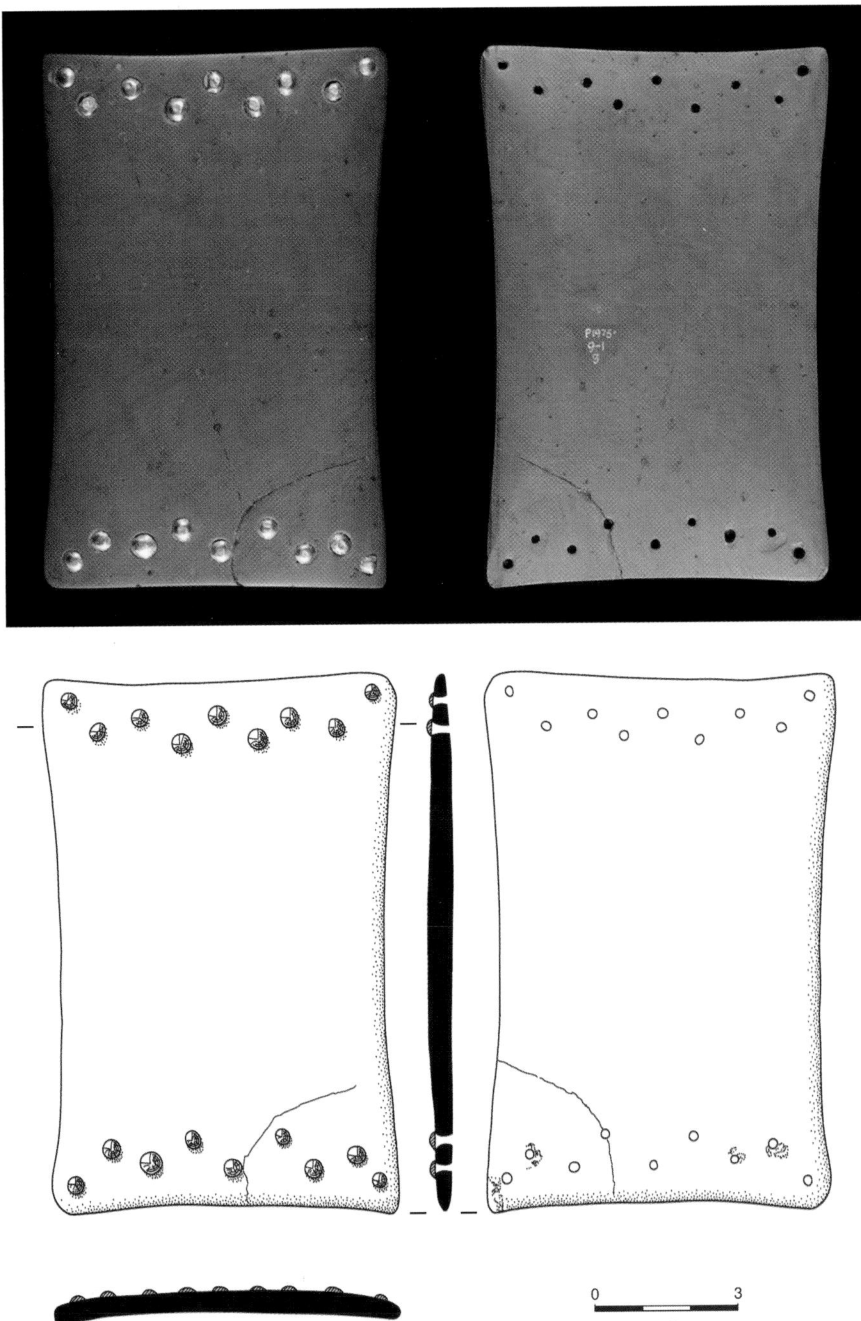

ID 9: Mildenhall

Stray find, Mildenhall, Suffolk.

British Museum unreg. Code Sturge 2305; no details in Smith 1937; 102.2 × 58.7 × 8.3mm; miscellaneous type, olive grey (5Y 4/1); 98% present at deposition; evidence of striations and polishing; four perforations; slightly worn.

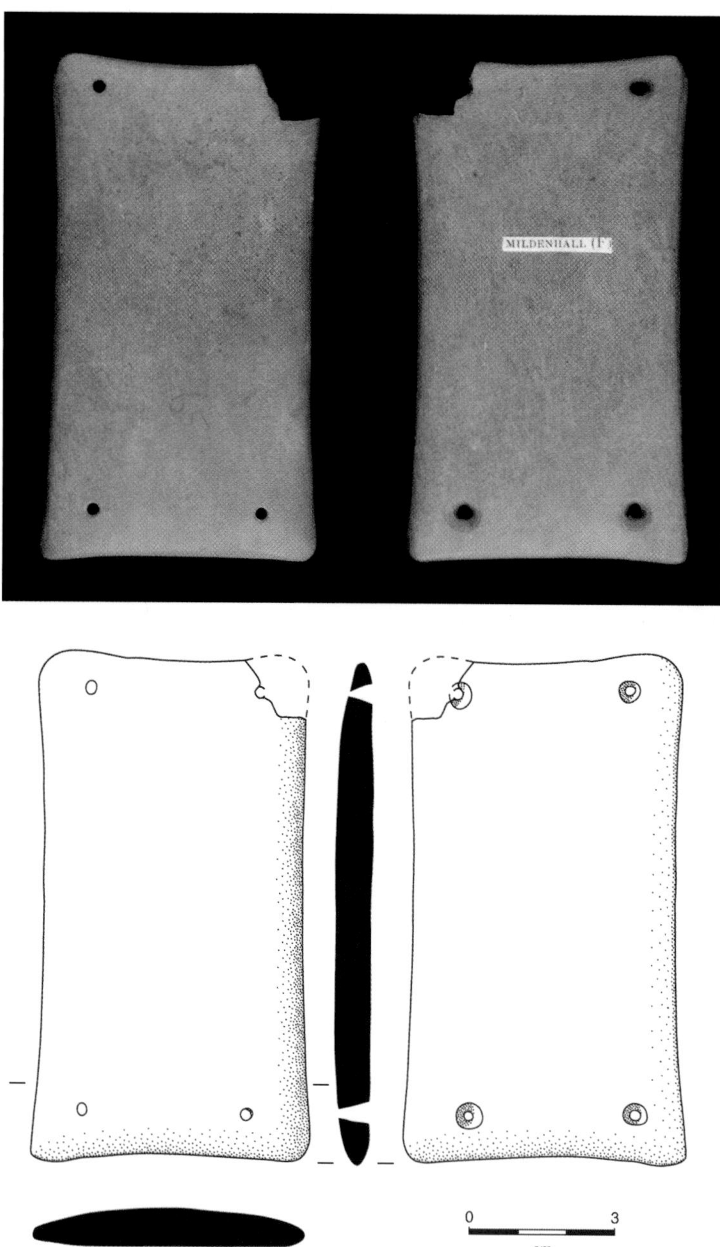

ID 10: Sittingbourne

Beaker inhumation grave, Sittingbourne, Kent.

British Museum 1892 5–17 3; Kinnes 1985, A13, 2; 96.8 × 35.7 × 6.7mm; amphibolite type, dark greenish grey (5GY 4/1); 99% present at deposition; evidence of striations and polishing; two perforations containing traces of copper; slightly worn.

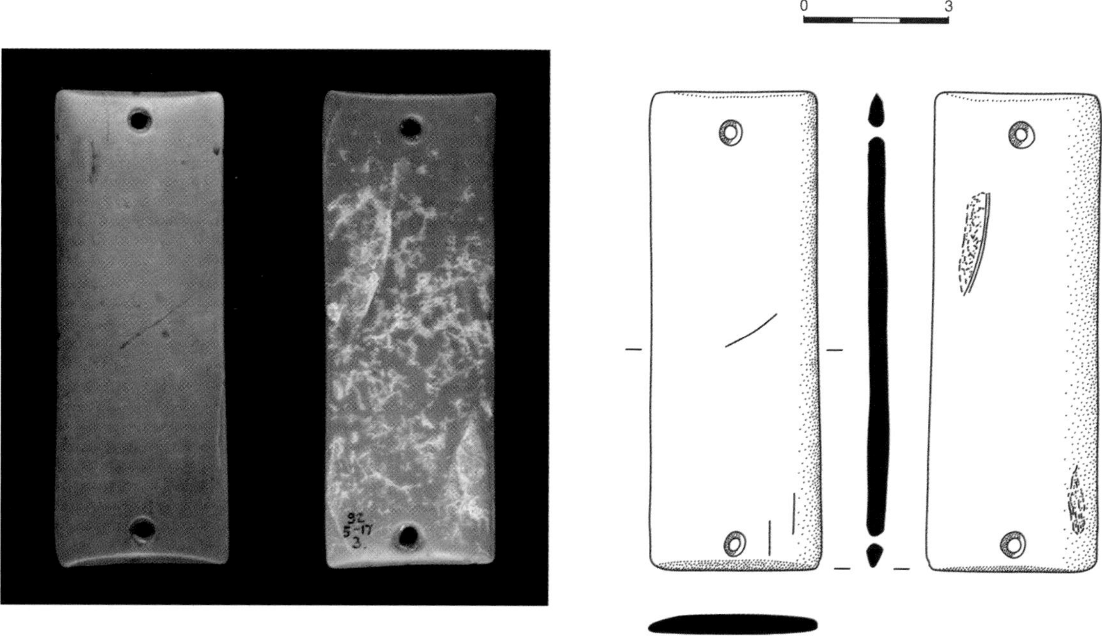

ID 11: Brandon

Non-burial archaeological context, Brandon, Suffolk.

British Museum POA 194.3; Franks 1873, 272; 115.2 × 36.4 × 4.9mm; amphibolite type, greenish grey (5GY 6/1); 95% present at deposition; evidence of striations and polishing; six perforations, outer four probably primary; worn.

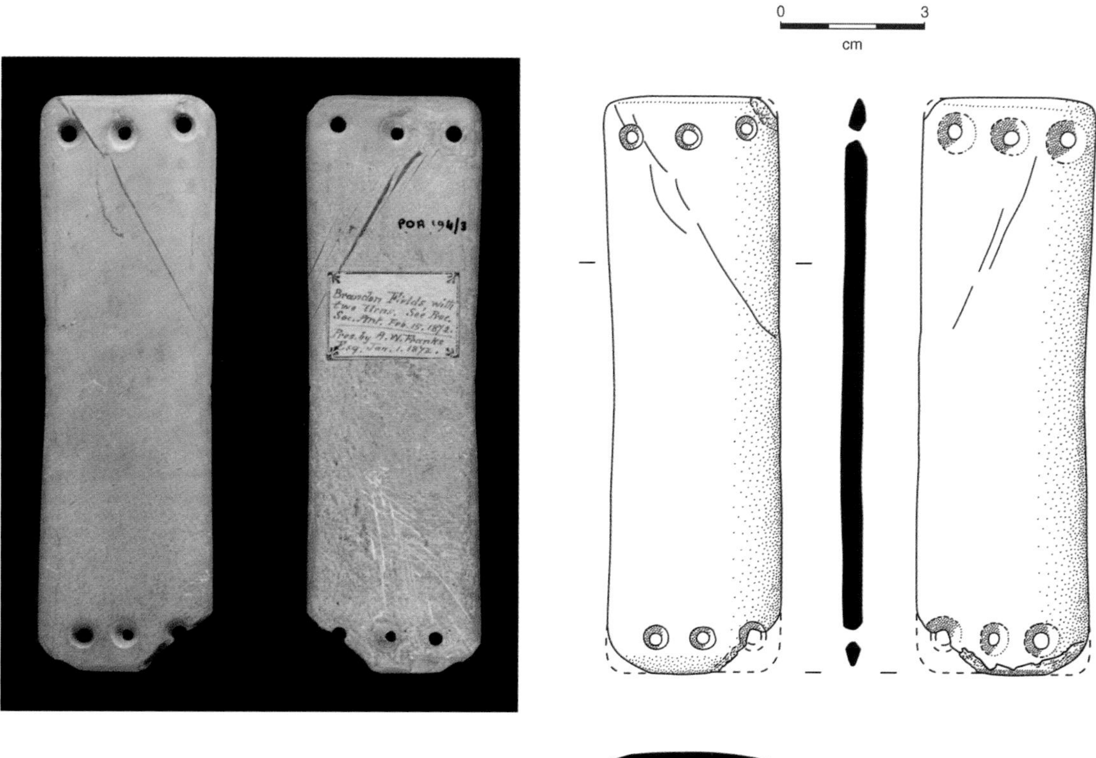

ID 12: Sewell

Beaker inhumation grave, Sewell, Bedfordshire.

British Museum 1976 4–1 3; Kinnes 1985, A9, 3; 102.2 × 42.0 × 5.8mm; amphibolite type, light greenish or bluish grey (5G 7/1 or 5B 7/1); 100% present at deposition; evidence of striations and polishing; four perforations; slightly worn.

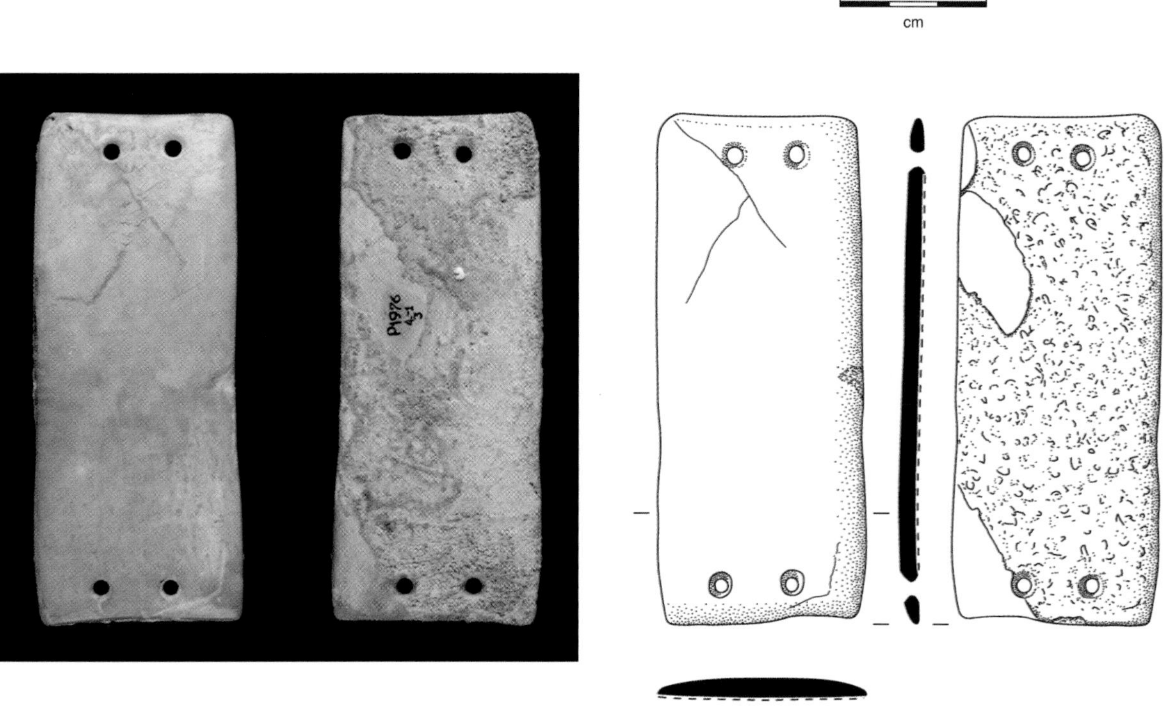

ID 13: Kelleythorpe

Beaker inhumation grave, Mortimer barrow 138, Driffield, East Yorkshire (East Riding).

British Museum 1884 5–20 1; Kinnes 1985, A11, 3; 127.1 × 33.8 × 7.0mm; Group VI type, dark greenish grey (5GY 4/1); 99% present at deposition; evidence of striations and polishing; four perforations with gold caps; slightly worn.

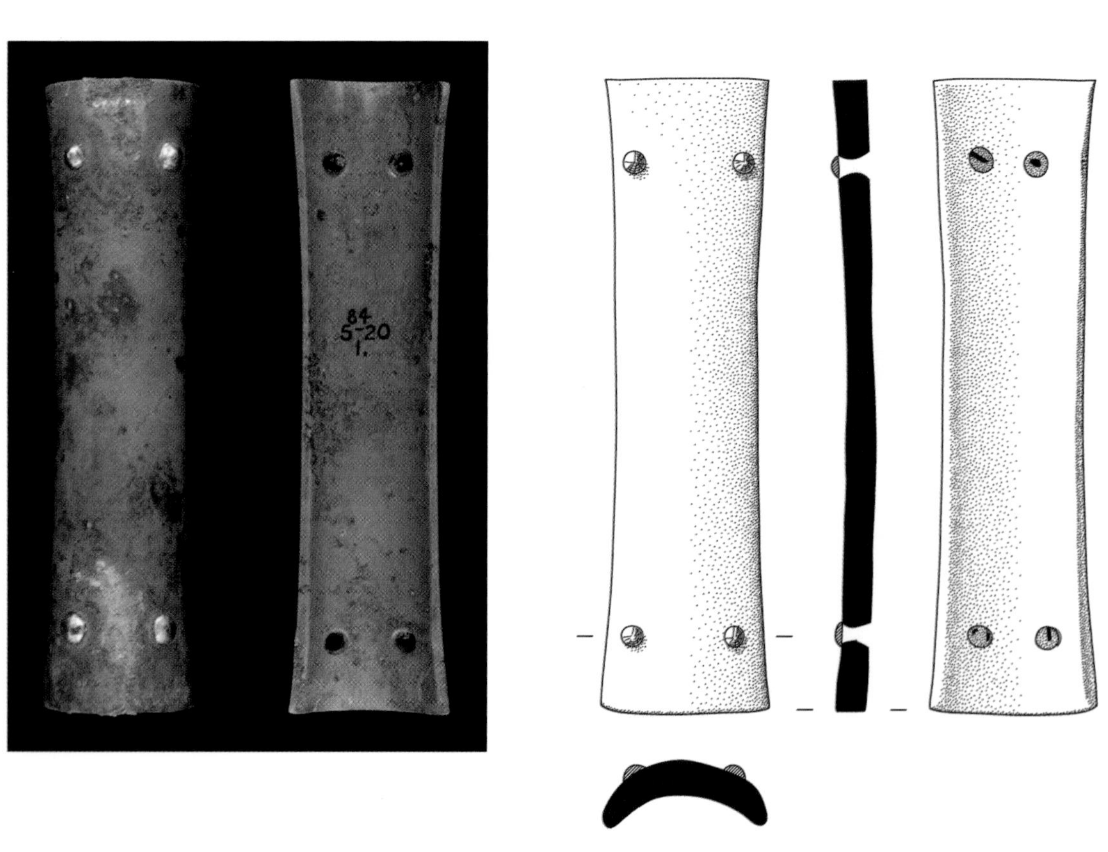

ID 14: Aldbourne

Early Bronze Age cremation burial, Aldbourne G13, Wiltshire.

British Museum 1879 12–9 1877; Kinnes and Longworth 1985, 284, 1; 58.7 × 33.5 × 5.8mm; amphibolite type, light bluish grey (5B 6/1); 100% present at deposition; reworked; evidence of striations and polishing; two surviving and two ?unfinished perforations; worn.

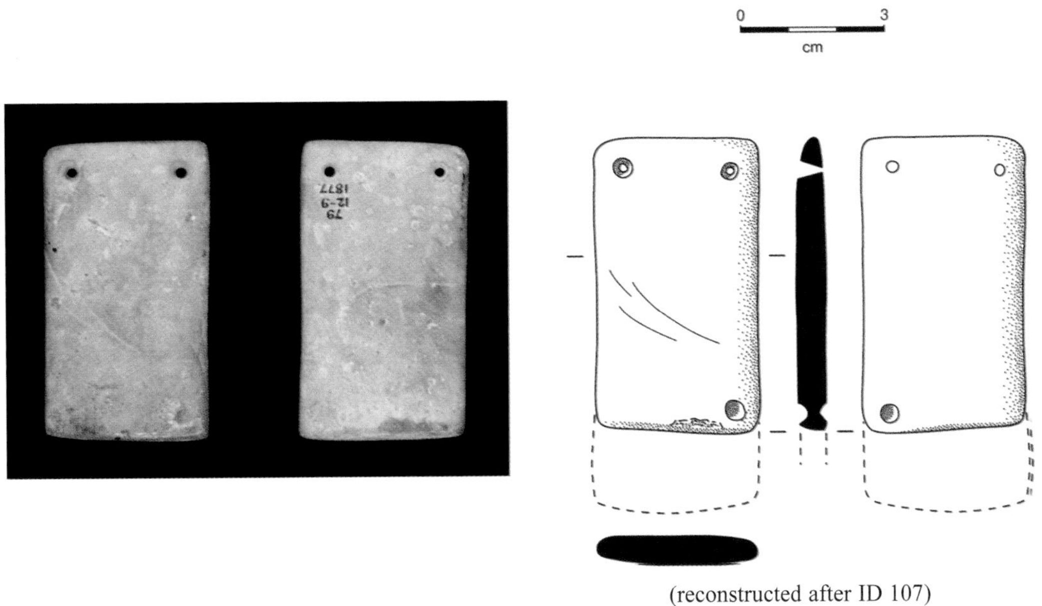

(reconstructed after ID 107)

ID 15: Calne

Inhumation grave, Calne, Wiltshire.

British Museum 1880 6–8 1; Evans 1897, 427; 122.6 × 46.8 × 6.5mm; Group VI type, dark greenish grey (5G 5/1); 99% present at deposition; evidence of striations and polishing; four perforations; slightly worn.

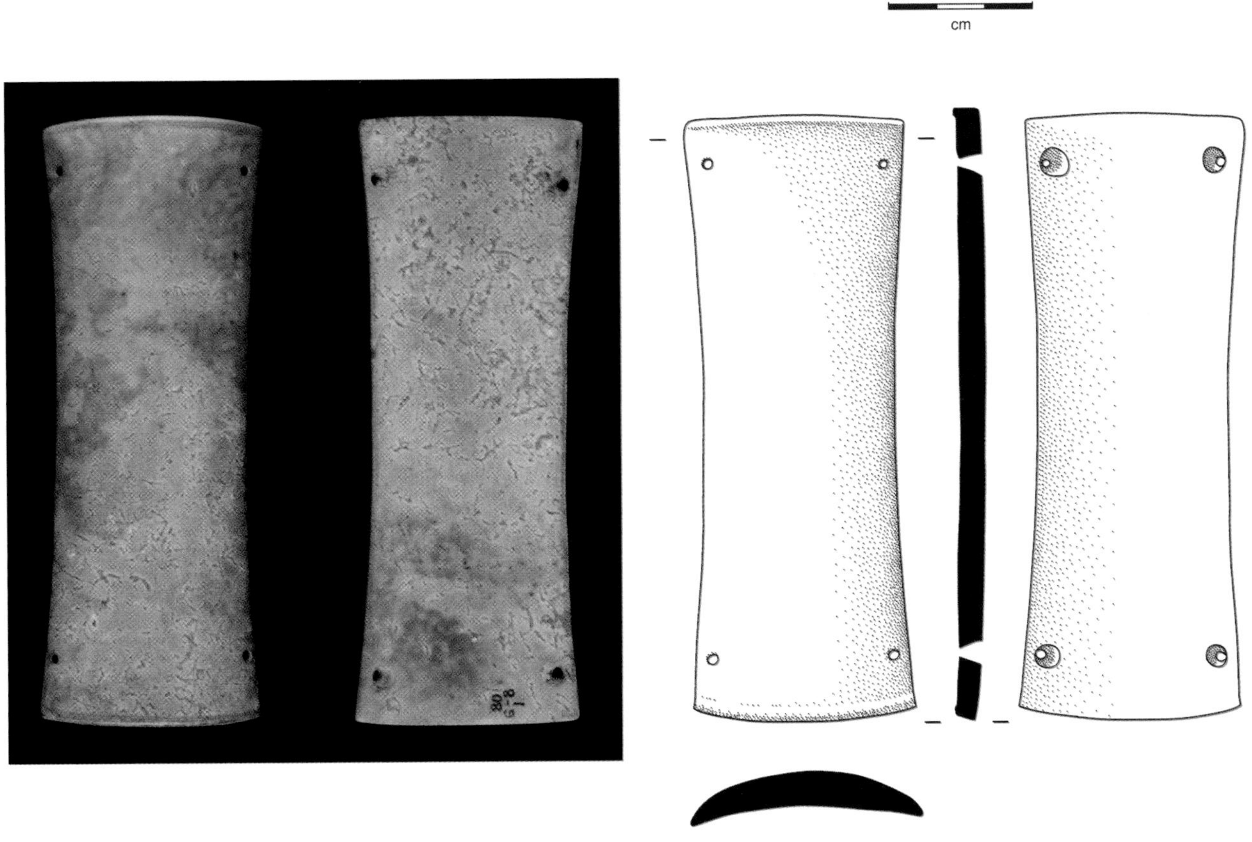

ID 18: Offham

Stray surface find, Offham, Kent.

Maidstone Museum, Portable Antiquities Scheme KENT 5254; unpublished; 78.5 × 44.5 × 4.9mm; amphibolite type, pale greenish grey; 60%? present at deposition; evidence of striations and polishing; one full perforation surviving, probably six originally; slightly worn.

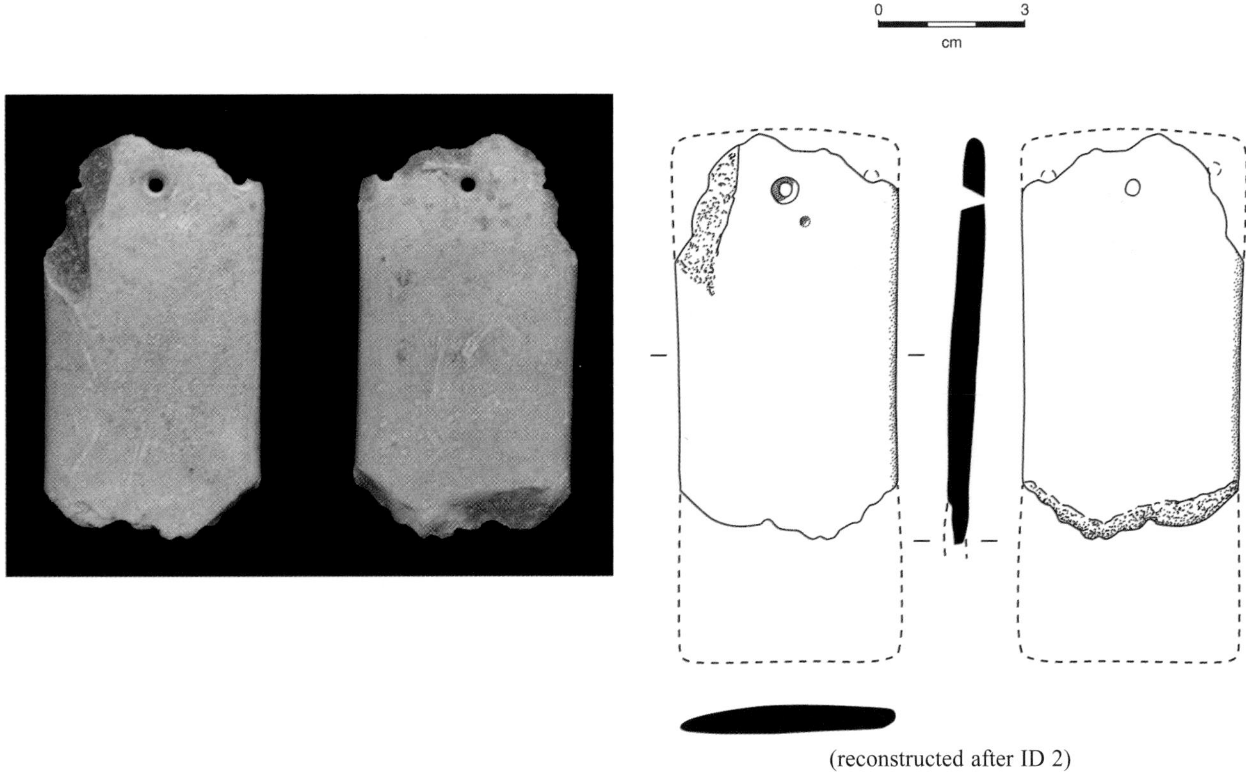

(reconstructed after ID 2)

ID 26: Wellington Quarry

Beaker inhumation grave, Marden, Herefordshire.

Worcestershire County Council HWCM 5522 Feb 96; Harrison *et al.* 1999, fig. 10; 29.5 × 21.0 × 4.0mm; amphibolite type, light bluish grey (5B 7/1); corner fragment only present at deposition; evidence of striations; one full perforation surviving, probably two originally; slightly worn.

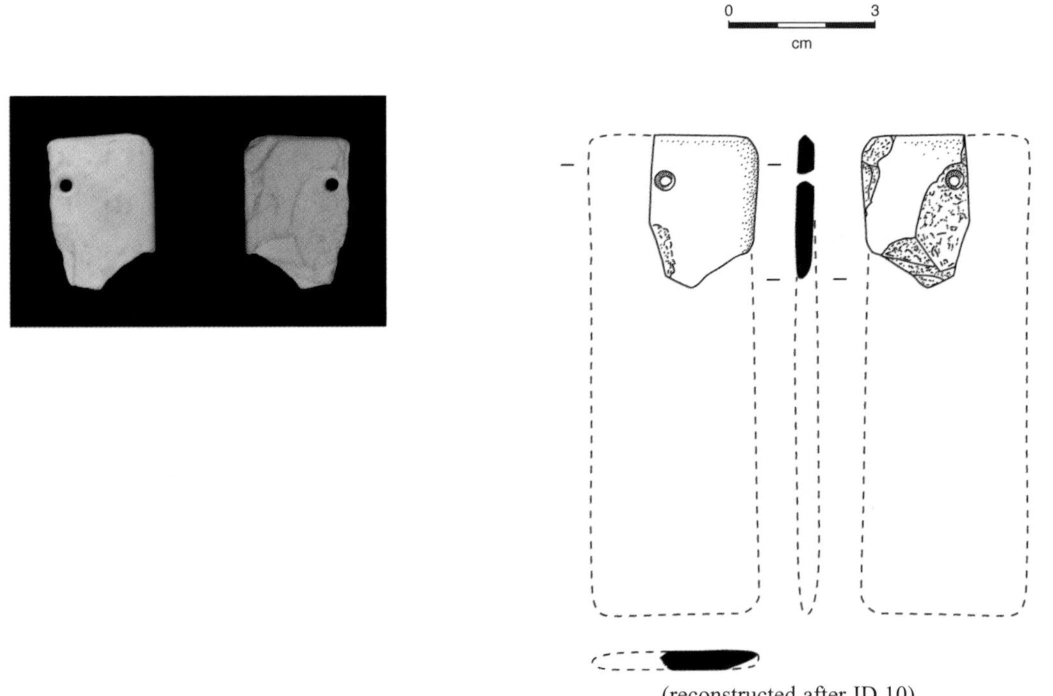

(reconstructed after ID 10)

ID 28: Roundway

Beaker inhumation grave, Roundway G8, Wiltshire.

Wiltshire Heritage Museum, DZSWS:X47; Cunnington 1857; Annable and Simpson 1964, no. 61; 112.3 × 33.6 × 4.7mm; amphibolite type, greenish grey (5GY 6/1); 98% present at deposition; evidence of striations and polishing; four perforations; slightly worn.

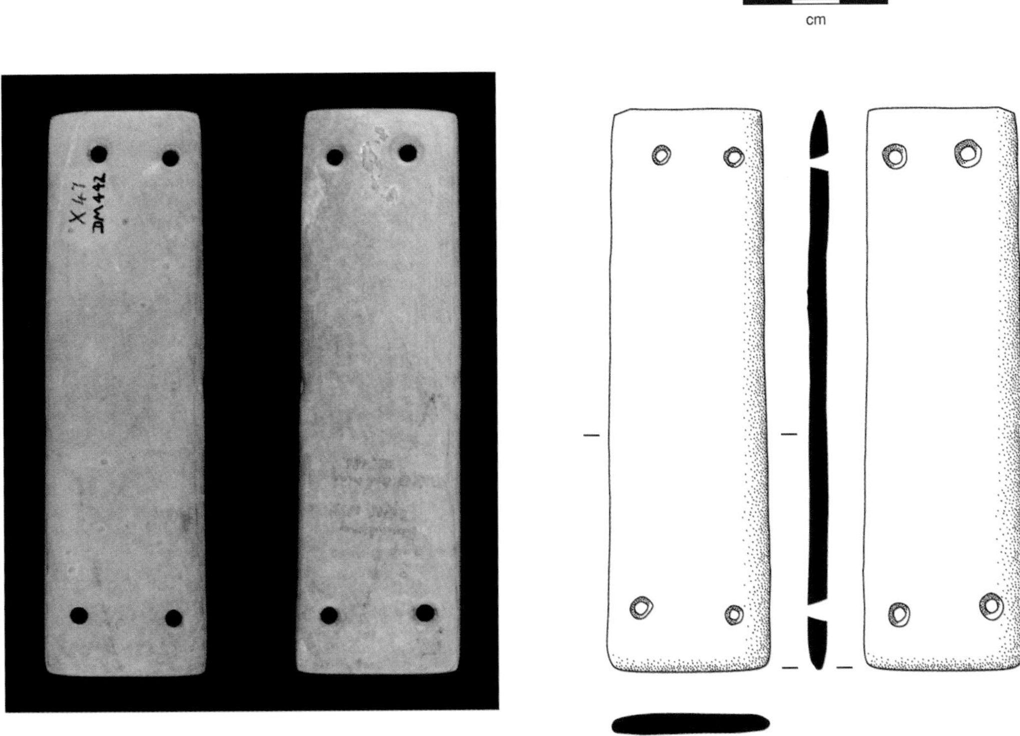

ID 29: Tytherington/Corton

Beaker inhumation grave, Tytherington/Corton boundary, probably Sutton Veny G11, Wiltshire.

Wiltshire Heritage Museum, DZSWS. STHEAD. 232; Colt Hoare 1812,103; Annable and Simpson 1964, no. 116; 105.5 × 47.5 × 4.0mm; miscellaneous type, light olive (5Y 6/1) to greenish grey (5gy 6/1); 99% present at deposition; evidence of striations and polishing; nine surviving perforations, twelve originally; worn.

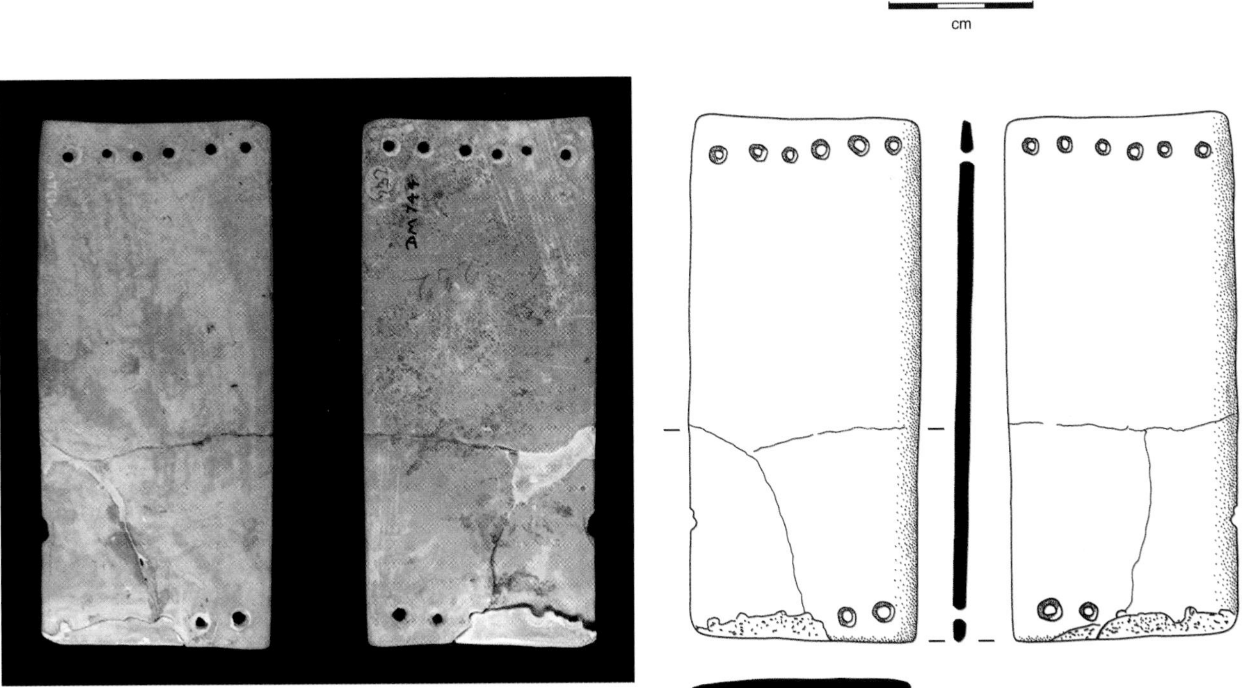

ID 30: Sutton Veny

Beaker cremation grave, Sutton Veny, Wiltshire.

Wiltshire Heritage Museum, DZSWS.STHEAD.63 (attached to mount in museum showcase); Colt Hoare 1812, pl. 12; Annable and Simpson 1964, no. 125; 115.5 × 71.8 × 4.6mm; amphibolite type, greyish yellow green (5GY 6/2); 98% present at deposition; evidence of striations and polishing; six perforations; slightly worn.

0 3
cm

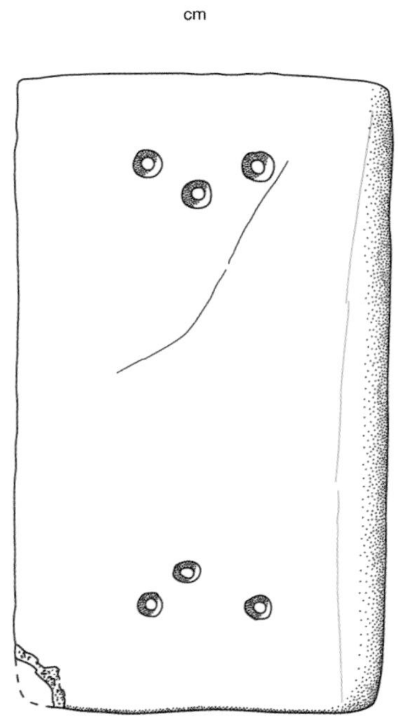

ID 31: Tring

Beaker inhumation grave, Tring, Hertfordshire.

Wiltshire Heritage Museum, DZSWS.STHEAD.326; Anon 1787, fig. 6; Annable and Simpson 1964, no. 126; 100.5 × 23.5 × 6.4m; Group VI type, dark greenish grey (5G 4/1); 99% present at deposition; evidence of striations and polishing; four perforations; slightly worn.

0 3
cm

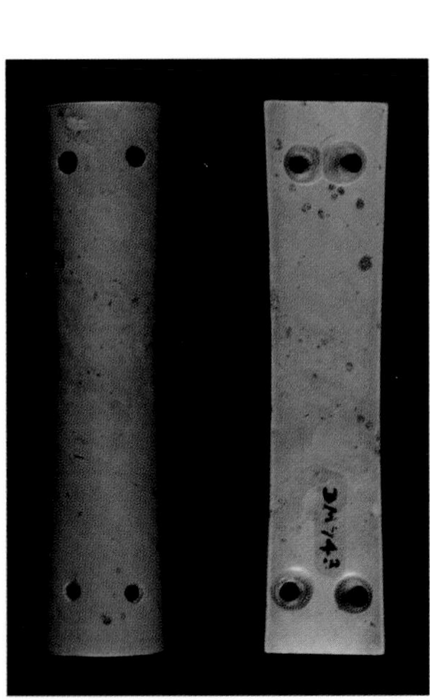

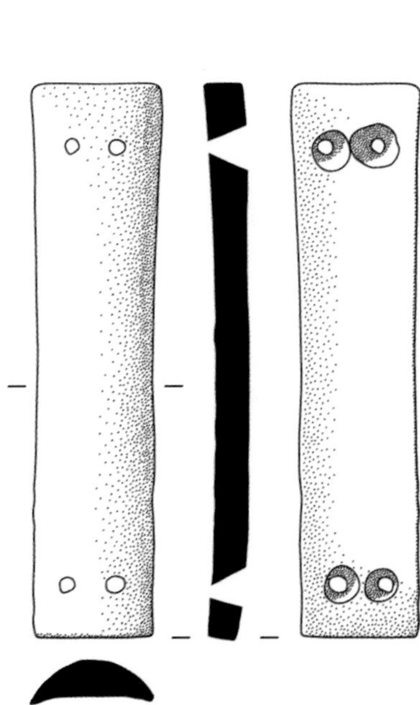

ID 32: Bishops Cannings

Probable Early Bronze Age burial, Bishops Cannings G11 or G12(?), Wiltshire.

Wiltshire Heritage Museum, DZSWS.STHEAD.232a; Annable and Simpson 1964, no. 447; 31.0 × 35.4 × 2.5mm; amphibolite type, greenish grey (5GY 5/1) to greenish grey (5G 6/1); fragment only present at deposition; reworked; evidence of striations and polishing; three perforations surviving, probably originally six; worn.

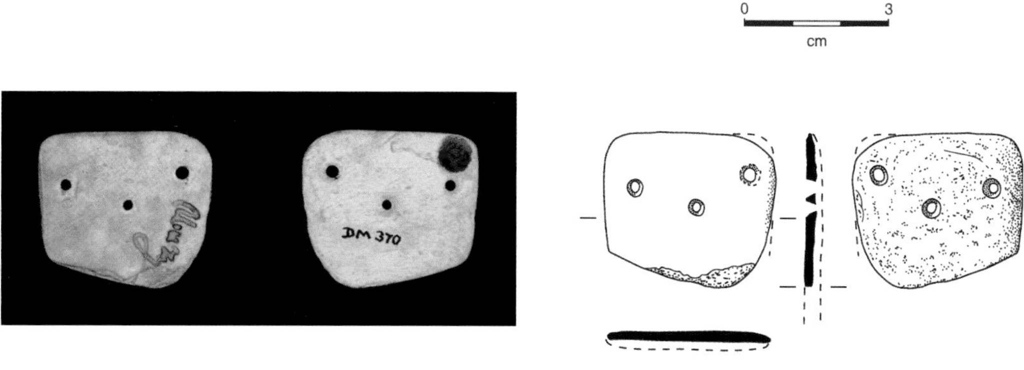

ID 56: Amesbury Archer (red)

Beaker inhumation grave, Amesbury, Wiltshire.

Salisbury and South Wiltshire Museum SBYWM 2003.23 (SF 6588); Fitzpatrick 2003 and 2011; 123.5 × 23.0 × 7.0mm; miscellaneous red/black type, red (5R 3/4); 100% present at deposition; evidence of striations and polishing; two perforations; slightly worn.

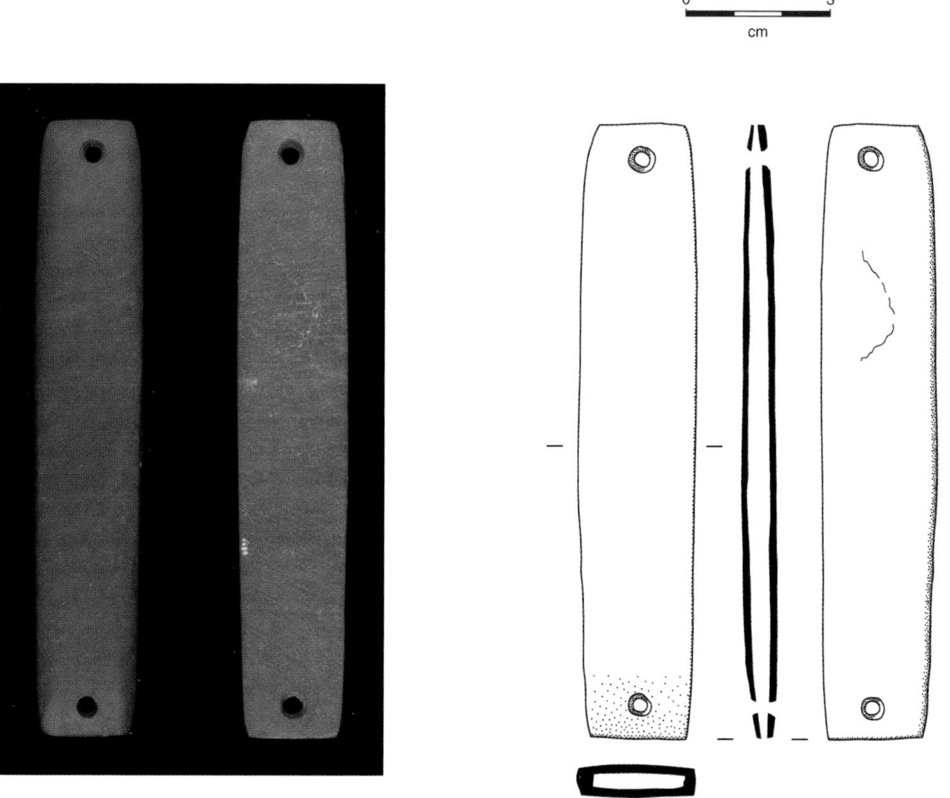

ID 57: Amesbury Archer (black)

Beaker inhumation grave, Amesbury, Wiltshire.

Salisbury and South Wiltshire Museum SBYWM 2003.23 (SF 6600); Fitzpatrick 2003 and 2011; 134.3 × 29.0 × 6.5mm; miscellaneous red/black type, dark grey (N3); 100% present at deposition; evidence of striations and polishing; two perforations; worn.

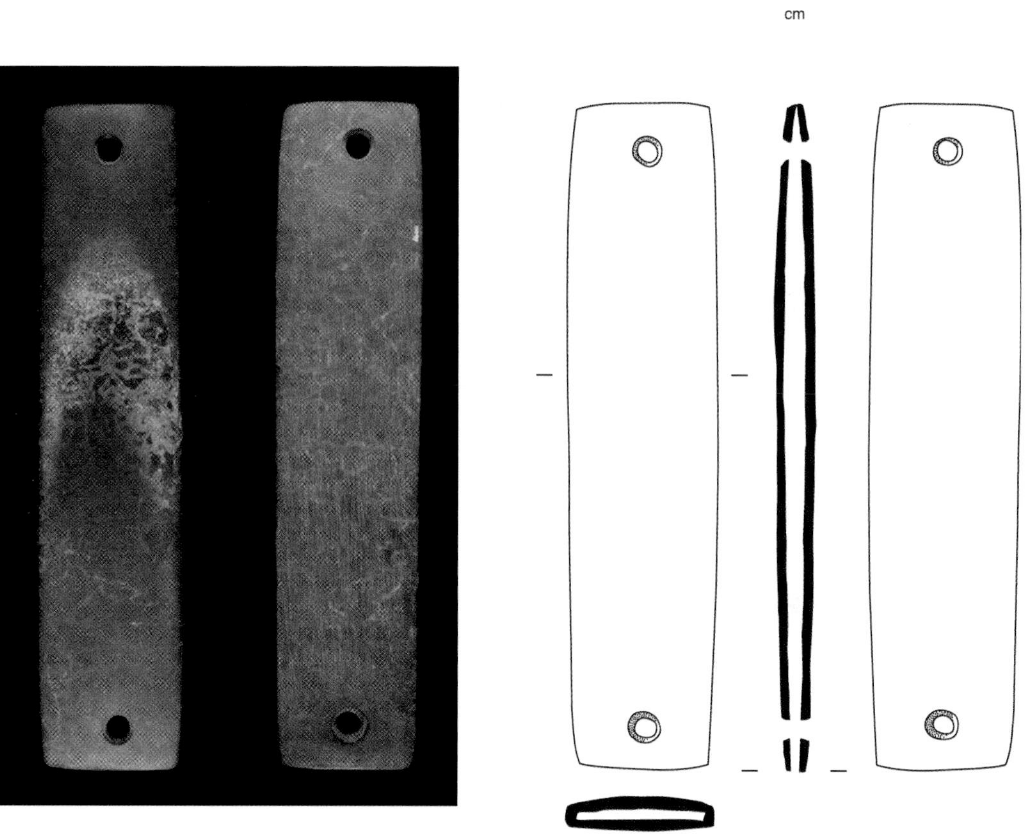

ID 58: Stonehenge

Beaker inhumation grave, Amesbury, Wiltshire.

Salisbury and South Wiltshire Museum 1983.7.2; Evans 1984, fig. 21, a; 110.0 × 29.0 × 9.0mm; miscellaneous red/black type, black (N4); 100% present at deposition; evidence of striations and polishing; two perforations; slightly worn.

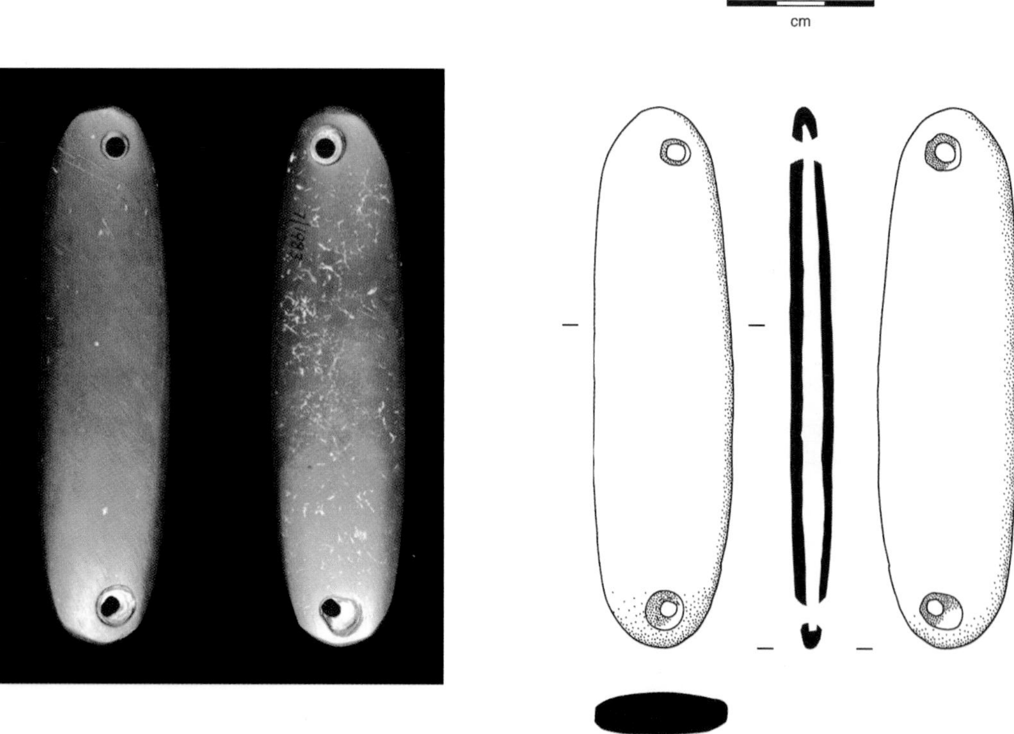

ID 66: West Stafford

Beaker inhumation grave, West Stafford, Dorset.

Dorset County Museum, Dorchester E6101; unpublished, AC archaeology; 115.5 × 39.0 × 5.0mm; amphibolite type, pale greenish yellow (10Y 8/2); 99% present at deposition; evidence of striations and polishing; four perforations; fresh.

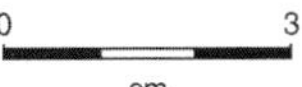

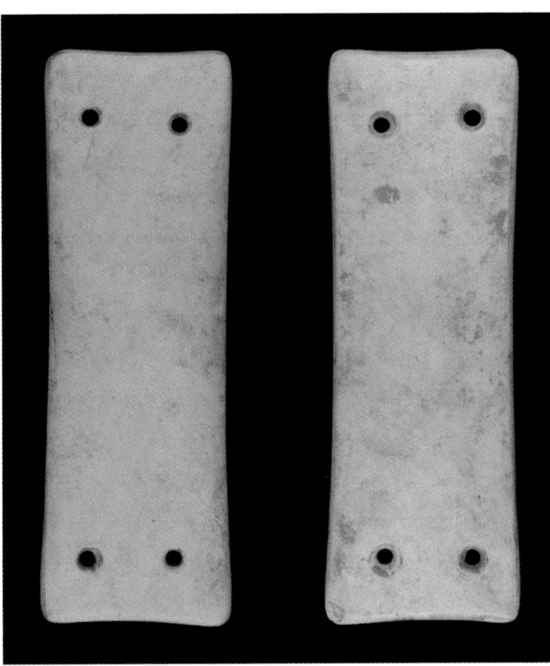

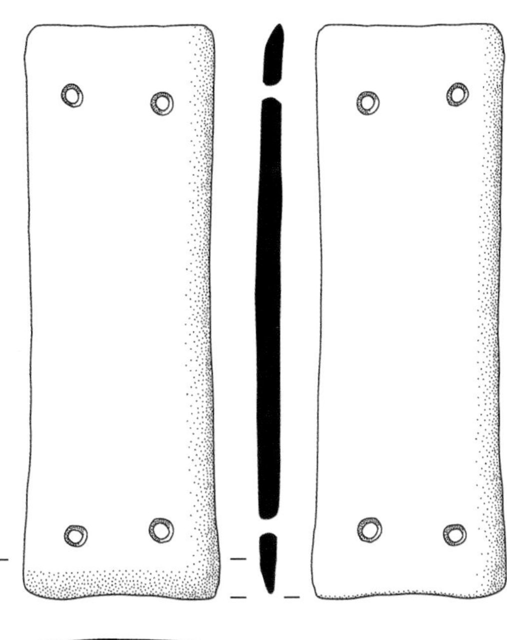

ID 67: Thomas Hardye School

Beaker inhumation grave 1643, barrow 1004, Dorchester, Dorset.

Dorset County Museum, Dorchester 2006 30 7; Gardiner *et al.* 2007, fig. 9b; 103.5 × 31.5 × 4.0mm; amphibolite type, mottled pale blue (5B 6/2); 100% present at deposition; evidence of striations; four perforations; fresh.

0 3
cm

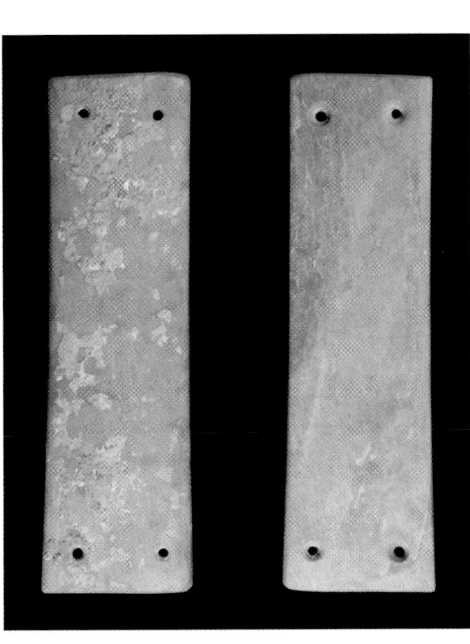

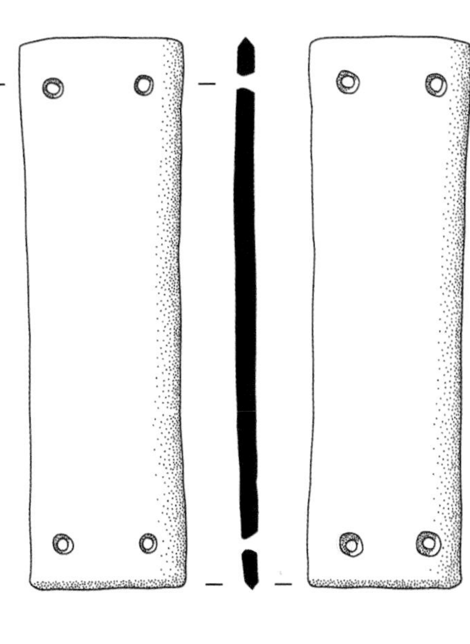

ID 73: Ferry Fryston

Beaker inhumation grave 2245, Ferry Fryston, West Yorkshire.

Oxford Archaeology North, and Wakefield Museum; Roe and Woodward 2007, fig. 168; 126.2 × 36.0 × 5.85mm; Group VI type, dark greenish grey (5G 5/1); 95% present at deposition; evidence of striations; four perforations; slightly worn.

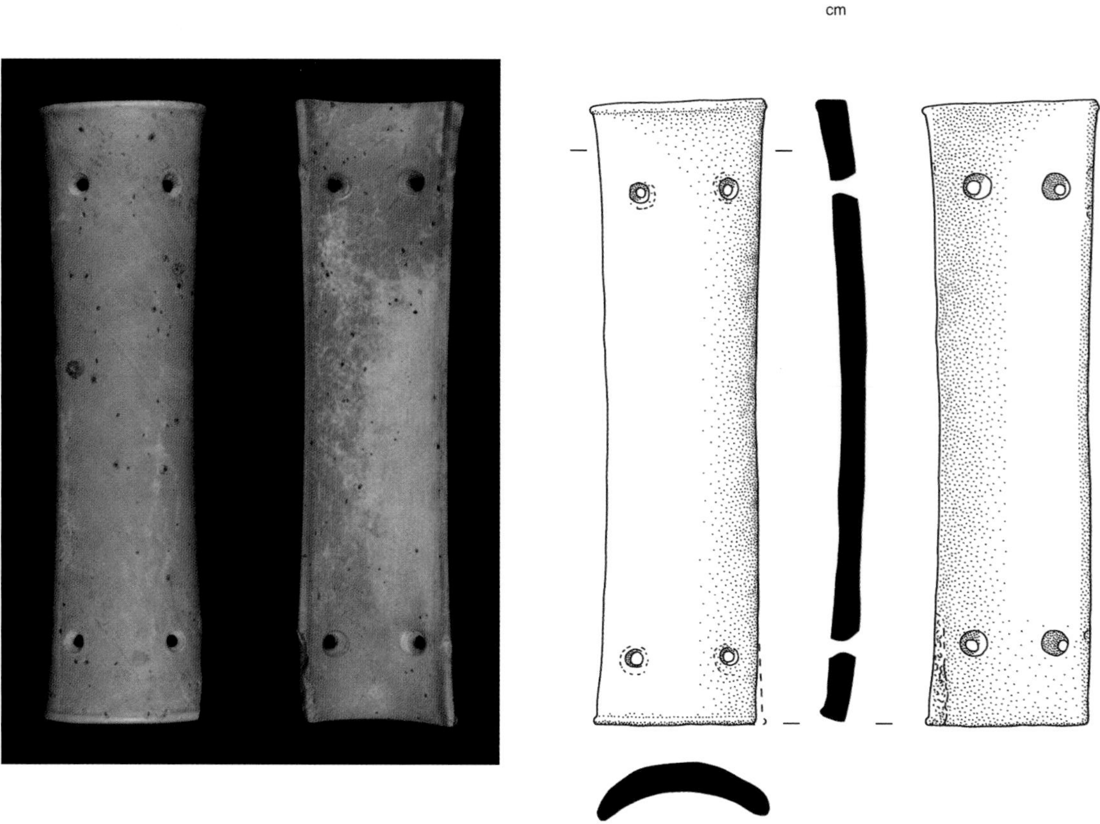

ID 74: Gravelly Guy

Beaker inhumation burial, Stanton Harcourt, Oxfordshire.

Oxford Archaeology and Ashmolean Museum; Lambrick and Allen 2004, fig. 2.18; 95.5 × 37.0 × 4.5mm; amphibolite type, light bluish grey (5B 8/1); 98% present at deposition; evidence of striations and polishing; four perforations; slightly worn.

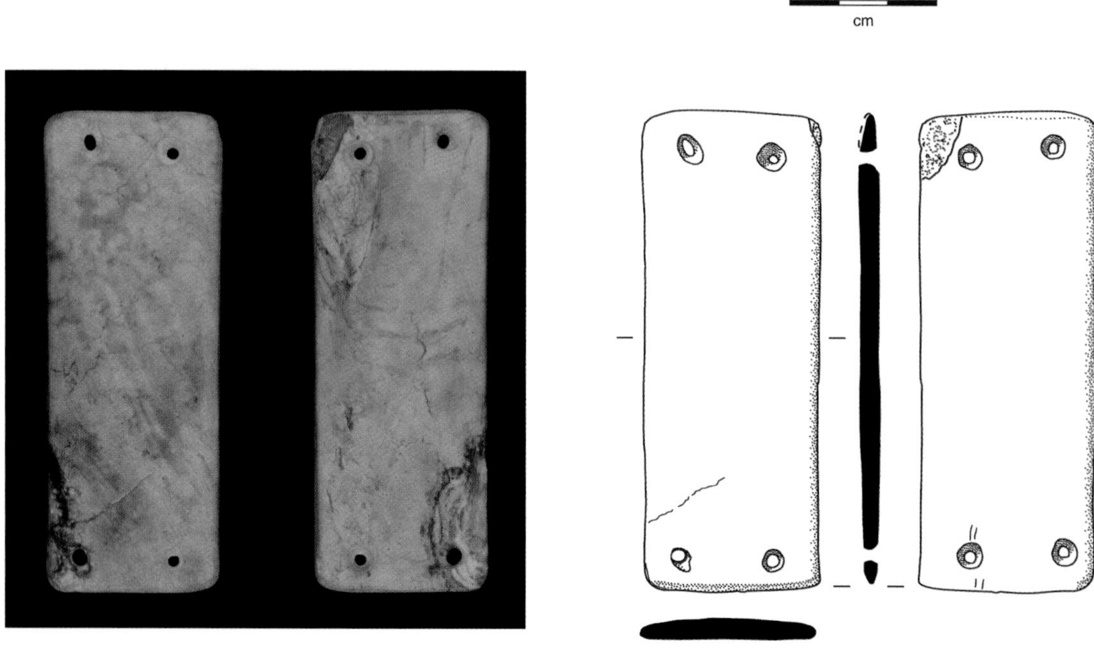

ID 75: Shorncote

Beaker inhumation grave, Cotswold Community, Gloucestershire.

Oxford Archaeology and Corinium Museum Cirencester, Shaffrey and Roe 2010; 44.0 × 28.0 × 2.4mm; amphibolite type, greenish grey (5GY 6/1); fragment only ?33% present at deposition; evidence of striations and polishing; one perforation surviving, probably two originally; wear indeterminate.

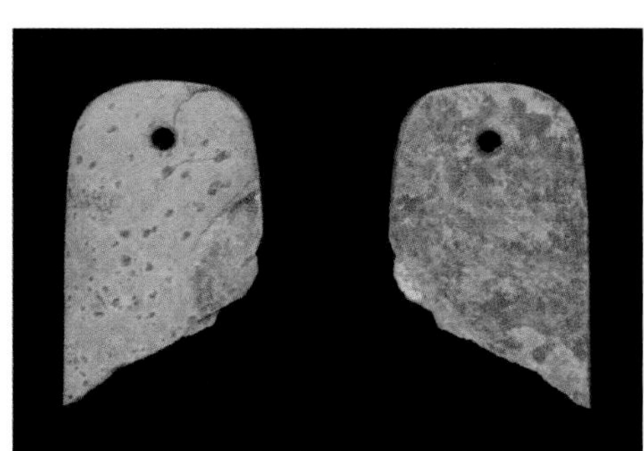

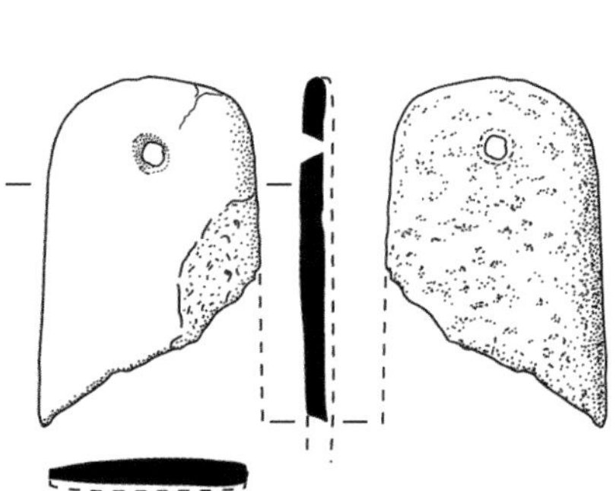

ID 77: Glenluce

Stray find, Glenluce, Wigtownshire (Dumfries and Galloway).

NMS Edinburgh X.AT 1; Wilson 1876, 580–7; 55.7 × 14.5 × 4.5mm; miscellaneous type, light olive grey (5Y 6/1); 95% present at deposition; reworked from larger bracer?; evidence of striations and polishing; two perforations; worn.

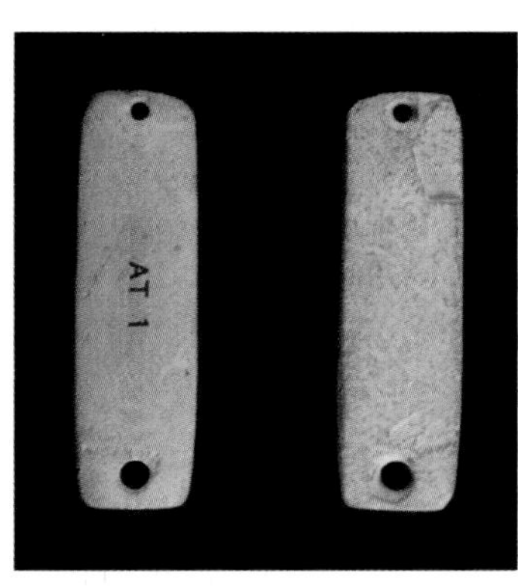

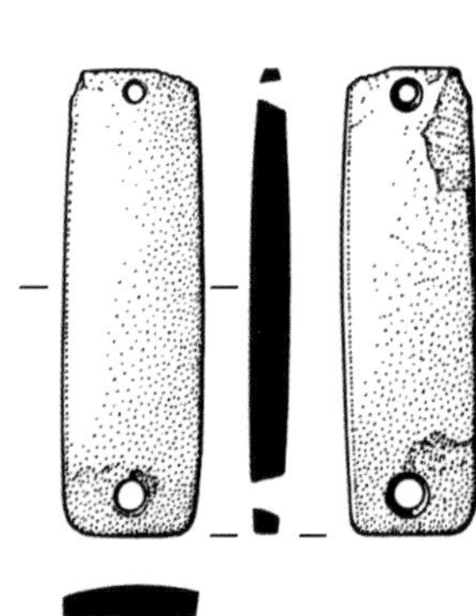

ID 78: Fyrish

Beaker cist burial, Evanton, Ross and Cromarty (Highland).

NMS Edinburgh X.EQ 133; Anon 1868; Evans 1897, 426, fig. 354; 114.0 × 29.0 × 5.2mm; Group VI type, dark greenish grey (5G 5/1); 98% present at deposition; evidence of striations and polishing; four perforations; slightly worn.

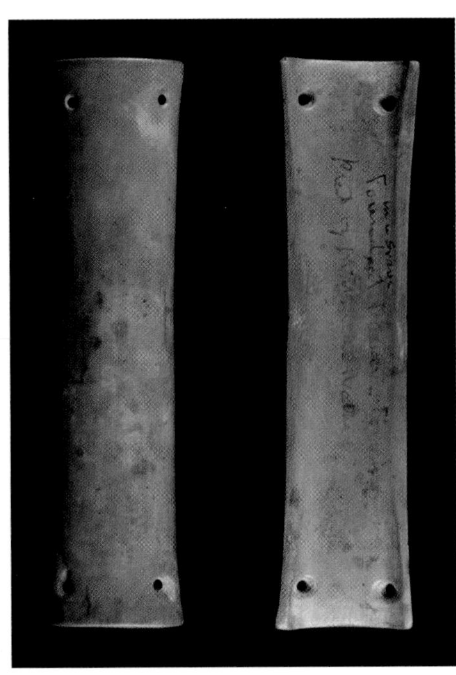

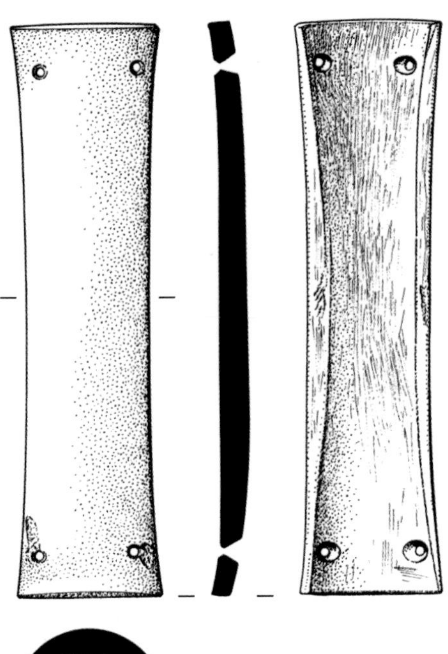

ID 79: Culduthel Mains

Beaker cist burial, Culduthel Mains, Inverness-shire (Highland).

NMS Edinburgh X.EQ 844; Clarke *et al.* 1985, 267 and fig. 4.16; 117.5 × 37.2 × 5.5mm; Group VI type, greenish grey (5G 6/1); 99% present at deposition; evidence of striations and polishing; four perforations with gold caps; slightly worn.

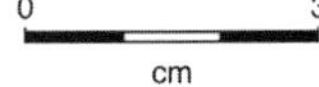

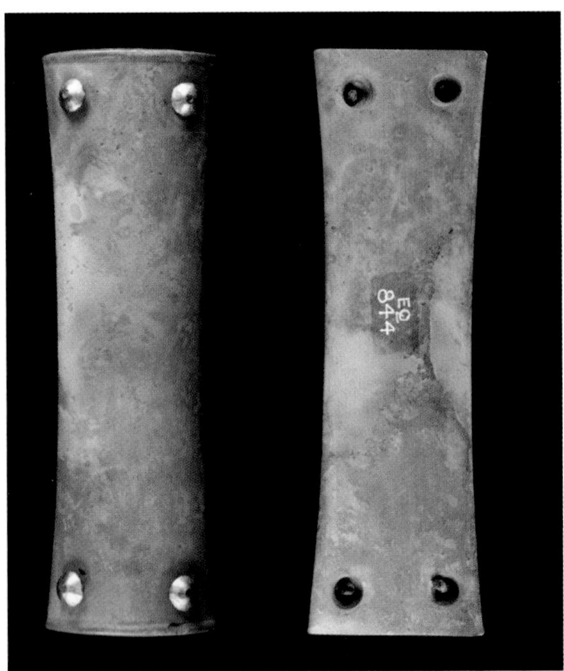

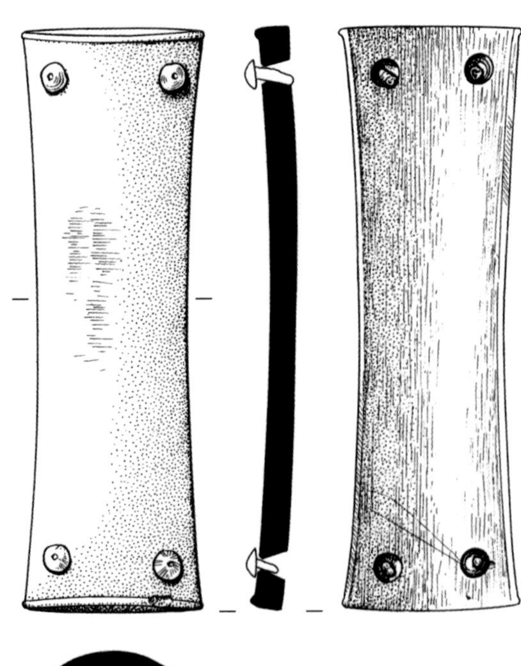

ID 80: Culbin Sands

Stray find, Culbin Sands, Moray.

NMS Edinburgh X. AT 9; Walker 1967, 90; 86.5 × 17.5 × 9.0mm; miscellaneous type, dark greenish grey (5GY 4/1); 99% present at deposition; possibly unfinished or used as pendant; evidence of striations and polishing; one perforation; slightly worn.

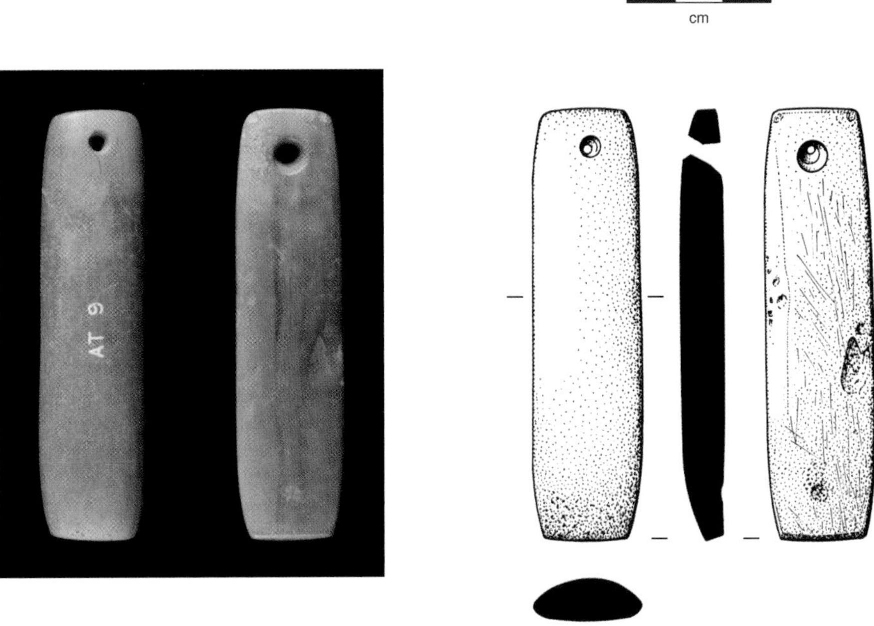

ID 82: Old Rayne

Cremation burial at centre of recumbent stone circle, Newhills, Aberdeenshire.

NMS Edinburgh X.AT 5; Dalrymple 1859; Coles 1902; 36.7 × 28.0 × 4.5mm; miscellaneous type, dark greenish grey (5GY 5/1); fragment (less than 50%) present at deposition; reworked as pendant?; evidence of striations and polishing; possible secondary perforation; three perforations, probably with six originally; two central perforations secondary; worn.

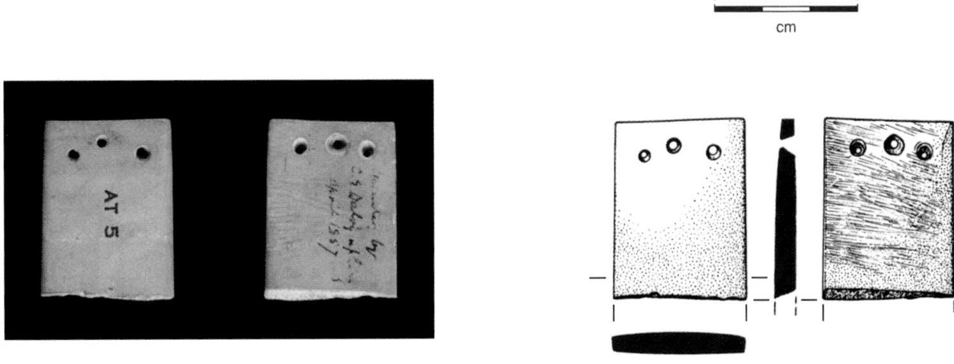

ID 84: Ballogie

Stray find, Ballogie, Aberdeenshire.

NMS Edinburgh X.AT 8; Anon 1893, 11; 75.5 × 13.5 × 6.5mm; miscellaneous type, greenish grey (5GY 5/1); 99% present at deposition; evidence of striations and polishing; two perforations; slightly worn.

0 3
cm

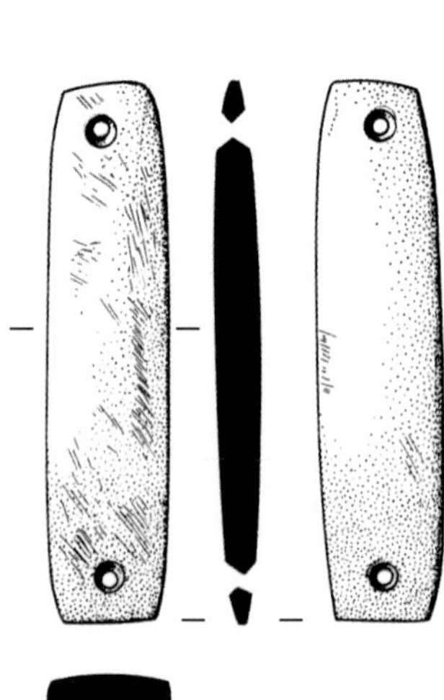

ID 86: Glen Forsa

Probable Beaker inhumation grave, Glen Forsa, Mull (Argyll and Bute).

NMS Edinburgh X.EQ 134; Anon 1873; 88.6 × 32.4 × 7.1mm; Group VI type, greenish grey (5G 7/1); 98% present at deposition; evidence of striations and polishing; two perforations; worn.

0 3
cm

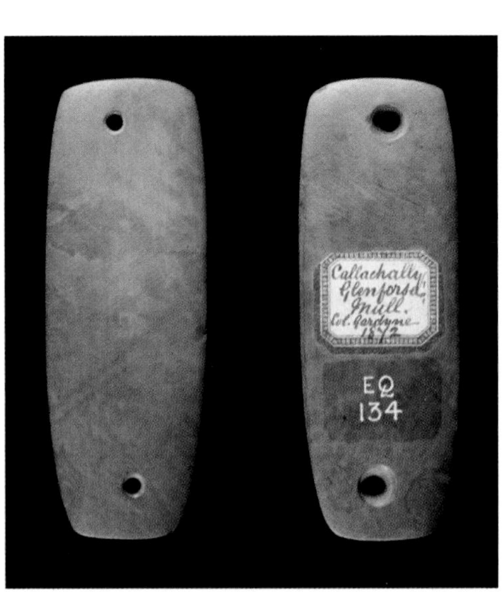

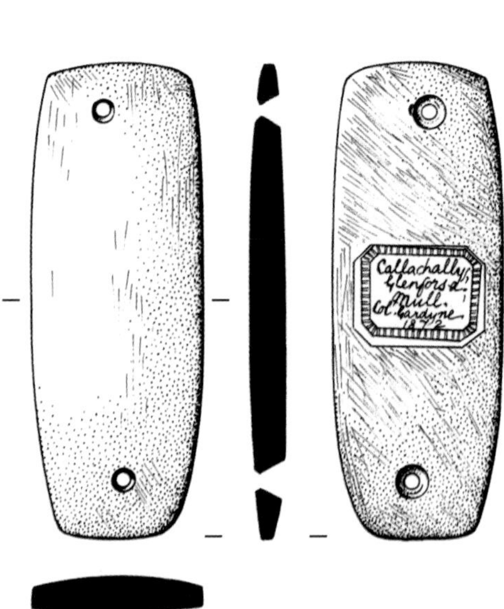

ID 87: Corry Liveras
In chamber of megalithic tomb SKY 6, Broadford Bay, Skye (Highland).
NMS Edinburgh X.AT4; Henshall 1972, 310, top left; 61.2 × 47.5 × 5.5mm; Group VI type, greenish grey (5G 6/1); 98% present at deposition; reworked; evidence of striations and polishing; four perforations; one end decorated with punctulations; worn.

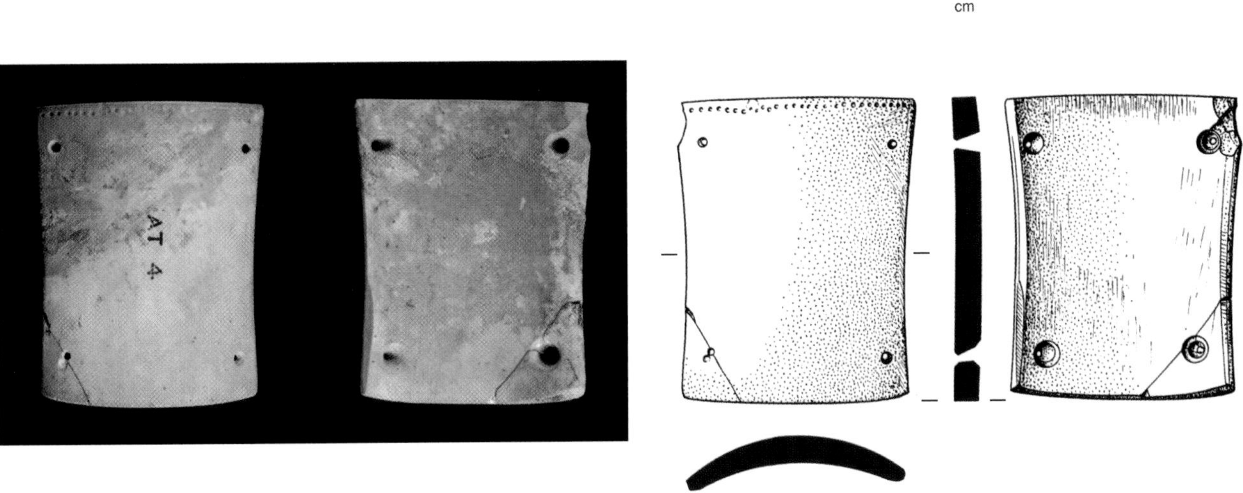

ID 88: Broadford Bay
Adjacent to megalithic tomb SKY 6, Broadford Bay, Skye (Highland).
NMS Edinburgh X. AT 3; Henshall 1972, 484–5 (not ill); 82.0 × 13.2 × 7.5mm; miscellaneous type, dark greenish grey (5G 6/1) with pinkish grey band (5YR 8/1); 100% present at deposition; evidence of striations and polishing; two perforations; worn.

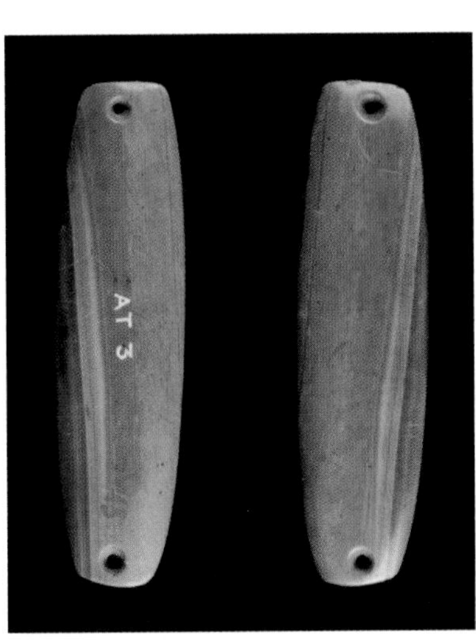

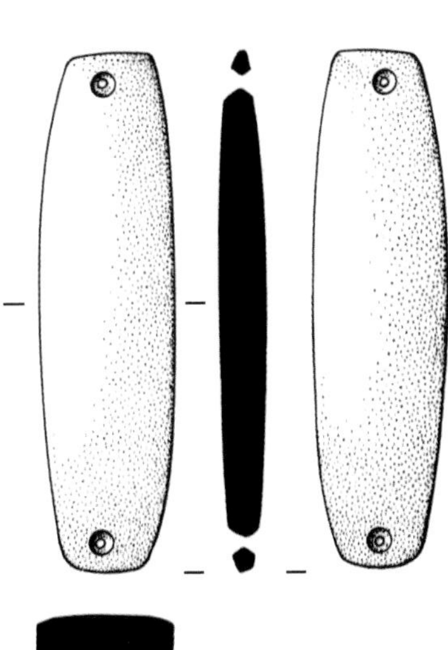

ID 89: Borrowstone

Beaker cist burial, Newhills, Aberdeenshire (City of Aberdeen).

Marischal Museum, Aberdeen 14776; Shepherd 1986; 112.0 × 35.2 × 6.8mm; Group VI type, pale greenish yellow (10Y 8/2) to greyish olive (10Y 4/2); 99% present at deposition; evidence of striations and rivets; four perforations, three showing bronze rivets; slightly worn.

0 3
cm

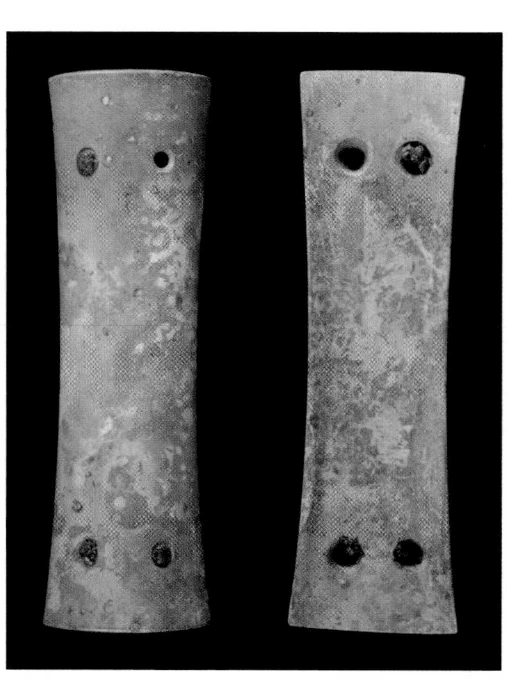

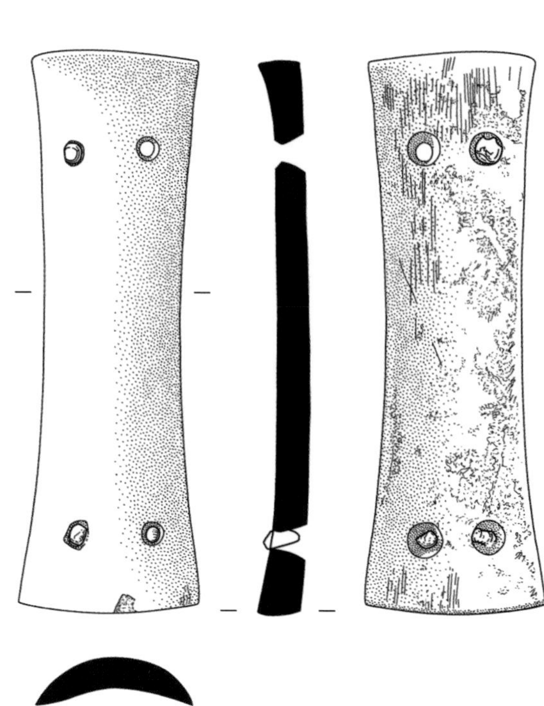

ID 90: Newlands, Oyne

Beaker cist burial, Newlands, Oyne, Aberdeenshire.

Marischal Museum, Aberdeen 14870; Low 1936, fig. 4; 83.0 × 28.0 × 10.5mm; miscellaneous type, dark grey (N3); 99% present at deposition; evidence of striations; four perforations; possible grooves for thongs; worn.

0 3
cm

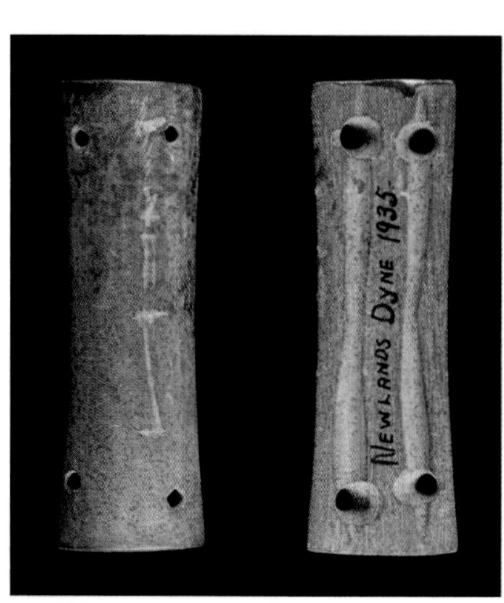

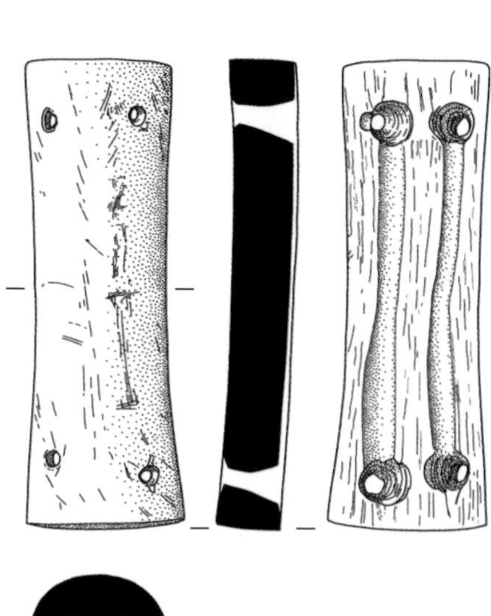

ID 91: Newlands, Oyne

Cist burial, Newlands, Oyne, Aberdeenshire.

Marischal Museum, Aberdeen 14780; Low 1936, fig. 3; 74.7 × 17.8 × 8.6mm; Group VI type, dark greenish grey (5GY 4/1) to light olive grey (5Y 6/1); 100% present at deposition; possibly reworked; evidence of striations; two perforations; slightly worn.

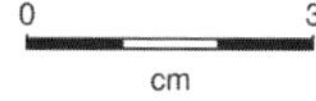

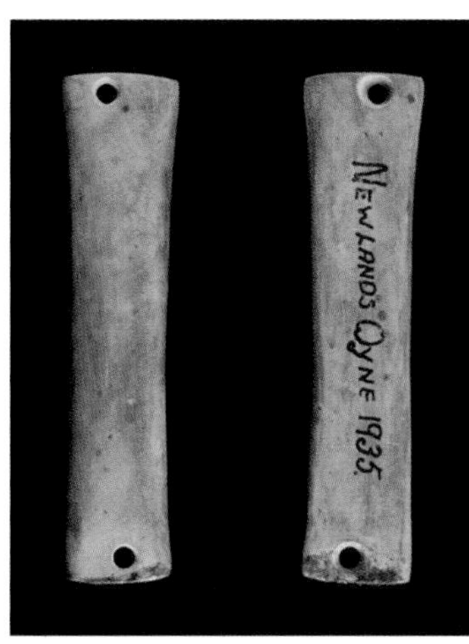

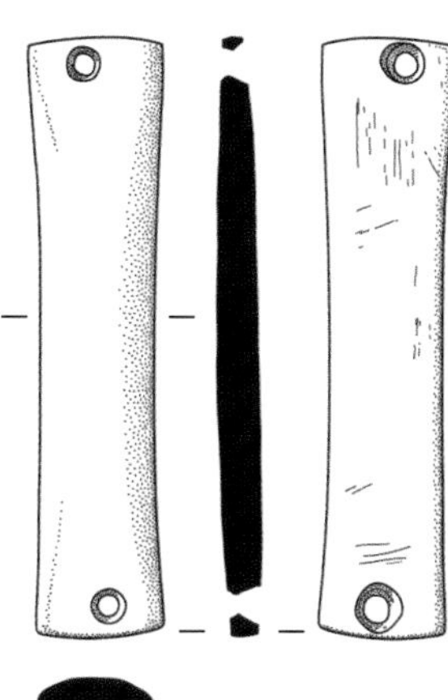

ID 92: ?Scotland

Stray find.

Hunterian Museum and Art Gallery, Glasgow A.122; unpublished; 92.0 × 18.0 × 6.8mm; miscellaneous red/black type, dusky red (10R 2/2); 100% present at deposition; evidence of striations; two perforations; slightly worn.

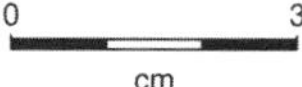

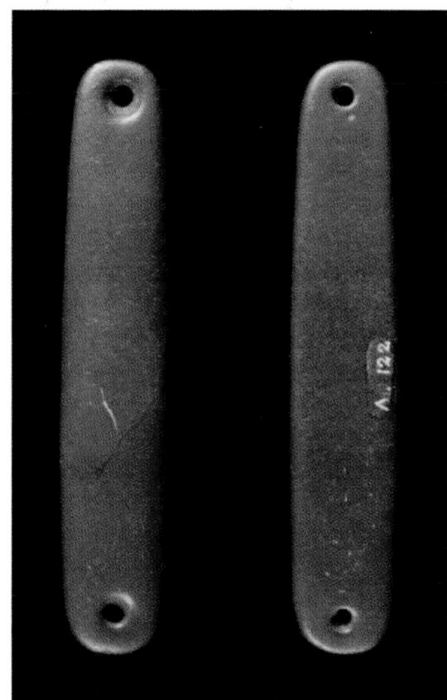

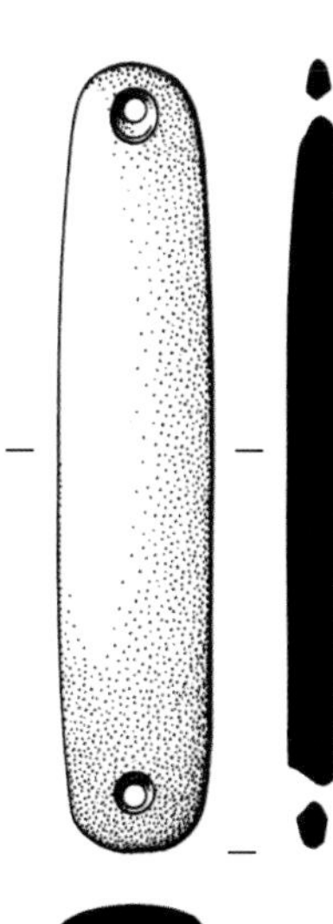

ID 93: Crawford

Stray find, Crawford, Lanarkshire (South Lanarkshire).

Hunterian Museum and Art Gallery, Glasgow B 1951.907; RCAHMS 1978, 4; 59.5 × 26.2 × 5.2mm; miscellaneous type, dark yellowish brown (10YR 8/2); 100% present at deposition; evidence of striations; two perforations; worn.

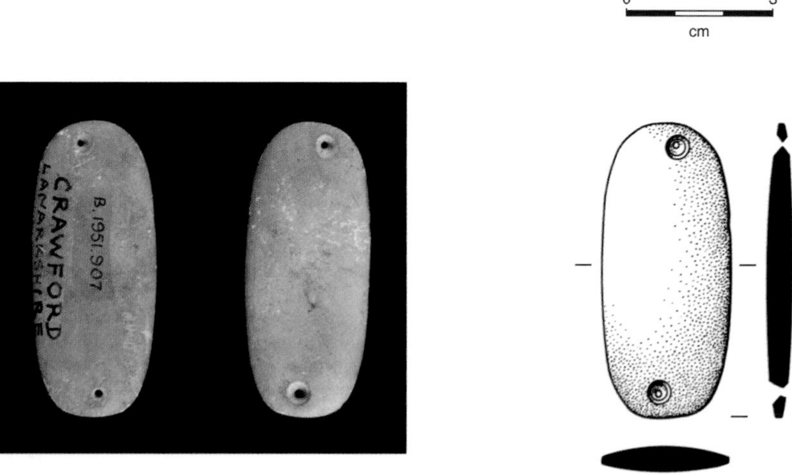

ID 94: Dornoch Nursery

Beaker cist burial, Dornoch Nursery, Sutherland (Highland).

Inverness Museum and Art Gallery 980.19; Ashmore 1989, fig. 6b, 6; 94.8 × 10.2 × 6.0mm; miscellaneous red/black type, greyish red (10YR 4/2); 100% present at deposition; evidence of striations; two perforations; worn.

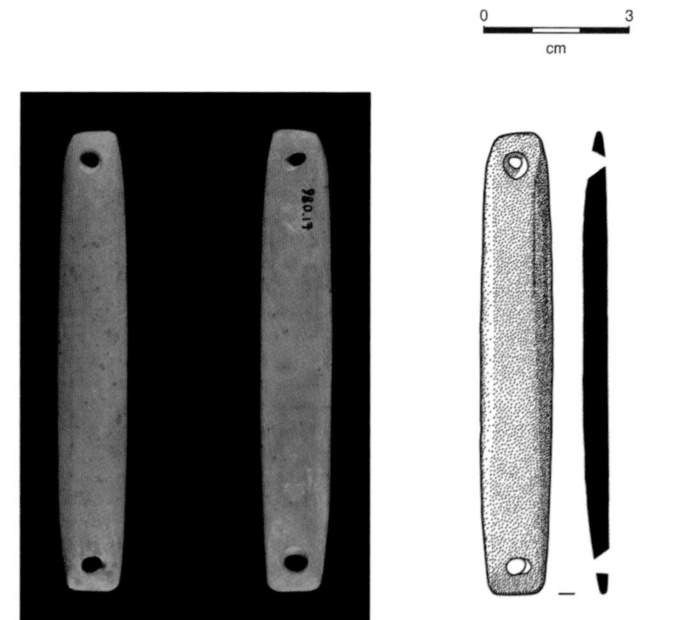

(from publication, after Ashmore 1989, fig. 6b)

ID 101: Ardiffery (replica)
Beaker cist burial, Cruden, Aberdeenshire.
Peterhead Museum, NMS Edinburgh (cast) X.EQ 622; Anderson and Black 1888; Kenworthy 1979; *c.*100 × 27 × 5.65mm; Group VI type inferred, dark green; 99% present at deposition; four perforations; condition N/A.

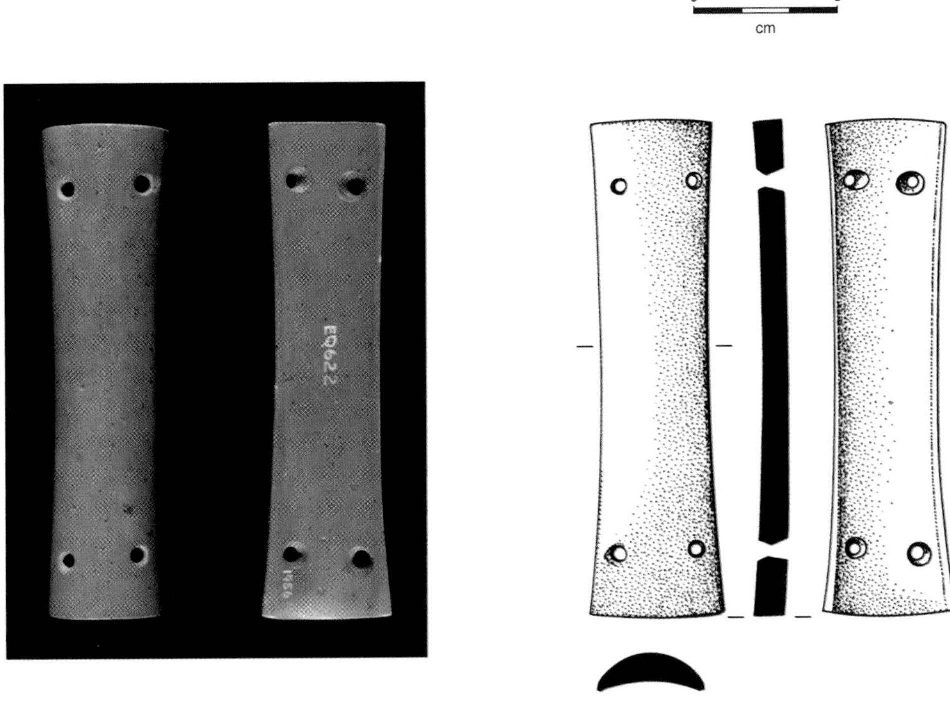

ID 102: Duston
Stray surface find, Duston, Northamptonshire.
Northampton Museum and Art gallery D66.1973; Clough and Cummins 1988, 186; 60.8 × 28.5 × 4.7mm; amphibolite type, greenish grey (5G 6/1); 90% present at deposition; reworked; evidence of striations and polishing; one perforation, probably two originally; worn.

0 3
cm

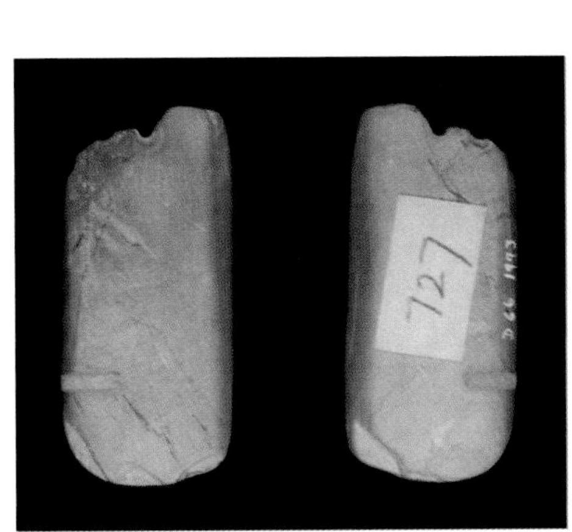

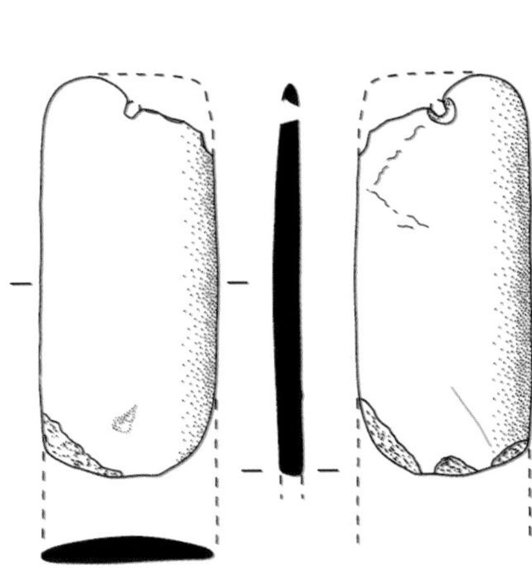

ID 103: Upper Heyford

Stray find in pipe trench, Upper Heyford, Northamptonshire.

Northampton Museum and Art Gallery D309. 1957–8; Kennett 1969; 72.5 × 28.8 × 5.7mm; amphibolite type, light greenish grey (5GY 7/1); 90% present at deposition; evidence of striations and polishing; two perforations; slightly worn.

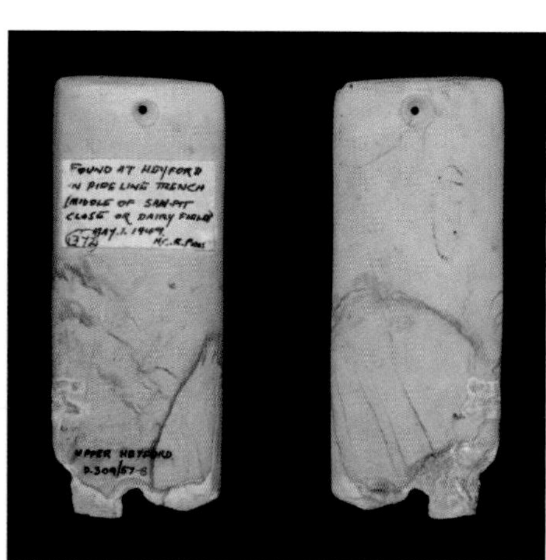

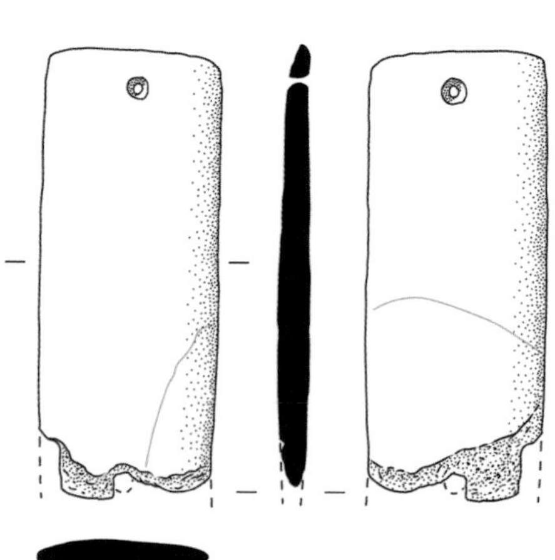

ID 104: Nr Scarborough

No context details, nr Scarborough, North Yorkshire.

Saffron Walden Museum, Loan 742; unpublished; 59.5 × 31.2 × 5.7mm; miscellaneous type, light grey (N8); 95% present at deposition; evidence of striations; two perforations; slightly worn.

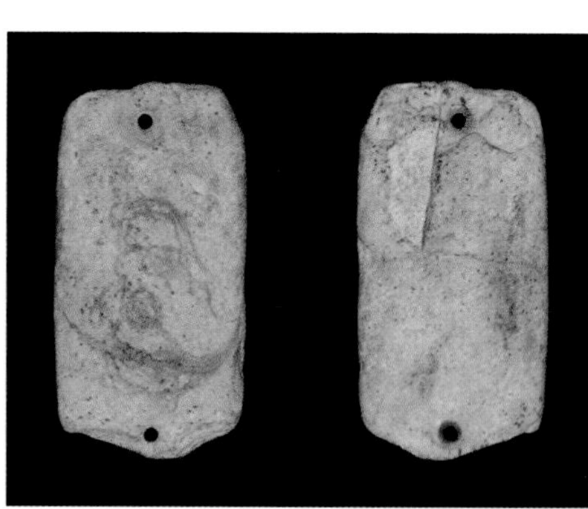

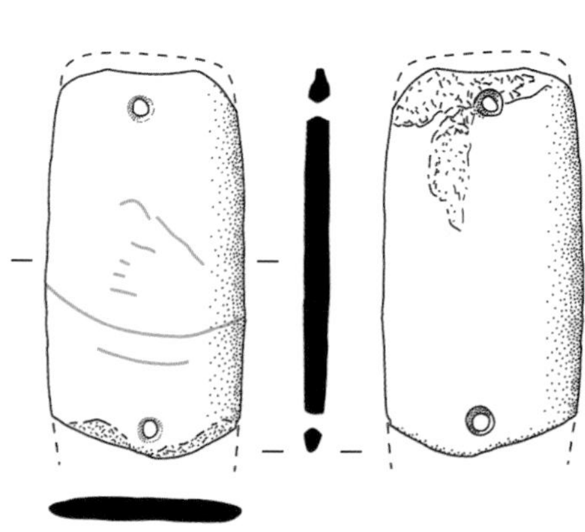

ID 105: Melton Quarry

Beaker inhumation grave, Melton Quarry, East Yorkshire (East Riding).

Hull and East Riding Museum 68.60.6; Bartlett 1963, fig. 2, 2a; 86.0 × 23.0 × 4.0mm; Group VI type, greyish olive green (5GY 4/2); 99% present at deposition; evidence of striations and polishing; two perforations; four locations of possible mounts; slightly worn.

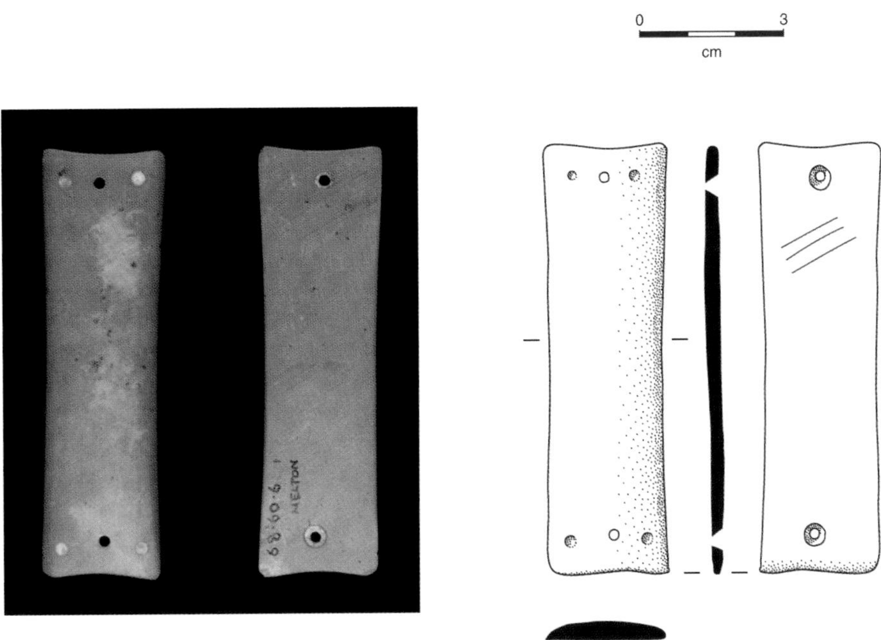

ID 106: Hockwold

Surface find near Beaker settlement site, Hockwold-cum-Wilton, Norfolk.

Norwich Castle Museum L.1968.1; Clough and Green 1972, fig. 14, left; 89.0 × 22.0 × 3.5mm; amphibolite type, yellowish grey (5Y 8/1); 90% present at deposition; evidence of striations and polishing; two perforations; slightly worn.

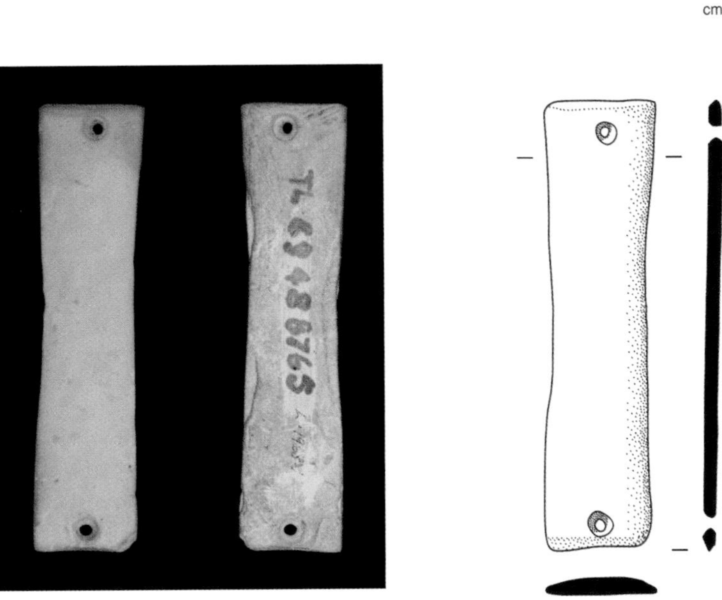

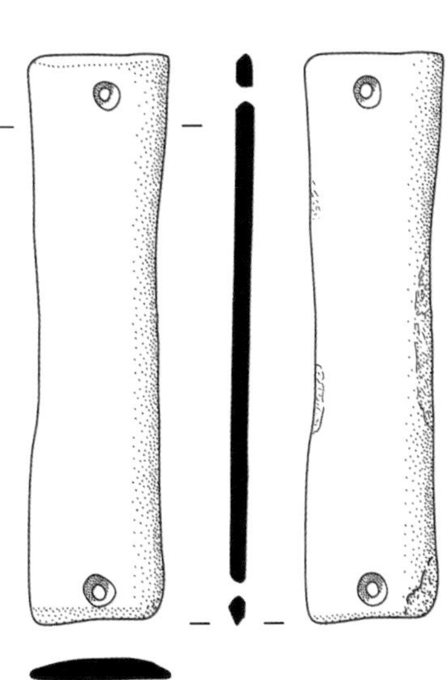

ID 107: Aston

Beaker inhumation grave, Aston-on-Trent barrow 1, Derbyshire.

Derby Museum and Art Gallery (A235) 810-3-67; Reaney 1968, 68–81 (not ill); Vine 1982, 315, no. 167; 74.5 × 38.0 × 4.5mm; amphibolite type, greenish grey (5G 7/1); 98% present at deposition; evidence of striations and polishing; four perforations; slightly worn.

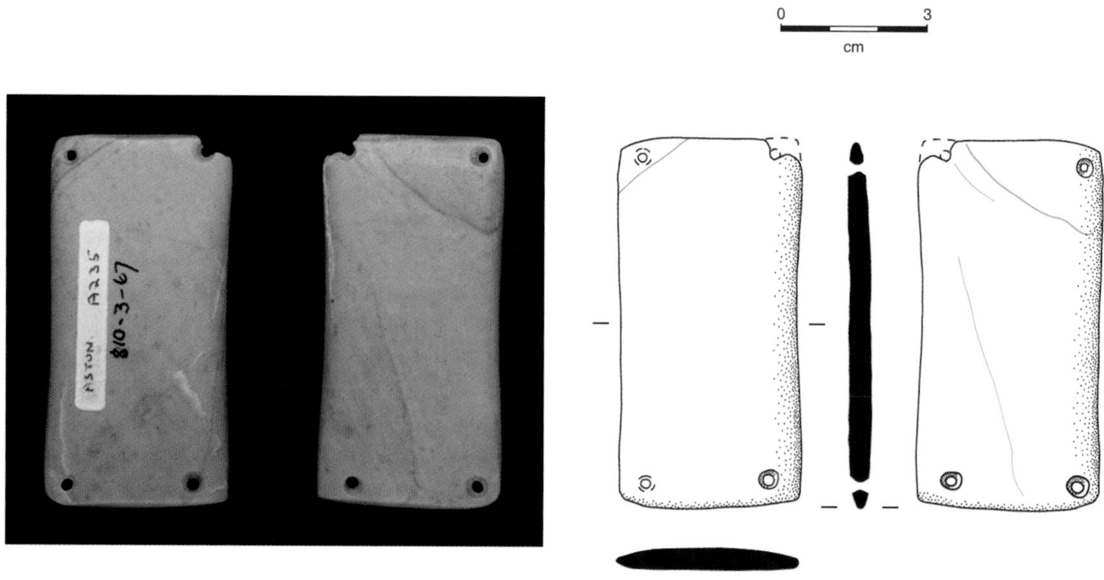

ID 108: Ben Bridge

Beaker pit, Ben Bridge, Somerset.

Bristol City Museum and Art Gallery F3647; Rahtz and Greenfield 1977, fig. 91, 11; 44.8 × 12.5 × 5.0mm; miscellaneous red/black type, dark grey (N3); 100% present at deposition; evidence of striations and polishing; two perforations; worn.

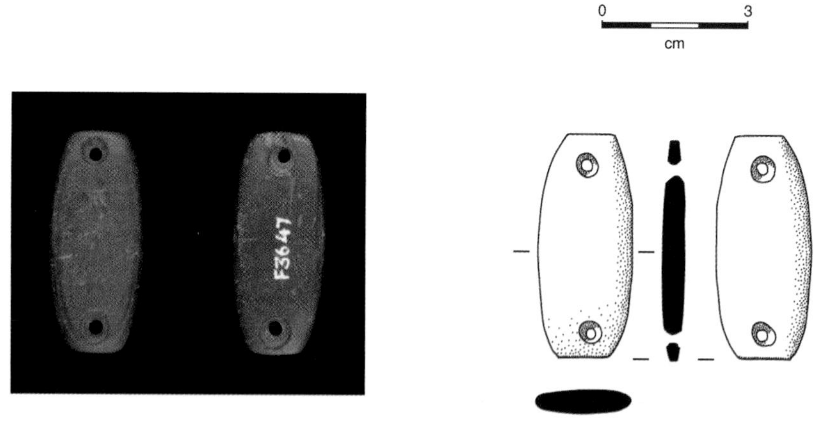

ID 111: Lindridge

Stray find 6 feet down in gravel pit, Sundridge, Worcestershire.

Worcester City Museum, no accession no; Allies 1849, 409; 27.7 × 26.2 × 6.7mm; miscellaneous type, olive black (5Y 2/1); 100% present at deposition; reworked?; evidence of striations and polishing; two perforations (originally four?); central location of possible mount; slightly worn.

0 3
cm

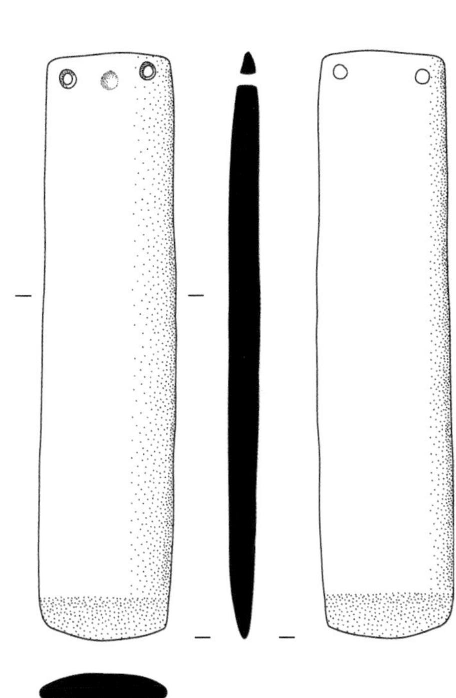

ID 112: Aldington

Stray find 5 feet down in gravel pit, Aldington, Worcestershire.

Worcestershire County Museum, Ingram Coll. 4; Ingram 1867, pl. 6; 138.5 × 47.0 × 6.2mm; Group VI type, olive grey (5Y 4/1); 99% present at deposition; evidence of striations and polishing; four perforations; worn.

0 3
cm

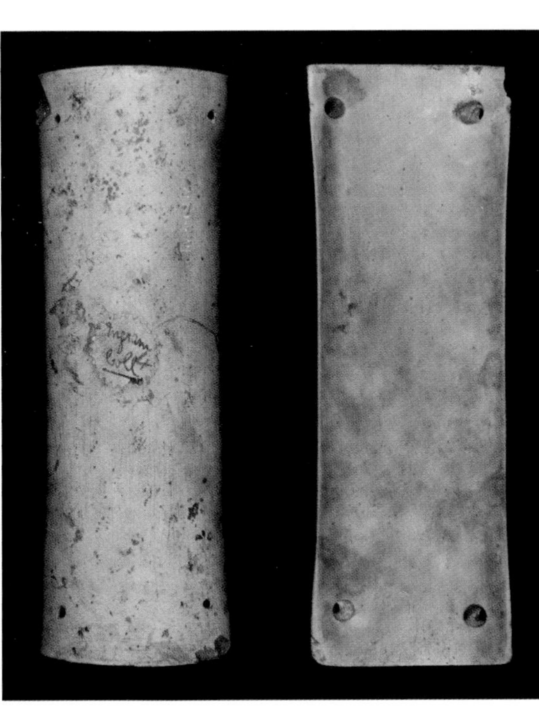

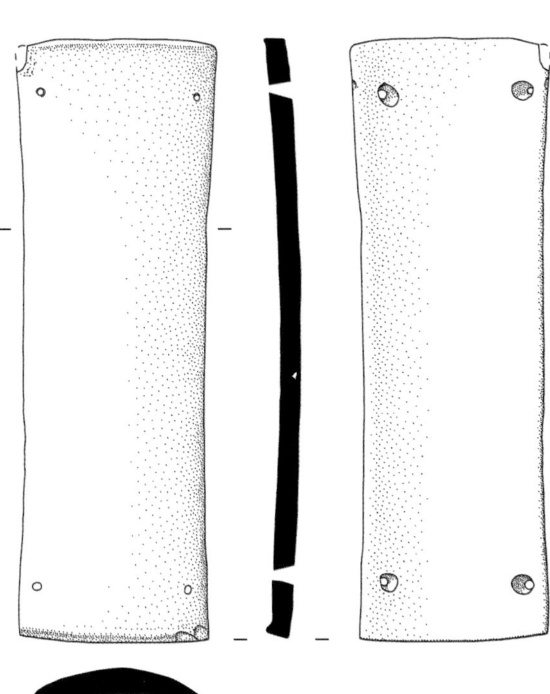

ID 113: Llantrithyd

Stray find on medieval site, but location uncertain, Llantrithyd, S Glamorgan (Glamorgan Gwent).

NMW Cardiff 76.4H/20; Savory 1973; Savory 1980, 20 and footnote; 127.0 × 24.0 × 5.6mm; amphibolite type, greenish grey (5GY 6/1); 100% present at deposition; evidence of striations and polishing; two perforations; fresh.

0 3
cm

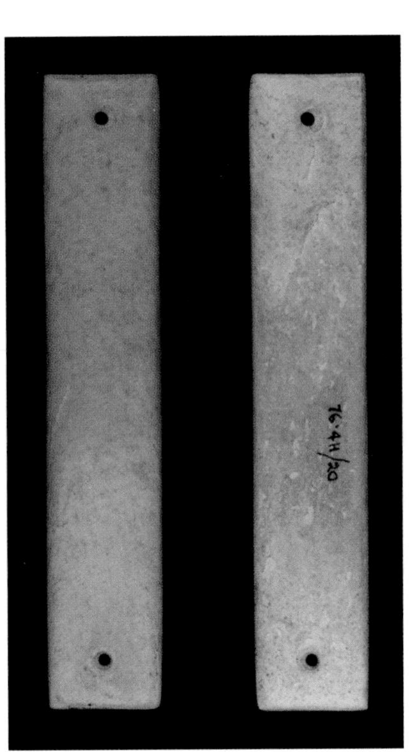

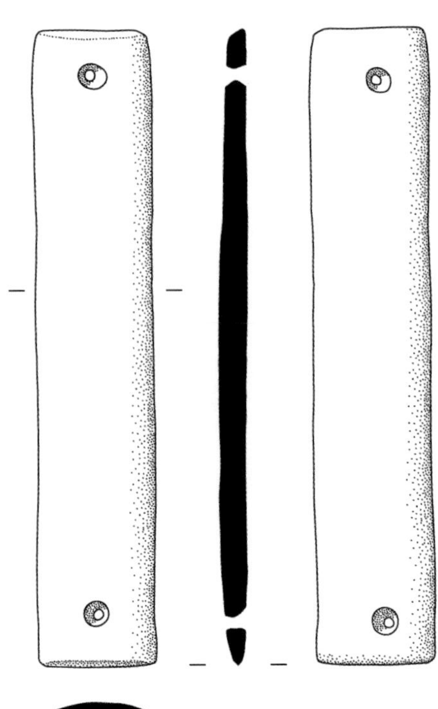

ID 114: Dyffryn Ardudwy

Disturbed in East Chamber of megalithic cairn, Dyffryn Ardudwy, Merioneth (Gwynedd).

National Museum of Wales, Cardiff; 64.357/1 and 64.357.2; Powell 1973, fig. 10, 1–2; 39.5 × 19.5 × 2.5mm; miscellaneous type, yellowish grey (10YR 6/2); two fragments present at deposition; evidence of striations and polishing; two perforations; one fragment slightly worn; one fragment worn.

0 3
cm

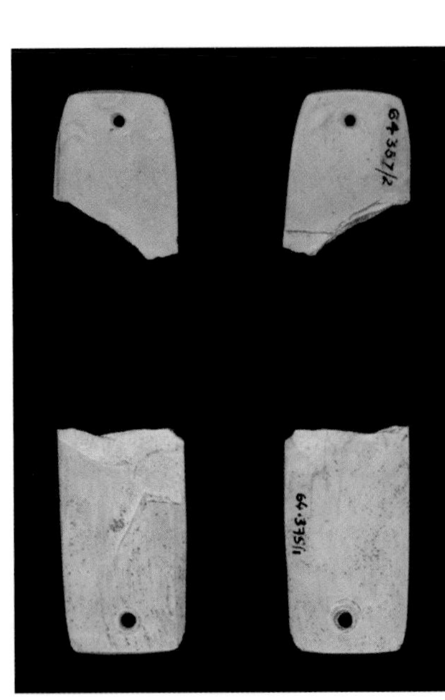

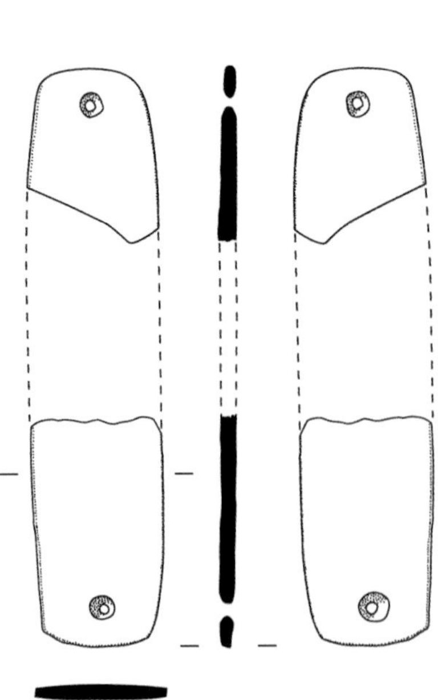

ID 115: Sonning

Stray find from River Thames, Sonning, Berkshire.

Reading Museum and Art Gallery 1945. S 243.1; Salzman 1939, 266a; Clough and Cummins 1988, 143; 84.3 × 32.1 × 4.3mm; amphibolite type, olive grey (5Y 4/1); 95% present at deposition; evidence of striations and polishing; six perforations; worn.

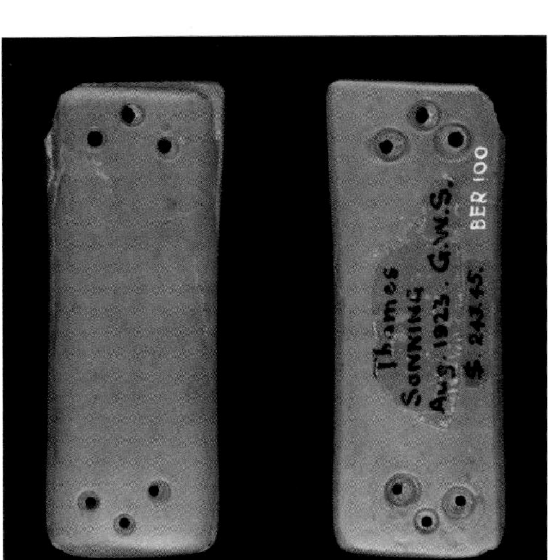

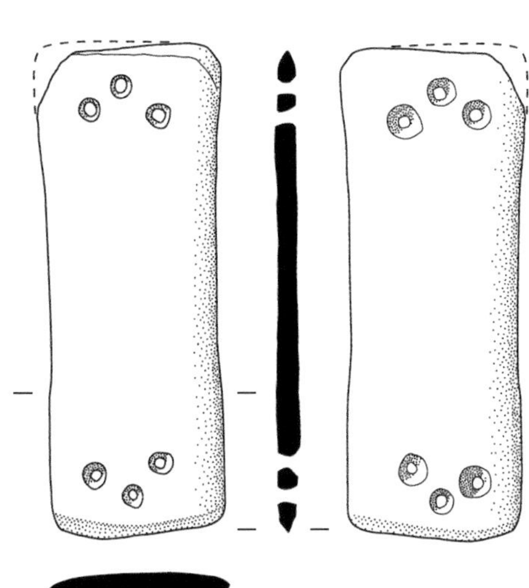

ID 116: Raunds

Beaker inhumation grave, Raunds, Northamptonshire.

English Heritage, Fort Cumberland SF 35125; Harding and Healy 2007, 236 and 252–3; 57.0 × 38.5 × 3.3mm; Group VI type, greyish olive green (5GY 3/2); 50% present at deposition; reworked; evidence of striations and polishing; two perforations (formerly four?); one location of ?mount/unfinished perforation; very worn.

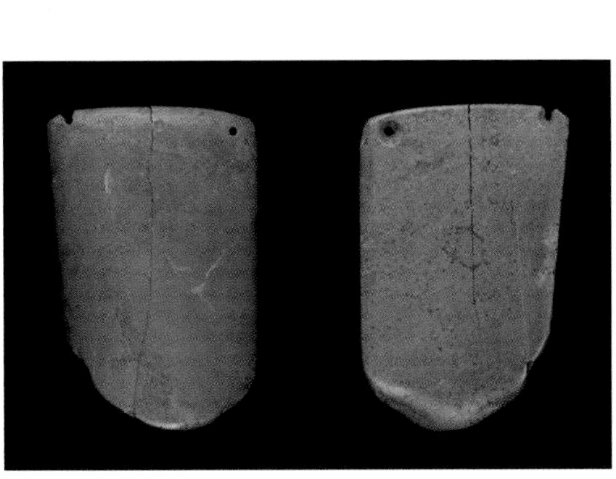

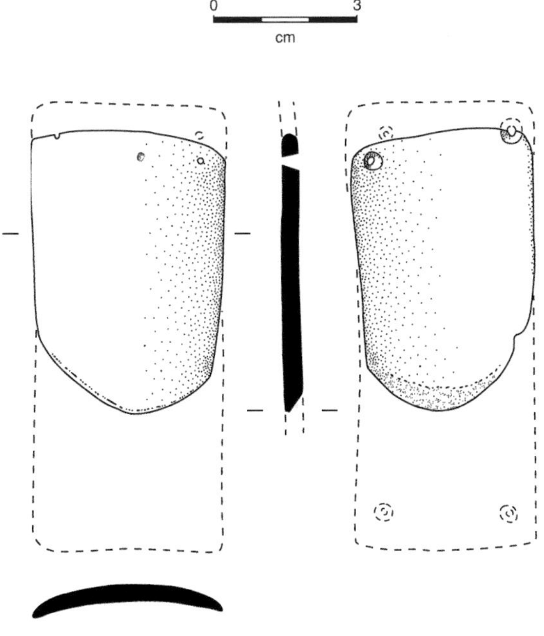

(reconstructed after ID 1)

118: Rauceby

No context details, Rauceby, Lincolnshire.

The Collection, Lincoln, 'Rauceby'; Petch 1958, fig. 2, 3; 68.3 × 20.3 × 4.5mm; Group VI type, brownish grey (5YR 3/2); 99% present at deposition; evidence of striations and polishing; two perforations; worn.

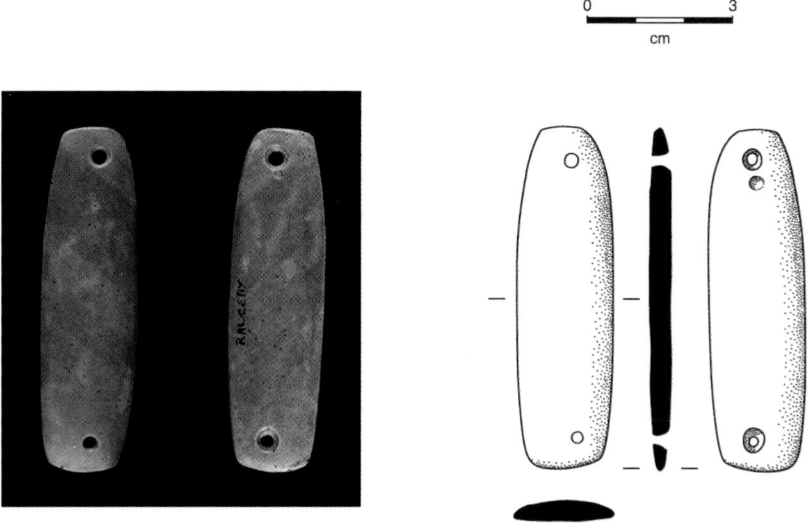

ID 119: Winteringham

Stray find in sand pit, Winteringham, Lincolnshire.

North Lincolnshire Museum, Scunthorpe, WGMAA23; Dudley 1949, 71; Petch 1958, 92, footnote 4; 33.5 × 28.5 × 4.5mm; Group VI type, greyish olive (10Y 3/2); estimated 20% present at deposition; evidence of striations; three perforations surviving, originally ?six; worn.

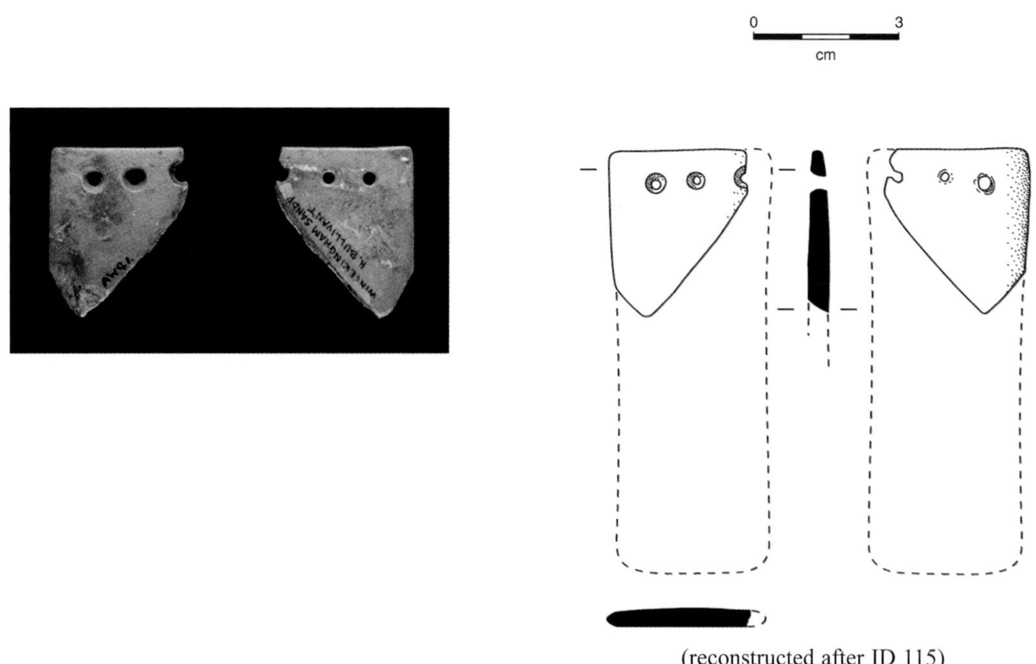

(reconstructed after ID 115)

ID 120: Littleport

Stray find, Burnt Fen, Littleport, Cambridgeshire.

Cambridge University Museum of Archaeology and Anthropology Z. 14825 – A; Salzman 1938, 264 and fig. 12, 2; 74.7 × 24.2 × 7.5mm; miscellaneous type, medium dark grey (N4); 99% present at deposition; evidence of polishing (lacquer?); two perforations; very worn.

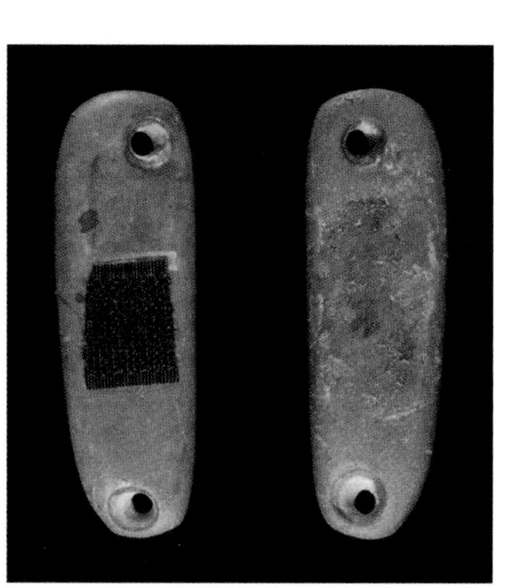

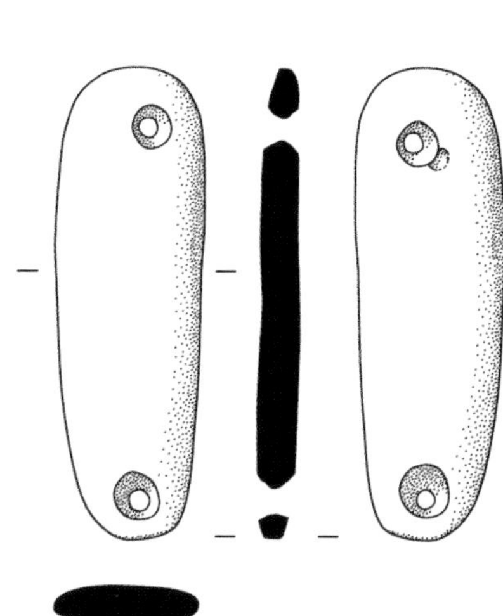

ID 121: Calceby

Stray find, Calceby, Lincolnshire.

The Collection, Lincoln 74.57; Petch 1958, fig. 2, 4; 76.5 × 33.6 × 5.5mm; amphibolite type, pale olive (10Y 7/2); 98% present at deposition; ?reworked; evidence of striations and polishing; four perforations; fresh.

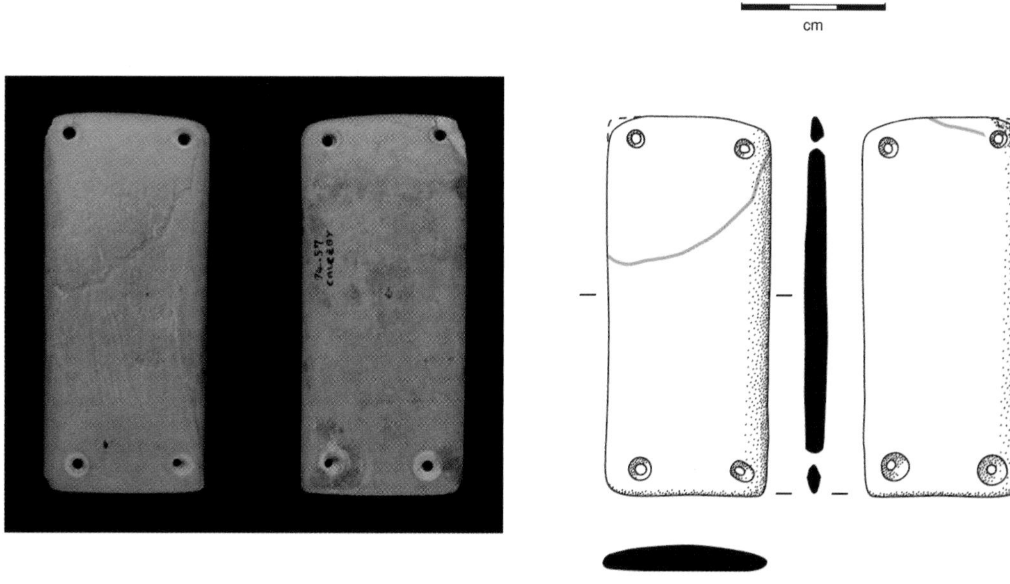

ID 122: Bridlington (not studied)
Stray find, Bridlington, East Yorkshire (East Riding).
Hull and East Riding Museum; not found; Sheppard 1930, 72, fig. (not numbered); recorded as B2 type (flat with four perforations).

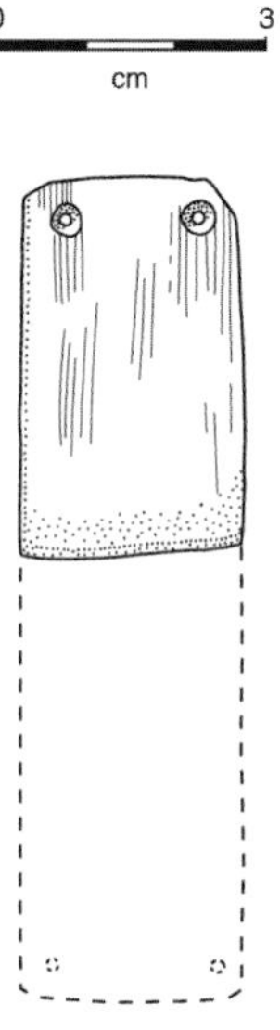

(from publication,after Sheppard 1930)

ID 123: Ferniegair (from photographs)
Early Bronze Age cremation burial, Hamilton, Lanarkshire (South Lanarkshire).
Kelvingrove Art Gallery and Museum 55–96; Welfare 1975, fig. 3, 4; 94 × 43 × 4mm; miscellaneous type (photo only); pale grey/red; four perforations.

0 3
cm

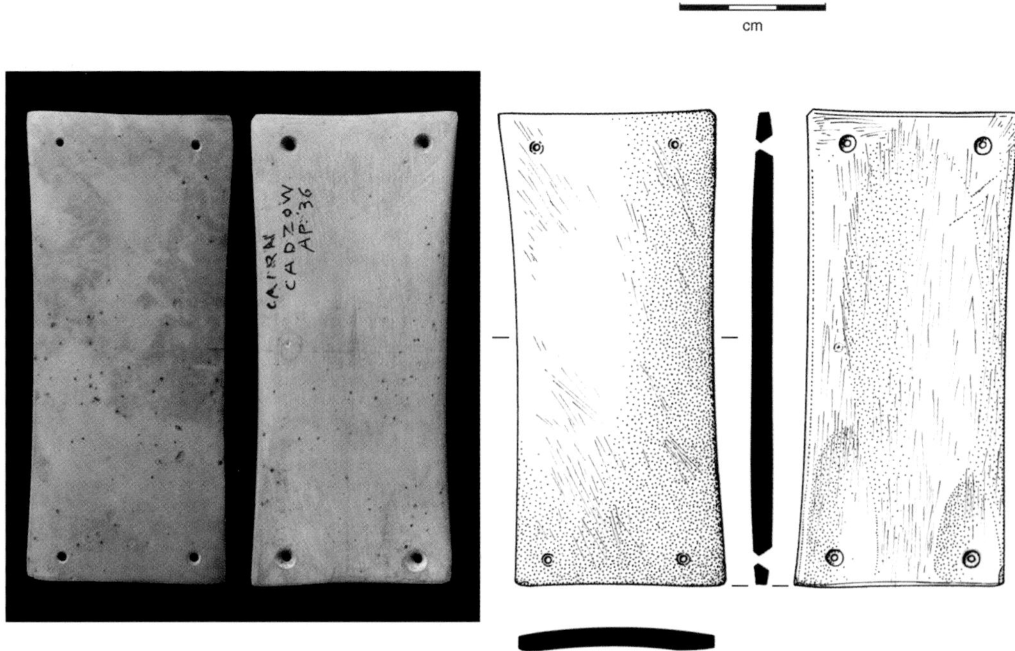

ID 124: Thoresway (not studied)
Near Beaker barrow, Thoresway, Lincolnshire.
The Collection, Lincoln; not found; Everatt1971, fig. II, 4.

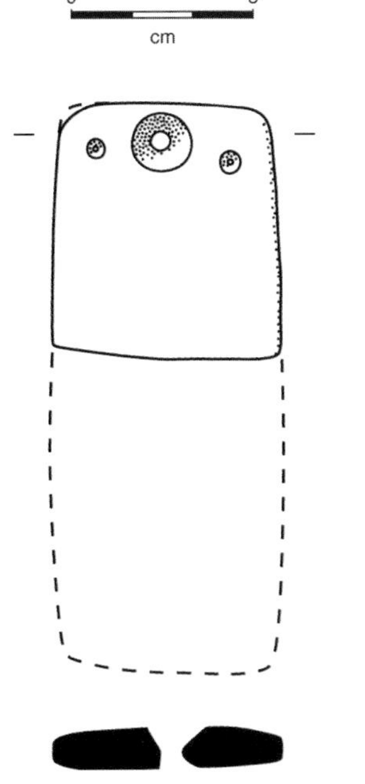

(from publication, after Everatt 1971)

ID 126: Lanarkshire (not studied)
No context details; Lanarkshire; Harbison 1976, 28; recorded as type A1 (flat with convex edges and two perforations); assumed lost.

ID 127: Dalmore. Alness (not studied)
In cist burial; Dalmore, Alness, Ross and Cromarty (Highland). Previously at Ardross Castle; Jolly 1879, fig. 4; 43 × 28 × 4mm (from published drawing); assumed lost.

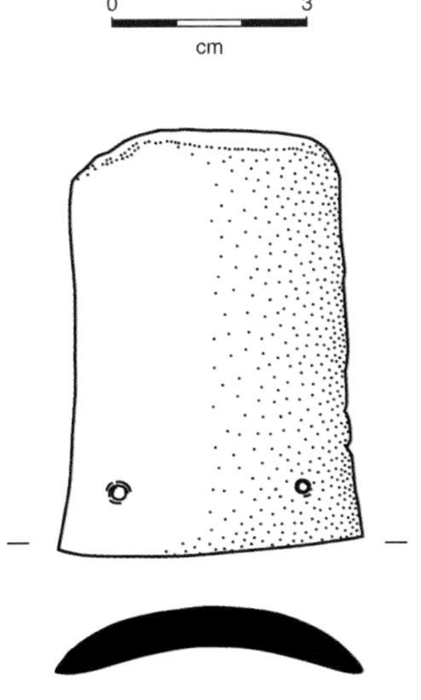

(from publication, after Jolly 1879)

ID 128: Gainsborough (not studied)
Near Gainsborough, Lincolnshire.
The Collection, Lincoln, recorded as type B2 (flat with four perforations, inf. N. Moore); assumed lost.

ID 129: High Dalby (not studied)
High Dalby, NorthYorkshire.
Unknown context; Yorkshire Museum; unpublished; not made available for study.

ID 130: Bowerham Barracks (from photograph)
Early Bronze Age cremation burial; Bowerham Barracks, Lancaster, Lancashire.
Lancaster Museum; Harker 1877; Longworth 1984, pl. 84c; 102 × 24 × 6mm (from published drawing); miscellaneous type, pale purple; two perforations.

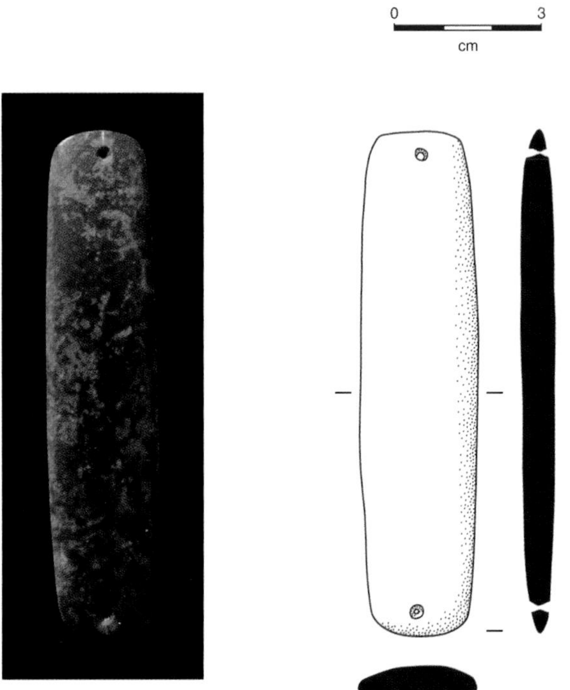

(from publication, after Longworth 1984)

ID 132: Hockwold (not studied)
Unstratified Beaker site, Hockwold-cum-Wilton, Norfolk.
Private ownership; Clough and Green 1972, fig. 14, right; w.30mm, th.3mm (from published drawing); slightly curved; six perforations originally.

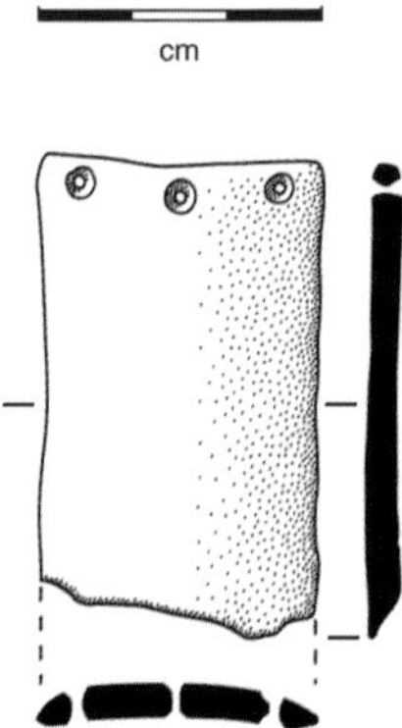

(from publication, after Clough and Green 1971)

ID 133: Archerton Newtake
Cist burial, Sittaford Down, Devon.
Plymouth City Museum and Art Gallery 1912.30; Baring-Gould 1901, fig. 3; 69.5 × 34.0 × 5.0mm; miscellaneous type, whitish grey; 98% present at deposition; evidence of striations and polishing; four perforations; use wear not recorded.

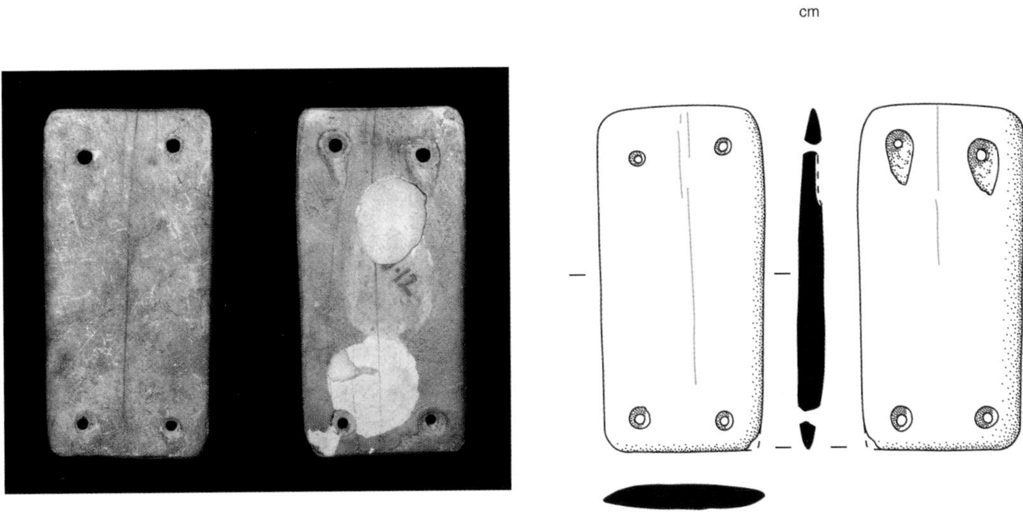

ID 134: Fox Hole
Stray find, Padstow, Cornwall.
Royal Cornwall Museum, Truro 1996/17; unpublished; 39.0 × 37.0 × 4.0mm; amphibolite type, green grey; fragment c.35% present at deposition; evidence of striations; two perforations, probably four originally; use wear not recorded.

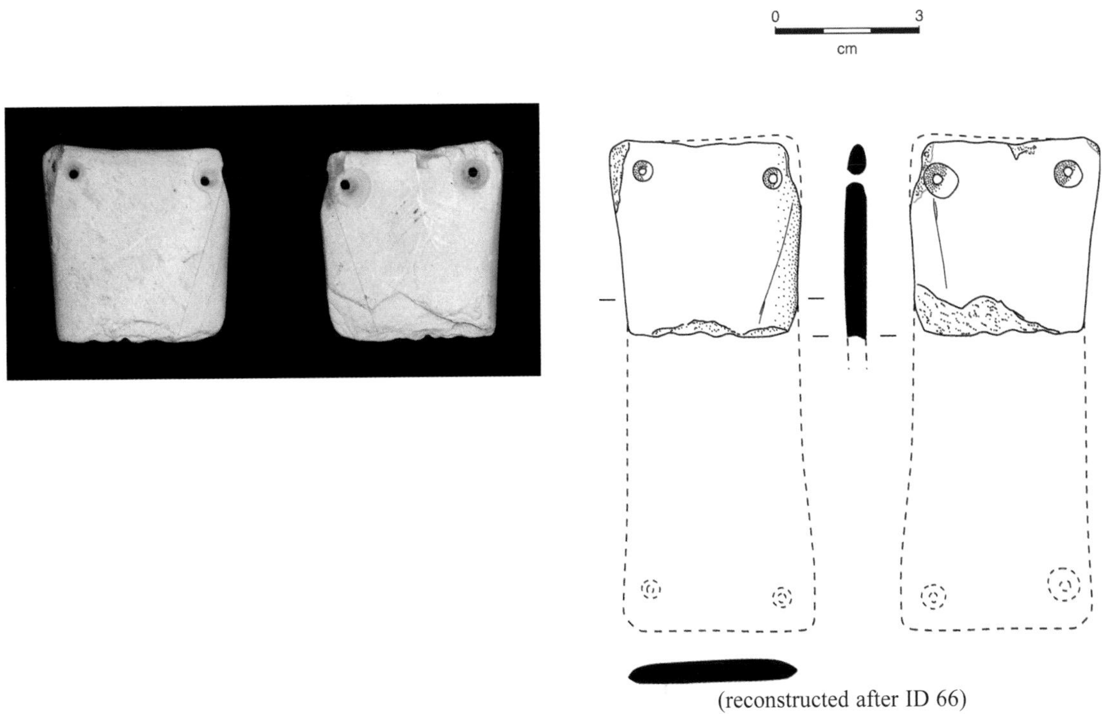

(reconstructed after ID 66)

ID 135: Cassington

Probable grave in gravel pit, Purwell Farm, Cassington, Oxfordshire.

Teaching collection, Queen's University, Belfast; Case and Sturdy 1959, 98 (not ill); 86.7 × 31.0 × 4.8mm; miscellaneous type, light greenish grey (5GY 7/1); 95% present at deposition; evidence of striations and polishing; two perforations; worn.

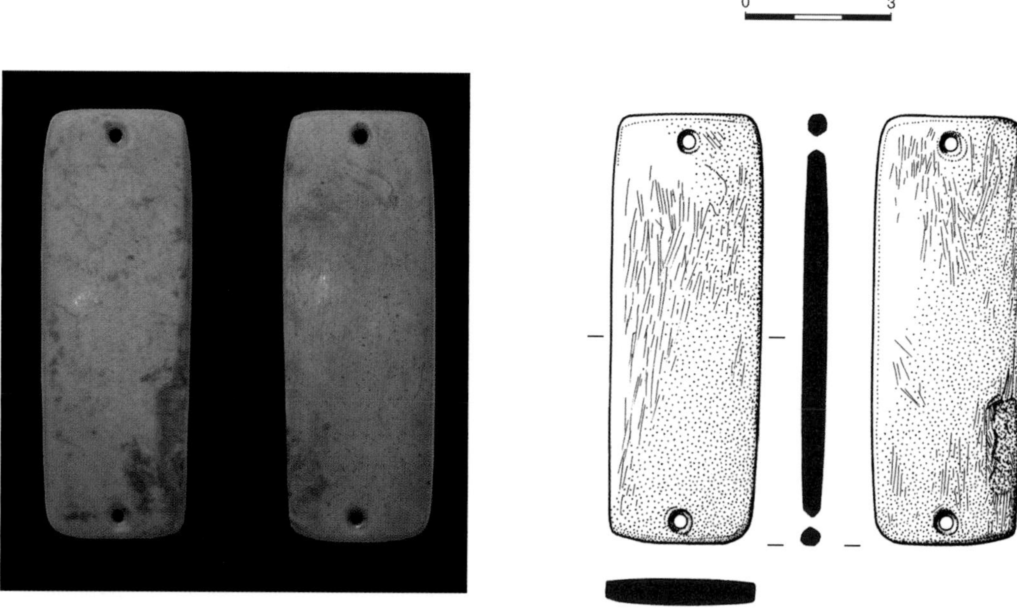

ID 136: Black Knoll (not studied)

No context details, Black Knoll, Church Stretton, Shropshire.

Chitty 1967, 80f cited in Harbison 1976, 29; B2 type (flat with four perforations); location unknown.

ID 137: Pyecombe

Beaker inhumation burial, Pyecombe, West Sussex.

Lewes Castle Museum, Sussex; Butler 1991, fig. 6, 2; 76.9 × 30.9 × 5.1mm; amphibolite type, blue grey; 96% present at deposition; four perforations; evidence of striations and polishing; worn.

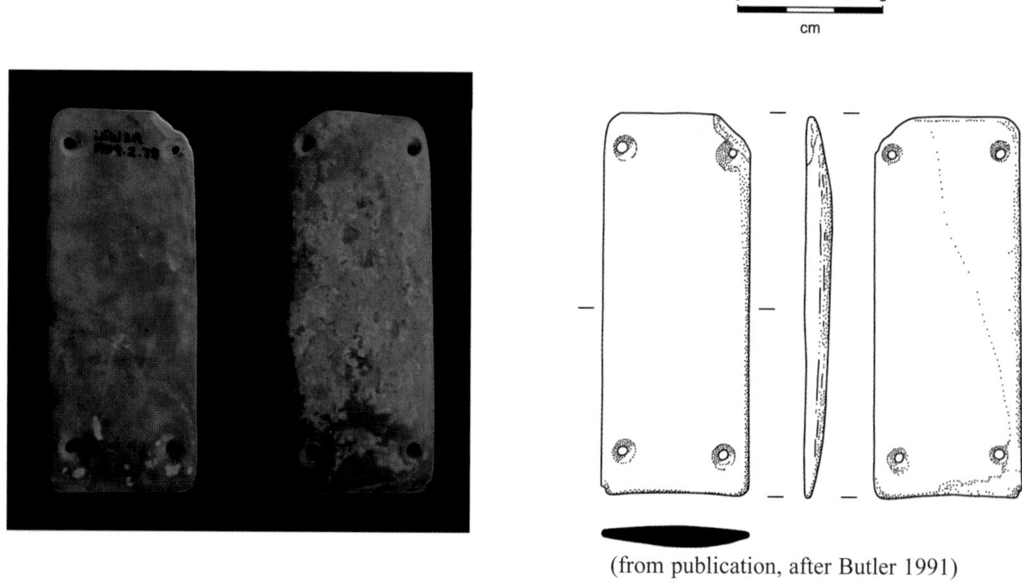

(from publication, after Butler 1991)

ID 139: Mola (from photographs)
Stray find, Nr Mola, Castlemartin, Pembrokeshire (Dyfed).
Carmarthen Museum 76.2756; Figgis 1999 (catalogue entry only, otherwise unpublished); 37 × 23 × 2mm; miscellaneous type, pinkish brown; four perforations, broken.

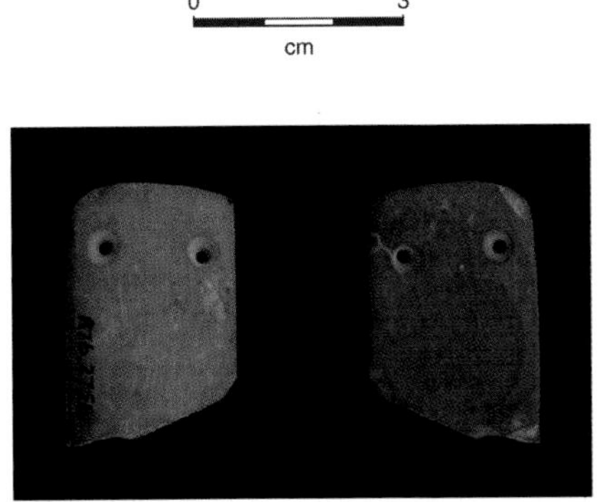

(photo copyright Steve Burrow, National Museum of Wales)

ID 140: Unprovenanced (not studied)
Probably East Yorkshire (East Riding).
Hull and East Riding Museum, 93a.42; Manby (pers comm) sketch and record; 97 × 27 × 6mm (from drawing), 'fine-grained greenstone with white flecks'; not found.

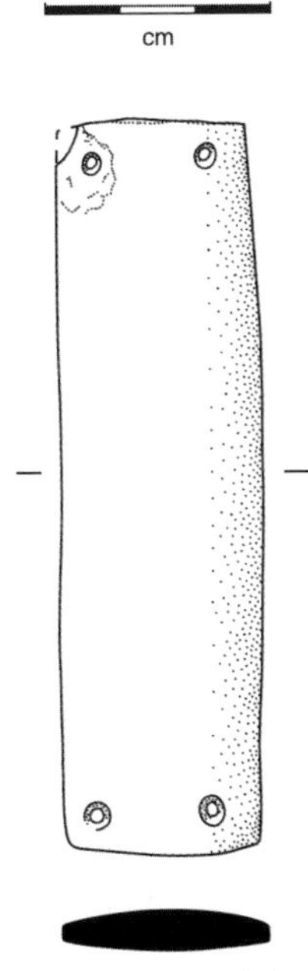

(after T. Manby)

ID 141: Broughton-in-Craven

Early Bronze Age cremation burial, Broughton-in-Craven, North Yorkshire (West Riding).

Burton Constable Hall, BCF 100; Manby 2000, fig. 2; 79.5 × 23.4 × 6.0mm; Group VI type, dark olive green; 99% present at deposition in secondary form; evidence of striations and polishing; probably two perforations originally; reused as pendant; slightly worn.

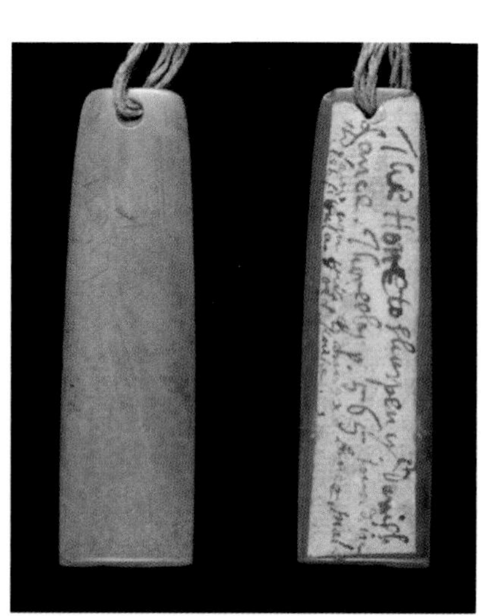

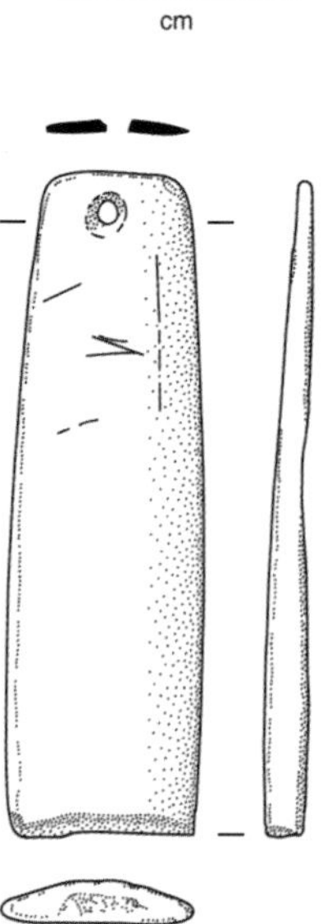

(from publication, after Manby 2000)

ID 142: Bulford (not studied)

Probably a burial in a barrow, Bulford, Wiltshire.

Anon 1849, 319; two perforations, assumed lost.

ID 144: Mere (not studied)

Beaker inhumation burial, Mere G6a, Wiltshire.

Colt Hoare 1812, pl II; Clarke 1970, fig. 130; c. 96 × 18mm (no record of thickness), 'grey slaty stone' according to Colt Hoare; lost.

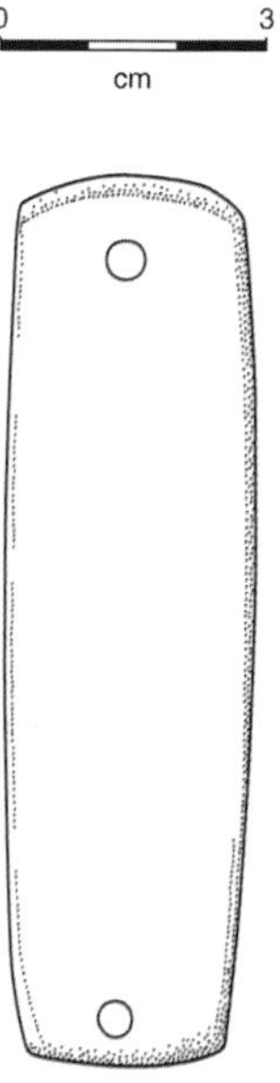

(from publication, after Clarke 1970)

ID 146: Tring (not studied)
Beaker inhumation grave, The Grove, Tring, Hertfordshire.
Anon 1787, fig. 7; 'four inches long and 1 inch broad' (= c. 20 × 2.5mm); curved with straight sides and unfinished; one end apparently broken; lost.

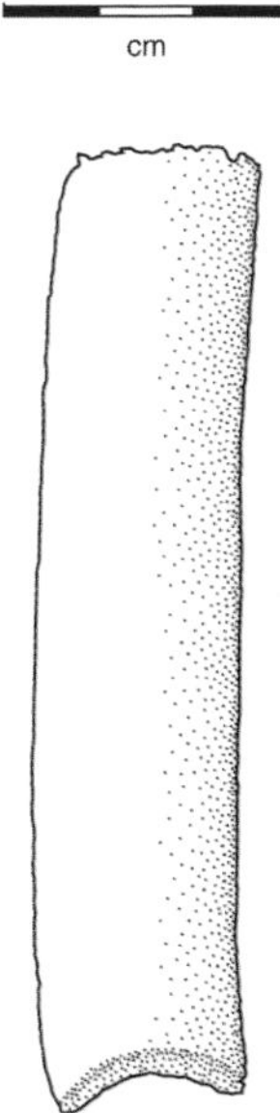

(from publication, after Anon 1787, fig.

ID 147: Sandy (not studied)
No context details, Sandy, Bedfordshire.
Evans 1897, 427; lost.

ID 148: Carneddau
In hearth near cist 5 in Early Bronze Age barrow, Carneddau Hengwm, Carno, Montgomery (Powys).
Powysland Museum, Welshpool; Gibson 1993, fig. 17, 4; 85 × 31 × 10mm; miscellaneous red/black group, red; 98% present at deposition; broken.

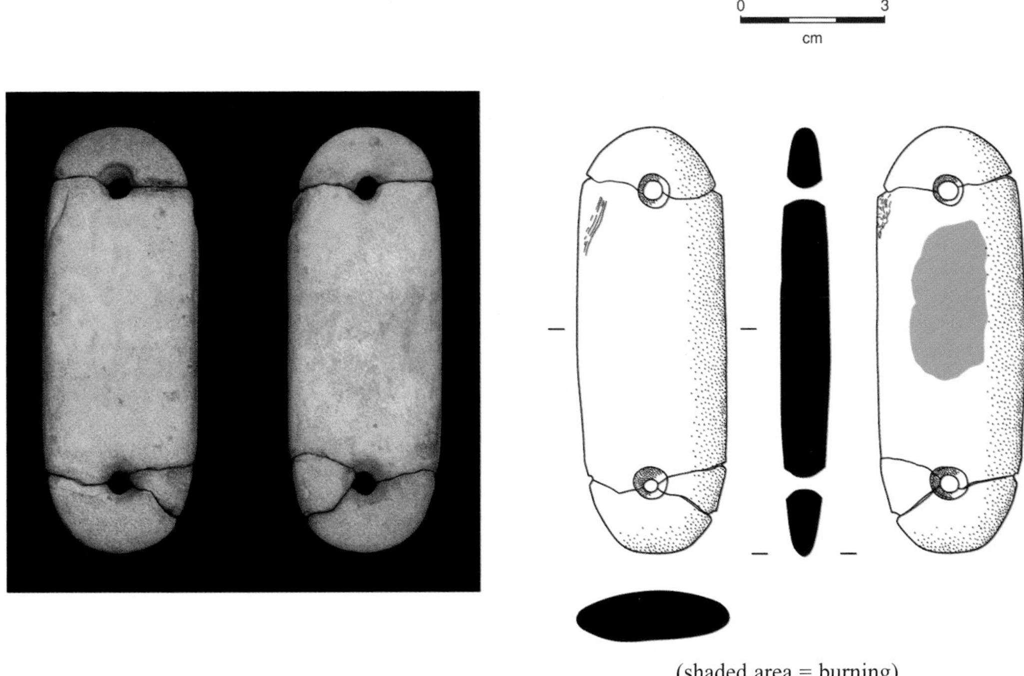

(shaded area = burning)

ID 149: Thanet (from photograph)
Beaker inhumation burial, St Peter's Refuse Tip, Broadstairs, Kent.
Trust for Thanet Archaeology, unpublished but see http://www.thanetarch.co.uk/Virtual%20Museum/3displays/GBeaker%20Displays/GBeakerDisplay1 ; 92 × 30mm; miscellaneous type, grey; two perforations; not fully studied.

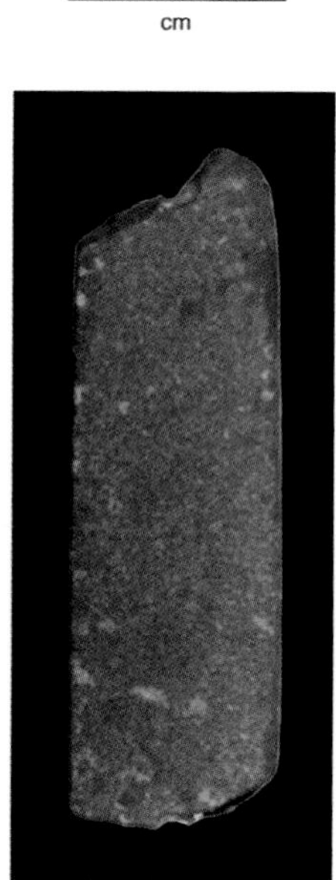

(photo copyright Trust for Thanet Archaeology)

ID 150: Lockerbie (from photographs)
Early Bronze Age cremation burial, Lockerbie, Dumfries (Dumfries and Galloway).
NMS Edinburgh; Sheridan and Jackson 2011; 73 × 18 × 6mm; miscellaneous rock type, brown; 97% present at deposition; no record of striations or polishing; two perforations; orange staining possibly from proximity to cremated remains; 'no obvious signs of wear'.

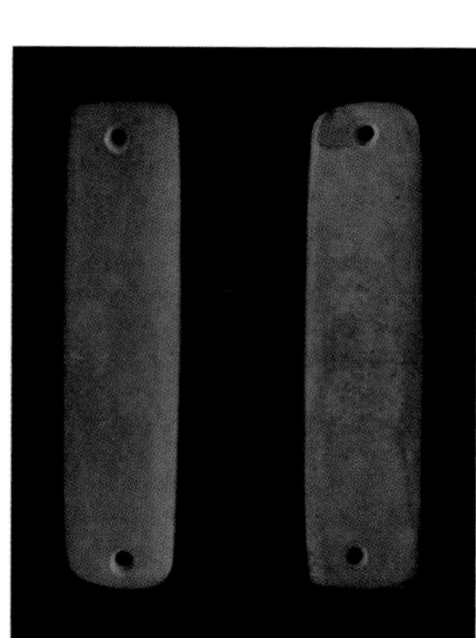

ID 151: Swindon (not studied)
Beaker inhumation grave recorded in Wiltshire Sites and Monuments Record; Old Town, Swindon, Wiltshire.
Swindon Museum, no record, assumed lost.

ID 152: Hartington (not studied)
Stray find, Aleck Low, Hartington, Derbyshire.
Private ownership; Vine 1982, no. 168; Hart 1985, fig. 3.4; 78 × 32 × 2.5mm (from published drawing); rock type unknown, colour not known; six perforations.

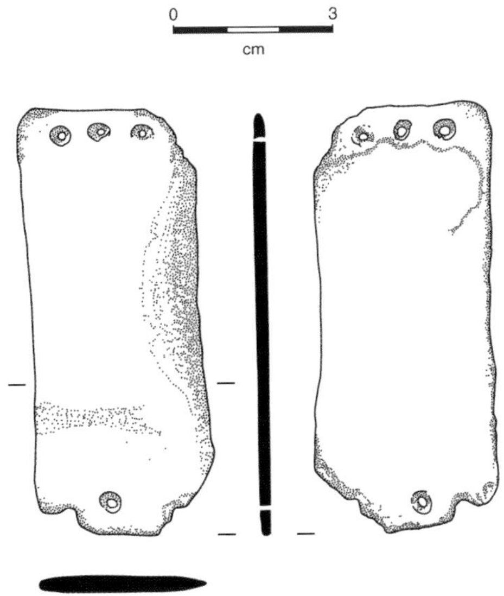

(from publication, after Hart 1985)

ID 153: Cliffe
Beaker inhumation grave, Cliffe, Kent.
British Museum; Kinnes and Cook 1998, fig. 34; 56 × 18 × 6mm; shale; miscellaneous (red/black) rock type; evidence of striations; two perforations; broken-through V-perforation on rear; part of larger plaque(?).

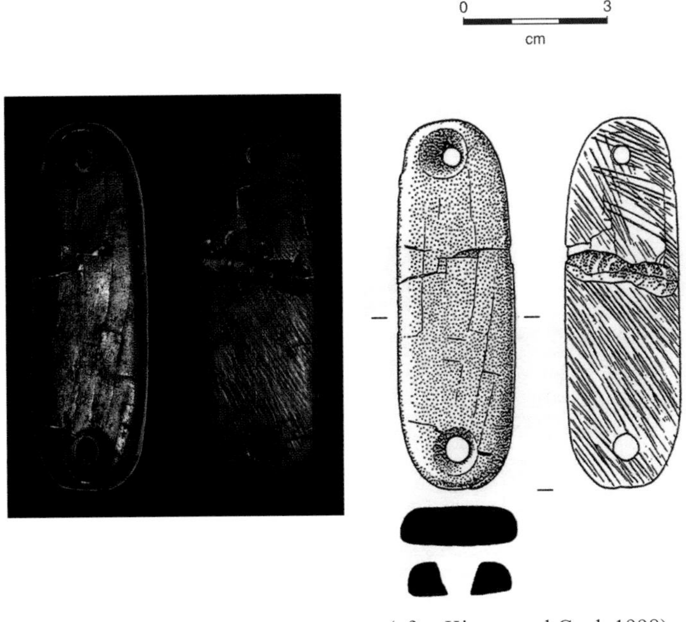

(after Kinnes and Cook 1998)

ID 154: Monkton

Beaker inhumation grave, Monkton Road Farm, Monkton, Thanet, Kent.

Canterbury Archaeological Trust; Rady 2009, 22–23 fig. and http://www.canterburytrust.co.uk/thanetearth.html ; 92.8 × 41.9 × 4.7mm; amphibolite type, grey-green (5GY 6/1); 95% of original form present at deposition; re-worked; no evidence of striations or polishing; six perforations originally; slightly worn.

Addendum

A further seven bracers were brought to our notice during 2010 and 2011 by Peter Harp, Dr Stuart Needham, Dr Alison Sheridan and Anna Tyacke. With the kind assistance of Anna Tyacke it proved possible for ID 156 and ID 157 to be studied by Fiona Roe. These bracers are not included in any analyses or maps within the volume, nor in the digital catalogue.

ID 155: Butterbumps

2m from a secondary cremation in round barrow, associated with a Camerton-Snowshill dagger, Butterbumps, Willoughby-with-Slootby, Lincolnshire.

May 1976, 81–2, not illustrated, described as a perforated whetstone; recorded and sketched at the Ancient Monuments Laboratory *c.*1980 by Stuart Needham; rock type unknown, pale grey; 95% surviving at deposition; reworked: one end broken and apparently re-smoothed; two perforations (originally four), one of which may never have been completed, possibly due to catastrophic breakage at this corner; any use wear not recorded.

ID 156: Paul

Stray find, Paul, near Mousehole, Cornwall, SW 453264.

Truro Museum; Mossop 2010, 33 with line illustration; 57 × 30 × 3mm; miscellaneous type, light buff; *c.*60% survives; two hourglass perforations, one broken (four originally); breaks at surviving end and near original centre of the bracer are all fresh/recent (possibly plough damage); any use wear not recorded.

Description of stone (FR): pale-coloured, fine-grained and laminated; appears to be the local Devonian sediment known as killas.

ID 157: Walsingham

Context unknown, Walsingham, Norfolk, TF 934368.

Private collection, Simon Camm, Penzance; unpublished; 80 × 27 × 8mm; possibly amphibolite, dark green; 98% surviving at deposition; multi-directional striations on both main surfaces; six hourglass perforations; very similar morphologically to ID 10 Sonning; any use wear not recorded.

Description of stone (FR): dark green, fine-grained stone with small darker veins running lengthways; there are no laminations and no spots, it is suggested that this could be an amphibolite bracer, unusually dark in colour, but comparable to the one from Sittingbourne (ID 115); no fresh surfaces exposed.

ID 158: Liffs Low

Uncertain context, possibly with a Beaker, in barrow, Liffs Low, Biggin, Derbyshire.

Buxton Museum; Barnatt 1996, fig. 2.12, 5002; 67 × 20 × 6.5mm; 'fine-grained, pale green-brown volcanic ash' (Barnatt 1996, 117); more than 50% surviving; one hourglass perforation (probably two originally); probably re-used as pendant.

ID 159: Armadale

Early Bronze Age cist (Cist 4) containing decayed remains of unburnt individual with bipartite Vase Food Vessel, Pier Road, Armadale, Skye (Highland).

Currently c/o the excavator pending allocation through Treasure Trove system; Sheridan forthcoming; 32 × 23 × 6mm; miscellaneous type (talcose schist, identified by Simon Howard, geologist, National Museums Scotland), cream with green and light brown tinges; evidence of striations; one hourglass perforation (probably two originally); wear at fractured surface and at perforation, broken and re-used as pendant.

ID 160: Flixton

Beaker inhumation grave with 'short-necked' Beaker and two amber boat-shaped objects, Flixton Quarry (Cemex), Flixton, Suffolk. Adult buried on left side, head at south-east.

Information from Suffolk County Council Archaeological Service and Alison Sheridan; 112 × 22.5 × 8mm; Group VI rock (identified by Simon Howard, geologist, National Museums Scotland); evidence of mainly longitudinal striations, plus rilling in the perforations; 99% surviving; two hourglass perforations, slightly waisted, minimally concavo-convex with lipped ends; two small circular hollows at one end; at the other end two diagonally drilled perforations which, at their upper end, are linked by narrow incised grooves to one of the main perforations; few signs of ancient damage; no obvious signs of wear.

ID 161: no provenance

Information from Peter Harp (Surrey) and Ben Roberts, British Museum; 92mm long, 6mm thick; 'slightly green slate' (Peter Harp); two hourglass perforations; possibly broken and reworked, modern chip on one corner.

IRISH BRACERS

ID 16: Ireland A

Stray find, no specific location.

British Museum 1854 12–27 19; Harbison 1976, no. 7, pl. 3, 7; 96.36 × 24.4 × 9.5mm; jasper, dusky red (5R 3/4); 100% present at deposition; evidence of striations and polishing; two perforations; slightly worn.

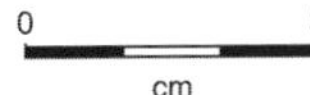

ID 17: Ireland B

Stray find, no specific location.

British Museum 1920 11–9 16; Harbison 1976, no. 61, pl. 13, 61; 94.0 × 17.6 × 6.1mm; jasper, dusky red (5R 3/4); 99% present at deposition; evidence of striations and polishing; two perforations; slightly worn.

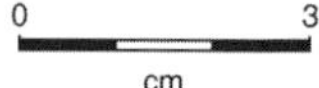

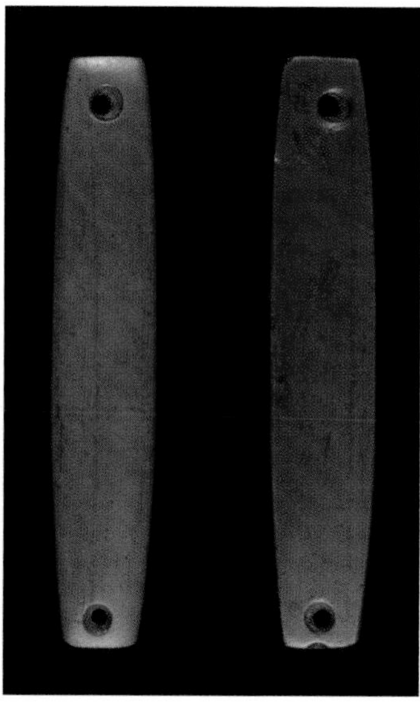

ID 95: Ireland

Stray find, no specific location.

NMS Edinburgh AU1; Harbison 1976, no. 69, pl. 14; 80.8 × 20.6 × 6.9mm; ?Volcaniclastic tuff, yellowish grey (5Y 7/1) to greenish grey (5GY 6/1); 99% present at deposition; evidence of striations and polishing; two perforations; worn.

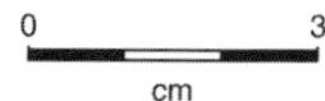

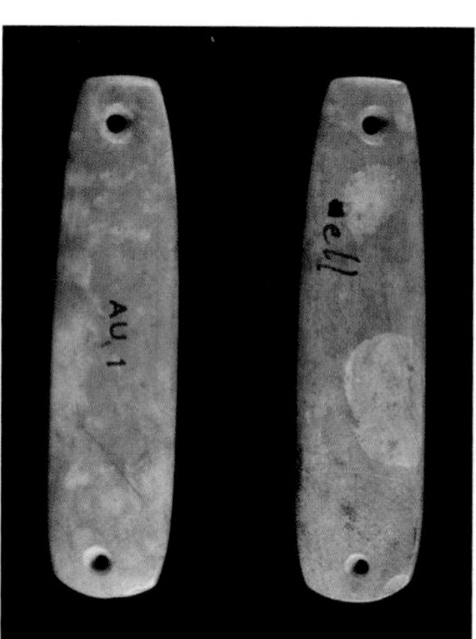

ID 96: Northern Ireland

Stray find, no specific location.

NMS Edinburgh AU2; Harbison 1976, 26, no. 33, pl. 7; 83.0 × 19.5 × 5.6mm; ?Volcaniclastic tuff, greyish olive green (5GY 3/2); 95% present at deposition; evidence of striations and polishing; two perforations; slightly worn.

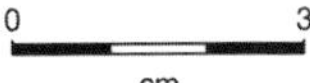

ID 97: Ireland (Co Antrim)

Stray find, County Antrim, Ireland.

NMS Edinburgh AU3; Anon 1879, 73, no. 3; Harbison 1976, no. 35, pl. 8; 86.5 × 19.0 × 6.2mm; ?Meta-volcaniclastic, greenish black (5GY 3/1); 98% present at deposition; evidence of striations and polishing; two perforations; worn.

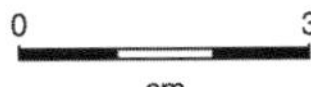

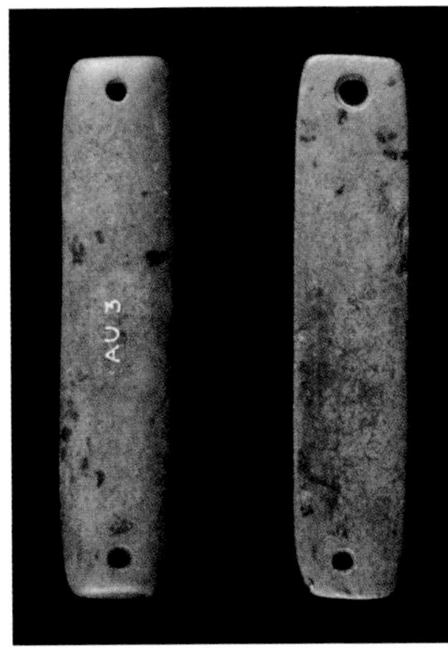

ID 98: Ireland (Co Antrim, red)

Stray find, County Antrim, Ireland.

Hunterian Museum and Art Gallery, Glasgow B 1914.259; Harbison 1976, no. 43, pl. 9; 57.0 × 16.2 × 5.7mm; jasper, greyish red (5R 4/2); 100% present at deposition; evidence of striations and polishing; two perforations; slightly worn.

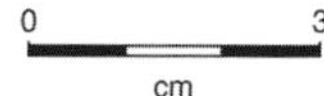

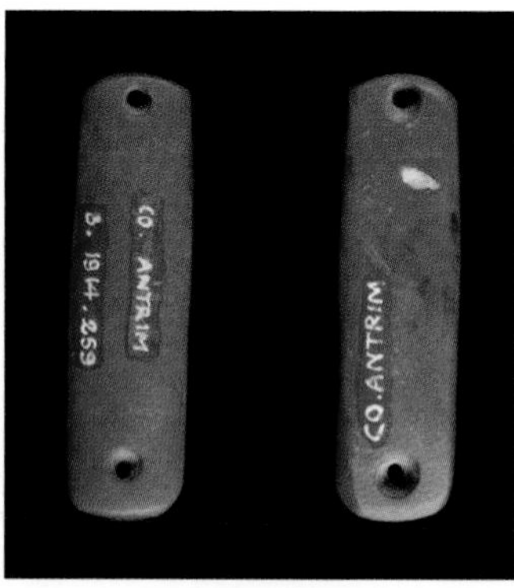

ID 99: Ireland (Co Antrim, black)

Stray find, County Antrim, Ireland.

Hunterian Museum and Art Gallery, Glasgow B 1951.2639; Harbison 1976, no. 25, pl. 6; 66.0 × 29.6 × 8.4mm; porcellanite, greyish black (N2); 99% present at deposition; evidence of polishing; two perforations; worn.

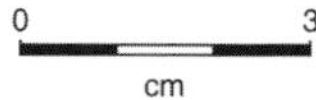

ID 100: Ireland (Co Westmeath)

Stray find, County Westmeath, Ireland.

Hunterian Museum and Art Gallery, Glasgow B 1951.2676; Harbison 1976, no. 36, pl. 8; 101.2 × 26.0 × 8.0mm; fine grained sandstone, light brown (5YR 6/4) to pale yellowish brown (10YR 6/2); 99% present at deposition; evidence of striations and polishing; two perforations; worn.

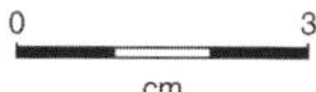

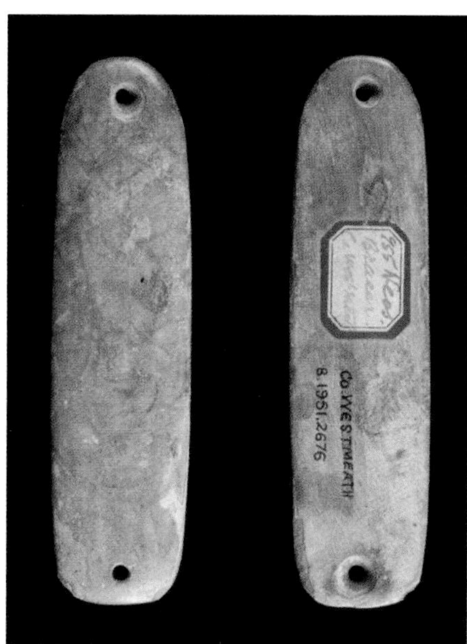

BIBLIOGRAPHY

Allies, J. 1849. 'Antiquities and works of art exhibited', *Arch. J.* VI, 409.

Anderson, J. and Black, G. F. 1888. 'Reports on local museums in Scotland, obtained through Dr. R. H. Gunning's Jubilee gift to the Society', *Proc. Soc. Antiq. Scot.* 22, 331–422.

Annable, F. K. and Simpson, D. D. A. 1964. *Guide Catalogue of the Neolithic and Bronze Age Collections in Devizes Museum*. Devizes: Wiltshire Archaeological and Natural History Society.

Anon 1787. 'Exhibits at ballots. Feb 9, 1764', *Archaeologia* 8, 429 and Pl. XXX, fig. 6.

Anon 1849. 'Archaeological Intelligence', *Arch. J.* VI, 319.

Anon 1868. 'Donations to the Museum', *Proc. Soc. Antiq. Scot.* 6 (1864–6), 233.

Anon 1873. 'Donations to the Museum', *Proc. Soc .Antiq. Scot.* 9 (1870–1872), 537–40.

Anon 1879. 'Donations to the Society', *Proc. Soc. Antiq. Scot.* 13, (1878–9), 73.

Anon 1893. 'Purchases for the Museum', *Proc. Soc. Antiq. Scot.* 27, (1892–3), 7–14.

Ashmore, P. J. 1989. 'Excavation of a Beaker cist at Dornoch Nursery, Sutherland', *Proc. Soc. Antiq. Scot.* 119, 63–71.

Bailloud, G. 1964. *Le Néolithique dans le Bassin Parisien. IIe supplément à Gallia Préhistoire,* C.R.N.S., Paris.

Baker, L., Sheridan, A. and Cowie, T. 2003. 'An Early Bronze Age 'dagger grave' from Rameldry Farm, near Kingskettle, Fife', *Proc. Soc. Antiq. Scot.* 133, 85–123.

Bamford, H. M. 1982. *Beaker Domestic Sites in the Fen Edge and East Anglia.* Gressenhall: East Anglian Archaeology No.16.

Bantelmann, N. 1982. *Endneolithische Funde im rheinisch-westfälischen Raum*, Offa-Bücher Band 44. Neumünster: Wacholtz.

Barclay, A. and Halpin, C. 1999. *Excavations at Barrow Hills, Radley, Oxfordshire.* Oxford: Oxford Archaeological Unit. Thames Valley Landscapes Vol 11.

Barclay, A., Gray, M. and Lambrick, G. 1995. *Excavations at the Devil's Quoits, Stanton Harcourt, Oxfordshire 1972–3 and 1988.* Oxford: Oxford Archaeological Unit. Thames Valley Landscapes: the Windrush Valley, Vol 3.

Baring-Gould, S. 1901. 'Seventh report of the Devon Exploration Committee', *Report and Trans.of the Devon Association* 33, 129–138.

Barnatt, J. 1996. 'A multiphased barrow at Liffs Low', in Barnatt, J. and Collis, J., *Barrows in the Peak District.* Sheffield: J. R. Collis Publications, 95–136.

Bartlett, J. 1963. *Beaker burials from Brantingham, Melton and South Cave.* Hull Museum Publications 214. Hull: Hull Museum.

Bateman, T. 1861. *Ten Years'Diggings in Celtic and Saxon Grave Hills, in the Counties of Derby, Stafford and York.* London: J. R. Smith.

Bell, M. 1990. *Brean Down Excavations 1983–1987.* London: English Heritage Arch Report no. 15.

Benz, M. and van Willigen, S. (eds.) 1998. *Some New Approaches to the Bell Beaker 'Phenomenon'. Lost Paradise…?* Oxford: British Archaeological Reports International Series 690.

Billard, C., Querre, G. and Salanova, L. 1998. 'Le phénomène campaniforme dans la Basse vallée de la Seine: chronologie et relation habitats-sépultures', *Bulletin de la Société Préhistorique Française* 95, 351–63.

Blanchet, J-C. 1984. *Les premiers métallurgists en Picardie et dans le nord de la France, Chalcolithique, âge du Bronze et début du premier âge du fer,* Mémoires de la Société Préhistorique Française 27, Paris.

Bradley, R. and Edmonds, M. 1993. *Interpreting the Axe Trade.* Cambridge: Cambridge University Press.

Brandherm, D. 2009. 'The Social Context of Early Bronze Age Metalworking in Iberia: Evidence from the burial record', in Kienlin, T. B. and Roberts, B. V. W. (eds.), *Metals and Societies: Studies in Honour of Barbara S Ottaway*, 172–80. Universitätsforschungen zur Prähistorischen Archäologie aus dem Institut für Archäologische Wissenschaften der Universität Bochum Fach Ur- und Frűhgeschichte. Bonn: Habelt.

Briard, J. 1993. 'Relations between Brittany and Great Britain during the Bronze Age' in Scarre, C. and Healy, F. (eds.), *Trade and Exchange in Prehistoric Europe*, 183–90, Oxford: Oxbow Monograph 33.

Briard, J. and Mohen, J-P. 1974. 'Le Tumulus de la fôret de Carnoët à Quimperlé (Finistère)', *Antiquités Nationales* 6, 46–60.

Brindley, A. L. 2007. *The Dating of Food Vessels and Urns in Ireland.* Galway: National University of Ireland.

Brown, F., Howard-Davis, C., Brennand, M., Boyle, A., Evans, T., O'Connor, S., Spence, A., Heawood, R. and Lupton, A. 2007. *The Archaeology of the A1(M) Darrington to Dishforth DBFO Road Scheme.* Oxford: Lancaster Imprints.

Bursch, F. C. 1933. 'Die Becherkultur in den Niederlanden', *Oudheidkundige Mededeelingen* 14, 39–123.
Butler, C. 1991. 'The excavation of a Beaker bowl barrow at Pyecombe, West Sussex', *Sussex Archaeological Collections* 129, 1–28.
Butler, J. J. and Van der Waals, J. D. 1966. 'Bell Beakers and early metal-working in the Netherlands', *Palaeohistoria* 12, 41–139.
Canby, J.V. 2002. 'Falconry (hawking) in Hittite lands', *Journal of Near Eastern Studies* 61, no.3, 161–201.
Cardoso, J. L. and Monge Soares, A. M. 1992. 'Cronologia absoluta para o campaniforme', *O Arqueólogo Português* IV (1990–92), 8–10, 203–28.
Carrington, A. 1996. 'The horseman and the falcon: mounted falconers in Pictish sculpture', *Proc. Soc. Antiq. Scot.* 126, 459–468.
Case, H. J. 1963. 'Notes on finds and on ring-ditches and other sites at Stanton Harcourt', *Oxoniensia* 28, 1–19.
Case, H. J. 1965. 'A tin-bronze in Bell-Beaker association', *Antiquity* 39, 219–22.
Case, H. J. 1977. 'The Beaker Culture in Britain and Ireland', in Mercer, R. (ed.), *Beakers in Britain and Europe.* Oxford: British Archaeological Reports Supplementary Series 26: 71–101.
Case, H. J. 1993. 'Beakers: deconstruction and after', *Proc. Prehist. Soc.* 59, 241–268.
Case, H. J. 2004a. 'Bell Beaker and Corded Ware Culture burial associations: A bottoms-up rather than top-down approach', in Gibson, A. and Sheridan, A. (eds.), *From Sickles to Circles: Britain and Ireland at the Time of Stonehenge*, 201–14. Stroud: Tempus.
Case, H. J. 2004b. 'Beakers and the Beaker Culture', in J. Czebreszuk (ed.), *Similar but Different: Bell Beakers in Europe*, Poznán, Adam Mickiewiez University, 11–33.
Case, H. and Sturdy, D. 1959. 'Archaeological Notes', *Oxoniensia* 24, 98–102.
Chapman, J. 2000. *Fragmentation in Archaeology: People, Places and Broken Objects in the Prehistory of South Eastern Europe.* London: Routledge.
Cherryson, A. K. 2002. 'The identification of archaeological evidence for hawking in medieval England', *Acta zoological cracoviensia* 45 (special issue), 307–314.
Chitty, L. 1967. *Trans. Caradoc and Severn Valley Field Club* 16, (1961–7), 80–81.
Claris, P. and Quartermaine, J. 1989. 'The Neolithic quarries and axe-factory sites of Great Langdale and Scafell Pike: a new field survey', *Proc. Prehist. Soc.*, 1–25.
Clark, J. G. D. 1952. *Prehistoric Europe: The Economic Basis.* London: Methuen.
Clark, J. G. D. 1963. 'Neolithic bows from Somerset, England, and the prehistory of archery in north-west Europe', *Proc. Prehist. Soc.*, 29, 50–98.
Clarke, D. L. 1970. *Beaker Pottery of Great Britain and Ireland.* Cambridge: Cambridge University Press.
Clarke, D. V., Cowie, T. G. and Foxon, A. 1985. *Symbols of Power at the Time of Stonehenge.* Edinburgh: National Museum of Antiquities of Scotland.
Clough, T. H. McK. and Cummins, W. A. (eds.). 1988. *Stone Axe Studies Volume 2.* London: C.B.A Research Report 67.
Clough, T. H. McK. and Green, B. 1972. 'The petrological identification of stone implements from East Anglia', *Proc. Prehist. Soc.* 38, 108–155.
Coles, F. R. 1902. 'Report on stone circles in Aberdeenshire', *Proc. Soc. Antiq. Scot.* 36 (1901–2), 488–581.
Coles, J. M. and Minnitt, S. 1995. *Industrious and Fairly Civilized. The Glastonbury Lake Village.* Taunton: Somerset Levels Project and Somerset County Council Museums Service.
Colt Hoare, R. 1812. *Ancient Wiltshire, Vol. 1.* London.
Cooney, G. and Mandal, S. 1998. *The Irish Stone Axehead Project: Monograph 1.* Dublin: Wordwell.
Coope, G. R. 1979. 'The influence of geology on the manufacture of Neolithic and Bronze Age stone implements in the British Isles', in Clough, T. H. McK. and Cummins, W. A. (eds.), *Stone Axe Studies.* London: C.B.A Research Report 23, 98–101.
Cressey, M. and Sheridan, A. 2003. 'The excavation of a Bronze Age cemetery at Seafield West, near Inverness, Highland', *Proc. Soc. Antiq. Scot.* 133, 47–84.
Cunliffe, B. 2001. *Facing the Ocean: The Atlantic and its Peoples 8000 BC–AD 1500.* Oxford: University Press.
Cunnington, W. 1857. 'A barrow on Roundway Hill nr Devizes opened in April 1885', *Wilts. Arch. Mag.* III, 185–8.
Curtis, N., Wilkin, N., Hutchison, M., Jay, M., Shepherd, L., Sheridan, A. and Wright, M. 2007. 'Radiocarbon results from the Beakers and Bodies Project', *Discovery and Excavation in Scotland.* N.S. Vol 8, 223–4.
Czebreszuk, J. 1998. 'The north-eastern borderland of the Bell Beakers. The case of the Polish lowland', in Benz, M. and van Willigen, S. (eds.), 161–174.
Czebreszuk, J. and Szmyt, M. (eds.) 2003. *The Northeast Frontier of Bell Beakers.* Oxford: British Archaeological Reports International Series 1155.
Dalrymple, C. E. 1859. 'Notes of the excavation of a tumulus at Auchleven, in the parish of Premnay and the district of Garioch, Aberdeenshire', *Proc. Soc. Antiq. Scot.* 2, 431–2.
Darvill, T. 1989. 'The circulation of Neolithic stone and flint axes: a case study from Wales and the mid-west of England', *Proc. Prehist. Soc.* 55, 27–43.
Darvill, T., Davies, R. V., Morgan Evans, D., Ixer, R. A. and Wainwright, G. 2007. 'Strumble-Preseli Ancient Communities and Environment Study (SPACES): Fifth Report 2006', *Archaeology in Wales* 46, 100–107.
Dobney, K. 2002. 'Flying a kite at the end of the Ice Age: the possible significance of raptor remains from Proto- and Early-Neolithic sites of the Middle East', *Archaeozoology of the Near East V,* 74–84.
Dobney, K. and Jacques, D. 2002. 'Avian signatures for identity and status in Anglo-Saxon England', *Acta zoological cracoviensia* 45 (special issue), 7–21.
Dudley, H. 1949. *Early Days in North-West Lincolnshire: a regional archaeology.* W. H. and C. H. Caldicott.
Endrodi, A. 1998. 'Results of settlement archaeology in Bell Beaker culture research in Hungary', in Benz, M. and van Willigen, S. (eds.), 141–160.
Evans, J. 1897. *The Ancient Stone Implements, Weapons and Ornaments of Great Britain.* London: Longman.
Evans, J. G. 1984. 'Stonehenge – the environment in the late Neolithic and Early Bronze Age and a Beaker-age burial', *Wilts. Arch. Mag.* 78, 7–30.
Everatt, D. 1971. 'A flint sickle and an archer's bracer fromThoresway', *Lincs. Hist and Arch.* 6, 15.
Felix, R. and Hantute, G. 1969. 'La sepulture campaniforme d'Aremberg (commune De Wallers – Nord)', *Bulletin de la Société Préhistorique Française* 66, 276–82.
Ferreira, O. da Veiga, Zbyszewski, G., Leitao, M., North, C. T. and Reynolds de Sousa, H. 1975. 'The Megalithic Tomb of Pedra Branca, Portugal. Preliminary Report', *Proc. Prehist. Soc.* 41, 167–78.
Field, D. 2008. *Use of Land in Central Southern England*

during the Neolithic and Early Bronze Age. Oxford: British Archaeological Reports British Series 458.
Figgis, N. P. 1999. *Catalogue of accessions in the County and Local Museums of Wales and Other Collections*. Machynlleth: Atelier Productions.
Fitzpatrick, A. P. 2003. 'The Amesbury Archer', *Current Archaeology* 184, 146–152.
Fitzpatrick, A. P. 2004. 'The Boscombe Bowmen: Builders of Stonehenge?' *Current Archaeology* 193, 10–16.
Fitzpatrick, A. P. 2011. *The Amesbury Archer and the Boscombe Bowmen*. Salisbury: Wessex Archaeology Report 27.
Fleming, A. 1995. 'St Kilda: stone tools, dolerite quarries and long term survival', *Antiquity* 69, 25–35.
Fokkens, H., Achterkamp, Y. and Kuijpers, M. 2008. 'Bracers or Bracelets? About the functionality and meaning of Bell Beaker wristguards' *Proc. Prehist. Soc.* 74, 109–140.
Ford, E. 1992. *Falconry. Art and Practice.* Blandford Press.
Franks, A.W. 1873. 'Exhibits at ballots', *Proc. Soc. Ant. Lond.* 2 set V, 271–5.
Freising, H. 1938. 'Die Hinterlassenschaften der GBK aus dem Gerichtsbezirk Nikolsburg (Mähren)', *Wiener Prähistorische Zeitschrift* 25, 47–58.
Freudenberg, M. 2009. 'Steingeräte zur Metallbearbeitung – Eine Neue Aspekte zum Spätneolitischen und Frühbronzezeitlichen Metallhandwerke vor dem Hintergrund des Schleswig-Holsteinischen Fundmaterials', *Archäologisches Korrespondenzblatt* 39 (3), 341–59.
Gardiner, J., Allen, M. J., Powell, A., Harding, P., Lawson, A. J., Loader, E., McKinley, J. I., Sheridan, A. and Stevens, C. 2007. 'A matter of life and death: Late Neolithic, Beaker and Early Bronze Age settlement and cemeteries at Thomas Hardye School, Dorchester', *Proc. Dorset NHAS* 128, 17–52.
Garrido-Pena, R. 1997. 'Bell Beakers in the southern Meseta of the Iberian Peninsular: Socioeconomic contexts and new data', *Oxford J. Arch.* 16 (2). 187–209.
Gebers, W. 1978. *Endneolithikum und Frühbronzezeit im Mittelrheingebiet: Katalog*, Saarbrücker Beiträge zur Altertumskunde Band 28, Bonn: Rudolf Habelt.
Gebers, W. 1984. *Das Endneolithikum im Mittelrheingebiet: Typologische und Chronologische Studien*, Saarbrücker Beiträge zur Altertumskunde Band 27, Bonn: Rudolf Habelt.
Gerloff, S. 1975. *The Early Bronze Age Daggers in Great Britain, and a reconsideration of the Wessex Culture*, Munich: Praehistorische Bronzefunde VI, 2.
Gibson, A. 1993. 'The excavation of two cairns and associated features at Carneddau, Carno, Powys, 1989–90', *Arch. J.* 150, 1–45.
Grant, A. 1988. 'Animal resources', in Astill, G. G. and Grant, A. (eds.) *The countryside of Medieval England.* Oxford: Blackwell, 149–187.
Gray, H. St G. 1966. *The Meare Lake Village. Volume III.* Taunton: Taunton Castle.
Green, H. S. 1980. *The Flint Arrowheads of the British Isles.* Oxford: British Archaeological Reports British Series 75.
Guilaine, J., Claustre, F., Lemercier, O. and Sabatier, P. 2001. 'Campaniformes et environment culturel en France méditerranéenne' in Nicolis, F. (ed.), 229–75.
Harbison, P. 1976. *Bracers and V-perforated Buttons. The Beaker and Food Vessel Cultures of Ireland.* Archaeologia Atlantica Research Report 1. Moreland: Bad Bramstedt, W Germany.
Harcourt, R. A. 1971. 'Appendix II. The Animal Bones', in Wainwright, G. J. and Longworth, I. H., *Durrington Walls: Excavations 1966–1968.* London: Society of Antiquaries Research Report 29, 338–350.
Harding, J. and Healy, F. 2007. *The Raunds Area Project. A Neolithic and Bronze Age Landscape in Northamptonshire.* London: English Heritage.
Harker, J. 1877. 'British Interments at Lancaster', *J. Brit. Arch. Ass.* XXXIII, 125–7.
Harrison, R. J. 1980. *The Beaker Folk. Copper Age archaeology in Western Europe*, London: Thames and Hudson.
Harrison, R. J., Jackson, R. and Napthan, M. A. 1999. 'A rich Bell Beaker burial from Wellington Quarry, Marden, Herefordshire', *Oxford J. Arch.* 18(1), 1–16.
Hart, C. R. 1985. 'Aleck Low and Upper House Farm, Derbyshire: prehistoric artefact scatters', in Spratt, D. and Burgess, C. (eds.), *Upland Settlement in Britain. The Second Millennium B.C. and After.* Oxford: British Archaeological Reports British Series 143; 59–69.
Hartenberger, B., Rosen, S. and Matney, T. 2000. 'The Early Bronze Age blade workshop at Titris Hoyuk: lithic specialisation in an urban context', *Near Eastern Archaeology* 63:1, 51–58.
Hawkes, J. 1937. *The Archaeology of the Channel Islands II.* Jersey: Société Jersiaise.
Healy, F. and Harding, J. 2004. 'Reading a burial: the legacy of Overton Hill', in Gibson, A. and Sheridan, A. (eds.), *From Sickles to Circles*, 176–193. Stroud: Tempus.
Henshall, A. 1972. *The Chambered Tombs of Scotland.* Vol 2. Edinburgh.
Heyd, V. 1998. 'Die Glochenbecherkultur in Suddeutschland. Zum stand der forschung einfer regionalprovinz entlang der Donau', in Benz, M. and van Willigen, S. (eds.), 87–106.
Heyd, V. 2000. *Die Spätkupferzeit in Süddeutschland.* Saarbrücker Beiträge zur Altertumskunde Band 73. Bonn: Rudolph Habelt.
Heyd, V. 2007. 'Families, Prestige Goods, Warriors and Complex Societies: Beaker Groups and the 3rd Millenium cal BC along the Upper and Middle Danube', *Proc. Prehist. Soc.* 73, 327–79.
Holland, C. H. 1981. *A Geology of Ireland.* Edinburgh: Scottish Academic Press.
Husty, L. 2004. 'Glockenbecherzeitliche Funde aus Landau a.d. Isar', in Heyd, V., Husty, L. and Kreiner, L. (eds.), *Siedlungen der Glockenbecherkultur in Süddeutschland und Mitteleuropa,* 15–102. Arbeiten zur Archäologie Suddeutschlands. Büchenbach: Dr Faustus Verlag.
Ingram, A. H. W. 1867. 'On a piece of perforated slate found at Aldington, Worcestershire, and illustrative of the ancient use of slate tablets discovered in barrows in Wiltshire'. *Wilts. Arch. Mag.* 10, 109–113.
Jacobs, R. 1991. 'Arm(schutz)platten und Funde im Trierer Land', *Bulletin de la Société Préhistorique Luxembourg* 13, 97–130.
Jenkins, D. 1986. *The Law of Hywel Dda: Law Texts from Medieval Wales Translated and Edited.* Dyfed.
Jessup, R. F. 1933. 'Early Bronze Age Beakers', *Archaeologia Cantiana* 45, 174–178.
Jolly, W. 1879. 'Notice of the excavation and context of ancient graves at Dalmore, Alness, Ross-shire', *Proc. Soc. Antiq, Scot.* 13, (1878–9), 252–64.
Keiller, A., Piggott, S. and Wallis, F. S. 1941. 'First report of the Sub-Committee of the South-Western Group of Museums and Art Galleries on the petrological identification of stone axes', *Proc. Prehist. Soc.* 7, 50–72.
Kennett, D. H. 1969. 'The New Bradwell Late Bronze Age Hoard', *Northampton Museums and Art Gallery Journal*, 6, 2–7.
Kenworthy, J. B. 1979. 'A reconsideration of the "Ardiffery" finds, Cruden, Aberdeenshire', *Proc. Soc. Antiq. Scot.* 108, 80–93.

Kinnes, I. A. 1985. *British Bronze-Age Metalwork A7–16, Beaker and Early Bronze Age Grave Groups*. London: British Museum.

Kinnes, I. and Cook, J. 1998. 'The burials' in Kinnes, I., Cameron F., Trow, S. and Thomson, D. 1998. *Excavations at Cliffe, Kent.* BM Occasional Paper no. 69. London: British Museum, 59–62.

Kinnes, I. A. and Longworth, I. H. 1985. *Catalogue of the Excavated Prehistoric and Romano-British Material in the Greenwell Collection*. London: British Museum.

Kinnes, I, Gibson, A., Ambers, J., Bowman, S., Leese, M. and Boast, R. 1991. 'Radiocarbon dating and British Beakers: the British Museum programme', *Scottish Archeaeological Review* 8, 35–68.

Kitzinger, E. 1993. 'Interlace and icons: form and function in early insular art', in Spearman, R. M. and Higgit, J. (eds.), *The Age of Migrating Ideas: Early Medieval Art in Northern Britain and Ireland.* Edinburgh: National Museums of Scotland, 3–15.

Kopacz, J., Prichystal, A., Sebela, L. and Skrdla, P. 2003. 'Contribution to the chipped stone industry of the Moravian Bell Beaker culture', in Czebreszuk, J. and Szmyt, M. (eds.), 215–230.

Köster, C. 1966. 'Beiträge zum Neolithithikum und zur Frühen Bronzezeit am nördlichen Oberrein', *Prähistorische Zeitschrift* (1965/6) 43/44, 2–95.

Lambrick, G. and Allen, T. 2004. *Gravelly Guy, Stanton Harcourt, Oxfordshire. The Development of a Prehistoric and Romano-British Community*. Oxford: Oxford Archaeology. Thames Valley Landscapes Monograph 21.

Lanting, J. N. and Van der Waals, J. D. 1972. 'British Beakers as seen from the Continent', *Helinium* 12, 20–46.

Lanting, J. N. and Van der Waals, J. D. 1976. 'Beaker Culture Relations in the Lower Rhine Basin', in Lanting, J. N. and Van der Waals, J. D. (eds.), *Glockenbecher Symposium, Oberreid 1974, 1–80.* Fibula van Dishoeck: Bussum/Haarlem.

Lawson, A. 2000. *Potterne 1982–5 Animal Husbandry in Later Prehistoric Wiltshire.* Salisbury: Wessex Archaeology.

Leivers, M. and Moore, C. 2008. *Archaeology on the A303 Stonehenge Improvement.* Salisbury: Wessex Archaeology.

Le Roux, C-T. 1979. 'Stone Axes of Brittany and the Marches', in Clough, T. H. McK. and Cummins, W. A. (eds.), *Stone Axe Studies: Archaeological, Petrological, Experimental and Ethnographic*. London: C.B.A. Research Report 23, 49–56.

Lillios, K. 2002. 'Some new views of the engraved slate plaques of southwest Iberia', *Revista Portuguesa de Arqueologia* 5 No 2, 135–51.

Londesborough, Lord. 1851. 'An account of the opening of some tumuli in the East Riding of Yorkshire', *Archaeologia* 34, 251–8.

Longworth, I. H. 1984. *Collared Urns of the Bronze Age in Great Britain and Ireland.* Cambridge: Cambridge University Press.

Low, A. 1936. 'A short cist containing a Beaker and other relics at Newlands Oyne, Aberdeenshire', *Proc. Soc. Antiq. Scot.* 70, 326–331.

Makarowicz, P. 2003. 'Northern and southern Bell Beakers in Poland', in Czebreszuk, J. and Szmyt, M. (eds.), 137–154.

Manby, T. G. 2000. 'The Early Bronze Age grave assemblage from Broughton-in-Craven', *Prehistory Research Section Bulletin (York)*, 7–13.

Martín C., Fernández-Miranda, A., Fernández-Posse, M. D. and Gilman, A. 1993, 'The Bronze Age of La Mancha', *Antiquity* 67, 23–45.

May, J, 1976. *Prehistoric Lincolnshire.* Lincoln: Lincolnshire Local History Society.

Mortimer, J. R. 1905. *Forty Years' Researches in British and Saxon Burial Mounds of East Yorkshire.* London: Brown and Sons.

Mossop, M. 2010. 'The stone collector', *British Archaeology* 113, 30–33.

Müller, J. and Van Willigen, S. 2001. 'New radiocarbon evidence for European Bell Beakers and the consequences for the diffusion of the Bell Beaker Phenomenon', in Nicolis, F. (ed.), 59–80.

Needham, S. P. 2000. 'Power pulses across a cultural divide: cosmologically driven acquisition between Armorica and Wessex', *Proc. Prehist. Soc.* 66, 151–207.

Needham, S. P. 2002. 'Analytical implications for Beaker metallurgy in North-West Europe', in Bartelheim, M., Pernicka, E. and Krause, R. (eds.), *Die Anfänge der Metallurgie in der Alten Welt/The Beginnings of Metallurgy in the Old World,* Rahden: Marie Leidorf, 99–133.

Needham, S. 2004. 'Migdale-Marnoch: sunburst of Scottish metallurgy', in Shepherd, I. A. and Barclay, G. (eds.), *Scotland in Ancient Europe. The Neolithic and Early Bronze Age of Scotland in their European Context.* Edinburgh: Society of Antiquaries of Scotland, 217–245.

Needham, S. P. 2005. 'Transforming Beaker Culture in north-west Europe; processes of fusion and fission', *Proc. Prehist. Soc.* 71, 171–217.

Needham, S. 2007. 'The dagger blade and hilt furnishings from Site D (Ferry Fryston), burial 2245', in Brown, F. *et al.*, 279–289.

Neugebauer, C. and Neugebauer, J-W. 1998. 'Zum Forschungsstand der Glockenbecherkulture in Ostösterreich', in Fritsch, B., Mante, M., Matuschik, I., Müller, J. and Wolf, C. (eds), *Tradition und Innovation: Prähistorische Archäologie als Historische Wissenschaft*, 307–24. Rahden: Verlag Marie Leidorf.

Nicolis, F. (ed.). 2001. *Bell Beakers Today. Pottery, people, culture, symbols in prehistoric Europe. Proceedings of the International Colloquium, Riva del Garda (Trento, Italy), 11–16 May 1998.* Trento: Ufficio Beni Archeologici.

O'Connor, B. 2010. 'From Dorchester to Dieskau: some aspects of relations between Britain and central Europe during the Early Bronze Age', in Meller, H. and Bertemes, F. (eds.), *Der Griff nach den Sternen. Internationales Symposium in Halle (Saale) 16–21. Februar 2005.* Halle: Tagungen des Landesmuseums für Vorgeschichte Halle Vol. 2.

Parent, R. 1975. 'La grotte sépulcrale de vichel-nanteuil (aisne) et l'habitat de la civilisation "seine-oise-marne" dans le bassin moyen de l'ourcq', *Cahiers Archéologiques de Picardie* 1, 13–18.

Parker, A. J. 2007. 'The birds of Roman Britain', *Oxford J. Arch.* 7(2), 197–226.

Petch, D. F. 1958. 'Archaeological Notes for 1958', *Lincolnshire Architectural and Archaeol. Soc. Reports and Papers* VIII (1959–60), 19–22.

Petrequin, P., Croutsch, C. and Cassen, S. 1998. 'A propos du dépot de la Bégude: haches alpines et haches carnacéennes pendant le V millenaire', *Bulletin de la Société Française* 95, 239–54.

Piggott, S. 1958. 'Segmented bone beads and toggles in the British Early and Middle Bronze Age', *Proc. Prehist. Soc.* 24, 227–9.

Potts, P. J., Webb, P. C. and Williams-Thorpe, O. 1997a.

'Investigation of a correction procedure for surface irregularity effects based on scatter peak intensities in the field analysis of geological and archaeological rock samples by portable X-ray fluorescence spectrometry', *Journal of Analytical Atomic Spectrometry* 12, 769–776.

Potts, P. J., Williams-Thorpe, O. and Webb, P. C. 1997b. 'The bulk analysis of silicate rocks by portable X-ray fluorescence: The effects of sample mineralogy in relation to the size of the excited volume', Geostandards Newsletter, *The Journal of Geostandards and Geoanalysis* 21, 29–41.

Powell, T. G. E. 1963. 'The chambered cairn at Dyffryn Ardudwy', *Antiquity* 37, 19–24.

Powell, T. G. E. 1973. 'Excavation of the megalithic chambered cairn at Dyffryn Ardudwy, Merioneth, Wales', *Archaeologia* 104, 1–49.

Price, T. D., Knipper, C., Gruper, G. and Smrcka, V. 2004. 'Strontium isotopes and prehistoric migration: the Bell Beaker period in central Europe', *Journal of European Archaeology* 7 (1), 9–40.

Rady, J. 2009. 'Thanet Earth Site, Monkton, Barrow 1', *Canterbury Archaeology, 2007–2008*. Canterbury: Canterbury Archaeological Trust.

Rahtz, P. and Greenfield, E. 1977. *Excavations at Chew Valley Lake, Somerset*. London: HMSO.

RCAHMS 1978. (=Royal Commission on the Ancient and Historical Monuments of Scotland) *Lanarkshire: an inventory of the prehistoric and Roman monuments*. Edinburgh: HMSO.

Reaney, D. 1968. 'Beaker burials in south Derbyshire', *Derbys. Arch. J.* 88, 68–81.

Richards, J. 1990. *The Stonehenge Environs Project*. London: English Heritage Arch Report no. 16.

Robertson-Mackay, M. E. 1980. 'A "head and hoofs" burial beneath a round barrow with other Neolithic and Bronze Age sites, on Hemp Knoll, near Avebury, Wiltshire', *Proc. Prehist. Soc.* 46, 123–176.

Roe, F. 1966. 'The battle-axe series in Britain', *Proc. Prehist. Soc.* 32, 199–245.

Roe, F. and Woodward, A. 2007. 'The wristguard from burial 2245', in Brown *et al.* 298–304.

Roe, F. and Woodward, A. 2009. 'Bits and pieces: Early Bronze Age Stone bracers from Ireland', in Edmonds, M. and Davis, V. (eds.), *Stone Tools in Analytical and Cultural Perspective, Current Research*. Internet Archaeology 26: http://intarch.ac.uk/journal/issue26/index.html.

Russel, A. D. 1990. 'Two Beaker burials from Chilbolton, Hampshire', *Proc. Prehist. Soc.* 56, 153–172.

Salanova, L. 2000. *La question du Campaniforme en France et dans les îles anglo-normandes: productions, chronologie et rôles d'un standard céramique*, Paris: C. T. H. S./Société Préhistorique Française.

Salzman, L. F. (ed.) 1938. *Victoria County History, Cambridgeshire Vol 1*. Oxford: OUP.

Salzman, L. F. (ed.) 1939. *Victoria County History, Oxfordshire Vol 1*. Oxford: OUP.

Sangmeister, E. 1964. 'Die Schmalen "Armschutzplatten" ', in von Usler von R. and Narr, K. J. (eds), *Studien aus Alteuropa 1, Festschrift für Kurt Tackenburg, Beihefte der Bonner Jahrbücher Band 10,* 93–122, Köln: Böhlau.

Sangmeister, E. 1974. 'Zwei Neufunde der Glockenbecherkultur in Baden-Württemberg. Ein Beitrag zur Klassifierung der Armschutzplatten in Mitteleuropa', *Fundberichte aus Baden-Württemberg* 1, 103–156.

Savory, H. N. 1973. 'The prehistoric finds', in Charlton, P., Roberts, J. and Vale, V. *Llantrithyd: a Ringwork in South Glamorgan*, 57–60 and fig 3. Cardiff: Cardiff Archaeological Society.

Savory, H. N. 1980. *Guide Catalogue of the Bronze Age Collections, National Museum of Wales*. Cardiff: Cardiff Archaeology Society.

Schmotz, K. 1992. 'Eine Gräbergruppe der Glockenbecherkultur von Künzing, Lkr. Deggendorf', *Vorträge des Niederbayerischen Archäologentages* 10, 41–68.

Schüle, W. and Pellicer, M. 1966. 'El Cerro de la Virgen en Orce (Granada) I', *Excavaciones Arqueologicas en España* 46, 3–66.

Scothern, P. M. T. 1989. 'A comparison of the medieval White Castle flute with the Chalcolithic example from Veyreau', *Proc. Prehist. Soc.* 55, 257–260.

Serjeantson, D. 2009. *Birds*. Cambridge: Cambridge University Press.

Shaffrey, R. and Roe, F. 2010. 'Chapter 5: Worked Stone', in Smith, A. Powell, K. and Booth, P. *Evolution of a Farming Community in the Upper Thames Valley. Excavation of a Prehistoric, Roman and Post-Roman Landscape at Cotswold Community, Gloucestershire and Wiltshire. Volume 2: The Finds and Environmental Reports,* 75–84. Oxford: Oxford Archaeology.

Shepherd, I. A. G. 1981. 'Bronze Age jet working in north Britain', *Scottish Archaeological Forum* 11, 43–51.

Shepherd, I. A. G. 1984. 'Borrowstone (Newhills) short cists', *Discovery and Excavation Scotland* 1984, 13–14.

Shepherd, I. A. G. 1985. 'Jet and amber'. In Clarke, D. V. *et al.*, (eds.), 204–216.

Shepherd, I. A. G. 1986. *Powerful Pots*. Aberdeen: University of Aberdeen.

Shepherd, I. A. G. 2005. 'Radiocarbon dates sponsored by Aberdeenshire Archaeology in 2004', *Discovery and Excavation in Scotland 2005*, 184.

Sheppard, T. 1930. 'Bronze Age bracer from east Yorks' in Sheppard, T. (ed.), *Bronze Age Remains*. Hull: Hull Museum Publications 169, 71–72.

Sheridan, A. 2007. 'Scottish Beaker dates: the good, the bad and the ugly' in Larsson, M. and Parker Pearson, M. (eds.), *From Stonehenge to the Baltic: Living with cultural diversity in the third millennium BC*. Oxford: British Archaeological Reports International Series 1692, 91–123.

Sheridan, A. 2008. 'Upper Largie and Dutch-Scottish connections during the Beaker period', in Fokkens, H., Coles, B. J., van Gijn, A. L., Kleijne, J. P., Ponjee, H. H. and Slappendel, C. G. (eds.), *Between foraging and farming: an extended broad spectrum of papers presented to Leendert Louwe Kooijmans*, Analecta Praehistorica Leidensia. Leiden: University of Leiden, 247–60.

Sheridan, J. A. forthcoming. 'The wristguard fragment from cist 4, Armadale', in Peteranna, M., *Pier Road, Armadale: Excavation of a Bronze Age Cemetery*.

Sheridan, A. and Jackson, A. 2011. 'The stone wristguard from F34, in Kirby, M., *Lockerbie Academy: Neolithic and Early Historic timber halls, A Bronze Age cemetery, an undated enclosure and a post-medieval drying kiln in south-west Scotland*. Scottish Archaeological Internet Report 46, 33–34. www.sair.org.uk/sair46.

Sheridan, A., Kochman, W. and Aranauskas, R. 2003. 'The grave goods from the Knowes of Trotty, Orkney: reconsideration and replication', in Downes, J. and Ritchie, A. (eds.), *Sea Change: Orkney and Northern Europe in the later Iron Age AD 300–800*. Balgavies: The Pinkfoot Press, 177–188.

Smith, R. 1937. *The Sturge Collection. Vol II. An illustrated*

Selection of Foreign Stone Implements bequeathed in 1919 by William Allen Sturge to the British Museum. London: British Museum.

Smith, J. 2006. 'Early Bronze Age stone wrist-guards in Britain: archers's bracers or social symbol?' *http://www.geocities.com/archchaos1/article1/1.html*.

Smith, I. F. and Simpson, D. D. A. 1966. 'Excavation of a round barrow on Overton Hill, north Wiltshire, England', *Proc. Prehist. Soc.* 32, 122–155.

Stevens, F. and Stone, J. F. S. 1939. 'The barrows of Winterslow', *Wilts. Arch. Mag.* XLVIII, 174–182.

Strutt, J. 1810. *Glig Gamena Angel Theoth: Or the Sports and Pastimes of the People of England* (2nd edition). London: White.

Thurnam, J. 1871. 'On ancient British barrows, especially those of Wiltshire and the adjoining counties (Part II. Round barrows)', *Archaeologia* 43: 285–552.

Treinen, F. 1970. 'Les Poteries Campaniformes en France', *Gallia Préhistore* 13, 53–107 & 263–332.

Turek, J. 1998. 'The Bell Beaker period in north-west Bohemia', in Benz, M. and van Willigen, S. (eds.), 107–120.

Turek, J. 2004. 'Nátepní destičky z období zvoncovitých pohárů, jejich suroviny, technologie a společenský význam' (Bell Beaker wristguards, their raw materials, technology and social significance), in Kazdová, E., Měřinský, Z. and Šabatová, K. (eds.), *Poctě Vladimíru Podborskému,* Ústav archeologie a museologie, Filozofická Faculta Masarykovy univerzity v Brně, 207–26, Brno.

Van der Vaart, S. 2009a. *Bell Beaker Wristguards Reconsidered.* Unpublished Batchelor thesis, Faculty of Archaeology, Leiden University.

Van der Vaart, S. 2009b. *Beaker wristguards, how are they made and what was their use?* Internal report, Laboratory for Artefact Studies, Faculty of Archaeology, Leiden University.

Vander Linden, M. 2006. *Le phénomène campaniforme dans l'Europe du 3éme millénaire avant notre ère: synthèse et nouvelles perspectives*, Oxford: British Archaeological Reports International Series 1470.

Van Giffen, A. E. 1930. *Die Bauert der Einzelgräber: Beitrag zur Kenntnis der älteren individuellen Grabhügelstrukturen in den Niederlanden*, Leipzig: Mannus.

Vine, P. M. 1982. *The Neolithic and Bronze Age Cultures of the Middle and Upper Trent Basin*. Oxford: British Archaeological Reports British Series 105.

Walker, I. C. 1967. 'The counties of Nairnshire, Moray and Banffshire in the Bronze Age: part 1', *Proc. Soc. Antiq. Scot.* 98, 76–125.

Weinig, J. G. 1991. 'Ein neues Gräberfeld der Kupfer- und Frühbronzezeit bie Weichering, Landkreis Neuburg-Schrobenhausen, Oberbayern', *Das Archäologische Jahr in Bayern 1990*, 64–7.

Welfare, H. G. 1975. 'A Bronze-age cemetery at Ferniegair, Lanarkshire, Hamilton', *Proc. Soc. Antiq. Scot.* 106, (1974–5), 1–14.

Whittle, A., Atkinson, R. J. C., Chambers, R. and Thomas, N. 1992. 'Excavations in the Neolithic and Bronze Age complex at Dorchester-on-Thames, Oxfordshire, 1947–1952 and 1981', *Proc. Prehist. Soc.* 58, 143–201.

Williams-Thorpe, O. and Thorpe, R. S., 1993. 'Magnetic susceptibility used in non-destructive provenancing of Roman granite columns', *Archaeometry* 35, 185–95.

Williams-Thorpe, O., Potts, P. J. and Webb, P. C. 1999. 'Field-portable non-destructive analysis of lithic archaeological samples by X-ray fluorescence instrumentation using a mercury iodide detector: comparison with wavelength-dispersive SRF and a case study in British stone axe provenancing', *Journal of Archaeological Science* 26, 215–237.

Wilson, G. 1876. 'Notes on a collection of stone implements and other antiquities, from Glenluce, Wigtownshire', *Proc. Soc. Antiq. Scot.* 11 (1874–6), 580–7.

Woodward, A. 2002. 'Beads and Beakers: heirlooms and relics in the British Early Bronze Age', *Antiquity* 76, 1040–7.

Woodward, A., Hunter, J. R., Ixer, R., Roe, F., Potts, P. J., Webb, P. C., Watson, J. S. and Jones, M. C. 2006. 'Beaker age bracers in England: sources, function and use', *Antiquity* 80, 530–543.

Woodward, A., Hunter, J. R. and Bukach, D. In prep. *Ritual in Early Bronze Age Grave Goods*. Oxford: Oxbow.

Woolley, A. R. 1983. 'Jade axes and other artefacts', in Kempe, D. R. C. and Harvey, A. P. (eds.), *The Petrology of Archaeological Artefacts*, Oxford: Clarendon Press, 256–76.